ROUND MOUNDS AND MONUMENTALITY IN THE BRITISH NEOLITHIC AND BEYOND

Round Mounds and Monumentality in the British Neolithic and Beyond

Neolithic Studies Group Seminar Papers 10

Edited by

Jim Leary, Timothy Darvill and David Field

Oxbow Books
Oxford and Oakville

Neolithic Studies Group Seminar Papers
Series Editor Timothy: Darvill

Published by
Oxbow Books, Oxford, UK

© Oxbow Books and the individual authors, 2010

ISBN 978 1 84217 404 3

This book is available direct from

Oxbow Books, Oxford, UK
(Phone: 01865-241249; Fax: 01865-794449)

and

The David Brown Book Company
PO Box 511, Oakville, CT06779
(Phone: 860-945-9329; Fax: 860-945-9468)

or

from our website
www.oxbowbooks.com

A CIP record for this book is available from the British Library

Library of Congress Cataloging-in-Publication Data

Round mounds and monumentality in the British Neolithic and beyond / edited by Jim Leary, Timothy Darvill, and David Field.
    p. cm. -- (Neolithic Studies Group seminar papers ; 10)
  Papers from a seminar held Nov. 3, 2008 at the British Museum.
  Includes bibliographical references.
  ISBN 978-1-84217-404-3 (pbk.)
 1. Mounds--Great Britain--Congresses. 2. Monuments--Great Britain--Congresses. 3. Neolithic period--Great Britain--Congresses. 4. Great Britain--Antiquities--Congresses. 5. Mounds--Congresses. 6. Monuments--Congresses. 7. Neolithic period--Congresses. 8. Antiquities--Congresses. I. Leary, Jim. II. Darvill, Timothy. III. Field, David, 1950-
  GN805.A2R68 2010
  936.1--dc22
                              2010029113

Printed in Great Britain by
Information Press, Eynsham, Oxfordshire

This book presents the proceedings of a seminar held under the aegis of the Neolithic Studies Group (NSG), one of an ongoing series of NSG Seminar Papers. The NSG is an informal organization comprising archaeologists with an interest in Neolithic archaeology. It was established in 1984 and has a large membership based mainly in the UK and Ireland, but including workers from the nations of the European Atlantic seaboard. The annual programme typically includes a seminar in London during the autumn and, in spring-time, a field meeting in an area of northwest Europe known to be rich in Neolithic remains.

Membership is open to anyone with an active involvement in the Neolithic of Europe. The present membership includes academic staff and students, museum staff, archaeologists from government institutions, units, trusts, and those with an amateur or avocational interest. There are no membership procedures or application forms, and members are those on the current mailing list. Anyone can be added to the list at any time, the only membership rule being that the names of those who do not attend four consecutive meetings are removed from the list (in the absence of apologies for absence or a request to remain on the list).

The Group relies on the enthusiasm of its members to organize its annual meetings; the two coordinators maintain the mailing lists and finances. Financial support for the Group is drawn from a small fee payable for attendance of each meeting.

Anyone wishing to contact the Group and obtain information about forthcoming meetings should contact the coordinators or visit the NSG website at:

http://www.neolithic.org.uk/

Timothy Darvill and Kenneth Brophy
NSG Coordinators

Contents

Round mounds have been a feature of Neolithic archaeology since the period was defined in the mid-nineteenth century. Liffs Low, Derbyshire, excavated in 1843 by Thomas Bateman set the scene, followed by work at notable sites such as Duggleby Howe, North Yorkshire, and Linch Hill, Oxfordshire. By the time Stuart Piggott published his magisterial *Neolithic Cultures of the British Isles* in 1954 more than a dozen burials under round barrows were associated with his "Secondary Neolithic" in addition to the wide scatter of round mounds covering passage graves and various other kinds of megalithic chamber tomb. However, it was Ian Kinnes's *Round barrows and ring-ditches in the British Neolithic* published in 1979 that really defined the nature and extent of these otherwise rather neglected monuments. Focusing on the non-megalithic barrows, Kinnes catalogued just under a hundred examples across England, Wales, and Scotland, mainly in small geographically discrete clusters, and showed that as a class of monument there were many different types and regional variations. He amply demonstrated that round mounds represented a long-lived tradition spanning the fourth and third millennia BC, initially integral to the insular British Neolithic whose defining and commemorative role survived as a distinctive factor into later phases.

Thirty years on from Kinnes's review it seemed appropriate to look again at these monuments, and the papers published here are largely those presented at a Neolithic Studies Group seminar on the subject that took place at the British Museum on Monday 3 November 2008, organised by the present editors. The seminar was entitled "Round mounds and monumentality", and aimed to consider the chronology and development of Neolithic round mounds, their changing form and use, relationship to contemporary cultural, ancestral and natural landscapes, the extent to which they provide scope for identifying local and regional social organization and, not least, why they were round. Following the conference further papers were offered for this edited volume, and thus our reach extended into parts of the British Isles not considered during the tight programme at the original seminar and includes material from further afield across the Atlantic Ocean in order to consider the role of round mounds in comparable situations elsewhere in the world. At the original London seminar we were privileged to have a short introductory paper by Ian Kinnes and Marcus Brittain as a retrospective of Neolithic round barrow studies over the period 1979 to 2008 and a taster of a more substantial piece to be published elsewhere in due course.

We have arranged the papers here in rough geographic order starting in the north and working southwards. Following a wide-ranging introduction we start in Scotland, moving down to the Isle of Man, Yorkshire, the Peak District, the Cotswolds, Wessex and Wales before leaping across to Ireland and then to North America where mound-building traditions are widely scattered through the Mid-West in particular. We conclude with another wide-ranging essay on the nature of round mounds. We recognize that not everything that could be considered is covered here, but hope that as a whole these papers show the state of play at this point in time. Radiocarbon dating, both for individual round barrows and for regional barrow-building traditions, features in many of the papers included here. Throughout the book a simple prehistoric chronology based on a back-projection of the prevailing Western Christian Calendar is used, with dates cited as solar years BC (BCE) or AD (CE) in years, decades, centuries, or millennia. Where neither BC nor AD is indicated reference is being made to a date AD. Where radiocarbon ages have been calibrated as date ranges (usually given at 2σ) these are cited as cal BC followed by the laboratory number, original determination in years BP (before AD 1950), and the relevant standard deviation expressed at 1σ. The editors would like to thank the British Museum, in particular Gill Varndell from the Department of Prehistoric and Roman Antiquities for allowing and facilitating the smooth running of the seminar at which the papers in this volume were given. We would also like to thank Clare Litt and latterly Julie Gardiner at Oxbow for help and assistance in getting this volume into print.

Front cover image used by kind permission of James O'Davis (© *English Heritage*).

Timothy Darvill, Dave Field and Jim Leary
July 2009

List of Contributors

MARTYN BARBER
SENIOR INVESTIGATOR
English Heritage
NMRC
Kemble Drive
Swindon
SN2 2GZ

ALISTAIR BARCLAY
SENIOR POST-EXCAVATION MANAGER
Wessex Archaeology (Salisbury)
Portway House
Old Sarum Park
Salisbury
Wiltshire
SP4 6EB

ALEX BAYLISS
SCIENTIFIC DATING CO-ORDINATER
English Heritage
138–142 Waterhouse Square
Holborn
London
EC1N 2ST

KENNETH BROPHY
LECTURER
Department of Archaeology
University of Glasgow
Glasgow
G12 8QQ

STEVE BURROW
CURATOR OF NEOLITHIC ARCHAEOLOGY
Amgueddfa Cymru – National Museum Wales
Cathays Park
Cardiff. CF10 3NP

EDWARD CARPENTER
INVESTIGATOR
English Heritage
NMRC
Kemble Drive
Swindon
SN2 2GZ

TIMOTHY DARVILL
PROFESSOR OF ARCHAEOLOGY
Centre for Archaeology, Anthropology
    and Heritage
School of Conservation Sciences
Bournemouth University
Fern Barrow
Poole
Dorset
BH12 5BB

DAVID FIELD
ARCHAEOLOGICAL INVESTIGATOR
English Heritage
NMRC, Kemble Drive
Swindon
SN2 2GZ

ALEX GIBSON
READER IN BRITISH PREHISTORY
Division of Archaeological, Geographical
    and Environmental Sciences
University of Bradford
BD7 1DP

TIM INGOLD
PROFESSOR OF SOCIAL ANTHROPOLOGY
Department of Anthropology
School of Social Science
University of Aberdeen
Aberdeen
AB24 3QY

MANDY JAY
POSTDOCTORAL RESEARCH ASSOCIATE
Department of Archaeology
Durham University
South Road
Durham
DH1 3LE

AND: Department of Human Evolution
Max Planck Inst. for Evolutionary Anthropology
Deutscher Platz 6
04103 Leipzig
Germany

TATJANA KYTMANNOW
VISITING RESEARCH FELLOW
School of Geography, Archaeology
    and Palaeoecology
Queen's University Belfast
Post: Lackagh Drumfin
Co. Sligo, Ireland

JONATHAN LAST
HEAD OF RESEARCH POLICY (PREHISTORY)
English Heritage
Fort Cumberland, Fort Cumberland Road
Eastney
Portsmouth
PO4 9LD

JIM LEARY
ARCHAEOLOGIST (PREHISTORY)
English Heritage
Fort Cumberland, Fort Cumberland Road
Eastney
Portsmouth
PO4 9LD

ROY LOVEDAY
HONORARY VISITING FELLOW
School of Archaeology and Ancient History
University of Leicester
University Road
Leicester
LE1 7RH

LOUISE MARTIN
GEOPHYSICIST
English Heritage
Fort Cumberland
Fort Cumberland Road
Eastney
Portsmouth
PO4 9LD

STUART NEEDHAM
HONORARY RESEARCH FELLOW AT NATIONAL
    MUSEUM WALES
Langton Fold
North Lane, South Harting
West Sussex
GN31 5NW

MIKE PARKER PEARSON
PROFESSOR OF ARCHAEOLOGY
Department of Archaeology
University of Sheffield
Northgate House
Western Street
Sheffield
S10 2TN

MIKE RICHARDS
PROFESSOR OF ARCHAEOLOGY
Department of Archaeology
Durham University
South Road
Durham
DH1 3LE

AND: Department of Human Evolution
Max Planck Institute for Evolutionary
    Anthropology
Deutscher Platz 6
04103 Leipzig
Germany

ALISON SHERIDAN
HEAD OF EARLY PREHISTORY
Department of Archaeology
National Museums Scotland
Chambers Street
Edinburgh
EH1 1JF

CATHY STOERTZ
INVESTIGATOR
English Heritage
NMRC
Kemble Drive
Swindon
SN2 2GZ

GERALDINE STOUT
FIELD ARCHAEOLOGIST
Archaeological Survey of Ireland
Department of the Environment
Heritage and Local Government
6 Ely Place Upper
Dublin 2, Ireland

PETER TOPPING
HEAD OF ARCHAEOLOGICAL SURVEY
    & INVESTIGATION
English Heritage
37 Tanner Row
York
Yorkshire
YO1 6WP

HELEN WINTON
SENIOR INVESTIGATOR
English Heritage
NMRC
Kemble Drive
Swindon
SN2 2GZ

Chapter 1

Design, Geometry and the Metamorphosis of Monuments

David Field

INTRODUCTION

One intriguing result of participating in sustained periods of archaeological fieldwork is how focussed direct engagement leads inevitably on to enquiry about how sites develop and why they appear the way that they do. Persistent queries arise concerning to what degree forms of monument might have been shaped by later landscape activities or even how they were altered, enhanced or influenced by some pre-existing feature. Questions arise regarding the very nature of field monuments being single deliberately planned and constructed entities as, for example, might be the case with say village war memorials. Instead we see them as something developing, constantly evolving and changing, metamorphosing from one form to another. Geometric shape, whether round, square or pentagonal, is not likely to occur to someone breaking and cultivating new ground in a land full of trees or stony moorland. This is equally true of domestic as well as ceremonial structures. Even fields don't have to be square and only when two amorphous shapes are put together is a tangent created and a straight edge between them, a compromise, occurs. Geometry is influenced by surroundings, that is, local context and relationships and it is these relationships that influence the final emerging shape of "things".

Creating a circular pile of earth, stones, turf or any other material you would have thought, couldn't be easier. Just pile it together and a round mound results. In his seminal volume on round mounds, Ian Kinnes (1979) rightly suggested that creating a round mound was the most "economical method of creating all round visual impact" – and indeed it is. However, as those who have pushed wheelbarrow loads of spoil will recognise, the larger the pile gets, the more difficult it is to retain the shape and instead material tends to be placed alongside as satellites, or at one or other end creating a linear dump. Amorphous shaped dumps are the natural result of unplanned earth moving. To use another familiar example, that of the garden bonfire – once material gets too high, hedge cuttings tend to be placed on one side and it is often a lack of space, or a wish to contain the fire within a small area so that it doesn't burn the lawn or engulf other managed areas that ensures that form is maintained. In some cases, for example, on 5 November there may be a desire to build higher quite deliberately in order to create an impression – to provide a memorable occasion – and there may even be social drivers to this involving status, perhaps conspicuous consumption and other influences. Sometimes there might be communal effort and in such cases ladders or even tractors and fork lift trucks may be employed to place material on the summit. The additional effort assumes the availability of certain resources, equipment, machinery, and labour, not to mention goodwill and organisational ability. So the difficulties of increasing the height of a heap of material that could need elaborate revetment and organised barrow runs might be eased by simply creating a long or sinuous mound.

Laying out a series of points in different directions at a common distance from a given position can be carried out in a relatively straightforward manner and we see the results as pit and post circles of which there are many good examples (Case 2004). However, applied to earthworks, the creation of large circles is not exactly straightforward. Unguided, it is difficult to walk in a circle, indeed even corn circles invariably need a template and simple mechanical devices such as board and string to lay them out. Disc barrows (the most aesthetic and sophisticated of monuments) aside, few prehistoric monuments are precisely circular and even those that we come to think of as round such as the henge and stone "circle" at Avebury, in Wiltshire, are instead a series of straight lengths even if at a certain scale they give the impression of circularity. Yet we should not dismiss, what to a modern eye, is lack of perfection, for some importance is curiously given to asymmetry during the Neolithic period. The asymmetrical mound at Wayland's Smithy, for example, deliberately incorporated the asymmetry of an earlier structure, *i.e.* Wayland's Smithy I, the general form evidently being of considerable importance. Similarly, the incidence of asymmetry among monuments in the Carnac region, where long mounds have one side deliberately made longer or more curved or angled than the other, has been specifically remarked upon (Laporte *et al.* 2002). This can also be observed as present in material culture; many ground axes, for example, being manufactured as lop-sided (as distinct from differential use wear). When considering prehistoric mounds it becomes evident that even at a relatively simple level there is an architectural concept, the circularity, the dome, the ditch and encircling bank, the layered deposits of coloured soils, even if this only existed as a mental template rather than a formal plan.

Preoccupation with burial rite has influenced our investigations with round mounds. This has certainly proved useful, for it has provided chronology, but it is often overlooked that many mounds contain no such burials. Many of those excavated by Hoare and Cunnington were "without result" (Hoare 1812). Of a cemetery of nine Bronze Age mounds excavated at West Heath, Sussex, by Peter Drewett only two had primary burials (Drewett *et al.* 1988), while Andy Jones's assessment of barrows on the southwest peninsular concluded that human remains are invariably treated no differently from animal bone or indeed other cultural items (Jones 2005) and consequently his term "ceremonial monuments" is a useful one. Any assessment of Beaker and early Bronze Age burials in Wessex invariably relies upon evidence from 200 year old excavations and consequently we know little of the structure of mounds themselves, or of the events that they mask. Where modern excavation has taken place there is often evidence of repeated use. Just like those of causewayed enclosures, ditches are invariably cut, backfilled, re-cut, re-backfilled *etc.*, or post or stake circles replaced and cairn rings added, although the nature of the superstructure is largely unknown as most encounters are on already levelled sites. In recent times we have become used to the idea that the mound simply seals these events and marks the end of a complex series of activities.

It's not simply the monument that undergoes change but the surrounding landscape also comes into focus. The collection of rocks to build cairns or kerbs involves clearing patches of land allowing other activities to take place there. Indeed it is not inconceivable that the two are unrelated. The very process of removing rocks may be tempered with contemporary taboos and restrictions but it will also have had a practical consequence of allowing new vegetation to take hold in the cavities. What of turf, a component of many barrows? Unless the surrounding de-turfed area is managed in some way, the monument will soon be disguised, camouflaged, by rank vegetation – or even poppies. The usual reconstruction drawing of such monuments is of clean architecture, but where the mound comprises turf (and not of the variety familiar at Wembley or the Chelsea Flower Show) or has a capping of earth it will also support new vegetation.

The relationship between long and round barrows is clearly of some importance and deserving of further study. It is not simply a matter of chronology, for there are early examples of round mounds, while circular structures, rotunda (*e.g.* Darvill 2004) or earthen or turf mounds (Eagles & Field 2004), lie at the heart of some long mounds in both Britain and Brittany. Kinnes (1979) was clear that round mounds are "integral to insular early Neolithic practice in all areas" and pointed out that the earliest chambers at Clyde tombs are encased in round cairns, while the same is true of some portal dolmens. In Brittany, the round cairn La Table de Marchands was constructed *c*.3900–3700 BC, late in the Brittany sequence but contemporary with many early Neolithic events in Britain. Construction of the passage tomb at Newgrange is dated to 3370–2920 BC but it also overlies an earlier circular turf mound (Stout & Stout 2008). Whereas for the most part long mounds appear to disappear from the record some time before 3000 BC, round mounds continue through a mature stage of the Neolithic (Kinnes 1979). Given the recent advances in the dating of long barrows and emerging indications that use may have been restricted to a few, potentially even a single, generation, it is almost as if the circular construction was normal practice and long structures were something that marked an aberration. As Whittle *et al.* (2007, 117–8) discuss in the case of Wayland's Smithy, such mounds could potently mark "special or unusual circumstance...burial of a chieftain...attendants and dependants....illness" or even shamen, or, as was suggested long ago, the result of battle. If this indeed proves to be so, like village war memorials, the long mounds might be seen as monuments in a modern sense, constructed to commemorate an important and remarkable occurrence or series of events.

Isolated round mounds often occur in remarkably close spatial proximity to long mounds. A number of examples, such as Kings Barrow or Beckhampton Road, Wiltshire (Ashbee *et al.* 1979: Eagles & Field 2004, 154), Whitchurch, South Wonston or Rockbourne in Hampshire (RCHME 1979, xxiii), or placed on top of long mounds such as Seamer Moor or Kilham, Yorkshire (Manby 1976; 1988), spring to mind. In the case of the latter, chronological relationship is clear, but it by no means follows that this applies to the others.

SILBURY HILL

It comes as a surprise to realise that, like many other monuments, the massive final phase mound at Silbury Hill isn't circular and that instead it is composed of a series of straight lengths; this is demonstrated by a model of 10,000 spot heights taken during a recent survey (Figure 1.1) (Field 2002). There is of course much erosion on the slopes, not to

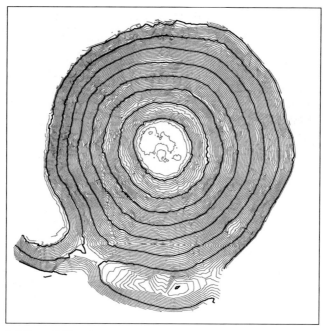

Figure 1.1: Plan of Silbury Hill with contours at 0.5m intervals showing the strength-sided nature of the mound © English Heritage.

mention the effects of 4000 years of human activity to take into account, nevertheless, nine straight lengths can be identified, although one of these is more correctly concave. Towards the summit the number decreases, the sharp angles being particularly noticeable on aerial photographs. This observation was, of course, entirely unexpected and the reason for it is unknown, although dumping material in straight lengths is easier than placing spoil in a regular curve. At other earthworks such as henges or hillforts explanations of "gang" construction are commonplace to explain straight segments, but while that is possible at Silbury, the mounded geometric nature of the site leads to an alternative suggestion that it may in some way reflect an internal construction technique that could involve features such as bracing pillars, spokes or buttresses even though these are not apparent at the summit where walls or revetment of a different nature are present (Atkinson 1967; 1968; 1969; 1970; Leary, this volume Chapter 8). This and other structural devices contained in the mound such as the "tiers" proposed by Atkinson implies the existence of a grand plan for the final phase. It is implicit that some individual or group of people already versed in the knowledge of construction projects had a guiding hand. However, modern survey coupled with a reading of the published excavated tunnel sections (Whittle 1997) suggests that there may have been greater "movement" or change, for example, at least five phases of ditch construction, can be detected or implied (Field 2002) one of them, if circular, is some 100m in diameter, which in terms of size would place it alongside Flagstones and the first phase of Stonehenge. Careful study of the new excavation data has cast light on this and there are further interpretations in Jim Leary's contribution to this volume (Chapter 8).

Figure 1.2: Mound near Tomsky, Russia, published in Archaeologia 1773. Note the tree-lined path to the summit

SPOKES

Unique structures illicit a search for comparative material and it is no surprise that Silbury Hill has often been considered on an international basis. Its massive bulk has been compared to the pyramids and the mounds in the United States. It is higher than Monks Mound at Cahokia –although the latter has three times the bulk. In terms of internal structure, it might be worth considering Krakus' mound in Krakow, Poland, alongside these. Half the size of Silbury but still a massive 16m in height, this was excavated in the 1930s and thought to date to the tenth century AD, but intriguingly its construction was based around a central post from which seven fence lines separated nine different radially segmented deposits (Słupecki 2006, 127–8). It is noteworthy that suggestions have been made that a central post existed at Silbury (Cannon & Constantine 2004; Gough 1789; Leary, this volume Chapter 8; and Edwards 2010), although no support for this was encountered during Atkinson's or the recent excavations. Four thousand miles away in the United States are a series of spoked monuments without covering mounds. One of the best known, the Medicine Wheel at Bighorn, Wyoming has twenty-eight spokes, a number thought to represent the lunar cycle, the symbolism of which is retained in the rafters of ceremonial lodges. Here too there is thought to have been a central post (Hall 1985). Four thousand miles away in the opposite direction, the Chakra or wheel is neatly emblazoned on the flag of India, a twenty-four-spoke spinning wheel version of the ancient eight-spoked chariot or Dharma wheel. The overall shape, a circle is considered to represent perfection, while each spoke represents a virtue: kindness, justice, love, courage, patience *etc.* It is not suggested that Silbury was constructed in this manner, simply that we become aware of the possibilities.

In 1773 the second volume of a new journal concerned with antiquities, *Archaeologia*, was published in which an article gave an account of tumuli on the Russian steppes many of which, when opened, produced rich grave furnishings. In particular, an illustration of the largest of these mounds, a barrow of Silbury-like proportions situated near Tomsky will have caught the eye (Figure 1.2) (Demidoff 1773). The mound was so large that the Tsar sent an officer and troops to dig into it. The diggings found burials then interpreted as those of a prince, his princess and his horse. Both human skeletons lay between sheets of gold; the male draped in a gold bordered and jewel bedecked cloth; the female similarly accompanied by gold and jewels. Just three years before the investigation of Silbury Hill, the paper will almost certainly have caught the imagination of antiquaries and, perhaps provided a catalyst for funding, for in November 1776 what appears to have been a press release was issued in at least three newspapers of the day announcing the first excavation of Silbury Hill in which the "antiquaries promise themselves wonders from the bowels of this mountain" (Field 2002). The investigators were not named and it is only later that we learn that it was the Duke of Northumberland and Colonel Drax of Dorset. Little is known of the exploration and the fact that dramatic finds were not encountered, coupled with the nation's attention on the war in North America may explain the a silence on the matter. Nevertheless, the presumed lack of backfill to this operation may have led directly to the recent interventions and a fresh look at the surface and the surrounding area, as well as crucially, the interior of the mound (see Leary, this volume Chapter 8).

While antiquarian thought was progressing, the assumption on the part of Colonel Drax and the Duke of Northumberland that there was a rich burial or burials at the centre is implicit in the press release. Although not explicitly stated, Atkinson was on the same track and the BBC who funded the excavation and invested in outside broadcast production clearly expected something dramatic to emerge. Since Atkinson's time, interpretation of Silbury as a three stage construction, I, II and III, with III being constructed in tiers like a wedding cake, has been widely accepted. Stage I, a small mound of gravel, turf and earth and perhaps a sarsen peristalith or kerb will have been nothing special as Neolithic mounds go. Even in Wiltshire, the Hatfield Barrow and the Compton Barrow will have been more monumental. Atkinson's Stage II will have been of similar proportions to Newgrange, Dowth, or Maes Howe and comparable to many other large mounds in Europe of different dates such as Leeberg, Großmugl, Austria, or the Butte de Warlencourt, Belgium, or many in Brittany or elsewhere; or even some of the mounds in the United States.

The final stage is where Silbury stands alone, Atkinson's III, incorporated a series of ledges, said to have been polished by the passage of many feet and therefore by implication those of the builders. Notwithstanding the fact that these were demonstrated by excavation to incorporate early medieval revetting, with a Saxon stone bowl placed on one ledge, they were nevertheless held to be Neolithic in origin. Survey of these terraces quickly demonstrated that they do not form concise self-contained circuits but instead, at least in the upper part of the mound, a spiral which in terms of getting things, material, and people to the higher levels makes much more sense both as ancient and more recent construction technique. Such spirals were certainly present in some early structures such as the ziggurats of Iraq and the Egyptian pyramids, but the method is also widely known in seventeenth and eighteenth century garden features such as the Marlborough Mount with its own inherited Christian symbolism largely drawn from artistic depictions of the Tower of Babel.

CIRCLES

Neolithic and early Bronze Age preoccupation with circles is evident from the sheer number of these monuments scattered across Britain and it is likely that this represents more than a fascination with geometry (Field 1998). More than half a century ago H. Taylor pointed out that the primary purpose of the ditch around a Bronze Age ceremonial monument at Tyning's Farm in the Mendips could not have been as a quarry for mound material since the mound overlay it. Neither could it be an architectural feature as it was covered over. Being a slight affair it did not constitute an obstacle to humans. Instead he thought that it must represent some magical or religious function (Taylor 1951, 162). Perhaps he had in mind the need to keep malign spirits in or out and the possibility that they might get trapped or bogged down in the ditch as is believed in the case of some earthworks in Africa (Darling 1998). Circular churches (especially in Scotland *e.g.* Bowmore, Islay) were built like that in order that the devil could not hide in the corners.

Across continents and time there are beliefs that the circle is a sacred form, that it represents the passage of human life, the cycle of the year, of the month and day, of the sun and moon and of the cosmos; or in the natural world of ripples in water, or the shape of nests and beaver lodges. A circle has no end – to the Native Americans it symbolises life, for example, the seven sacred circles of the Lakota encapsulate life and its key ceremonies. The juxtaposition of circles and squares in the earthworks at Newark, Ohio remains unexplained (Brine 1894, 66), but five thousand miles away, similar contrasts at the enormous spiritual complex known as Temple of Heaven in Beijing reflect the ancient Chinese belief that heaven is round and the earth is square. Set within an outer wall 6.4km in length and aligned to the points of compass, the complex encloses 273ha and was a sacred place where the wishes of people were conveyed to heaven. Sacrificial activities took place at the winter solstice reporting results of good harvest and at the summer solstice asking for rain while Ming and Qing dynasty emperors prayed for a good harvest. Its position in the landscape is instructive. Deliberately constructed on a slope, the northern end of the complex is higher and considered closer to heaven, while the southern is lower and closer to the earth. The northern part of the outer wall is semi-circular to reflect the dome of heaven, while the southern is square to reflect the flat earth. Internally, circular structures reflect heaven and square ones of the earth. The symbolism inherent in the construction extends to numbers, sound and colour. Deep blue tiled conical roofs and ceilings indicate that heaven is round and blue. The height and form of individual structures is related to celestial figures. Odd numbers are considered to be heavenly with multiples of three, particularly nine, being most powerful, as heaven was said to have been built of nine layers. The features, stone slabs, pillars and railings all reflect these numbers being, for example, 9m high or in multiples of nine. The three tiers of the circular mound altar, each 5m high is interrupted at the cardinal points by flights of nine steps. On the summit are shrines to the elements and to the sun and moon. Harmonious sound effects include a whispering wall whereby sound waves travel and return around the circle (Anon 1993).

None of this provides answers. How on earth can events 5000 miles away influence or have relevance to the British Neolithic? There is no need to rehearse the cautionary arguments and caveats regarding space and time, or to have to make out a case for the shedding of cultural preconceptions, for this essay has certainly been wide ranging in that respect; quite deliberately so. It outlines some of the possibilities and is perhaps a sign of the times that we are willing to entertain non-western perceptions. The important change is the recognition that at many, perhaps most, Neolithic monuments there is little evidence of blueprint, but instead of continually perhaps, intermittently shifting perceptions and requirements. Those who laid the first turves at the core of Silbury could not have known what eventual form the huge mound would take. At the same time the intense investigation and new dating programmes that have taken place for the Stonehenge and Avebury sites in recent years might soon allow us to get to the heart of Neolithic society. Almost certainly, throughout the latter half of the third millennium BC local occupants will have had direct contact, through parent, grandparent, with a family member who worked on one of the great monuments and passed on their skills and stories. Did construction of the Avebury monuments take place using "gangs" of labour or family or clan units? Or by slaves, or was it done differently? Was each bucketful of chalk, or each deposited sarsen boulder, the offering of an individual who had travelled a distance to a powerful religious location? Given the amount of material and numbers of trees required in the various monuments, might we be able to identify division of labour – logging, carpentry, earthmoving, catering – similar to that known for certain types of stone tool manufacture in the United States and New Zealand (*e.g.* Topping 2004; 2005: Best 1912)? In this volume we hope to be able to point to some new directions in the investigation of the long-lived fascination with mounds. While it might be expected that burial mounds reflect society as a whole, each with its centre and periphery and with the third dimension being the visible dome of the sky, how can we reconcile different views of the monuments, one of meaningful architecture; the other of metamorphosis, of continual, if intermittent, change?

BIBLIOGRAPHY

Anon (1993) *Tiantan-Temple of Heaven Beijing: China*. Esperanto Press.
Ashbee, P., Smith, I. F., and Evans, J. G. (1979) Excavation of three long barrows near Avebury, Wiltshire. *Proceedings of the Prehistoric Society* 45, 207–300.
Atkinson, R. J. C. (1967) Silbury Hill. *Antiquity* 41, 259–62
Atkinson, R. J. C. (1968) *Silbury Hill*. London, BBC.
Atkinson, R. J. C. (1969) The date of Silbury Hill. *Antiquity* 43, 216.
Atkinson, R. J. C. (1970) Silbury Hill, 1969–70. *Antiquity* 44, 313–14.
Best, E. (1912, edition 2005) *The stone implements of the Maori*. Wellington, A R Shearer.
Brine, L. (1894, edition 1996) *The ancient earthworks and temples of the American Indians*. Royston, Oracle Publishing.
Cannon, J. and Constantine, M. A. (2004) A Welsh bard in Wiltshire: Iolo Morganwg, Silbury Hill and the sarsens. *Wiltshire Archaeological and Natural History Magazine* 97, 78–88.
Case, H. (2004) Circles, triangles, squares and hexagons. In R. Cleal and J. Pollard (eds.) *Monuments and material culture*, 109–19. Salisbury, Hobnob Press.
Darling, P. (1998) Aerial archaeology in Africa: the challenge of a continent. *AARGnews: the Newsletter of the Aerial Archaeology Research Group* 17, 9–18.
Darvill, T. (2004) *Long barrows of the Cotswolds and surrounding areas*. Stroud, Tempus.

Demidoff, P. (1773) Some account of certain Tartarian Antiquities. In a letter from Paul Demidoff, Esquire, at Petersburg, to Mr Peter Collinson, dated September 17, 1764. *Archaeologia* 2, 222–226

Drewett, P., Rudling, D. and Gardiner, M. (1988) *The south-east to AD 1000*. London, Longmans.

Eagles, B. and Field, D. (2004) William Cunnington and the long barrows of the River Wylye. In R. Cleal and J. Pollard (eds.) *Monuments and material culture*, 47–69. Salisbury, Hobnob Press.

Edwards, B. (2010) Silbury Hill: Edward Drax and the Excavations of 1776. *Wiltshire Archaeological and Natural History Magazine* 103, 257–68.

Field, D. (1998) Round barrows and the harmonious landscape: placing early Bronze Age burial mounds in south-east England. *Oxford Journal Archaeology* 17, 309–26.

Field, D. (2002) *The investigation and analytical survey of Silbury Hill*. Archaeological Investigation Report Series, AI/22/2002, London, English Heritage (unpublished report).

Gough, R. *trans* 1789 *William Camden's Britannia* (originally pub 1610).

Hall, R. L. (1985) Medicine wheels, sun circles, and the magic of world center shrines. *Plains Anthropologist* 30(109), 181–194.

Hoare, R. C. (1812) *The ancient history of Wiltshire, vol. 1*. London, Miller.

Jones, A. M. (2005) *Cornish Bronze Age ceremonial landscapes c.2500–1500 BC*. Oxford, Archaeopress (BAR British Series 394).

Kinnes, I. (1979) *Round barrows and ring-ditches in the British Neolithic*. London, British Museum (Occasional Paper 7).

Laporte, L., Jousaume, R. and Scarre, C. (2002) The perception of space and geometry. In C. Scarre (ed.) *Monuments and landscape in Atlantic Europe*, 73–83. London and New York, Routledge.

Manby, T. G. (1976) The excavation of Kilham long barrow, East Riding of Yorkshire. *Proceedings of the Prehistoric Society* 42, 111–60.

Manby, T. G. (1988) The Neolithic period in eastern Yorkshire. In T. G. Manby (ed.) *Archaeology in eastern Yorkshire: essays in honour of T. C. M. Brewster FSA*, 35–88. Sheffield, Department of Archaeology and Prehistory.

RCHME (1979) *Long barrows in Hampshire and the Isle of Wight*. London, HMSO.

Słupecki, L. P. (2006) Large burial mounds of Cracow. In L. Smejda (ed.) *Archaeology of burial mounds*, 119–42. Czech Republic, University West Bohemia.

Stout, G. and Stout, M. (2008) *Newgrange*. Cork, Cork University Press.

Taylor, H. (1951) The Tynings Farm barrow group. Third report. *Proceedings University of Bristol Speleological Society* 6, 111–73.

Topping, P. (2004) The South Downs flint mines: Towards ethnography of flint extraction. In J. Cotton and D. Field (eds.) *Towards a New Stone Age: aspects of the Neolithic in southeast England*, 177–90. York, Council for British Archaeology (CBA Research Report 23).

Topping, P. (2005) Shaft 27 Revisited: an ethnography of Neolithic flint extraction. In P. Topping and M Lynott (eds.) *The cultural landscape of prehistoric mines*, 63–93. Oxford, Oxbow.

Whittle, A. (1997) *Sacred mound, holy rings. Silbury Hill and the West Kennet palisade enclosures: a later Neolithic complex in north Wiltshire*. Oxford, Oxbow Books (Monograph 74).

Whittle, A., Bayliss, A. and Wysocki, M. (2007) Once in a lifetime: the date of the Wayland's Smithy long barrow. *Cambridge Archaeological Journal* 17(1) Supplement, 103–121.

"... a place where they tried their criminals": Neolithic Round Mounds in Perth and Kinross

Kenneth Brophy

Round mounds are difficult sites to deal with. They are recognisable across eastern lowland landscapes within Scotland, more often than not viewed from the car in passing, isolated mounds within fields, covered in trees, and sometimes surrounded by a fence or wall. These sites have often suffered; landscaped, altered, ploughed, quarried, explored or robbed by antiquarian diggers. Their origin is often unclear, or contested, clouded by medieval and post-medieval associations, or fragmented antiquarian reports of associated (but now lost) stone coffins, standing stones, stone circles and cup-marked stones. Typical of this ambiguity is Sair Law, Perth and Kinross (Figure 2.1), the "place where they tried their criminals" (Cowan 1909, 59) mentioned in my title. This large round mound, measuring 22m by 21.5m in diameter, and up to 2m in height, has a long tradition of being a place of trial and execution, but also of being a burial mound, yet remarkably was only formally recognised as potentially prehistoric in 1991 (Barclay 1991, 73). Yet beyond this tantalising possibility, what more can we say about this mound? A lack of archaeological excavations of the round mounds of eastern lowland Scotland has left most open to multiple interpretations. The situation is similar elsewhere where such traditions may exist; Linge (1987) re-evaluated a small group of large flat-topped mounds in north Ayrshire long thought to be mottes, and concluded that these may be just as likely be prehistoric in origin.

Round mounds could be many things, and Neolithic is probably the least likely. In 1979, Kinnes suggested that there may be something like 800 Neolithic round barrows in Britain, representing less than five per cent of identified non-megalithic burial mounds (1979, 49). It seems likely that a much smaller proportion still represent an artificial mound without a burial at their core. What of the other mounds? Most are likely to be Bronze Age cairns or barrows. Other sites may be early medieval or more recent in origin, characterised variously (rightly or wrongly) as mottes or court hills. A fair proportion of the sites within the archaeological record may be natural glacial mounds. Finally, some of them may be multi-phase sites; in such cases the Neolithic origins of a round mound may be obscured by later activity or antiquarian associations as was the case at Droughduil, Dumfries and Galloway (Thomas 2001, 138). This diverse range of sites cannot easily be pinned down to specific dates, but do seem to reflect a largely east coast tradition of late Neolithic and early Bronze Age mound building.

In this paper, I want to consider some of the Scottish evidence for Neolithic round mounds. After this brief summary, I will then highlight the difficulties in dealing with these

Figure 2.1: Sair Law round mound, Perth and Kinross: "… a place where they tried their criminals" and putative prehistoric burial mound. (Photograph: K. Brophy)

monuments by focusing on Strathtay, Perth and Kinross, the location of Pitnacree, long regarded as the classic example of the Scottish Neolithic round barrow. At the time of its excavation, it was regarded as being one of a number of such sites in Strathtay (Coles and Simpson 1965, 48–9), and so I will revisit this group, drawing on the limited work that has been undertaken on these monuments since the 1960s and my own field visits. This paper is only the beginning of my engagement with these monuments, and I hope to develop a longer term in-depth analysis of round mounds more generally in Perth and Kinross. There are almost certainly more Neolithic round mounds waiting to be confirmed, and these could well be viewed as another monumental element of an apparently distinctive monumental tradition in eastern lowland Scotland (Barclay *et al.* 2002, 131). However, before considering the Strathtay group of round mounds, it is worth reminding ourselves of the confirmed sites. These illustrate that while the mound is what survives today, there is more to these monuments than meets the eye.

NEOLITHIC ROUND MOUNDS AND BARROWS IN EASTERN SCOTLAND

There are surprisingly few confirmed Neolithic round mounds and barrows in Scotland. Kinnes (1979), in his initial review of such monuments in Britain in the 1970s, identified only two round barrows in Scotland: Pitnacree and Boghead. A third site identified in Scotland, Hilton on the island of Bute, may have had a non-megalithic mortuary element, but this was replaced by a megalithic cairn (Marshall 1976; Kinnes 1992, 95). The identification of two round barrows in all of Scotland at this time in such a comprehensive review not only illustrates the limited extent of understanding of such sites then, but was also indicative of a wider lack of engagement with Neolithic non-megalithic round barrows within Neolithic studies (Kinnes 1979). Furthermore, both Pitnacree and Boghead demonstrated that Neolithic round mounds could be complex monuments with an extremely long history of use; this would become a recurring theme for such mounds in Scotland.

Pitnacree will be discussed in more detail, below (and see Sheridan, this volume Chapter 3). Boghead, Fochabers, Moray, was excavated in 1972 and 1974 (Burl 1984). As with many

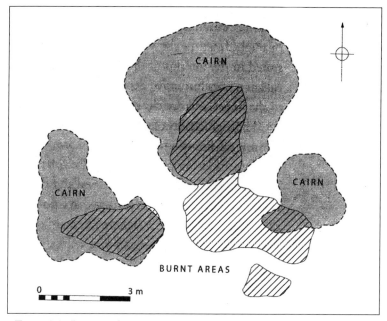

Figure 2.2: Pre-mound features at Boghead, Moray. (After Burl 1984, illus 6)

Neolithic mounds, this site is perhaps better known for what the barrow was built over, than the barrow itself. A cluster of hollows, stakeholes and pits (Figure 2.2) that pre-dated the barrow were interpreted by Burl (1984, 53) as evidence for a seasonally occupied spot, with windbreaks and flint-working areas (*cf.* Noble 2006, 63; Jones 2007). Sherds of carinated early Neolithic pot were associated with this cluster of features; however, radiocarbon dates from these phases subsequently came to be regarded as of little use (Ashmore *et al.* 2000; Sheridan, this volume Chapter 3). These features were subsequently followed by a sequence of mortuary activities, including an extensive pyre, and the construction of a series of stone cairns, finally capped by a sandy mound some 15m in diameter which consisted of material scraped from the surface of a nearby stream bed. Later Bronze and Iron Age burials focused on this mound simply emphasised the longevity of significance of this place.

In a subsequent general overview of Scotland's Neolithic a few years later, Kinnes (1985, 33*ff.*) included a useful discussion on non-megalithic mortuary practice in Scotland, and added a further three round barrows to the two already known, all in Aberdeenshire. Midtown of Pitglassie, excavated in 1978, consisted of a low mound that covered two or three concentric banks of rounded pebbles; these in turn post-dated various early Neolithic pits containing cremation deposits and Carinated Bowl pottery (Shepherd 1996; Kinnes 1985, 46). The excavator of this site characterised the monument as a "Neolithic ring-mound" but was happy to see it as part of Kinnes's non-megalithic round mound tradition (Shepherd 1996, 48). The other two sites were identified as part of a catalogue of Neolithic pottery sherds in northeast Scotland compiled by Henshall (1983). Atherb cairn 1 (Henshall 1983, 39–40) – destroyed in the nineteenth century (Milne 1892) – was apparently a low stone cairn containing charred wood, burnt bone, flint arrowheads and sherds of Carinated Bowl pottery (Henshall 1983, 39). However, Sheridan (this volume

Chapter 3) regards this site as a long mound or cairn. The round mound at East Finnercy has been excavated several times (summarised in Leivers *et al.* 2000) although exact details of the structure remain unclear. Some pre-mound features were recorded including "hearths", cremated bone and an oval pit containing sherds of seven different early Neolithic vessels. This surface was sealed by the construction of a large mound of earth and stone; this may have been a late Neolithic or early Bronze Age development (Leivers 2000, 194).

In a further review of non-megalithic mortuary sites, Kinnes (1992) drew out the "eclectic" nature of the known round barrows. He identified eleven possible round barrows in Scotland (Kinnes 1992, 84–5), although at least one of these, Achnacreebeag, Argyll and Bute, has more recently been re-interpreted in terms of passage grave architecture (*e.g.* Sheridan 2000). Kinnes added to his list the intriguing site of Courthill, Ayrshire, excavated in the nineteenth century. Here, a large mound was found to cover a timber hall-type structure (Cochran Patrick 1874). With the limited information we have about this monument, it could represent an early Historic hall beneath a motte (Scott 1989) or a Neolithic hall beneath a prehistoric mound (Linge 1987). (See Brophy (2007) for a wider discussion of ambiguity between Neolithic and early historic halls.). Kinnes's excellent summary of the diverse monuments does not need to be repeated here (1992, 92–9). Nonetheless, in his discussion of this small group of sites, Kinnes importantly starts to tease out the different elements of these monuments, notably separating the mortuary activity from the mound.

Only one Neolithic "round mound" has been excavated in Scotland since 1992, Droughduil, adjacent to the Dunragit palisaded enclosure cropmark complex (Thomas 2002). Although long believed to be a motte, the alignment of the palisaded enclosure avenue on the mound led to an investigation in 2002. The huge oval mound was shown to be an artificial augmentation of a sand dune in this location, and in the Neolithic would have appeared as a stepped and flat-topped sandy mound. No evidence was found for any kind of revetment for this structure, although it was covered in a deposit of windblown sand. A Bronze Age kerbed cairn was constructed on top of the mound, and subsequently a nineteenth century folly (Thomas 2002). Unlike any other Neolithic round mounds identified in Scotland, the closest parallel for Droughduil appears to be Silbury Hill. The recognition that such an artificial feature exists in Scotland offers another possible interpretation for a range of large unexcavated mounds. However, the sheer scale of this mound (up to 50m across at the base, and with a height of almost 10m in the Neolithic (Figure 2.3)) is out of character with any other excavated Neolithic mounds.

There have been few other excavations recently that could be interpreted as identifying Neolithic round mounds. The remarkable barrow at Fordhouse, Angus, excavated in 1994–7, consists of a sunken passage grave in a location where there had already been early Neolithic activity (Peterson & Proudfoot 1997). The passage grave was sealed by a mound of stone, earth and large burnt timbers; oak from one of these timbers was dated to the early Neolithic (Proudfoot 1999). This was then remodelled somewhat in the Bronze Age with the addition of a ring-cairn. This monument seems to fit well with the tradition of complex activities at such sites in eastern lowland Scotland, with mortuary activity being capped by a mound, although this was played on in a remarkable form. A ring-ditch within the northern terminal of Holywood South cursus was excavated in 1997. With a diameter of about 10m, this site was first identified as a cropmark and as such, only survives as a truncated ditch. Excavation

Figure 2.3: The Droughduil Neolithic mound, Dumfries and Galloway. The trees give some indication of scale. (Photograph: K Brophy)

could not demonstrate if this was indeed initially a mound, and its location was such that it could have pre-dated, or post-dated the early Neolithic cursus (Thomas 2007, 196–7). Finally, a sub-circular ditched enclosure with an internal timber setting excavated at Brownsbank, South Lanarkshire, in 2005–06 could tentatively be interpreted as a ploughed-out mound site surrounded by a ditch (Brophy & Noble in prep).

There have been no recent attempts to pull together information on Neolithic round mounds in Scotland since Kinnes's brief synthesis (1992) although an update of Kinnes's 1970s research is ongoing (Kinnes & Brittain, November 2008 Neolithic Studies Group Lecture). No sites were positively identified by RCAHMS during their survey work in Perthshire, for instance, although some possible Neolithic barrows were identified as standing monuments and cropmarks (RCAHMS 1990, 1994, 20). However, this work did not add to the solitary confirmed site, Pitnacree (Barclay 1999, 24). Recent reviews of Scotland's Neolithic have, variously, offered a description of a few sites (Ashmore 1996; Barclay 2005), presented a reinterpretation of pre-mound structures (Noble 2006) or added little to this discussion at all (Brophy 2006).

In reviewing this evidence, it is clear that there is a problem in dealing with a wider corpus of possible Neolithic round mounds. The discussion thus far has only been possible due to the fine-grained detail afforded by excavation. The vast majority of round mounds visible with the landscape of eastern lowland Scotland remain extremely difficult to interpret without some kind of invasive work. In embarking on analysis of the possible evidence, therefore, it is important to try to think about how we can work usefully with *unexcavated* mounds. Is it possible to develop a field methodology for identifying mounds more likely to be Neolithic than later? Can mound size and form, and possibly other factors like landscape location and local archaeological context, start to tease apart differences within groups of round mounds? Ultimately, such a methodology could only be tested by excavation, but could perhaps allow a better understanding of the potential and frequency of such Neolithic monuments at minimal cost. In the next section of this paper, I will focus on a specific case-study to test some ideas along these lines. However, ultimately, it may well be that Neolithic round mounds will remain concealed within the large group of unclassified and perhaps unclassifiable round mounds found within the landscape across eastern lowland Scotland.

PITNACREE AND THE STRATHTAY ROUND MOUNDS

> *"A field survey of the area between Loch Tay and Dunkeld … suggests that at least twenty barrows comparable in external appearance to Pitnacree still remain in Strathtay … only further excavation will reveal whether or not the structure and finds at Pitnacree are to be considered as typical of these sites" (Coles & Simpson 1965, 43).*

Given the paucity of confirmed Neolithic round mounds and barrows known in Scotland, even in the forty or so years since Pitnacree was excavated, it seems remarkable to suggest that as many as twenty alone could exist within Strathtay, to the north of Perth. Yet testing this group of round earthen mounds was precisely why Pitnacree was excavated in 1964. Stewart (1959) recorded eleven "earth tumuli" in Strathtay; these earthen mounds were regarded as being distinct from stone cairns and were all located at a low level, near the Rivers Tay and Lyon. Stewart attributed them to an invasive culture contemporary with Beaker people, with stone cairns restricted to upland reaches of the valley, and an apparent absence of beaker burials and cists in the Strath (Stewart 1959, 84). Coles and Simpson (1965) added to this list, identifying at least eighteen possible "barrow" sites (Figure 2.4).

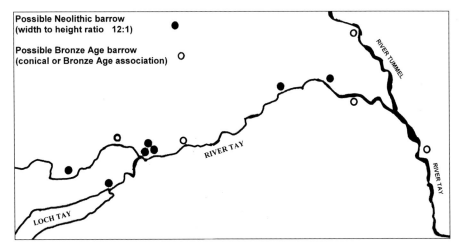

Figure 2.4: Possible earthen barrows in Strathtay. (After Stewart 1959 and Coles & Simpson 1965)

Figure 2.5: Pitnacree round barrow in 2009. (Photograph: K. Brophy)

They appeared "superficially to be of earthen construction … many are of very great size, up to 130 feet [40m] in diameter and 30 feet [9m] in height" (Coles & Simpson 1965, 34). To test the date of such an apparently cohesive and discrete group of monuments, Pitnacree (Figure 2.5) was chosen as one of the more accessible to excavate.

The excavations at Pitnacree were a great success, and demonstrated that Pitnacree was a multi-phase Neolithic round barrow, with no direct parallels in Britain (see Sheridan, this volume Chapter 3, for more detail). The excavators identified three main phases, focused on a location that may already have been cultivated in the early Neolithic (Coles & Simpson 1965, 40). Initially, two large timber uprights were erected, probably a split-post feature (*cf.* Scott 1992; Noble 2006), and these timbers were left to decay *in situ*. Subsequently, the location of the posts was enclosed by a horseshoe-shaped stone bank, possibly associated with cremation deposits in its interior; a stone rectangular structure sealed these deposits in roughly the same location as where the post-setting had been. These features were associated with various sherds of relatively high quality Neolithic Carinated Bowl pottery (Cowie 1993, 15). Almost immediately, this was covered by a round mound of earth, stone and turf some 28m in diameter and supported by an unusual drystone kerb. The "third phase" consisted of secondary burials and a standing stone set into the top of the barrow (Coles & Simpson 1965, 41), with one cremation deposit recently dated to the early Bronze Age (Sheridan, this volume Chapter 3). It seems to me that the complexity – and perhaps date – of this monument would have been unexpected to the excavators. It is also interesting that parallels discussed for Pitnacree were not parallels for the monument as a whole, but for each architectural element (Coles & Simpson 1965, 44*ff.*), almost as if this was a hybrid monument, drawing on a range of different traditions (see discussion below).

Regardless of how we explain this sequence, the excavations at Pitnacree demonstrated that such mounds *can* be Neolithic. However, this did not mean that the other round mounds identified in Strathtay were certainly contemporary, and a lack of any further excavation at any of these mounds since 1964 has left Pitnacree isolated in a Strath of undated mounds (Barclay 1999, 24). In the intervening years, and in the absence of invasive investigations at any of these monuments, some gradually started to "drop off" the possible Neolithic round mound list, due to reclassification as natural features by Ordnance Survey (OS) archaeological field visits or re-interpretation as being Bronze Age barrows.

For instance, four "barrows" on the Coles and Simpson list were discounted as being prehistoric, and re-interpreted as natural glacial mounds during one field visit in May 1975 alone (Strathtay, Mains of Taymouth and two oval mounds at Dalmartaig House). Nonetheless, superficial geomorphological analysis of these mounds is not always accurate, with barrows such as North Mains (Barclay 1983) and Little Trochry (G. J. Barclay pers. comm.), both Perth and Kinross, discounted at one time as natural, with the former shown through excavation to be Bronze Age, and the latter now a Scheduled Ancient Monument. There certainly is an issue here; is it possible in the field to be sure a monument is artificial or natural from surface and morphological inspection alone? The supposed glacial mound in Strathtay golf course (Figure 2.6) is now regarded as a glacial knoll, but appears very similar to Pitnacree, albeit more irregular. This mound sits in the shadow of two much larger and certainly natural glacial mounds. The nearby mound at Mains of Taymouth is also characterised as being natural, even though an OS fieldworker notes (recorded in the National Monuments Record of Scotland) that when a farmer dug into the mound to establish water tanks, he felt the mound was composed of rubble and was artificial. It is interesting in itself that so many putative mounds exist within a landscape characterised by sand and gravel round, oval and long glacial knolls at the edge of the valley floor, suggesting that burial monuments have a certain fittedness within this landscape. Interestingly, the putative barrow at Kindallachan, near Pitlochry, has been shown through two episodes of rescue excavation to be an entirely natural mound with cist burials inserted into it (Stewart 1956; Suddaby 2007). As such, there may have been a certain ambiguity between natural and artificial mounds even in prehistory, and an element of mimicry in monument form.

Still more mounds from the Coles and Simpson list could be characterised as Bronze Age barrows, as opposed to Neolithic monuments. Barclay (Barclay & Maxwell 1998, 115–7, Barclay 1999, 24–6) has considered the form of many round mounds in Tayside, drawing on the very different forms of two prehistoric round mounds – the Neolithic barrow of Pitnacree and the Bronze Age barrow at North Mains – as exemplars for a crude rule of thumb characterisation of unexcavated round mounds. Barclay noted that: "In the field, I have observed that individual round barrows in Perthshire, Angus and Fife seem to fall into one class or the other – broad and low, like Pitnacree, or high and bowl-shaped, like North Mains" (1999, 24).

Barclay's simple characterisation (see Figure 2.6 and Figure 2.7) is that round mounds of greater than 20m width at base and with width to height ratio of 12:1 are more likely to have been constructed in the Neolithic. High but less broad mounds ("pudding bowl shaped") are more likely to have been Bronze Age in origin (although these may still overlie evidence

Figure 2.6: Low and broad Pitnacree-type mound – Strathtay 'barrow', Strathtay. (Photograph: K. Brophy)

Figure 2.7: High and conical North Mains-type mound – Balnaguard, Strathtay. (Photograph: K. Brophy)

for Neolithic activity). Although this observation is of course contingent on this being a characterisation of a modern – potentially denuded – version of these monuments, it is a useful rule of thumb to consider in the lack of any other real information on such sites.

Using this criterion, a few of the Strathtay mounds could be considered to be more likely to be Bronze Age than Neolithic, notably the impressive but mutilated mound at Balnaguard (Figure 2.7), just a few kilometres from Pitnacree. This mound measures some 29m in diameter across the base, and is 5m high. It has suffered somewhat from modern quarrying, tree growth and a location sandwiched between houses, but it has a distinctive conical profile unlike lower mounds like Pitnacree and Strathtay golf course (Mercer & Midgley 1997, 285). Other mounds in the area have a similar profile to North Mains, such as Court Hill (a site with an interesting name). Still others seem to be more likely to be Bronze Age in origin, such as Balhomais, a much denuded monument only 14m in diameter and possibly associated with a stone circle (Coles 1908, 128–30; Stewart 1959, 84) and Dunfallandy, which looks rather like Pitnacree, but has a width: height ration of 8:1, and is only 16m across.

Are there any other mounds in the valley that have a comparable morphology to Pitnacree? Remarkably, there may be a concentration of three at Tirinie, near Aberfeldy. These tree-covered low mounds have gone through various different interpretations, initially regarded as being "motes" on the OS 6-inch map sheet, but then listed by Coles and Simpson (1965) as possible barrows. Although subsequently they came to be regarded as possibly natural in origin (D. Strachan pers. comm.), more recently they have been designated Scheduled Ancient Monuments and have been characterised once again as "tumuli" (*e.g.* Stewart & Barclay 1997, Illus. 19). These earthen mounds each fall into the low, broad, Neolithic criteria set out by Barclay, measuring 16m, 22m and 23m in diameter, with heights ranging from 1m to 2m, and are set about 200m apart almost in a line. These mounds lie just down slope from a putative stone setting and an unusual four-poster stone setting at Carse Farm; this early Bronze Age funerary monument was associated with a cremation urn (Stewart & Barclay 1997, 48*ff.*). Rather like Pitnacree, these mounds sit near the Tay, although in this case they sit on the floodplain itself.

Ultimately, Barclay was able with confidence to attribute only two of the barrows in Strathtay to a Neolithic round barrow tradition (Figure 2.8) – Pitnacree and Mains of Taymouth (Barclay & Maxwell 1998, 116). Yet from field observation, it seems to me impossible to rule out sites that have at some point been interpreted as wholly natural, including the three low mounds at Tirinie and the low and broad mound on Strathtay golf course. Still other sites from the initial Coles and Simpson (1965) list can be assigned with some confidence to slightly later in prehistory, notably Balnaguard and Balhomais. Field visits to these sites, of course, can only get us so far, and other possible strategies will be discussed below. It is also worth considering another form of evidence in this respect, that of cropmarks. Aerial reconnaissance in the 1990s identified cropmarks of a possible long barrow and several round barrows at Haugh of Grandtully on the bank of the River Tay opposite Pitnacree, adjacent to an area of Neolithic pits and a Bronze Age cremation cemetery (Coles & Simpson 1990). Other barrows have been recorded in the Strath as cropmarks, such as Camserney and Drumdewan; nothing further can be said about these sites without excavation. A cropmark "ring-ditch" has been identified near the excavated Bronze Age ring cairn at Sketewan, on the south side of the Tay between Pitnacree and

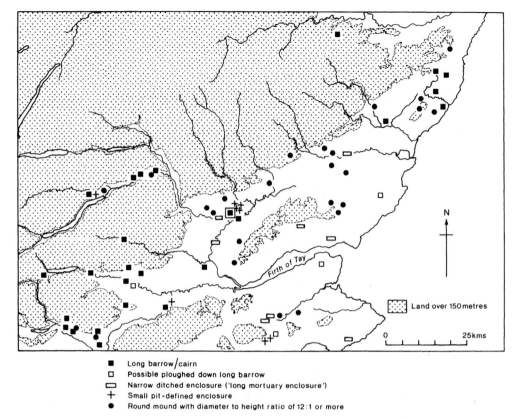

Figure 2.8: Barclay's map showing location of various Neolithic monument types in Tayside. (After Barclay & Maxwell 1998, illus 86; and Barclay 1999, 24)

Balnaguard barrows (Mercer & Midgely 1997), although Bradley (2007, 78–9) has sounded a note of caution about how we define round barrows, ring-ditches and hengiforms when dealing with such unexcavated cropmarks, and it would certainly be interesting in this context to consider what Pitnacree would have looked like as a cropmark. Nonetheless, the round mounds that are known are almost all set back from arable fields at the edge of the valley floor; the location of the Tirinie sites on the valley floor itself and accumulating cropmark evidence suggest that earthwork barrows may not entirely represent the full potential for Neolithic round mounds in this Strath.

Given the paucity of excavation evidence, and the potentially dozens, if not hundreds, of round mounds (of natural and artificial origin) in eastern lowland Scotland, Barclay's "measurable" approach seems a pragmatic one and allows a way into further, more focussed analysis of this group of monuments. When dealing with large numbers of sites, and the obvious logistical problems of a large-scale invasive fieldwork programme, such a strategy may allow energy and resources to be focused on refining a smaller dataset which can then be tested in different ways. In Strathtay for instance, an unwieldy list of eighteen sites can be narrowed down to about a third of that through field visits alone, albeit with the proviso other sites have only been cautiously "ruled out". However, although Barclay's morphological observation is based on excavation evidence (North Mains / Pitnacree), it has not yet been tested by subsequent excavation in Perth and Kinross. It seems to me the next step in this process is a project aimed at testing his 20m / 12:1 "rule" through excavation and perhaps geophysical survey.

Given a small group of sites, such as the Strathtay group, a short campaign of excavation need not be impossible. Mounds are responsive to trial and small-scale excavation; Barclay and Maxwell (1998, 117–8) carried out a very limited excavation at Herald Hill, Perth and Kinross, a supposedly natural long mound near The Cleaven Dyke. A trial excavation (in the form of a 1m square test pit) in 1997 demonstrated that this was in fact a long barrow augmenting a natural glacial feature (Barclay & Maxwell 1997). Therefore the character of a mound could quite rapidly be recovered by limited excavation, although each individual mound would require different levels of analysis. Only a very small trench (relative to the overall size of the mound) was opened at Droughduil, but it would be fair to say that this was a major undertaking (Thomas 2002). There may also be a role for geophysical survey, notably Ground Penetrating Radar, in both characterising the nature of a mound and establishing, for instance, the presence of a flanking ditch (Oliver O'Grady pers. comm.). GPR survey has been successful is identifying elements of the underlying form of the Tynwald Hill, Isle of Man (Darvill, this volume Chapter 4).

The round mounds of Strathtay, then, present an opportunity to test a localised Neolithic round barrow tradition thus far unparalleled in Scotland. In the 1960s, barrows were defined as being possibly Neolithic and analogous with the remarkable Pitnacree site based only on the materiality of the mound ("earthen"), rather than the form of the mound. Subsequent field interpretation of many of these sites discounted them based on similarities to natural knolls in the landscape, rather than consider that the similarity may reflect monumental mimicry and augmentation in the Neolithic. More recently, Barclay's field observations have allowed a middle ground, where sites unlikely to be Neolithic can be discounted with some confidence, while others can stay firmly on the radar for future analysis and fieldwork. It may also be possible to rethink or refine Barclay's observation. For instance, Droughduil has a width to height ratio of only about 5:1 but is Neolithic; could it be that some of the very large conical monuments could be Neolithic artificial mounds, not Bronze Age barrows? Is the presence of a flat top another factor we should consider (*cf.* Linge 1987)? Furthermore, given that we know the mound at Pitnacree was the final Neolithic alteration of that location, we should acknowledge that mounds of any date may seal deposits from centuries or more before, so labels such as "Bronze Age" could have limited usefulness. Nonetheless, Pitnacree and similar low, broad mounds in the Strath, and the untapped cropmark record, offers an excellent opportunity for a field project to understand a round mound landscape, but also to understand what came before those mounds.

DISCUSSION

I want to finish this paper with a brief wider discussion on elements on these monuments, trying to make sense of them in a Scottish context, given the inherent problems with the record as already outlined. As stated previously, my engagement with these monuments is only just beginning, so these observations are provisional.

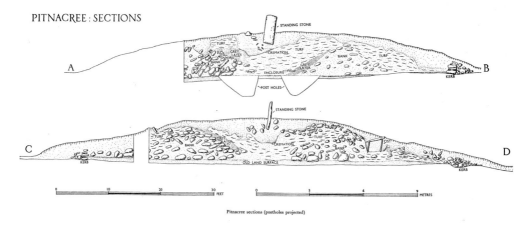

PITNACREE : SECTIONS

Figure 2.9: Section through Pitnacree round barrow. (After Coles & Simpson 1965, Plate XVII)

Firstly, of course, there is the mound itself, the physical element of the monument by which we recognise, define and classify these sites. I recognise that it is inherently problematic to classify monuments purely by external form, especially given that almost all excavation evidence suggests that mounds were often only the last alteration or "phase" of these monuments in the Neolithic. Indeed, the creation of round mounds of earth, turf and stone could and should be seen as distinctive and separate acts from what came before. At some sites, such as Pitnacree and Boghead, there is strong evidence for substantial periods of time between initial activities at these sites and final barrow construction. Those partaking of funerary ceremonies, cutting down and preparing large tree trunks, cultivating and so on at these specific places were not the same people who buried the traces of these processes under a mound. The uniformity of the round mound form disguises a variety of activities undertaken at different sites by earlier generations. This has long been recognised (*cf.* Kinnes 1979) but it has not stopped us defining these monuments by the mound.

The form and character of the mound is of interest, although not always considered in much detail. Where narratives are increasingly focused on pre-mound activities (*e.g.* Noble 2006), the mounds hardly seem to matter, a secondary development. At Pitnacree, the barrow did not even get a phase to itself in the final excavation report (Coles & Simpson 1965, 41), and yet the published sections of the barrow (Coles & Simpson 1965, plate XVII) (Figure 2.9) suggests a complex interplay of stone, turves and soil came together to shape the mound. We know that mound construction must have been an elaborate, time-consuming and almost certainly meaningful process, and this may be reflected in the growth of the mound and its temporality. Mounds may have reflected a range of materials from across the landscape – pebbles from a river, turf and soil from the fields, and so on. Scraping together soil and deturfing would have provided materials for the mound, but also altered the wider locality for years, or decades. The elaborate stake structure that acted as a frame and guide for the early Bronze Age barrow at North Mains, Perth and Kinross (Barclay 1983) reminds us that building a barrow would have involved more than heaping earth into a pile. The form of the mound may also have been significant, even if not stepped (as Droughduil) – mounds, as

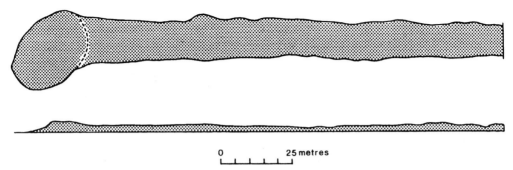

0   25 metres

Figure 2.10: Northwest terminal of the Cleaven Dyke – enlarged terminal and possible early Neolithic round mound / barrow. (After Barclay & Maxwell 1998, illus 90)

already noted in Strathtay, may have been modelled on natural features within the surrounding landscape. The modern confusion between artificial and natural round mounds in Strathtay alluded to above is in part because this is a glacial landscape with low knolls and drumlins. The confusion may also be in part because some prehistoric monuments are extensions of the natural topography upon which they sit, a notable example being the aforementioned Herald Hill long barrow. Round mounds then may have been responses to the landscape of the builders; any distinction between natural and artificial mounds in the Neolithic may have been problematic, or regarded differently from our clear categories. With time, these mounds would have grassed over and become part of the landscape.

Mounds may have tied together the local landscape in some way through their form and materiality, but we could also argue that they played a significant role in wider traditions of monumentality. Most notable in Perth and Kinross in this respect is the intriguing nature of the northwest terminal of The Cleaven Dyke (Figure 2.10). As with other cursus monuments (and bank barrows) in Scotland (Brophy 1998), there is an emphasis on enlarged terminals, a phenomenon apparent at the earthwork element of the Dyke. The terminal has the appearance of a large round mound, and there is a strong possibility that the earliest monument here may have been a free-standing round mound. Barclay and Maxwell (1998, 51) call this a Pitnacree-type burial mound. It is interesting to note that this would place this large round mound (28m by 22m and 2m high) in the early Neolithic, much earlier than the superficially similar Pitnacree mound. The possibility that this round mound is a burial monument is unproven, and it could just as easily be mimicking such a monument (Barclay & Maxwell 1998) or a natural feature, or be an artificial knoll. Aside from remaining the focus of a huge linear earthwork for decades, possibly centuries, this round mound also suggests that a tradition of such mounds may have its origins in the fourth, not the third, millennium BC in eastern Scotland.

The role, form and chronology of the round mound itself, then, seems rather ambiguous. Mounds brought together communal labour and permanently marked a place in the landscape. They may have been focal points for ceremony long after their construction. Yet they also served as a sort of closing act, essentially putting beyond use everything that had been there before, rather like blocking up a chambered cairn. Closer investigation of barrow mounds – materiality, anatomy, topography and temporality – may shed more light on all of these processes.

Finally, it is worth briefly considering the pre-barrow activities at these monuments. Round mounds did not spring up in places with no prior meaning or use. They were constructed over a range of features including hollows, hearths, spreads of burnt material, timber settings, cultivation traces and possible mortuary features. These included crematoria, pyres, split timber post-structures, rectangular settings, horseshoe and oval enclosures and various small-scale stone, even megalithic, structures. These activities were frequently associated with sherds of Carinated Bowl pottery (although unlike Yorkshire there does not seem to have been an emphasis on exotic or "prestigious" artefacts (Harding 1997, 286) or single inhumation burials (Kinnes 2004)). It seems in the late Neolithic it was appropriate to cover all sorts of places with round mounds; some of these processes may have left little physical surface traces, and mounds may have marked places picked out as special through memory or tradition. In some respects it is only the round mound that connects them all in the architectural record, but perhaps a process was going on in the late Neolithic, drawing together a series of important but diverse places through mound construction.

This is not to say that these places existed in complete isolation – there are recurring patterns such as split post structures (Scott 1992; Noble 2006) and oval / horseshoe settings at Pitnacree, Boghead and Midtown of Pitglassie (Shepherd 1996). This is where we can perhaps broaden out the role of round mound places (as opposed to the mounds themselves) within wider monumental traditions and connection. Split post structures, for instance, are not purely restricted to round barrows, and have been recorded under a range of other burial monuments, from Wayland's Smithy, Oxfordshire (Atkinson 1965), to Lochhill, Dumfries and Galloway (Masters 1973). The stone oval setting at Pitnacree is reminiscent of the oval setting at Croft Moraig, only a few kilometres to the west in Strathtay, although this phase of the monument has recently been attributed to the second millennium BC (Bradley & Sheridan 2005). In this respect it is also interesting to note the ambiguity in our labelling between oval and round mounds (Bradley 2007, 78*ff.*); the early round mound at The Cleaven Dyke (Figure 2.10) could be viewed as an *oval* mound with an alignment slightly different from the cursus as a whole. This conforms more closely to cursus traditions in the British Isles than a cursus / round mound relationship (Loveday 2006). The hollows and light structures suggested at Boghead are reminiscent of other early Neolithic "camp" locations recorded more recently in eastern Scotland (Brophy 2006, 22*ff.*) and so on. Cross-cutting traditions of monumentality are nothing new in Scotland's Neolithic, and it should perhaps not surprise us that the activities that occurred in these places that subsequently became "mounded" represent a range of forms and structures. Practices may have drawn elements of both activities and architecture from a wide palette of Neolithic activities, cutting across aspects of life that we view as ritual, funerary and domestic. However we see these connecting, it seems that in some cases, similar activities carried out in the earlier Neolithic were carried out at locations where different monumental trajectories were followed. At other diverse sites, with little in common, at some point in the later Neolithic it was deemed appropriate that they were marked with a low round mound. The story of round mounds in Scotland may be one of such divergences and convergences.

CONCLUSION

This paper has posed more questions than it has answered, but was written very much as a starting point in my wider investigation of the round mounds of Perth and Kinross. There is an inherent paradox in these sites, in that we have to isolate monuments that appear superficially similar in order to dig deeper and find variation. One of the enduring mysteries of these sites is not necessarily what the mound was for, but why the mound was built at these specific places (and not others). What is especially interesting to me is that most sites marked by round mounds were special places for many generations. Covering these places, sealing them in and putting beyond use, was a special act that was more than a process of heaping earth upon earth. It is also useful – despite some west coast monuments having been identified – to consider these round mounds and what lies within in the context of other regionally distinctive monumental forms in eastern lowland Scotland, northeastern Scotland and perhaps further afield (*e.g.* Harding 1997). The Neolithic round mounds of Perth and Kinross may still represent notionally a small group of monuments, but the potential is there for a wider tradition to be identified, a tradition of mound builders burying not people, but places.

ACKNOWLEDGEMENTS

I am indebted to research previously undertaken by Gordon Barclay, which I "inherited" from him in the form of a floppy disk a few years ago. Gordon has also offered much advice during the final preparation of this paper, for which I am extremely grateful as ever. I would like to thank my colleagues Steve Driscoll and Gordon Noble; our Strathearn Environs and Royal Forteviot (SERF) Project supported my trip to London to deliver the paper at the initial Neolithic Studies Group event. This paper also benefited from discussion with Oliver O'Grady and Davy Strachan, and some helpful comments on an earlier draft by Alison Sheridan.

BIBLIOGRAPHY

Ashmore, P. (1996) *Neolithic and Bronze Age Scotland*. London, Batsford.
Ashmore, P., Cook, G. T. and Harkness, D. D. (2000) A radiocarbon database for Scottish samples. *Radiocarbon* 42(1), 41–8.
Atkinson, R. J. C. (1965) Wayland's Smithy. *Antiquity* 39, 126–33.
Barclay, G. J. (1983) Sites from the third millennium bc to the first millennium ad at North Mains, Strathallan, Perthshire. *Proceedings of the Society of Antiquaries of Scotland* 113, 122–281.
Barclay, G. J. (1991) Sair Law (Fowlis Wester): burial mound. *Discovery and Excavation in Scotland* 1991, 73.
Barclay, G. J. (1999) A hidden landscape: the Neolithic of Tayside. In A. F. Harding (ed.) *Experiment and design: archaeological studies in honour of John Coles*, 20–9. Oxford, Oxbow Books.
Barclay, G. J. (2005) *Farmers, temples and tombs: Scotland in the Neolithic and early Bronze Age*. Edinburgh, Birlinn.
Barclay, G. J., Brophy, K. and MacGregor, G. (2002) Claish, Stirling: an early Neolithic structure in its context. *Proceedings of the Society of Antiquaries of Scotland* 132, 65–138.
Barclay, G. J. and Maxwell, G. S. (1997) Herald Hill (Caputh Parish), long barrow. *Discovery and Excavation in Scotland* 1997, 62.

Barclay, G. J. and Maxwell, G. S. (1998) *The Cleaven Dyke and Littleour: monuments in the Neolithic of Tayside.* Edinburgh, Society of Antiquaries of Scotland (Monograph Series 13).

Bradley, R. (2007) *The prehistory of Britain and Ireland.* Cambridge, Cambridge University Press.

Bradley, R. and Sheridan, J. A. (2005) Croft Moraig and the chronology of stone circles. *Proceedings of the Prehistoric Society* 71, 269–81.

Brophy, K. (1998) Cursus monuments and bank barrows of Tayside and Fife. In G. J. Barclay and G. S. Maxwell (eds.), *The Cleaven Dyke and Littleour: monuments in the Neolithic of Tayside,* 92–108. Edinburgh, Society of Antiquaries of Scotland.

Brophy, K. (2006) Rethinking Scotland's Neolithic: combining circumstance and context. *Proceedings of the Society of Antiquaries of Scotland* 136, 7–46.

Brophy, K. (2007) From big houses to cult houses: Neolithic timber halls in Scotland. *Proceedings of the Prehistoric Society* 73, 75–96.

Brophy, K. and Noble, G. (in prep.) Excavations at Brownsbank, South Lanarkshire. *Scottish Archaeological Journal.*

Burl, H. A. W. (1984) Report on the excavation of a Neolithic mound at Boghead, Speymouth Forest, Fochabers, Moray, 1972 and 1974. *Proceedings of the Society of Antiquaries of Scotland* 114, 35–73.

Cochran Patrick, R. W. (1874) Note on some explorations in a tumulus called the "Court-Hill", in the parish of Dalry and county of Ayr. *Proceedings of the Society of Antiquaries of Scotland* 10 (1872–4), 281–5.

Coles, F. R. (1908) Report on stone circles surveyed in Perthshire – northeastern section; with measured plans and drawings. *Proceedings of the Society of Antiquaries of Scotland* 42, 95–162.

Coles, J. M. and Simpson, D. D. A. (1965) The excavation of a Neolithic round barrow at Pitnacree, Perthshire, Scotland. *Proceedings of the Prehistoric Society* 31, 34–57.

Coles, J. M. and Simpson D. D. A. (1990) Excavations at Grandtully, Perthshire. *Proceedings of the Society of Antiquaries of Scotland* 120, 33–44.

Cowan, S. (1909) *Three Celtic earldoms: Atholl, Strathearn, Mentieth.* Edinburgh.

Cowie, T. (1993) A survey of the Neolithic pottery of eastern and central Scotland. *Proceedings of the Society of Antiquaries of Scotland* 123, 13–41.

Harding, J. (1997) Interpreting the Neolithic: monuments of North Yorkshire. *Oxford Journal of Archaeology* 16(3), 279–95.

Henshall, A. S. (1983) The Neolithic pottery from Easterton of Roseisle, Moray. In A. O'Connor and D. V. Clarke (eds.) *From the Stone Age to the 'Forty-five: studies presented to R. B. K. Stevenson,* 19–44. Edinburgh, John Donald.

Jones, A. (2007) *Memory and material culture.* Cambridge, Cambridge University Press.

Kinnes, I. (1979) *Round barrows and ring-ditches in the British Neolithic.* London, British Museum (Occasional Paper 7).

Kinnes, I. (1985) Circumstance not context: the Neolithic of Scotland as seen from the outside. *Proceedings of the Society of Antiquaries of Scotland* 115, 15–57.

Kinnes, I. (1992) Balnagowan and after: the context of non-megalithic mortuary sites in Scotland. In N. Sharples & J. A. Sheridan (eds.), *Vessels for the ancestors: essays on the Neolithic of Britain and Ireland in honour of Audrey Henshall,* 83–103. Edinburgh, Edinburgh University Press.

Kinnes, I (2004) "A truth universally acknowledged": some more thoughts on Neolithic round barrows. In A. Gibson and J. A. Sheridan (eds.) *From sickles to circles. Britain and Ireland at the time of Stonehenge,* 106–15. Stroud, Tempus.

Leivers, M., Roberts, J. and Peterson, R. (2000) The cairn at East Finnercy, Dunecht, Aberdeenshire. *Proceedings of the Society of Antiquaries of Scotland* 130, 183–95.

Linge, J. (1987) Re-discovering a landscape: the barrow and motte in north Ayrshire. *Proceedings of the Society of Antiquaries of Scotland* 117, 23–32.

Loveday, R. (2006) *Inscribed across the landscape. The cursus enigma.* Stroud, Tempus.

Marshall, D. (1976) The excavation of Hilton cairn. *Transactions of the Bute Natural History Society* 20, 9–27.

Masters, L. (1973) The Longhill long cairn. *Antiquity* 47, 96–100.

Mercer, R. J. and Midgley, M. (1997) The early Bronze Age cairn at Sketewan, Balnaguard, Perth and Kinross. *Proceedings of the Society of Antiquaries of Scotland* 127(1), 281–338.

Milne, J. (1892) Traces of early man in Buchan. *Transactions of the Buchan Field Club 2* (1891–92), 97–108.

Noble, G. (2006) *Neolithic Scotland: timber, stone, earth and fire.* Edinburgh, Edinburgh University Press.

Peterson, R. and Proudfoot, E. (1997) Fordhouse barrow excavations 1994–1997, *PAST* 27.

Proudfoot, E. (1999) Fordhouse barrow, Duns [radiocarbon dates]. *Discovery and Excavation in Scotland* 1999, 111.

RCAHMS (1990) *North-east Perth, an archaeological landscape.* Edinburgh, HMSO.

RCAHMS (1994) *South-east Perth, an archaeological landscape.* Edinburgh, HMSO.

Scott, J. (1989) The hall and motte at Courthill, Dalry, Ayrshire. *Proceedings of the Society of Antiquaries of Scotland* 119, 217–8.

Scott, J. (1992) Mortuary structures and megaliths. In N. Sharples and J. A. Sheridan (eds.) *Vessels for the ancestors: essays in honour of Audrey Henshall,* 104–19. Edinburgh, Edinburgh University Press.

Shepherd, A. (1996) A Neolithic ring-mound at Midtown of Pitglassie, Auchterless, Aberdeenshire. *Proceedings of the Society of Antiquaries of Scotland* 126, 17–51.

Sheridan, J. A. (2000) Achnacreebeag and its French connections: vive the Auld Alliance. In J. C. Henderson (ed.) *The prehistory and early history of Atlantic Europe,* 1–15. Oxford, British Archaeological Reports (BAR International Series 861).

Stewart, M. (1956) Guay, Dunkeld. *Discovery and Excavation in Scotland* 1956, 19.

Stewart, M. (1959) Strath Tay in the second millennium BC. A field survey. *Proceedings of the Society of Antiquaries of Scotland* 92, 71–84.

Stewart, M. and Barclay, G. J. (1997) Excavations in burial and ceremonial sites of the Bronze Age in Tayside. *Tayside and Fife Archaeological Journal* 3, 22–54.

Suddaby, I. (2007) A9 Kindallachan Junction improvements. *Discovery and Excavation in Scotland New Series* 8, 154.

Thomas, J. (2001) Neolithic enclosures: reflections on excavations in Wales and Scotland. In T. Darvill and J. Thomas (eds.) *Neolithic enclosures in Atlantic Northwest Europe,* 132–43. Oxford, Oxbow Books (Neolithic Studies Group Seminar Papers 6).

Thomas, J. (2002) *Excavations at Dunragit, 2002.* Unpublished interim report (see http://orgs.man.ac.uk/research/dunragit/)

Thomas, J. (ed.) (2007) *Place and memory. Excavations at the Pict's Knowe, Holywood and Holm Farm, Dumfries and Galloway 1994-1998.* Oxford, Oxbow books.

Chapter 3

Scotland's Neolithic Non-Megalithic Round Mounds: New Dates, Problems and Potential

Alison Sheridan

INTRODUCTION

The purpose of this contribution is to review briefly the non-megalithic round mounds of definite and probable Neolithic date in Scotland, and to draw attention to some accelerator mass spectrometry (AMS) radiocarbon dates, relating to the use of four of these monuments – Midtown of Pitglassie, one of the cairns of Atherb, East Finnercy and Pitnacree – that have been commissioned by the author over the past seven years as part of an ongoing, and broad-ranging, National Museums Scotland (NMS) radiocarbon dating initiative. The issues involved in obtaining these dates, and in seeking to obtain others for Scottish non-megalithic round mounds, will be outlined. Where the potential exists to obtain further new dates, this is pointed out.

BACKGROUND: THE NMS RADIOCARBON DATING INITIATIVE

Since the early 1990s, and in addition to commissioning fieldwork-related dates, the NMS Archaeology Department has undertaken radiocarbon dating programmes to target specific aspects of Scotland's archaeology (Sheridan 2002 and see annual NMS datelists in *Discovery and Excavation in Scotland* from 2001 onwards). Until 1998, this work was principally geared to providing information for the Early People displays in what was then called the Museum of Scotland (now part of the National Museum of Scotland), and it tended to focus on organic finds from peat bogs, such as wooden bowls and pieces of clothing (Sheridan *et al.* 2002, and see Oxford Radiocarbon Accelerator Unit (ORAU) *Datelists* 16, 20 and 29 in *Archaeometry*). Thereafter, and taking advantage of developments that allowed the structural carbonate in cremated bone to be dated (Lanting *et al.* 2001), human bone associated with Beaker pottery (Sheridan 2007a), early Bronze Age cinerary urns (Sheridan 2003, 2007b), Food Vessels (Sheridan 2004) and various other early Bronze Age artefact types including jet jewellery (Sheridan 2006a; 2007b) was dated. Additional dates relating to Scottish Beaker, Food Vessel and aceramic early Bronze Age graves have recently been produced by Mike Parker Pearson's *Beaker People Project* (Sheridan *et al.* 2006; 2007) and Neil Curtis's *Beakers and Bodies* project (Curtis *et al.* 2007). Funding for the NMS-commissioned dates has come from NMS, Historic Scotland, the Society of Antiquaries of Scotland, Aberdeenshire Archaeology and NERC (through the ORADS scheme); in addition, the University of Groningen kindly provided a number of determinations at no cost.

The dating of Neolithic funerary monuments has been a long-standing interest of NMS Archaeology, and working in collaboration with Rick Schulting (University of Oxford), Finbar McCormick (Queen's University Belfast) and Richard Jones (Glasgow University), it has been possible to obtain a number of useful new dates for Scottish megalithic chamber tombs (*e.g.* Cuween passage tomb, Orkney: Sheridan 2005a and b; 2006a; *cf.* Schulting 2004 for some of the others and see Schulting and Sheridan in prep. for a synthesis). Among these, of considerable interest have been the results of dating eagle bones from Isbister chamber tomb, Orkney, which revealed that the eagles had been deposited in the tomb during the second half of the third millennium BC, long after its construction (Pitts 2006; Sheridan 2005b).

The quest to improve the dating of Scotland's Neolithic non-megalithic round mounds was a logical part of this overall desire to maximise the potential of the existing body of evidence. Accordingly, attempts were made, from 2003 onwards, to locate and date suitable samples – especially those of cremated bone which, until shortly before then, had not been datable. Funding for these dates again came from various sources; particular thanks are extended to the late Ian Shepherd, of Aberdeenshire Archaeology, who kindly arranged sponsorship of the Atherb date, and to Tom Higham of ORAU, for the East Finnercy date.

All the dates cited here have been calibrated with OxCal v.4.1, using the IntCal 04 calibration curve (Reimer *et al.* 2004); values at 2σ are cited, rounded to ten years, as advocated by Mook and Waterbolk (1985).

NEOLITHIC NON-MEGALITHIC ROUND MOUNDS IN SCOTLAND

Credit for confirming the existence of this class of monument in Scotland must go to John Coles and the late Derek Simpson, whose excavation at Pitnacree, Perth and Kinross – part of a study of the barrows, standing stones and stone circles of Strathtay – demonstrated the Early Neolithic date of this particular round mound (Coles & Simpson 1965). In discussing other possible Scottish examples, they cited East Finnercy in Aberdeenshire and Courthill, Dalry, North Ayrshire.

Ian Kinnes subsequently reviewed the evidence for this class of monument, on a nationwide basis, in 1979; he returned to the subject in 1985, 1992 and 2004, and his current work with Marcus Brittain will update and refine the *corpus* further. The number of Scottish sites has remained small, and the list of candidates has varied between publications (*cf.* Brophy, this volume Chapter 2); this author would exclude Kinnes's 1992 suggestions of Gullane, East Lothian and Achnacreebeag, Argyll and Bute, on the grounds that the former is very likely to be of Iron Age date, and the latter is a megalithic monument lying at the beginning of Scotland's passage tomb tradition. Whether one should follow Kinnes in including Mid Gleniron B, Dumfries and Galloway, with its stone chamber under a round mound, and Hilton, on Bute – a partly slab-built chamber built against a rock outcrop, with a roughly semi-circular mound – is debatable, although the early Neolithic date of at least the latter monument is not to be doubted. Hilton, together with the simple megalithic stone chambers under round or oval cairns forming the Phase 1 structures at Mid Gleniron 1 and 2 (Corcoran 1969), and indeed the simple megalithic chamber at Cairnholy 1, Dumfries and Galloway, associated with a façade and long rectilinear cairn (Piggott & Powell 1949), may well represent the translation of a wooden chamber form into a slab-built stone chamber. Indeed, the emergence of the "Clyde cairn" monument type is clearly part of this process (Sheridan 2006b). Such monuments, although not unrelated to the sites discussed in this paper, broaden the debate about early Neolithic funerary monuments beyond the scope of this contribution.

This paper will focus on the candidates that provide the strongest evidence for (or best chance of) being Neolithic non-megalithic round mounds, and of these, all but one are to be found in northeast and east-central Scotland, at Boghead, Moray; Midtown of Pitglassie, Atherb cairns numbers 2 (Pow Sod/Powsode), 3 and possibly 4, and East Finnercy, all Aberdeenshire; and Pitnacree, Perth and Kinross. The exception, at Courthill, Dalry in North Ayrshire, lies in southwest Scotland (Figure 3.1). Others may well exist, of course, but without excavation it is impossible to determine whether they are of Neolithic or of Bronze Age (or even later) date. In Strathtay, for instance, excavation of a large (20m in diameter, 1.3m high) cairn at Sketewan Farm, Balnaguard, just 2km from Pitnacree on the opposite side of the Tay, revealed that it was of early Bronze Age date (Mercer & Midgley 1997).

The reader is referred to the published reports for full details of the sites in question; what follows is a brief description of the mounds, their associated finds, pre-existing dates, potential for obtaining new dates, and (in the case of some of the mounds) dates that the author has obtained.

THE SITES: DATES AND DATABILITY

1. Boghead, Fochabers, Moray

Excavated in 1972 and 1974 by Aubrey Burl, this round mound – consisting of a sandy capping over a cairn comprising three or four discrete heaps of stones, the whole around 15m in diameter and surviving to a height of *c*.1.5m high – was found to cover a 3cm-thick layer of charcoal, other carbonised plant remains and burnt sand, containing sherds, flints and a few comminuted fragments of cremated bone (Figure 3.2 and Burl 1984). This black layer overlay a patch of heavily-burnt sand, believed to represent the location of a pyre, and also a pit, with a hole for a substantial post close to it. Also present under the black layer were several stakeholes and two small hollows; there were also further stakeholes, and larger hollows, not covered by the black layer and not all covered by the stone heaps. Sherds from at least thirty-seven vessels in the modified Carinated Bowl (CB) tradition (Figure 3.3: Henshall's "North-Eastern style": Henshall 1984; henceforth, CBNE: Sheridan 2007c) were found, mostly in the black layer but also among the cairn stones, on the old ground surface, in the central pit, in a couple of the hollows and around the mound. Many of the sherds had been scorched. The flint finds (some of which were burnt) were also mostly found in the burnt layer and on the old ground surface. The charcoal was mainly of oak; other carbonised plant material included grains of emmer wheat and naked 6-row barley, and hazelnut shells. The burnt bone was too small to permit identification; the excavator assumed that it is human, and suggested that the body or bodies in question may first have been buried in the pit, prior to being cremated in skeletal (or at least decomposed) form. There was also evidence for later activity at Boghead, with a pit containing an early, undecorated Beaker (Burl 1984, illus 11.44); the possibility that this may have been an

Figure 3.1: Map showing the non-megalithic round mounds discussed in this paper. 1: Boghead; 2. Pitglassie; 3: Atherb; 4: East Finnercy; 5: Pitnacree; 6: Courthill

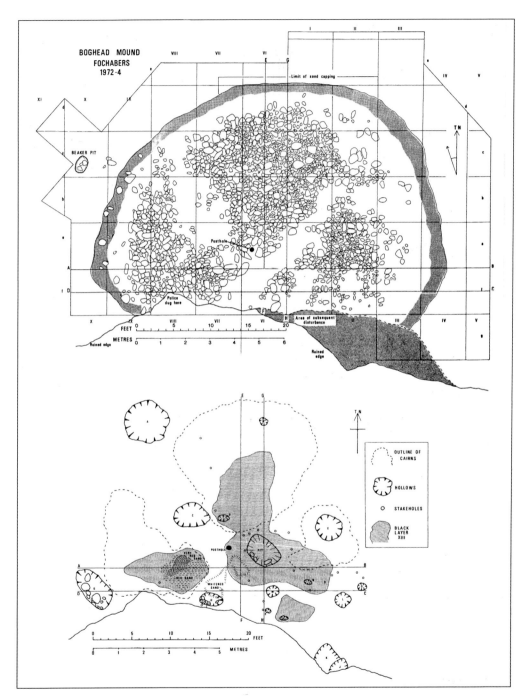

Figure 3.2a (above) and 3.2b (facing page): Boghead, Moray: plan and section of the mound, and plan of the sub-mound features. (From Burl 1984; I am grateful to the Society of Antiquaries of Scotland for permission to reproduce these images)

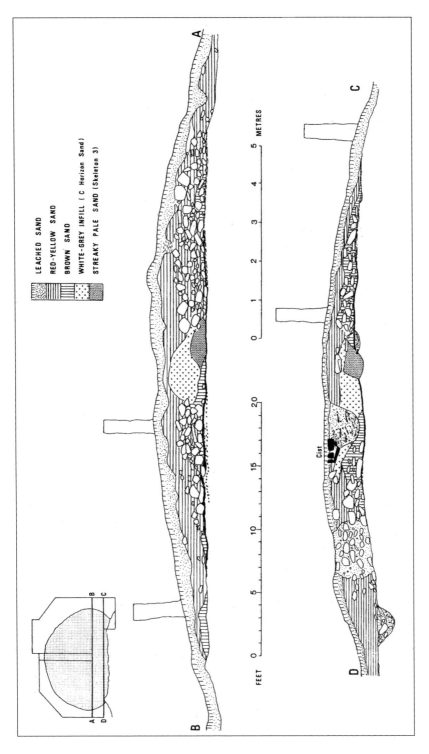

LEACHED SAND

RED-YELLOW SAND

BROWN SAND

WHITE-GREY INFILL (C Horizon Sand)

STREAKY PALE SAND (Skeleton 3)

Figure 3.2b

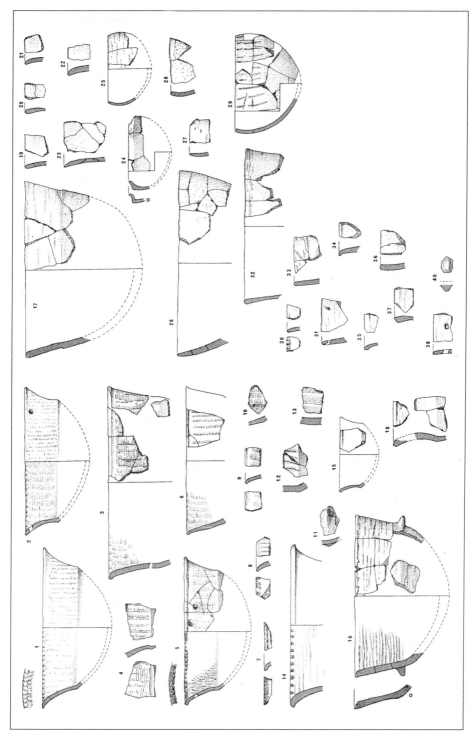

Figure 3.3: Boghead, Moray: the Early Neolithic pottery. (From Burl 1984; I am grateful to the Society of Antiquaries of Scotland for permission to reproduce these images)

Table 3.1

Dated material and context	Lab. No.	Date BP	Date as adjusted by Historic Scotland
Oak charcoal in infill of central pit	SRR-683	4946±175	4946±250
Charred oak, layer XIII under North Cairn	SRR-684	4823±60	4823±110
Oak charcoal, bottom of Hollow M	SRR-685	5031±100	5031±140
Charcoal (species unspecified), layer XIII	SRR-686	4898±60	4898±110
Charcoal (species unspecified), Beaker pit	SRR-687	3867±70	3867±110
Charcoal (species unspecified), above 'cobbling' under layer XIII	SRR-688	4124±200	4124±280
Charcoal (species unspecified), layer XIII	SRR-689	4959±110	4959±155
Charcoal (species unspecified), under West Cairn	SRR-690	6006±60	6006±110

early Beaker inhumation grave has recently been discussed (Sheridan 2008). A small cist near the surface of the mound, containing a little cremated bone from a young female and infant, may be of Bronze Age date; and the mound had also been re-used as a cemetery for extended inhumation graves orientated roughly east to west, probably during the first millennium AD.

Eight radiocarbon dates, from charcoal from various contexts, were obtained by Burl from the Scottish Universities Research and Reactor Centre (Table 3.1 and see the Historic Scotland on-line C14 database, whose URL is listed in the bibliography). Of these, three were of oak and may therefore be subject to the old wood effect; the species of the other five was not specified. Four of the dates have standard deviations of, or exceeding, ±100 years, rendering them of limited value. Furthermore, in their critical review of Scottish radiocarbon dates, Patrick Ashmore *et al.* (2000) recommended that the quoted errors for dates obtained before the mid-1980s should be multiplied, since in their view there was systematic bias and unexplained variability in these determinations. As a result, all of the Boghead dates have ended up with standard deviations in excess of ±100 years, meaning that they are effectively useless.

The Boghead finds archive was allocated to NMS in 1995, and in 2006 the cremated bone from underneath the mound was examined to determine whether it was viable for radiocarbon dating. Unfortunately, with one possible exception (still embedded in sediment), the comminuted fragments were found to be too small to constitute single-entity samples (and indeed, even if all the loose fragments from each find location under the mound were to be put together – a practice that would not be acceptable, given the need to submit single entity samples – they would not attain the minimum acceptable sample weight of 1.3g). Therefore, unless the technique of dating burnt bone develops so that much smaller samples can be dated – and unless the piece in sediment turns out to be of sufficient weight – this material is of no use for dating. The best chance of obtaining new radiocarbon dates lies with the carbonised cereal grains and hazelnut shells, but unfortunately these do not seem to have been delivered with the rest of the assemblage and enquiries have not succeeded in tracking them down – at least, not yet.

Some of the sherds have a thin layer of encrusted organic residue, and this might be usable for radiocarbon dating. One other potential source of datable material may exist, in the form of invisible organic residues absorbed within the potsherds; this is true of all the pottery from the sites considered in this contribution. Initial attempts to date such material, by Rob Berstan and colleagues using early Neolithic sherds from the Sweet Track, Somerset, have been claimed as successful (Berstan *et al.* 2008), and research continues to refine this technique, and to investigate further the issues surrounding the dating of visible encrusted organic residues on pottery (R. Evershed and A. Bayliss pers. comm.). This author would welcome seeing the results of further research on dating absorbed lipids before submitting sherds; but it appears to be a potentially useful approach. The only other source of dating for the Neolithic material is comparative dating of the modified (North-Eastern style) CB pottery (for a recent review of which, see Sheridan 2007c). Here, the growing number of dates – including those from the "hall" at Balbridie and from sites at Kintore, Aberdeenshire – indicates that this variant of the CB tradition developed rapidly after the first appearance of the tradition as a whole, and was in use by the thirty-eighth century. (See also below for the dates for Midtown of Pitglassie, where this kind of pottery was found.)

2. Midtown of Pitglassie, Aberdeenshire

This monument was excavated by Alexandra Shepherd in 1978, following earlier partial excavation by Alexander Fenton during the 1950s (Shepherd 1996). The sequence of activity, reconstructed by Shepherd, is as follows: a circular area was delimited by the stripping of turf; a funerary pyre was lit in the centre of this area and an individual was cremated. Several pits and scoops were dug, and that individual's remains were then placed in three pits and on the stripped surface, along with pieces of broken pots and of struck flint (including a leaf-shaped arrowhead) and quartz. The scoops may have been settings for uprights of stone or timber. A sticky layer of black-grey charcoal-rich soil, rich in potsherds, was deposited in the northeast arc of the mound (if not elsewhere as well) – around the pits and scoops. The stripped turves – along with stones and earth (containing potsherds, struck flint, quartz and quartzite and a few fragments of cremated bone) were then used to construct a ring-cairn (*c.*7.2m in maximum diameter) that covered the pits, and finally a capping of topsoil and gravelly clay was placed over the ring-bank, with struck quartz scattered on it (Figure 3.4). The ring-mound survives to a height of *c.*0.6m. The central area may have been filled in with cairn material at this point, or else later; its chronology is uncertain, because the area was heavily disturbed by Fenton's excavations in 1952. If this central cairn was a later addition, then it is likely to be associated with a putative cist structure, from which a complete, crushed, cord-impressed Beaker was found; sherds of two or three other cord-impressed Beakers were also deposited in the central area. Finally, the ring-mound was used in the recent past for a sheep burial.

The pottery found in the pre-mound levels and in the mound is, as at Boghead, of CBNE type; pieces from at least fifteen vessels are represented (Figure 3.5). Apart from the leaf-shaped flint arrowhead, no chronologically-diagnostic lithic item was found. The abundance of quartz was noted as being a feature not characteristic of early Neolithic monuments.

Two radiocarbon dates were obtained for the excavator, from bulk samples of charcoal of relatively short-lived trees (ash, alder, birch, beech and willow) sealed under the ring-mound. One, from Cremation Pit 1, produced a date of 3970–3520 cal BC (GU-2014: 4935±135 BP); note that, in the Historic Scotland on-line radiocarbon database, it is incorrectly stated that the dated material for GU-2014 was encrusted organic residue from a sherd.

The excavation publication makes it clear that charcoal was the dated material. The other, from the black layer, produced a date of 3630–3350 cal BC (GU-2049: 4660±50 BP). Since these dates were obtained after the mid-1980s, their standard deviation values have not been adjusted upwards by Ashmore *et al.*; that for GU-2014 is already unacceptably large. In 2007, the author commissioned a date from a fragment of the cremated human bone, from Cremation Pit 3. The result came out at 3940–3670 cal BC (GrA-34772: 4995±35 BP). Quite how the discrepancy between this result and GU-2049 is to be explained is unclear. There is scope for further dating, with more cremated bone (from the same individual) and more charcoal being available; one alternative is the encrusted organic residue that was noted on some of the sherds of pot ASH 13 (and possibly also any absorbed lipid that may exist inside these and other sherds).

3. One of the Cairns of Atherb, Aberdeenshire

An 1892 paper by John Milne, on *Traces of Early Man in Buchan*, describes four cairns at and near Atherb that had been "swept away by the march of improvement" (Milne 1892). Three of these (Nos 2–4) were round; the fourth (No. 1), long. Two of these will be described here in some detail, since the cremated bone from Atherb that was dated for the author in 2003 will have come from either No. 1 or No. 2.

Cairn No. 1 appears to have been a non-megalithic long cairn, about 100 yards (*c.*91m) long, *c.*27m wide and *c.*4.25m high at its centre. From its description it seems likely that it had contained a substantial wooden mortuary structure at its centre, which had been set alight, the heat of the fire vitrifying the cairn stones in this area to a depth of *c.*90cm. In addition to "the charred remains of oak logs, some of which must have been pieces of large trees" that "traversed the [cairn] in various directions", sherds of undecorated early Neolithic pottery and "vast quantities of calcined human bones" were found. The bones were recovered from among and below the vitrified cairn stones and the best-preserved examples were parts of skulls; jaws still with teeth present; and "joints of vertebrae"; bones from all other parts of the body were present, including the tips of fingers. Among the bones were "many flint arrow points, all heart or leaf-shaped, some entire and some broken, but all showing that they had passed through the fiery ordeal. They must have either been in the bodies or placed beside them prior to their calcinations". The sherds were mostly found outside the area of vitrification, on the old ground surface under the cairn; Milne argued that they had been deposited as sherds, rather than as complete pots.

Cairn No. 2, called "Pow Sod" (or "Powsode"), was round, 34m in circumference and 1.83m high. Excavated by Milne in 1854, the cairn was found to comprise a mixture of stones, earth and wood ash, but none of the stones was burnt (except where "hallow[e'en]-fires" had been lit in the recent past). "A good many" pieces of cremated human bone were found among the cairn material, with skull fragments predominating (as in Cairn 1). No reference was made to any sherds being associated with these bones, or of any pottery that sounds to be Neolithic being found in the cairn. A cist-like structure at the west of the cairn – not necessarily contemporary with its construction, but almost certain to be Neolithic – contained seventeen flint nodules, each missing a chip as if from testing its quality, together with a fine blade-polished axehead of black nodular flint and a large flint scraper/knife. Later activity is attested by the presence of an All-Over-Cord (AOC) decorated Beaker, found crushed on its side; a small pot, probably an early Bronze Age

Alison Sheridan

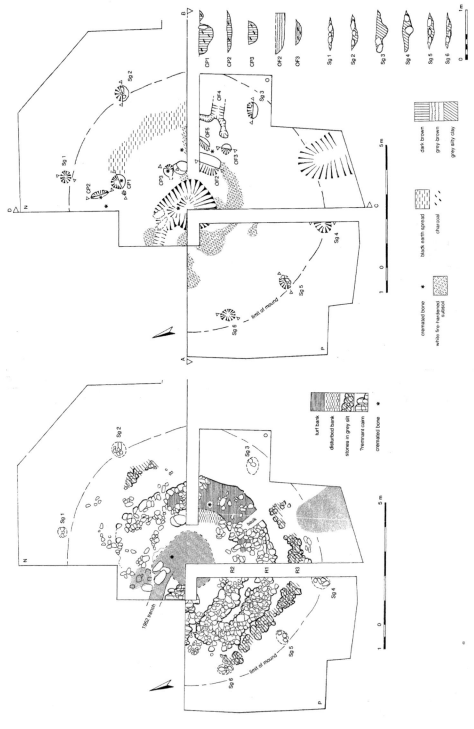

Figure 3.4a (this page) and 3.4b (facing page): Midtown of Pitglassie, Aberdeenshire: plan of ring-bank structure and subsoil features, and sections AB and CD. (From Shepherd 1996; I am grateful to the Society of Antiquaries of Scotland for permission to reproduce these images)

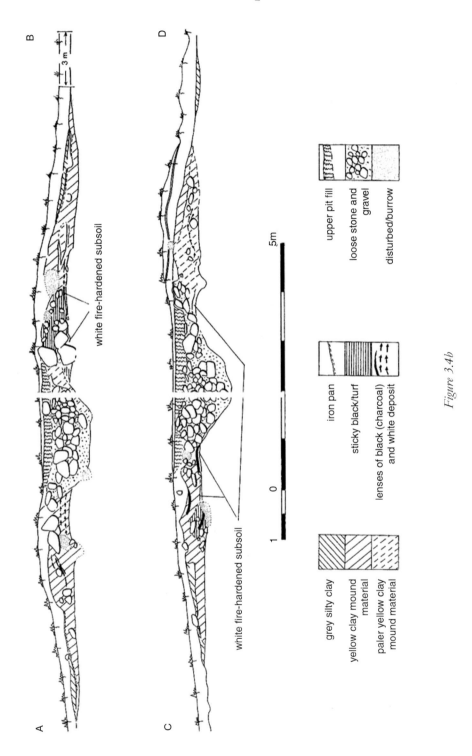

white fire-hardened subsoil

white fire-hardened subsoil

iron pan

sticky black/turf

lenses of black (charcoal)
and white deposit

upper pit fill

loose stone and
gravel

disturbed/burrow

grey silty clay

yellow clay mound
material

paler yellow clay
mound material

Figure 3.4b

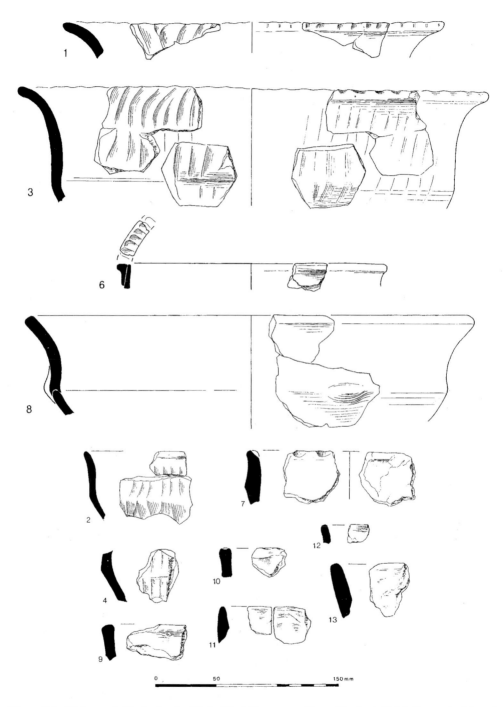

Figure 3.5: Midtown of Pitglassie: the Early Neolithic pottery. (From Shepherd 1996; I am grateful to the Society of Antiquaries of Scotland for permission to reproduce this image)

accessory vessel; and two small lined pits dug into the cairn, filled with small pebbles, ash, and minute fragments of calcined bones. No description was provided of the surface at the bottom of the cairn, but from Milne's account it seems likely that bodies had been cremated here, their remains becoming incorporated within the cairn, and so this appears to be a Neolithic non-megalithic round cairn, analogous to Boghead, with secondary re-use.

Cairn No. 3, "Tor Voe", seems to have matched Pow Sod in its size, appearance and the construction of the cairn, which was around 18m in diameter and 1.83m high; the farmer who had it cleared claimed that the bones were "far more numerous and in a better state of preservation" than those from Pow Sod. He "had the bones buried near the spot". Cairn No. 4, on the farm of Honeynook, had mostly been "carted away before I was interested in such things", and no bones seem to have been spotted during its demolition, but Milne noted "wood ashes and burnt stones" on the site when he visited, and stated that he suspected that the cairn had resembled No. 1. Other archaeological remains found on the Atherb farm where the cairns had stood comprise "vestiges of old fire-places, and sometimes the entire floors of pre-historic dwellings"; pottery from one of these, preserved in NMS, is of an AOC Beaker.

Some of the finds from Atherb have ended up in NMS. Milne reported having presented "a good few of the larger and best preserved bones from both cairns [*i.e.* Nos. 1 and 2] … along with the flint axe and knife, arrow points, broken urns and fused rock … to Dr (now Sir Arthur) Mitchell of Edinburgh", and most of the artefacts – along with sherds from at least one of the "hearth" sites – were acquired by the then-named National Museum of Antiquities of Scotland (NMAS), presumably from Mitchell, either in 1880, 1881 or 1896. (The record is ambiguous and the finds labelling somewhat confused. The relevant registration numbers are NMS X.AC 527–30, described as "fragments of steatite vessels" – not mentioned in Milne's account; NMS X.HH 52–3, vitrified stone, and NMS X.EO 909–925, pottery. The flint items are not present.) The Neolithic pottery has been described and illustrated by Audrey Henshall (1983, 39–40 and fig. 5); it falls within the CB tradition and represents either the earliest, "traditional" variant of that kind of pottery or its early regional variant, CBNE. The Beaker sherds were included in David Clarke's corpus of British and Irish Beakers (1970, 510). The bones did not accompany the artefacts, and had believed to be lost, but in 2002 they turned up in NMS, unexpectedly, among unregistered material that had been bequeathed to NMAS by Sir Francis Tress Barry, and received in 1908 after his death in 1907. The boxes in which they had been stored are clearly labelled "from the Cairns of Atherb", and the bones match Milne's description as being large, and mainly comprising skull fragments, so presumably Mitchell had passed them to Tress Barry (as a fellow antiquarian). Even though it was impossible to determine whether the bones had come from the long cairn No. 1, or the round cairn No. 2, it was deemed worthwhile to obtain a radiocarbon date, and the result came out at 3700–3390 cal BC (GrA-23971: 4815±45 BP). This is a little later than the date obtained for cremated bone from Midtown of Pitglassie, and it is particularly frustrating not to know whether it comes from the long cairn (and therefore dates the CBNE pottery), or from the round cairn, seemingly with no Neolithic pottery associated with it. The only scope for obtaining new dates, apart from by dating further pieces of cremated bone, would seem to lie in the absorbed lipids that may (or may not) exist within the pottery from Cairn 1, or in the organic encrustation noted on one of the sherds.

4. East Finnercy, Aberdeenshire

This relatively featureless round cairn – which survives as an oval mound 26.5m long, 22m wide and 2m high – has been investigated on at least three occasions: in 1924 or 1925 by the tenant farmer; again in 1925, under supervision by a Commissioner of the RCAHMS; and in 1952, by R. J. C. Atkinson. The results of all these interventions were finally published in 2000 (Leivers *et al.* 2000); the inadequacy of the records has made it difficult to establish a detailed structural description.

The cairn, of stones mixed with earth, had rested on the old ground surface which, apparently, had not been stripped. On this surface were found sherds of CBNE pottery (with sherds from three vessels found during Atkinson's excavations: Figure 3.6), along with cremated bone (in a degraded condition, but including possible sheep remains), charcoal and "hearths" (according to the 1950s documentation); towards the south-east end of Atkinson's trench was found a shallow oval pit. Further sherds, along with a leaf-shaped flint arrowhead and a fragment of an unburnt human femur (see below) were found in the cairn material; documentation from the 1920s excavations claimed that there were layers of ashes in the cairn, and that some of the cairn stones appear to have been burnt. At some point, it appears that a cord-impressed Beaker sherd was claimed to have been found at East Finnercy, but it seems likely that this is a case of accidental "accretion" of unrelated material, unless it was found during the 1920s; the sherd was not found in Leivers' review of the material held at the University of Cardiff, and it is not in the NMS collections (see Leivers *et al.* 2000, 193).

The surviving finds from the 1925 excavations, held by NMS, comprise thirty-two sherds, one small charcoal fragment and a single piece of flint debitage (NMS X.EO 385–92 and unregistered). In 2008, the documentary archive from the 1920s and from Atkinson's excavations was passed to NMS, for forwarding to the National Monuments Record of Scotland. Atkinson's finds accompanied the documentary archive; among this material was the unburnt femur shaft from the cairn.

No radiocarbon dates had previously been obtained for material from East Finnercy, and Historic Scotland – funders of Leivers' *et al.* work – had decided not to get the unburnt bone fragment dated, on the grounds that its contextual integrity could not be guaranteed. The current author decided, however, that even though there was a good chance that the bone may result from secondary activity, it would be useful to get some indication of its date, and accordingly a small sample was sent for radiocarbon dating in 2008. The result, through the kindness of ORAU, confirmed that the bone was indeed secondary to the early Neolithic activity: AD 830–990 (OxA-18374: 1124±27 BP). The δ13C‰ value is -21.21, indicating that no adjustment for any marine element in the individual's diet needs to be made: this is a normal signature for a terrestrial diet. Therefore, the individual dates to a period when Viking presence was being felt in parts of Scotland. The absence of any associated artefacts makes speculation as to the individual's identity fruitless. It should, however, be noted that the chances that the individual had been a Viking are slim, since the findspot lies well outside the main area of pagan Norse graves, notwithstanding the somewhat tenuous evidence from Fordhouse barrow, Angus (where a mid-tenth century copper alloy ringed pin was found at the top of a Neolithic mound and could conceivably have come from such a grave: Paterson & Proudfoot, unpublished MS 1936/06 in National Monuments Record of Scotland).

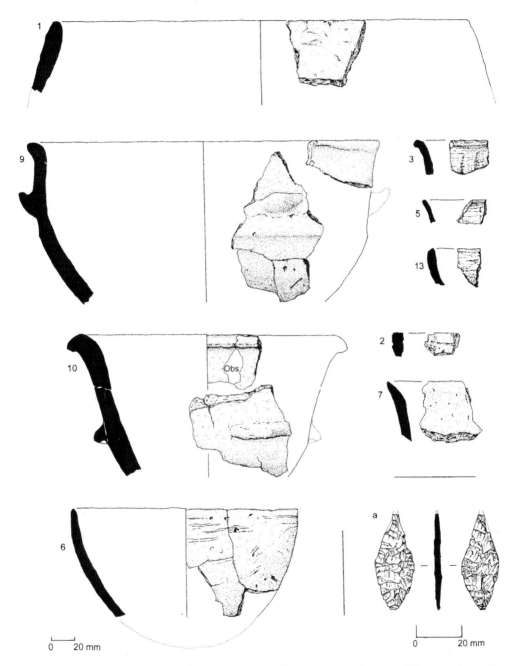

Figure 3.6: East Finnercy, Aberdeenshire: the Early Neolithic pottery and leaf-shaped flint arrowhead. (From Leivers et al. 2000; I am grateful to the Society of Antiquaries of Scotland for permission to reproduce this image)

The Atkinson finds included, in addition to the femur shaft fragment, several small pieces of charcoal and cremated bone ostensibly from relatively secure contexts. One piece of cremated bone is clearly of sufficient weight to be dated, and so this is next on the NMS' "To date" list; judgement will have to be exercised in deciding whether to date the charcoal (on the grounds that charcoal fragments could have been moved around by worm action. The same may be true of the cremated bone; one can only test this by dating). A couple of sherds have thin organic residues, but probably not enough material to be dated; once again, absorbed lipid may be present and datable.

5. Pitnacree, Perth and Kinross

Pitnacree is a large, earthen barrow, one of a distinctive group of imposing earthen round barrows in Strathtay. Before excavation it was slightly oval, *c.*27m in maximum diameter and 2.74m high (Coles & Simpson 1965). Coles and Simpson's excavations revealed the following sequence of activities (Figure 3.7):

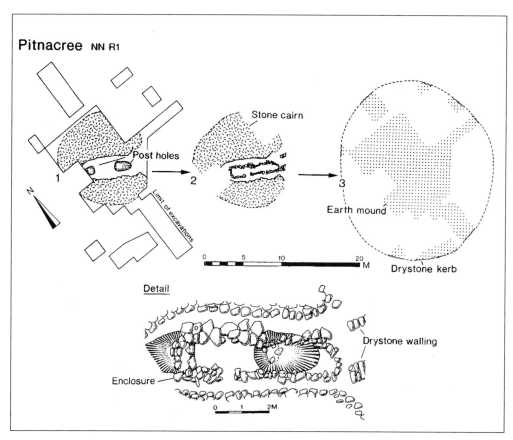

Figure 3.7: Pitnacree, Perth & Kinross: structural phases (from Kinnes 1992, reproduced with permission). Note that his phase '1' conflates phase 2 and part of Phase 3 (i.e. the erection of the horseshoe-shaped mound) in the description presented here)

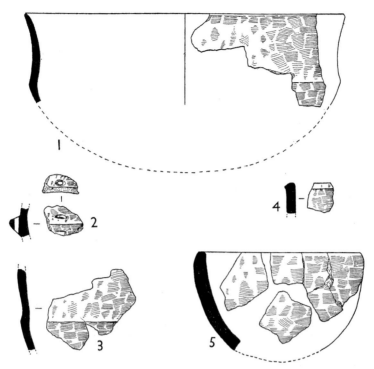

Figure 3.8: Pitnacree: the Early Neolithic pottery. (From Coles & Simpson 1965; reproduced by permission of the Prehistoric Society)

Pre-construction phase: Possible burning of – or else, burning on – the old ground surface (represented by "a considerable quantity of carbonized wood"), and deposition of sherds from at least eight pots (of "traditional CB" type: Figure 3.8), together with some flints. The fact that may of the sherds, flints, and natural schist fragments were found on their edge, and that the soil in this area seemed particularly thick, was interpreted as possible evidence of cultivation. The burning was interpreted as pre-construction clearance of vegetation.

Construction phase 1: Digging of two large oval pits and erection of two massive split-trunk posts, 2.75m apart, to create what Kinnes (1979) has termed a "linear zone". Some abraded sherds of traditional CB pottery found on the old land surface may relate to the use of this monument. The posts stood long enough for them to decay *in situ*.

Construction phase 2: Construction of a northwest to southeast orientated, horseshoe-shaped bank of stone in the same area, overlying the upcast from the post pits. A stone-capped, drystone entrance passage, 1.5m tall at its inner end, led east southeast from the open end of the bank. The inner surface of the stone bank was covered with a grey sandy deposit, possibly a deliberate lining. Erection of the bank must have been preceded by the deposition of further sherds on the old ground surface. Within the embanked area, four discrete deposits of cremated human remains, representing an adult male, an adult (probable) female and a child, were placed on the old ground surface (although the excavators argued that two of these deposits, from the adult male, must have been laid down when the turf mound was being constructed, as they were found 15cm apart, and separated by 5cm of mound material. However, disturbance of a pre-existing deposit when the turf mound was being erected seems an equally, or more plausible explanation.). These were then covered by the construction of a long rectangular stone "enclosure", represented by a mostly single course of stones set on edge, found leaning inwards. (Whether this had been a free-standing enclosure, or else a frame for some kind of wooden structure, was not discussed by the excavators, who clearly favoured the former interpretation; the presence of carbonized wood was, however, noted within the enclosure, along with sherds of coarse quartz-tempered Neolithic pottery.) The next actions were the blocking of the passageway with earth and boulders, filling in of the enclosure with boulders, and erection of the turf mound, covering the whole of the structure. The outer edge of the mound was defined by a low drystone wall revetment, but the excavators noted that this had been "blocked" by further, external revetment in the form of waterworn stones and pebbles.

There was evidence of secondary activity on the mound. At least one, probably two, short cists were inserted into the side of the mound, probably during the late third or early second millennium BC; and, on the summit of the mound, a pit was dug; cremated remains of an adult, possibly female, were deposited in it along with charcoal, probably from the pyre; and a standing stone was erected in the pit. The cremated remains "lay upon and mingled with a radial agglomeration of stones".

Coles and Simpson obtained two dates from charcoal (species unspecified), one (GaK-601: 4810±90 BP) from the material resting on the old ground surface (see 1 above), the other (GaK-602: 4220±90 BP) from the standing stone pit. In their review of Scottish radiocarbon dates Ashmore *et al.* (2000) were particularly critical of the radiocarbon dates obtained by the Gakusan laboratory, and accordingly in the Historic Scotland on-line C14 database, the standard deviations have each been increased to ±270, rendering them useless.

In an attempt to improve the dating of this site, in 2001 the author set out to find and date the cremated bone. Coles and Simpson had sent the bone, for identification, to osteologist Bernard Denston in the (then-named) Duckworth Laboratory of the Department of Physical Anthropology at Cambridge University. Through the kindness of Maggie Bellatti at the Laboratory, the present author searched through the human bone store there, but unfortunately, despite an extensive search, the Neolithic cremated bone could not be located. Only the bone from the standing stone pit was found. A fragment of this was duly dated, at the University of Groningen, producing the following result: 2340–1960 cal BC (GrA-21744: 3740±60 BP). Although this does not move forward the dating of the early Neolithic activity, it does nevertheless usefully locate the creation of this pit grave with standing stone to the period when Beaker (and, from the twenty-second century BC, Food Vessel) pottery was in use. The juxtaposition of the grave with the standing stone is reminiscent of a few other sites of this general period, including most notably the North Grave at Cairnpapple (Piggott 1949); and an echo of this practice was recorded at the nearby funerary monument at Sketewan where, during the pre-cairn phase of funerary activities, the position of a large cist was marked (albeit temporarily) by a post, 15cm in diameter (Mercer & Midgley 1997, 297).

The new Pitnacree date also helps to clarify the sequence of late third/early second millennium activities in this part of Strathtay. If the radiocarbon dates from Sketewan are accepted at face value, the inaugural episode/s of cremation that established that site as a focus for funerary activity may have been contemporary with, or slightly later than, the Pitnacree standing stone grave: the earliest date, from mixed oak and alder charcoal found (according to the publication) at the base of the pyre remains, is 2130–1770 cal BC (GU-2676: 3590±50 BP). The possibility of an "old wood" effect from the oak cannot be ruled out, however, although this date would not be inconsistent with that of the Food Vessel that was found in the aforementioned, central cist whose pit cut through the pyre debris.

6. Courthill, Dalry, North Ayrshire

This monument was the subject of a rescue excavation by R. W. Cochran Patrick in 1872, as it was imminently to be engulfed by tippings from iron-works; the quality of the description allows a clear impression of the nature of the sub-cairn structures to be made (Cochran Patrick 1874). The monument consisted of a flat-topped, sub-circular or oval earthen mound, 27m in diameter and 5 to 6m high (Figure 3.9); organic preservation was good, as pieces of still-green plant matter were found within it. At the base of the mound was found the burnt remains of a northeast to southwest orientated rectangular enclosure, 13.7m by 6m, made from oak stakes (some of which had fallen into the enclosure). Two pairs of much larger, grooved, squared-off stakes had been set at equivalent positions along the long sides, towards the northeast end; the *c.*1m-wide gap between each pair was filled by narrow hazel and birch posts. From this description it seems likely that the latter had been part of removable hurdle screens, capable of being slid up the grooves to form entrances into the enclosure. At the southeast entrance, an oar- or paddle-like piece of hard oak was found.

Within this enclosure, evidence for construction and other activity was found. A low wall of boulders and smaller stones ran close to, and in alignment with, the southwest side of the enclosure; immediately above these stones "were layers of burnt earth, mixed with pieces of charcoal and other burnt matter, and in this was found a very good flint arrow-head", together with some flint chips and fragments. Above this was found "a stratum of dark unctuous earth, with layers of vegetable matter composed principally of fern and moor moss." Elsewhere within the enclosure, set equidistant from its southwest and northeast ends, was a pair of pits for large oak posts, of which traces still survived; these were set 8.2m apart. The southwest post was found to be charred, and preserved tool-marks from where it had been squared off; a possible stake-hole was found around 1.2m away. Adjacent to the southwest post was an area where the old ground surface had been burnt by "a fierce and long-continued fire". Immediately above this was a thin layer, up to 5cm thick, of "grey and red ashes, with occasionally small fragments of bone. The largest of these was apparently part of the bone of a large deer." Flint chips and pieces of worked flint, including a scraper, were found immediately above this bed of ash; above that was a "thin layer of highly compressed moss and bracken", and on top of that was a thick layer, up to *c.*1 m deep, of "dark unctuous earth." containing "fern, moor-moss, coarse grass, reeds, *&c.*, mixed with small pieces of charred wood". The other large post towards the northeast end of the enclosure was described as "corresponding to the one first discovered", and so was presumably also burnt. Extending eastwards from this was "a deposit of ashes about 3 inches [*c.*7.5cm] thick, nearly 6 feet [1.83m] in length, and about 2½ [feet, *i.e. c.*0.75m] in breadth. Amongst the ashes were numerous small fragments of bone, and parts apparently of deer horn [*i.e.* antler]."

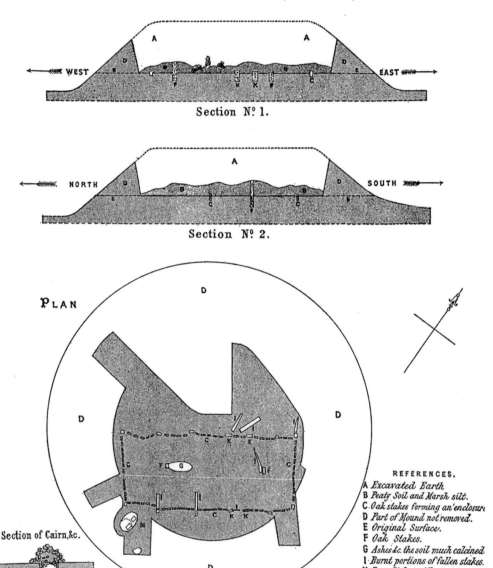

PLAN & SECTIONS OF EXCAVATIONS, COURTHILL, DALRY.

Figure 3.9: Courthill, North Ayrshire: plan and sections. (From Cochran Patrick 1874; I am grateful to the Society of Antiquaries of Scotland for permission to reproduce this image)

From this description it seems possible that some kind of "linear zone" mortuary structure (or structures) had stood within the enclosure and that the one/s associated with the large posts had been burnt down. Unfortunately, the positions of the ash layer extending from the northeast post, and of the low wall with burnt material on it, were not marked on the otherwise excellent published plan, and have to be interpolated from the description.

On the southwest side of the mound, and covered by mound material, was found a small cairn covering a cist-like structure; a broken Beaker lay inside, along with a "piece of blackened oak". Cochran Patrick argued that the fact that soil and gravel from the mound ran over and beyond this cairn indicated that it pre-dated the main mound; but it is at least possible that this Beaker grave had been a secondary addition, covered by mound slump.

While the precise structural arrangement at Courthill cannot be paralleled, each element – the paired large posts, the areas of burning, the rectangular enclosure and the round mound – can be matched among early Neolithic monuments elsewhere in Britain, and it seems reasonable to include Courthill in any review of Scottish Neolithic non-megalithic round mounds. That it may not have been alone in the area has been suggested by John Linge, whose review of survey evidence in North Ayrshire revealed the presence, or former presence, of nine other similar mounds within a 15km radius (Linge 1987).

Cochran Patrick recorded that a selection of finds from Courthill, including some small bone fragments that had "with difficulty been preserved", had been presented to the NMAS. The Beaker is certainly present (NMS X.EG 11), as are four flint scrapers, two flint knives and numerous flint chips (NMS X.AB 1–24); but unfortunately the bone is not with these; has never been registered; and has not been located in the NMS stores, despite an initial search. It is not impossible that it is lurking among the over one million items in the NMS Archaeology collections; alternatively, like some other unregistered material, it may have gone astray in the distant past.

CONCLUSIONS

It is hoped that this brief review of our current state of knowledge of Neolithic non-megalithic round mounds in Scotland will have highlighted some of the issues involved in trying to improve our understanding of their chronology. Old museum collections have the ability to produce both unexpected bonuses and mixed blessings (as in the case of the Cairns of Atherb bones) and, as seen above, in some cases all that the newly-obtained radiocarbon dates have been able to demonstrate is the date of secondary activity.

The existing dating evidence from the construction and primary use of these monuments suggests, that in Scotland, as elsewhere (*e.g.* Lyle's Hill, Co. Antrim), these mounds were constructed during the first half of the fourth millennium BC: at Pitnacree, the traditional CB pottery is indistinguishable from that found in earliest Neolithic sites elsewhere in Britain and Ireland (Sheridan 2007c) and may belong to the earliest Neolithic; elsewhere, the CBNE pottery present at Boghead, Pitglassie and East Finnercy relates to the generations that succeeded the earliest CB farming groups, not necessarily far removed in time. (The Atherb pottery could be classed as either "traditional" CB or as CBNE.) Why the builders chose the round format over the long format is a question that will remain to be answered; as Kinnes's work showed (1979), there seems to be a northern British bias to such sites.

(Here one excludes the non-megalithic round and oval barrows that post-date the Early Neolithic, such as Whitegrounds, North Yorkshire – although it may be that the frequency of such mounds in Yorkshire constitutes a reference to the older, pre-existing round mounds there that would constitute ancient ancestral monuments.)

The existing body of dates is far from adequate for undertaking the kind of Bayesian modelling as used by Alex Bayliss *et al.* for funerary monuments in southern England (Bayliss and Whittle 2007). Furthermore, even though there is scope, as indicated above, for obtaining a few additional dates (funding permitting) from the existing material – and from any additional material that may turn up – nevertheless the best "bet" for improving our knowledge would be to excavate several additional candidate sites (targeting the ones identified by Brophy, this volume Chapter 2), and apply the kind of rigour to the procurement and dating of samples as has been shown by the work of Bayliss and colleagues.

Meanwhile, as far as the NMS Archaeology Department are concerned, the search for datable material continues. Watch this space.

ACKNOWLEDGEMENTS

I am grateful to Jim Leary, Dave Field and Tim Darvill for inviting me to contribute this paper, and for their patience. All those who have assisted with the funding of the dates cited here are warmly thanked.

BIBLIOGRAPHY

Ashmore, P. J., Cook, G. T. and Harkness, D. D. (2000) A radiocarbon database for Scottish archaeological samples. *Radiocarbon* 42(1), 41–8.

Bayliss, A. and Whittle, A. W. R. (2007) Histories of the dead: building chronologies for five southern British long barrows. *Cambridge Archaeological Journal* 17(1) Supplement.

Berstan, R., Stott, A. W., Minnitt, S., Bronk Ramsey, C., Hedges, R. E. M. and Evershed, R. P. (2008) Direct dating of pottery from its organic residues: new precision using compound-specific carbon isotopes. *Antiquity* 82, 702–13.

Burl, H. A. W. (1984) Report on the excavation of a Neolithic mound at Boghead, Speymouth Forest, Fochabers, Moray, 1972 and 1974. *Proceedings of the Society of Antiquaries of Scotland* 114, 35–73 and fiche 1:A2–C10.

Clarke, D. L. (1970) *The Beaker pottery of Great Britain and Ireland.* Cambridge, Cambridge University Press.

Cochran Patrick, R. W. (1874) Note on some explorations in a tumulus called the "Court-Hill", in the parish of Dalry and county of Ayr. *Proceedings of the Society of Antiquaries of Scotland* 10 (1872–4), 281–5.

Coles, J. M. and Simpson, D. D. A. (1965) The excavation of a Neolithic round barrow at Pitnacree, Perthshire, Scotland. *Proceedings of the Prehistoric Society* 31, 34–57.

Corcoran, J. X. W. P. (1969) Excavation of two burial cairns at Mid Gleniron Farm, Glenluce, Wigtownshire. *Transactions of the Dumfriesshire & Galloway Natural History & Antiquarian Society* 46, 29–90.

Curtis, N., Wilkin, N., Hutchison, M., Jay, M., Sheridan, J. A. and Wright, M. (2007) Radiocarbon dating results from the Beakers and Bodies Project. *Discovery and Excavation in Scotland* 8, 223–4.

Evans, C. and Hodder, I. (2006) *A woodland archaeology: Neolithic sites at Haddenham. Volume 1.* Cambridge, McDonald Institute.

Henshall, A. S. (1983) The Neolithic pottery from Easterton of Roseisle, Moray. In A. O'Connor and D. V. Clarke (eds.) *From the Stone Age to the 'Forty-five: studies presented to R. B. K. Stevenson*, 19–44. Edinburgh, John Donald.

Henshall, A. S. (1984) The pottery from Boghead, Fochabers, Moray. In H. A. W. Burl, Report on the excavation of a Neolithic mound at Boghead, Speymouth Forest, Fochabers, Moray, 1972 and 1974, 59–66. *Proceedings of the Society of Antiquaries of Scotland* 114, 35–73 and fiche 1:A2–C10.

Historic Scotland on-line radiocarbon database: http://www.historic-scotland.gov.uk/index/ heritage/archaeology-techniques/radiocarbon-dating-search.htm (accessed May 2009)

Kinnes, I. (1979) *Neolithic round barrows and ring-ditches in the British Neolithic*. London, British Museum (Occasional Paper 7).

Kinnes, I. (1985) Circumstance not context: the Neolithic of Scotland as seen from outside. *Proceedings of the Society of Antiquaries of Scotland* 115, 15–57.

Kinnes, I. (1992) Balnagowan and after: the context of non-megalithic mortuary sites in Scotland. In N. Sharples & J. A. Sheridan (eds.), *Vessels for the ancestors: essays on the Neolithic of Britain and Ireland in honour of Audrey Henshall*, 83–103. Edinburgh, Edinburgh University Press.

Kinnes, I. (2004) "A truth universally acknowledged": some more thoughts on Neolithic round barrows. In A. Gibson and J. A. Sheridan (eds.), *From sickles to circles. Britain and Ireland at the time of Stonehenge*, 106–15. Stroud, Tempus.

Lanting, J. N. Aerts-Bijma, A. T. and van der Plicht, J. (2001) Dating of cremated bones. *Radiocarbon* 43(2), 249–54.

Leivers, M., Roberts, J. and Peterson, R. (2000) The cairn at East Finnercy, Dunecht, Aberdeenshire. *Proceedings of the Society of Antiquaries of Scotland* 130, 183–95.

Linge, J. (1987) Re-discovering a landscape: the barrow and motte in north Ayrshire. *Proceedings of the Society of Antiquaries of Scotland* 117, 23–32.

Mercer, R. J. and Midgley, M. (1997) The early Bronze Age cairn at Sketewan, Balnaguard, Perth and Kinross. *Proceedings of the Society of Antiquaries of Scotland* 127(1), 281–338.

Milne, J. (1892) Traces of early man in Buchan. *Transactions of the Buchan Field Club 2* (1891–2), 97–108.

Mook, W. G. and Waterbolk, H. T. (1985) *Radiocarbon dating*. Strasbourg, European Science Foundation. (Handbooks for Archaeologists 3).

Piggott, S. (1949) The excavations at Cairnpapple Hill, West Lothian, 1947–8. *Proceedings of the Society of Antiquaries of Scotland* 87 (1948–9), 68–123.

Piggott, S. and Powell, T. G. E. (1949) The excavation of three Neolithic chambered tombs in Galloway, 1949. *Proceedings of the Society of Antiquaries of Scotland* 83 (1948–9), 103–61.

Pitts, M. (2006) Flight of the eagles. *British Archaeology* 86, 6.

Reimer, P. J., Baillie, M. G. L., Bard, E., Bayliss, A., Beck, J. W., and Bertrand, C. J. H. (2004) IntCal04 terrestrial radiocarbon age calibration, 0-26 cal kyr BP. *Radiocarbon* 46(3), 1029–1058.

Schulting, R. J. (2004) Clachaig, Haylie House and Torlin, North Ayrshire, and Holm of Papa Westray North, Orkney. In P. J. Ashmore, A list of archaeological radiocarbon dates, 167–8. *Discovery and Excavation in Scotland* 5, 155–73.

Schulting, R. J. and Sheridan, J. A. (in preparation) New dates for human bones from Scottish Neolithic funerary monuments.

Shepherd, A. (1996) A Neolithic ring-mound at Midtown of Pitglassie, Auchterless, Aberdeenshire. *Proceedings of the Society of Antiquaries of Scotland* 126, 17–51.

Sheridan, J. A. (2002) The radiocarbon dating programmes of the National Museums of Scotland. *Antiquity* 76, 794–6.

Sheridan, J. A. (2003) New dates for Scottish Bronze Age cinerary urns: results from the National Museums' of Scotland Dating Cremated Bones Project. In A. Gibson (ed.) *Prehistoric pottery: people, pattern and purpose*, 201–26. Oxford, British Archaeological Reports (BAR International Series 1156).

Sheridan, J. A. (2004) Scottish food vessel chronology revisited. In A. M. Gibson and J. A. Sheridan (eds.), *From sickles to circles: Britain and Ireland at the time of Stonehenge*, 243–67. Stroud, Tempus.

Sheridan, J. A. (2005a) Cuween, Cuween-Wideford Project. In P. J. Ashmore, A list of archaeological radiocarbon dates, 177. *Discovery and Excavation in Scotland* 6, 165–81.

Sheridan, J. A. (2005b) The National Museums' of Scotland radiocarbon dating programmes: results obtained during 2004/5. *Discovery and Excavation in Scotland* 6, 182–3.

Sheridan, J. A. (2006a) The National Museums' Scotland radiocarbon dating programmes: results obtained during 2005/6. *Discovery and Excavation in Scotland* 7, 204–6.

Sheridan, J. A. (2006b) Creating (and using, amending and reacting to) appropriate dwellings for the dead in Neolithic Scotland. *Journal of Iberian Archaeology* 8, 103–25.

Sheridan, J. A. (2007a) Scottish Beaker dates: the good, the bad and the ugly. In M. Larsson and M. Parker Pearson (eds.), *From Stonehenge to the Baltic: living with cultural diversity in the third millennium BC*, 91–123. Oxford, Archaeopress (BAR International Series 1692).

Sheridan, J. A. (2007b) Dating the Scottish Bronze Age: "There is clearly much that the material can still tell us". In C. Burgess, P. Topping and F.M. Lynch (eds.), *Beyond Stonehenge: essays on the Bronze Age in Honour of Colin Burgess*, 162–85. Oxford, Oxbow Books.

Sheridan, J. A. (2007c) From Picardie to Pickering and Pencraig Hill? New information on the "carinated bowl Neolithic" in northern Britain. In A. W. R. Whittle and V. Cummings (eds.) *Going over: the Mesolithic–Neolithic transition in north-west Europe*, 441–92. Oxford, British Academy (Proceedings of the British Academy 144).

Sheridan, J. A. (2008) Upper Largie and Dutch-Scottish connections during the Beaker period. In H. Fokkens, B. J. Coles, A. L. van Gijn, J. P. Kleijne, H. H. Ponjee and C. G. Slappendel (eds.), *Between foraging and farming: an extended broad spectrum of papers presented to Leendert Louwe Kooijmans*, 247–260. Leiden, University of Leiden (Analects Praehistorica Leidensia 40).

Sheridan, J. A., Cowie, T. G. and Hunter, F. J. (2002) National Museums of Scotland dating programme: 1994–8. In C. Bronk Ramsey, T. F. G. Higham, D. C. Owen, A. W. G. Pike and R. E. M. Hedges, Radiocarbon dates from the Oxford AMS system: Archaeometry datelist 31, 55–61. *Archaeometry* 44(3), Supplement 1, 1–149.

Sheridan, J. A., Parker Pearson, M., Jay, M., Richards, M. and Curtis, N. (2006) Radiocarbon dating results from the Beaker People Project: Scottish samples. *Discovery and Excavation in Scotland* 7, 198–201.

Sheridan, J. A., Parker Pearson, M., Jay, M., Richards, M. and Curtis, N. (2007) Radiocarbon dating results from The Beaker People Project, 2007: Scottish samples. *Discovery and Excavation in Scotland* 8, 222.

Chapter 4

Tynwald Hill and the Round Mounds of the Isle of Man

Timothy Darvill

Leaving aside a rich selection of Bronze Age round barrows, Viking Age burial mounds, and early medieval mottes spread right across the Isle of Man, there is a recognizable tradition of using round mounds as the outwardly visible cover-structure for a variety of burial monuments during the fourth and third millennia BC. The Island was not one of the areas considered by Ian Kinnes in his original study of round barrows and ring-ditches in the British Neolithic (Kinnes 1979), although seven sites are identified on maps included in a later study (Kinnes 1992, figure 1A.2). Amongst these certain and probable Neolithic monuments with round mounds are examples with multiple megalithic cists, a range of passage graves, an entrance grave, and also the great stepped mound of Tynwald Hill that forms the traditional meeting place of the Island's parliament.

The Isle of Man is relatively small at 572 square kilometres, but its situation in the middle of the Irish Sea places it at a crossing-point in the pattern of north–south and east–west seaways (Davies 1946; Bowen 1970) and gives it a special interest as a cultural melting pot. In this paper the Neolithic round barrows and related monuments are reviewed within two broad but culturally meaningful chronological phases, and it is suggested that the morphology and what is known of the archaeology of these sites shows affinities with similar monuments elsewhere in the Irish Sea province and beyond.

FOURTH MILLENNIUM BC

Four sites can tentatively be assigned to the fourth millennium BC on the basis of radiocarbon dates and associations with Mull Hill pottery: a crematoria at Cashtal yn Ard, stone chambers at Port St Mary, a simple passage grave at Kew, and a multiple passage grave at Mull Hill itself. With the exception of Cashtal yn Ard, these sites all lie in the southern half of the Island (Figure 4.1), but Cashtal yn Ard is unusual in being sealed beneath a long barrow, one of four such monuments in the northern part of the Island. Chronological development may be at play here, such that by the middle of the fourth millennium BC the Island was divided between communities preferring long barrows in the north and those preferring round barrows in the south.

Cashtal yn Ard, Maughold [NGR: SC 462892]

The existence of a long barrow with a megalithic chamber on a prominent east-facing position overlooking the Irish Sea on the Island's northeast coast has been noted in the

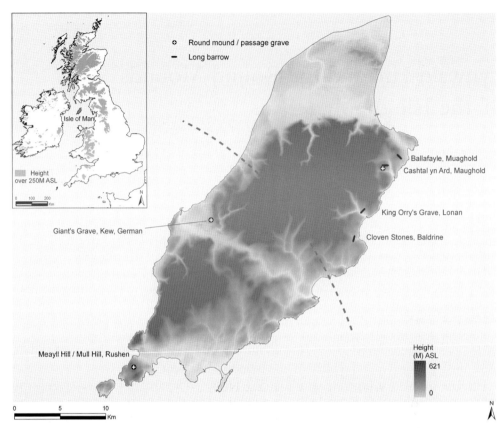

Figure 4.1: Map of the Isle of Man showing the position of megalithic monuments under round barrows and long barrows dated to the fourth millennium BC. (Sources: various. Illustration by Vanessa Constant)

antiquarian literature since the early nineteenth century. Small-scale investigations were carried out in 1884 by the Revd S. N. Harrison and Mr Llewellyn Jewitt (Jewitt 1885), and a far more extensive excavation by H. J. Fleure and G. H. Neely in 1932–33 (Fleure & Neely 1936). This second excavation revealed that underneath the long barrow, to the west of the main chambers, was a stone platform surrounded by a spread of burnt material. The excavators describe its discovery in terms typical of the time (Fleure & Neely 1936, 382): "After skinning away, over a considerable area, some 3ft thickness of loose stones, we came upon quantities of burnt shale fragments, reddish and brittle, along with some fragments of charcoal and black powdery material. ... Continued clearing revealed a mound of burnt material 20ft E–W, 12ft N–S, and some 4ft high. ... In the centre of the mound of burnt material were noticed some slabs, and after cleaning a portion of the small shaly burnt material, it was ascertained that the mound contained a central platform built by laying slab over slab. ... at the east end of our mound we found the burnt shale fragments going some 18ins down into the earth, and we examined and sieved material, finding two tiny fragments of whitish material but nothing that could be identified as bone."

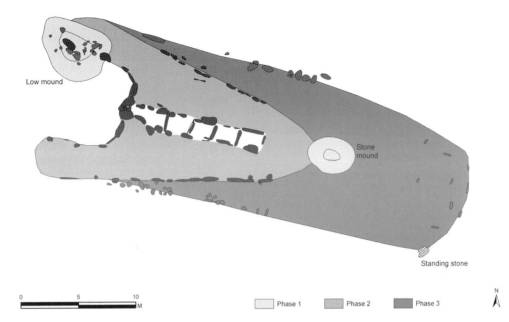

Low mound

Stone mound

Standing stone

0   5   10
M

Phase 1   Phase 2   Phase 3

N

Figure 4.2: Cashtal yn Ard, Maughold, Isle of Man. (After Darvill & Chartrand 2000. Illustration by Vanessa Constant)

Recognizing its unusual character Fleure and Neely did not investigate this structure any further, and it remains more or less intact to this day. Detailed topographic and geophysical surveys of the site in 1999 (Darvill & Chartrand 2000) confirmed the position, extent, and structure of what in Kinnes' terminology would be a "crematoria" under a round barrow. Details are rather vague, but its dimensions suggest a linear zone involving a stone platform of a kind well represented in other parts of the British Isles, especially northern England, with one possibly similar structure known in northern France pre-dating the multiple passage grave at la Houguette à Fontenay-le-Marmion, Calvados (Kinnes 1979, 58–9; Caillaud & Lagnel 1972). The results of the 1999 surveys, coupled with close scrutiny of the Fleure and Neely report, suggests that a standing stone stood *c*.10m to the southeast of the round barrow, and that a second round mound stood *c*.20m to the northwest (Figure 4.2). The overlying long barrow appears to have been built in two phases, the second representing a substantial enlargement of the original mound which had a deep forecourt to the northwest with access to a linear chamber comprising five cells. The long barrow has clear architectural affinities with court cairns in Ireland and to a lesser extent with the Clyde tombs in southwest Scotland (De Valera 1960; Scott 1969; Henshall 1972, 15–110). Its multi-phase construction, and the juxtaposition of successive components, invites comparison with Slewcairn, Dumfries and Galloway, where a paved area lies under the cairn south of a linear chamber (Kinnes 1992, 207), and Notgrove, Gloucestershire, where a rotunda grave was succeeded by a Cotswold-Severn style long barrow with a terminal chamber (Clifford 1936). Unfortunately, finds from the 1932–33 excavations at Cashtal yn Ard were scarce and dating is therefore difficult; nothing apart from charcoal and burnt material is noted from the central round barrow. However, no less than 125 beach-worn white quartz pebbles were associated with the standing stone and had clearly been brought to the site for ceremonial deposition (Fleure & Neely 1936, 388–9).

Port St Mary [NGR: SC 2167]

Investigations by Fredrick Swinnerton during the construction of the Alfred Pier at Port St Mary in 1885–8 revealed an interesting sequence of structures near to what would have been the coast during the late fifth millennium BC (Swinnerton 1890). Unfortunately, Swinnerton's records are scanty, based mainly on observations of sections exposed during construction works, and thus difficult to interpret. However, that he found a multi-period site including one or more megalithic structures is widely recognized (Clark 1935, 78–80).

Overlying the natural gravel was a preserved old soil horizon up to 0.3m thick, variously yellow and red in colour, in which Swinnerton found numerous worked flints, shells of periwinkle, limpet, dogwhelk, and crab, animal bones including a wild boar's tusk, and two pieces of quartz-tempered pottery. Taken together these finds led him to describe the deposit as a "refuse heap" or midden. Amongst the worked flints there are microliths dating back into the seventh and sixth millennia BC, while the pottery fragments and a radiocarbon date of 3950–3640 cal BC (OxA-2481: 4970±80 BP) on one of the marine shells shows continued use of the area into the early fourth millennium BC.

Four rectangular stone cists appear to have been built on the old ground surface, perhaps cutting into the midden, and possibly either singly or collectively covered in a mound or cairn (*cf.* Clark 1935, figure 4). Swinnerton provides a rather confused account of one cist which seems to have contained the remains of two inhumation burials with their heads to the northeast as well as a further internment immediately above the cover-slab of the cist with its head to the southwest. In all, there appears to have been an old adult, a young adult, and a child represented. Marine shells, a quartz scraper, and a broken leaf-shaped arrowhead were also present in the cist, together with a few bones from a small animal, at the time provisionally identified as a hare (Swinnerton 1890, 137–8). Similarities may be noted between these burials at Port St Mary and the rather better preserved examples at Téviec and Hoëdic in the Bay of Quiberon, Brittany, where at least some of the stone cists would have projected above the top of the midden into which they were cut (Schulting 1996). At Port St Mary a much larger cist appears to have been dug through the first structure and the midden below, its floor set below the top of the underlying gravel; it may represent a third phase to the use of the site. The capstone of this cist probably carried at least one panel of cup-mark style rock art, the whole structure seemingly set at the centre of a round barrow that also covered the earlier cists and part of the underlying midden. A limpet shell (*Patella* sp.) that may derive from this central cist has been radiocarbon dated to 1290–840 cal BC (OxA-2480: 2870±80 BP), suggesting that use of the site continued into the later second millennium BC.

This was an important site and it is disappointing that the records of its destruction are not better. The arrangement of cists in what may have been a round mound is highly reminiscent of Hedon Howe, North Yorkshire, investigated by J. R. Mortimer in 1893 and found to contain a central closed cist with four smaller closed cists evenly set round about (Mortimer 1905, 346–50). This site is classified by Kinnes (1979, 12 and figure 10.8) as a stone-chambered round barrow of Stage A. Multiple chambers are known at other sites around the Irish Sea, for example at Cerrig-y-Gof, Pembrokeshire (Lynch 1972, 80-2), the Glecknabae Cairn on the Isle of Bute which also seems to have been cut into a shell midden (Bryce 1904, 37–52), and are also a feature of the passage grave at Mull Hill only 2km east of Port St Mary on the Isle of Man.

Mull Hill, Rushen [NGR: SC 189677]

Mull Hill (also written Meayll Hill) lies on a slight terrace overlooking Port Erin Bay and the impressive tall sea-cliffs of Bradda Head in the southwestern part of the Island (Figure 4.1). Heavily denuded and excavated on several occasions, this monument is now extremely difficult to interpret (Gale *et al.* 1997). Its essential features comprise a set of six T-shaped chambers set in two arcs within a roughly round cairn 23m east to west by 20m north to south (Figure 4.3A). Each of the chambers consists of a short radial passage about 2.2m long leading from the outside of the mound to a pair of transeptally arranged cells, each about 1.8m long and with jambs and sillstones at their entrances and paving over the floors. In all cases the right-hand cell is smaller than the left-hand cell, although why this should be so is not known. Excavations by Audrey Henshall in 1971 showed the presence of a substantial outer-cairn wall defining the edge of the monument which might originally have stood more than 1m high (Henshall 1978, 174; forthcoming; Selkirk 1971, 96). Earlier excavations by W. Herdman and P. M. C. Kermode in 1893 brought to light the remains of at least eighteen Mull Hill Ware pots scattered through all but one of the six chambers (Piggott 1932). In their form these vessels find good parallels with the classic and slightly modified carinated bowls described by Sheridan (1995, figure 2.4) from northeastern Ireland. All but one chamber produced worked flints, including three leaf-shaped arrowheads. Cremated bone, marine shell, and quartz pebbles were also found in the chambers (Kermode & Herdman 1914, 44).

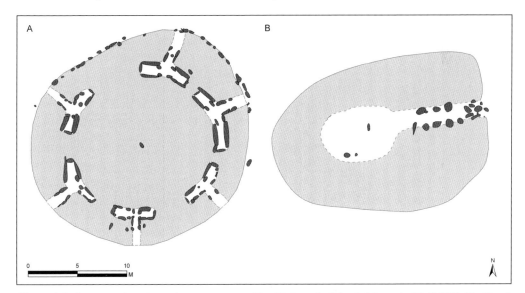

Figure 4.3: Interpretative plans of passage graves identified on the Isle of Man. A. Mull Hill. B. Giant's Grave, Kew. (Sources: various. Illustration by Vanessa Constant)

Although sometimes considered unique, Mull Hill finds a number of companions to the south, for example at Cerrig-y-Gof, Pembrokeshire (Lynch 1972, 80-2) already referred to, where a tomb with five chambers stands in a comparable position relative to the coast, sea-cliffs, and views westwards across the Irish Sea. Multiple passage graves are also known amongst the Bargrennan tombs of southwest Scotland (Henshall 1972, 2–14; 1978, 174; Murray 1992), in the Peak District of central England (Manby 1958), and most notably in northern France, for example the second phase of Fontenay-le-Marmion, Calvados, with six passage graves and a single closed chamber set within an oval mound (Daniel 1960, 58; Caillaud & Lagnel 1972), and Barnenez, Brittany, with five passage graves in the putatively early eastern part of the long mound and six in the westward extension (Giot 1987; Scarre 2002, 91). The T-shaped passage graves forming the chambered elements at Mull Hill are also well paralleled in central Wales at Ty Isaf, Brecknockshire, where a passage grave in an oval cairn arguably pre-dates a classic trapezoidal Cotswold-Severn style long barrow with lateral chambers (Grimes 1939; Darvill 2004a, 69). If Boujot and Cassen's (1993, 486) typological sequence for Breton passage graves is accepted, then the T-shaped chambers at Mull Hill stand fairly late in the overall European tradition, but comfortably within the local pattern of Neolithic monument building in the middle of the fourth millennium BC.

The Giant's Grave, Kew, German [NGR: SC 274834]

Simple passage graves with a single chamber are represented on the Isle of Man by the Giant's Grave at Kew (Figure 4.1). This rather dilapidated monument lies in a characteristically elevated position overlooking the fertile lowlands east of Peel with views westwards across the Irish Sea (Barnwell 1866, 53; Cubbon & Bruce 1928; Megaw 1938, 224). Much disturbed by the construction of field walls and a trackway, all that can be seen today is a double row of standing stones evenly spaced over a distance of about 8m, originally no doubt the orthostats forming the side walls of a passage (Figure 4.3B). They are roughly graduated in height along an east to west axis, the larger stones to the west where the main chamber should lie, confirmed perhaps by the presence of a few large but displaced stones in this area. Geophysical surveys have tentatively identified the outline of an oval cairn around about (Chartrand *et al.* 2003). No excavations are known, but it is certainly a monument that would repay further investigation.

Such simple passage graves find general parallels around the Irish Sea basin and are part of an extremely widespread tradition that also extends southwards into Brittany and Normandy (Herity 1974, 2–8; Lynch 1976, 74). Their form and arrangement overlaps considerably with what Kinnes (1979, 63) described as "trench chambers", exemplified by the sites of Black Beck, Cumbria, and Whitegrounds, North Yorkshire. Whitegrounds is especially interesting as it perhaps combines different materials in its construction – wood for the roofing and stone for the walls – an arrangement that yet again calls into question the separation of monuments into different classes simply on the basis of what was used to build them (on stone-chambered long cairns and timber-chambered earthen long barrows see Darvill 2004a, 39). Moreover, the form of the "trench chambers" themselves, with a narrow approach passage leading to a partially subterranean chamber area, blurs the boundary between these monuments and passage graves. Indeed, it is perhaps better to see them all as passage graves and follow Richard Bradley's simple but useful distinction between monuments with closed chambers (central cists *etc.*) and those with open access (passage graves), the degree of openness somehow reflecting social distance between the living and the dead, whether the chambers are in a round mound or a long one (Bradley 1998, 60). Developing such thinking further in light of the distribution of monuments already noted on the Isle of Man, it may be suggested that the chamber structures relate to beliefs and the relationships between the living and the dead while the mounds refer to issues of group identity and the projection of recognized cultural and social affiliations.

Other possible round barrows

A few other possible round barrows on the Island have been proposed as early examples, but can be rejected on various grounds. One is at Ballaterson Cronk, Maughold, excavated by Canon Harrison in 1908. Here he found a cairn about 10m in diameter within which was a circular chamber 7.3m in diameter that was approached from the northwest by a passage about 2.2m long (Harrison 1915; and see Darvill 2000, figure 32.5B for interpretative plan). Burnt bone and quartz pebbles were found within the chamber but little else is known about the site, and the records of Harrison's work are sufficiently poor that questions have been raised about its interpretation since it could well be a later prehistoric round-house

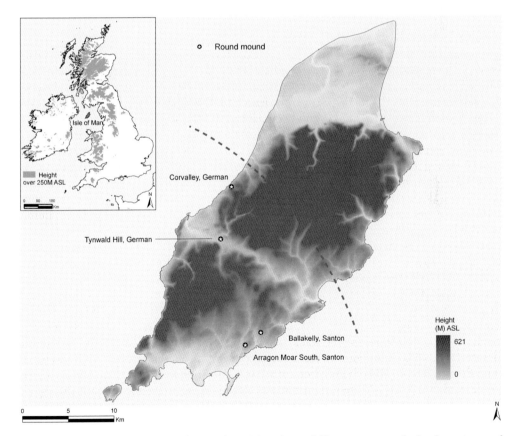

Figure 4.4: Map of the Isle of Man showing the position of megalithic monuments and related structures under round barrows dated to the third millennium BC. (Sources: various. Illustration by Vanessa Constant)

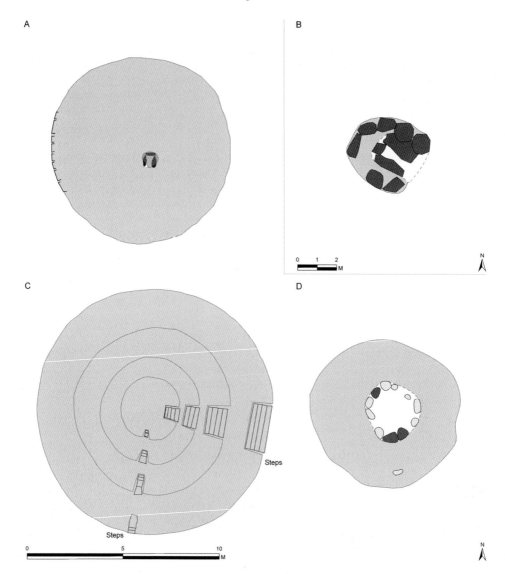

Figure 4.5: Interpretative plans of megalithic monuments and related structures under round barrows provisionally dated to the third millennium BC in the Isle of Man. A. Corvalley, German. B. Ballakelly, Santon. C. Tynwald Hill, German. D. Arragon Moar, Santon. (Sources: various. Illustration by Vanessa Constant)

(Megaw 1938, 225). Another is visible as a rectangular cist within a round mound on Clay Head, Lonan (Henshall 1978, 173), but given its position and local associations with a burnt mound (Cubbon 1964) it is best interpreted as a monument of the second millennium BC. There is little doubt, however, that other chambered tombs await discovery on the Island, and some known structures may one day be shown to be of Neolithic date. What appears to be a collapsed chamber within a low mound was surveyed at Cronk ny Arrey, Rushen in 2000, for example, but its date is not currently known (Darvill *et al.* 2001).

THIRD MILLENNIUM BC

Four monuments with round cover-mounds can be assigned to this period with greater or lesser certainty, all of them situated in topographically dominant positions (Figure 4.4). None of them have been extensively investigated in modern times, so dating is poor and based on analogy rather than radiocarbon or associations with the characteristic Ronaldsway pottery of this period (Burrow & Darvill 1997).

Ballakelly, Santon [NGR: SC 321719]

One late style of chambered tomb is known on the Island, the site of Ballakelly, Santon, overlooking the coastal plain east of Ronaldsway. It comprises a small rectangular chamber some 1.6m by 0.7m internally, built from just three large slabs, opening to the southeast (Figure 4.5B). The surrounding cairn is roughly circular in plan, little more than 3m across, with a neat kerb of eight uprights all but one of which survives (Figure 4.6). A stone in the northwest sector of the kerb carries more than twenty cup-marks on its outer surface and a further small panel of seven cup-marks on the lower part of the inner face. This slab is probably a re-used cup-marked boulder; others are known in the vicinity (Darvill & O'Connor 2005, 307: site 52). Excavations by F. C. Lukis in 1865 cleared the chamber, in the course of which one piece of pottery and some worked flints were apparently found but have since disappeared (Barnwell 1866; Daniel 1950, 180; Burrow 1997, 37).

A dozen or more stones scattered around the monument have served to confuse past interpretations of this site, but a detailed re-survey in 1997 shows that these extraneous blocks can be resolved as the displaced capstones and a rough ring of boulders set up to protect the site from potentially damaging agricultural activities (Gale & Darvill 1998). Some authors have suggested the site was a long barrow (Kermode 1929, 173; Clark 1935, 75), while Audrey Henshall proposed similarities with the simple passage graves of southwest Scotland (Henshall 1978, 172). However, the size, kerbing, chamber construction, and use

Figure 4.6: Ballakelly, Santon, looking north. (Photograph: Timothy Darvill)

of stones carrying rock-art panels strongly suggests analogies with the Scilly-Tramore tombs of the southern Irish Sea province once seen as rather early in the Neolithic (Ashbee 1982) but now recognized as dating to the early second millennium BC. The example at Brane in west Cornwall is extremely similar to Ballakelly (*cf.* Thomas 1985, 96). The presence of an example of this class of monument on the southern part of the Isle of Man should occasion no surprise in view of the scatter of examples in southeast Ireland (Ó Nualláin & Walsh 1986) and the established patterns of maritime movement within the Irish Sea basin (Davies 1946) perhaps based on fishing for herring (Clark 1977).

Tynwald Hill, German [NGR: SC 277818]

The largest round mound on the Island, and the best-known, is Tynwald Hill (*Cronk Keeill Eoin*), German (Darvill 2004b; Darvill in prep.). This site has been used since Norse times as a Thing-Mound, and has a good claim to be the oldest open-air parliament site still in active use anywhere in Europe. Local legend holds that the hill is a prehistoric burial mound re-used as an assembly place (Craine 1957), and there is long-lived folklore suggesting it was built from soil brought to the site from every part of the Island (Stranger 1836, 181). Whether these traditions are given any credence is a matter for debate, but it is certainly true that early medieval assembly sites often reused earlier mounds (Brink 2004), demonstrably so at Moat Low, Derbyshire, and Spellow Hills, Lincolnshire, which proved on excavation to be Bronze Age and Neolithic in origin respectively (Pantos 2004, 172). It may also be noted that there is increasing evidence for the use of stone taken from a range of geographically disparate sources in the construction of passage graves in the later fourth and third millennium BC, as for example at La Hougue Bie, Jersey (Patton 1992).

Tynwald Hill is situated on a gravel terrace above the River Neb. Unlike other large round mounds on the Island it does not command a sea-view. However, its position in the central valley means that it is easily accessible from all parts of the Island and this is perhaps what caused it to become the main assembly place. Today the mound stands in the western lobe of a dumb-bell shaped enclosure with St John's Chapel in the eastern lobe and a processional way linking the two. It is tempting to imagine the layout as having prehistoric origins, but in fact it was laid out in present form in the late eighteenth century with further aggrandizement when the chapel was rebuilt in the mid nineteenth century (Darvill 2004b, 223–4). During the course of these works a large stone cist in the centre of a round mound was discovered to the northeast of Tynwald (Barnwell 1866, 56–7). Tynwald Hill itself was further enhanced in 1979 when new furniture for the annual Tynwald Ceremony was acquired. However, a plan of the site by the antiquary Francis Grose made in 1774 shows the Hill and earlier cruciform Chapel within a rectangular enclosure with four entrances marked by stone gateposts. Tynwald Hill itself is clearly depicted as a stepped mound, a view confirmed by other broadly contemporary illustrations (Figure 4.7).

Today Tynwald Hill is approximately 25m in diameter at the base and 3.6m high. It has three steps or terraces on the site and a flat top forming the fourth tier with a diameter since 1979 of 3.6m but rather less in earlier times (Figure 4.5C). Topographic and geophysical surveys of the hill and its surroundings in 1993–6 and 2002 suggest that there may originally have been a ditch around the base of the mound. Preliminary results from a survey using ground penetration radar (GPR) show the presence of constructional features and a possible structure more or less in the centre of the mound (Figure 4.8).

Figure 4.7: Tynwald Hill, German. View of the hill c.1798 looking south. (After Feltham 1798, 214)

The size and form of Tynwald Hill invites comparison with a number of passage graves around the western seaways. To the north, Quanterness on Mainland Orkney has a similar overall diameter and with three concentric internal walls could easily be reconstructed as a stepped mound having three tiers and a flat top. Indeed, this is a possibility implicitly conveyed in the way that architect Alec Daykin reconstructed the mound in the published account of Colin Renfrew's excavations there in 1972–3, although Renfrew himself prefers to see the steps as having been infilled at a late stage in the construction sequence "so as to give a rounded effect to the cairn as a whole" (Renfrew 1979, 68 and *cf.* figure 32). To the south, in Brittany, stepped profiles on passage graves and long barrows have long been accepted with passage graves such as L'Ile Longue, Larmor-Baden and Le Notério, Carnac (L'Helgouach 1965, figure 3 and 4), providing close parallels for Tynwald Hill in terms of the size and form of their cover-mounds.

Arragon Moar I, Santon [NGR: SC 304704]

This flat-topped mound lies on a low ridge with extensive views east and south across the Irish Sea. The large round mound has a diameter at the base of 16m, and stands about 2m high on the west side but rather less on the upslope-eastern side (Figure 4.5D). There are traces of kerbing on the south side. On the top is a stone circle comprising eleven boulders, three of quartz and the remainder of local granite (Figure 4.9). A stone near the centre of the circle may originally have been a pillar stone that perhaps occupied one of the two gaps in the surviving ring. There are no recorded excavations at the site.

The existence of a stone circle on top of a round mound may not be so unusual as it first seems. At Croft Moraig, Perthshire, for example, surface evidence suggests that the central settings sit atop a natural knoll that has been elaborated to form a low cairn or platform about 18m across (Figure 4.10), defined by a kerb containing at least one cup-marked stone

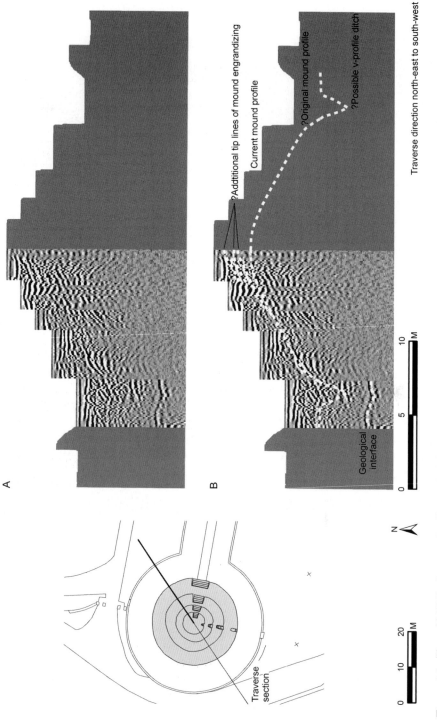

Figure 4.8: Tynwald Hill, German. Profile of the hill with preliminary plot of the results from a traverse using Ground Penetrating Radar (GPR). (Illustration by Paul Cheetham and Vanessa Constant)

Figure 4.9: Arragon Moar, Santon, looking north. (Photograph: Timothy Darvill)

Figure 4.10: Croft Moraig, Perthshire, looking east. (Photograph: Timothy Darvill)

identified by the excavators as a stone bank (Piggott & Simpson 1971, 6–8); it is a phasing not incompatible with later reinterpretations (Bradley & Sheridan 2005).

Corvalley, German [NGR: SC 289874]

Another large round mound is at Corvalley, German, situated on a dominant ridge with extensive views westwards across the Irish Sea. As preserved, the round barrow is 18.2m in diameter, over 3m high, with portions of an orthostatic revetment showing in the western sector at the base of the mound (Figure 4.5A). An accessible megalithic chamber 1.2m by 1.5m lies more or less in the centre of the mound; it is roofed and partly walled with

Figure 4.11: Corvalley, German, looking west. (Photograph: Timothy Darvill)

quartz slabs (Fleure & Neely 1936, 376). The site has never been excavated, but is highly deserving of further investigation in due course (Figure 4.11).

DISCUSSION

As the above summary catalogue shows, there is an interesting and fairly extensive range of certain and probable Neolithic round barrows on the Island. The best known are those datable to the fourth millennium BC. Architecturally, these structures accord well with traditions discussed by Ian Kinnes (1979) and show links across the Irish Sea in all directions in a way that underlines the role of human engagement with the material world and with one another (Cummings & Fowler 2004). Especially important in view of Alison Sheridan's findings on the distribution of pottery styles along the Atlantic seaways (2004) are the suggested connections southwards to Brittany and Normandy.

Where examined, round barrows of the fourth millennium BC show a common and widespread interest in the selection and deposition of white quartz, especially quartz pebbles that are found in the chambers and in associated external contexts. In many cases these pebbles appear to have been collected from beaches. They represent some of the earliest instances of a tradition that continues down into modern times in many parts of the west of Britain, and if recent belief and custom is any guide to ancient practices then these stones are regarded as tokens of the human spirit (Darvill 2002). In selecting a stone and placing it in a significant context a person can leave in that place a little piece of themselves that can survive to eternity. According to context, the presence of such stones may bring good fortune or bestow bad luck; they may restore health or serve as a vehicle to transmit ill-omens. Quartz was clearly a powerful and significant material, and its incorporation in monuments continues into the third millennium BC on the Island.

Two of the four possible round barrows of the third millennium BC certainly include quartz boulders in their construction: Arragon Moar and Corvalley. In both cases these are blocks either obtained locally from the numerous quartz veins that outcrop amongst the Manx Slates, or arrived near where they were used as glacial erratics. Whether these two sites and Tynwald Hill cover developed passage graves of some sort remains to be seen, but it is notable that the Island lies within the general distribution of such sites that includes eastern Ireland and the north Wales coastlands through to the most easterly example, now destroyed, at Calderstones in Liverpool that could be seen as an interaction sphere (Bradley & Chapman 1986).

The size and shapes of these putatively third millennium BC round barrows is interesting: Tynwald Hill was probably stepped like some passage graves; Arragon Moar is a truncated cone rather like Silbury Hill, Wiltshire, on a diminutive scale; and Corvalley is an amorphous bowl shape. The inspiration for this last-mentioned barrow might not be with the conventional megalithic architecture elsewhere in north-west Europe but rather with natural landscape forms found on the Island.

The Isle of Man was heavily glaciated during the middle and late Pleistocene with the result that sculpted landforms and glacial moraines deposited as small drumlins give the impression of substantial mounds. Cronk Howe Mooar (sometimes called Fairy Hill), Rushen, is one such feature situated within an area of boggy ground in the south of the Island. Its likeness to an ancient barrow was such that excavations were undertaken in 1914 with that expectation in mind (Kermode & Herdman 1914, 72–82). What the investigators found was a natural hillock artificially treated in early medieval times through the enclosure of the small level space on the top by an earthen embankment lined inside with large stone slabs set on end with walling between. Similarly, at Killeaba, Ramsey, in the north of the Island, excavations by Marshall Cubbon in 1968–9 revealed a wholly natural glacial mound with a long history of activity (Cubbon 1978). At the centre was an oval hollow 2.5m long and 0.7m wide which had been repeatedly used as a fire pit whose use started back in the fifth millennium BC. A radiocarbon date of 5470–5070 cal BC (BM-838: 6310±72 BP) related to this event and while the excavator dismissed it as being derived from old wood (Cubbon 1978, 87) it is possible that the pit has similarities with the early features at Billown Quarry Site (Darvill 1999, 15–16) where there is also a long history of interest in distinctive natural places. No cremated remains were found in the pit at Killeaba, but three cremations lay round about. Four smaller oval pits lay beyond the central feature, all between 1m and 3.5m across. Staining within the fills suggested that they had been timber-lined or had contained burials in wooden boxes. Two of the pits contained cremation burials, while a third held a Ronaldsway Ware jar. Radiocarbon dates of 3330–2890 cal BC (BM-839: 4381±58 BP) and 3090–2710 cal BC (BM-840: 4300±52 BP) show these burials to be of the early third millennium BC.

Rounding off the succession of Neolithic round barrows in the Isle of Man is Ballakelly with its obvious similarities with the Scilly-Tramore entrance graves of the southern Irish Sea basin. These generally small structures are increasingly recognized as one of several regional traditions of late megalithic structures spanning the late third and early second millennium across the British Isles – others include the Clava cairns of northeastern Scotland, the Bargrennan tombs of southwestern Scotland, and the Wedge tombs of Ireland. In many ways the style of these structures harks back to older traditions of passage graves and long barrows as if these communities were trying to perpetuate, or perhaps even reinvent, a heritage and a link with the past that others had already left behind. As the second millennium unfolded, however, it was the round barrow that became the ubiquitous burial monument of choice right across northwest Europe, a new tradition that in its way perhaps also owed much to Neolithic predecessors.

ACKNOWLEDGEMENTS

All radiocarbon dates cited in the text of this paper have been calibrated using OxCal v.4.0 with calibration curve Intcal04, and are expressed as age ranges at $c.95\%$ confidence limits (2σ) in calendar years BC (=cal. BC) rounded to the nearest decade. Thanks to Andrew Foxon and Andrew Johnston for comments and information about some of the sites discussed here, Paul Cheetham, John Gale, Steve Burrow, and Jeff Chartrand for assisting with surveys of these sites, and Vanessa Constant for the preparation of the accompanying figures.

BIBLIOGRAPHY

Ashbee, P. (1982) Mesolithic megaliths? The Scillonian entrance-graves: a new view. *Cornish Archaeology* 21, 3–22.

Barnwell, E. L. (1866) Notes on the stone monuments in the Isle of Man. *Archaeologia Cambrensis* 21, 46–60.

Boujot, C. and Cassen, S. (1993) A pattern of evolution for the Neolithic funerary monuments of the west of France. *Antiquity* 67, 477–91.

Bowen, E. G. (1970) *Britain and the Western Seaways*. London, Thames and Hudson.

Bradley, R. (1998) *The significance of monuments*. London, Routledge.

Bradley, R. and Chapman, R. (1986) The nature and development of long-distance relations in Later Neolithic Britain and Ireland. In C. Renfrew and J. Cherry (eds.), *Peer polity interaction and socio-political change*, 127–58. Cambridge, Cambridge University Press.

Bradley, R. and Sheridan, J. A. (2005) Croft Moraig and the chronology of stone circles. *Proceedings of the Prehistoric Society* 71, 269–81.

Brink, S. (2004) Legal assembly sites in early Scandinavia. In A. Pantos and S. Semple (eds.), *Assembly places and practices in Medieval Europe*, 205–16. Dublin, Four Courts Press.

Bryce, T. H. (1904) On the cairns and tumuli of the Island of Bute. *Proceedings of the Society of Antiquaries of Scotland* 38 (Fourth Series 2), 17–81.

Burrow, S. (1997) *The Neolithic culture of the Isle of Man: a study of the sites and pottery*. Oxford, Archaeopress (BAR British Series 263).

Burrow, S. and Darvill, T. (1997) AMS dating of the Ronaldsway Culture of the Isle of Man. *Antiquity* 71, 412–19.

Caillaud, R. and Lagnel, E. (1972) Le cairn et la crematoire néolithiques de la Hougette à Fontenay-le-Marmion (Calvados). *Gallia Préhistoire* 15, 137–97.

Chartrand, J., Cheetham, P., Darvill, T. and Hayes, T. (2003) The Giants Grave, Kew, German. In T. Darvill (ed.), *Billown Neolithic Landscape Project, Isle of Man, Seventh Report: 2002*, 37–47. Bournemouth and Douglas, Bournemouth University School of Conservation Sciences (Research Report 11).

Clark, G. (1935) The prehistory of the Isle of Man. *Proceedings of the Prehistoric Society* 1, 70–92.

Clark, G. (1977) The economic context of dolmens and passage-graves in Sweden. In V. Markotic (ed.), *Ancient Europe and the Mediterranean: Studies presented in honour of Hugh Henchen*, 35–50. Warminster, Aris and Phillips.

Clifford, E. (1936) Notgrove long barrow, Gloucestershire. *Archaeologia* 86, 119–61.

Craine, D. (1957) *Tynwald*. Douglas, Nelson Press.

Cubbon, M. (1964) Clay Head cooking-place sites excavation of a group of cairns. *Proceedings of the Isle of Man Natural History and Antiquarian Society* 6 (1956–1964), 566–96.

Cubbon, M. (1978) Excavation at Killeaba, Ramsey, Isle of Man. *Proceedings of the Prehistoric Society* 44, 69–95.

Cubbon, W. and Bruce, J. R. (1928) The Kew Giants Grave. *Proceedings of the Isle of Man Natural History and Antiquarian Society* 3(2), 239–41.

Cummings, V. and Fowler, C. (2004) Introduction: locating the Neolithic of the Irish Sea. In V. Cummings and C. Fowler (eds.), *The Neolithic of the Irish Sea: materiality and traditions of practice*, 1–8. Oxford, Oxbow Books.

Daniel, G. (1950) *The prehistoric chamber tombs of England and Wales*. Cambridge, Cambridge University Press.

Daniel, G. (1960) *The prehistoric chamber tombs of France*. London, Thames and Hudson.

Darvill, T. (1999) Billown Neolithic Landscape Project 1995–1997. In P. J. Davey (ed.), *Recent archaeological research on the Isle of Man*, 13–26. Oxford, Archaeopress (BAR British Series 278).

Darvill, T. (2000) Neolithic Mann in Context. In A. Ritchie (ed.), *Neolithic Orkney in its European context*, 371–85. Cambridge, McDonald Institute.

Darvill, T. (2002) White on Blonde: Quartz pebbles and the use of quartz at Neolithic monuments in the Isle of Man and beyond. In A. Jones and G. McGregor (eds.), *Colouring the past. The significance of colour in archaeological research*, 73–92. Oxford and New York, Berg.

Darvill, T. (2004a) *Long barrows of the Cotswolds and surrounding areas*. Stroud, Tempus.

Darvill, T. (2004b) Tynwald Hill and the "things" of power. In A. Pantos and S. Semple (eds.), *Assembly places and practices in Medieval Europe*, 217–32. Dublin, Four Courts Press.

Darvill, T. (ed.), (in preparation) *Moots and Things: An archaeological survey of Tynwald Hill and St John's Plain, German, Isle of Man*.

Darvill, T. and Chartrand, J. (2000) A survey of the chambered long barrow at Cashtal yn Ard, Maughold. In T. Darvill (ed.), *Billown Neolithic Landscape Project, Isle of Man, Fifth Report: 1999*, 34–44. Bournemouth and Douglas, Bournemouth University School of Conservation Sciences (Research Report 7).

Darvill, T., Cheetham, P., Madden, C. and Mundin, A. (2001) Investigations at Cronk ny Arrey, Rushen. In T. Darvill (ed.), *Billown Neolithic Landscape Project, Isle of Man, Sixth Report: 2000*, 48–51. Bournemouth and Douglas, Bournemouth University School of Conservation Sciences (Research Report 9).

Darvill, T. and O'Connor, B. (2005) The Cronk yn Howe Stone and the rock art of the Isle of Man. *Proceedings of the Prehistoric Society* 71, 283–332.

Davies, M. (1946) The diffusion and distribution pattern of the megalithic monuments of the Irish Sea and North Channel coastlands. *Antiquaries Journal* 26, 38–60.

De Valera, R. (1960) The court cairns of Ireland. *Proceedings of the Royal Irish Academy* 60C, 9–140.

Feltham, J. (1798) *A tour through the Island of Mann in 1797 and 1798*. London.

Fleure, H. J. and Neely, G. J. H. (1936) Cashtal yn Ard, Isle of Man. *Antiquaries Journal* 16, 373–95.

Gale, J. and Darvill, T. (1998) A survey of the Ballakelly chambered tomb, Santon. In T. Darvill (ed.), *Billown Neolithic Landscape Project, Isle of Man, Third Report: 1997*, 38–42. Bournemouth and Douglas, Bournemouth University School of Conservation Sciences (Research Report 4).

Gale, J., Chartrand, J., Fulton, A., Laughlin, B. and Darvill, T. (1997) The Mull Hill tomb. In T. Darvill (ed.), *Billown Neolithic Landscape Project, Isle of Man, 1996*, 52–60. Bournemouth and Douglas: Bournemouth University School of Conservation Sciences (Research Report 3).

Giot, P. R. (1987) *Barnenez, Carn, Guennoc*. Rennes, Travaux du Laboratoire d'Anthropologie, Préhistoire, Protohistoire et Quaternaire Armoricains.

Grimes, W. F. (1939) The excavation of Ty-Isaf long cairn, Brecknockshire. *Proceedings of the Prehistoric Society* 5, 119–42.

Harrison, S. N. (1915) Excavation of a round barrow on Ballaterson Cronk, Maughold. *Proceedings of the Isle of Man Natural History and Antiquarian Society* 1, 467–70.

Henshall, A. S. (1972) *The Chambered Tombs of Scotland. Volume 2*. Edinburgh, Edinburgh University Press.

Henshall, A. S. (1978) Manx megaliths again: an attempt at structural analysis. In P. J. Davey (ed.), *Man and Environment in the Isle of Man*, 171–76. Oxford, British Archaeological Reports (BAR British Series 54).

Henshall, A. S. (forthcoming) Excavations at the Mull Hill Circle. In A. Henshall and F. M. Lynch (eds.), *The chamber tombs of the Isle of Man*. Liverpool, Liverpool University Press.

Herdman, W. A. and Kermode, P. M. C. (1894) The excavation of the Neolithic Stone Circle on the Meayll Hill near Port Erin. *Transactions of the Biological Society of Liverpool* 8, 1–13.

Herity, M. (1974) *Irish passage graves*. Dublin, Irish University Press.

Jewitt, L. (1885) On Cashtal yn Ard. *The Reliquary* January 1885, 166–7.

Kermode, P. M. C. (1929) Presidential address. *Archaeologia Cambrensis* 84, 167–78.

Kermode, P. M. C. and Herdman, W. A. (1914) *Manks Antiquities (Second edition)*. Liverpool, Liverpool University Press.

Kinnes, I. (1979) *Round barrows and ring-ditches in the British Neolithic*. London, British Museum (Occasional Paper 7).

Kinnes, I. (1992) Non-megalithic long barrows and allied structures in the British Neolithic. London, British Museum (Occasional Paper 52).

L'Helgouach (1965) *Les sépultures mégalithiques en Armorique*. Rennes, Théses Présentées a la Faculté des Sciences de l'Université de Rennes.

Lynch, F. (1972) Portal dolmens in the Nevern Valley, Pembrokeshire. In F. Lynch and C. Burgess (eds.), *Prehistoric man in Wales and the West. Essays in honour of Lily F. Chitty*, 67–83. Bath, Adams and Dart.

Lynch, F. (1976) Towards a chronology of megalithic tombs in Wales. In G. Boon and J. M. Lewis (eds.), *Welsh Antiquity. Essays mainly on prehistoric topics presented to H. N. Savory upon his retirement as Keeper of Archaeology*, 63–79. Cardiff, National Museum of Wales.

Manby, T. (1958) The chambered tombs of Derbyshire. *Derbyshire Archaeological Journal* 78, 25–39.

Megaw, B. R. S. (1938) Manx megaliths and their ancestry. *Proceedings of the Isle of Man Natural History and Antiquarian Society* 4, 219–39.

Mortimer, J. R. (1905) *Forty years' researches in British and Saxon burial mounds of East Yorkshire*. London, Hull and York, A. Brown & Sons.

Murray, J. (1992) The Bargrennan group of chambered cairns. In N. Sharples and J. A. Sheridan (eds.), *Vessels for the ancestors. Essays on the Neolithic of Britain and Ireland in honour of Audrey Henshall*, 33–48. Edinburgh, Edinburgh University Press.

Ó Nualláin, S. and Walsh, P. (1986) A reconsideration of the Tramore passage-tombs. *Proceedings of the Prehistoric Society* 52, 25–9.

Pantos, A. (2004) The location and form of Anglo-Saxon assembly places: some "moot points". In A. Pantos and S. Semple (eds.), *Assembly places and practices in Medieval Europe*, 155–80. Dublin, Four Courts Press.

Patton, M. (1992) Megalithic transport and territorial markers: evidence from the Channel Islands. *Antiquity* 66, 392–5.

Piggott, S. (1932) The Mull Hill Circle, Isle of Man and its pottery. *Antiquaries Journal* 12, 147–57.

Piggott, S. and Simpson, D. D. A. (1971) Excavation of a stone circle at Croft Moraig, Perthshire, Scotland. *Proceedings of the Prehistoric Society* 37, 1–15.

Renfrew, C. (1979) *Investigations in Orkney*. London, Society of Antiquaries (Reports of the Research Committee 38).

Scarre, C. (2002) Coasts and cosmos. The Neolithic monuments of northern Brittany. In C. Scarre (ed.) *Monuments and landscape in Atlantic Europe*, 84–102. London, Routledge.

Schulting, R. J. (1996) Antlers, bone pins and flint blades: the Mesolithic cemeteries of Téviec and Hoëdic, Brittany. *Antiquity* 70, 335–50.

Scott, J. G. (1969) The Clyde Cairns of Scotland. In T. G. E. Powell, J. X. W. P. Corcoran, F. Lynch and J. G. Scott, *Megalithic enquiries in the west of Britain*, 175–222 and 309–28. Liverpool, Liverpool University Press.

Selkirk, A. (1971) Manx megaliths. *Current Archaeology* 3(27), 95–7.

Sheridan, J. A. (1995) Irish Neolithic pottery: the story in 1995. In I. Kinnes and G. Varndell (eds.) *"Unbaked urns of rudely shape" Essays on British and Irish pottery*, 3–22. Oxford, Oxbow Books (Monograph 55).

Sheridan, J. A. (2004) Neolithic connections along and across the Irish Sea. In V. Cummings and C. Fowler (eds.), *The Neolithic of the Irish Sea: materiality and traditions of practice*, 9–21. Oxford, Oxbow Books.

Stranger, A. (1836) *A six-days' tour through the Isle of Man*. Douglas.

Swinnerton, F. (1890) The early Neolithic cists and refuse heap at Port St Mary. *Yn Lioar Manninagh* 1(2), 137–9.

Thomas, C. (1985) *Exploration of a drowned landscape*. London, Batsford.

Chapter 5

Recent Work on the Neolithic Round Barrows of the Upper Great Wold Valley, Yorkshire

Alex Gibson and Alex Bayliss

With contributions by H. Heard, I. Mainland and A. R. Ogden, C. Bronk Ramsey, G. Cook, J. van der Plicht, and P. Marshall

INTRODUCTION

The valley of the Gypsey Race, or the Great Wold Valley, in eastern Yorkshire is well known for its Neolithic and Bronze Age archaeology, not only from the nineteenth century antiquarian researches of Greenwell (*e.g.* Greenwell 1877) and Mortimer (1905) but also from the works of more recent researchers such as Brewster, Manby and Kinnes (see Manby *et al.* 2003 for a summary). The Rudston cursus complex with the imposing Rudston monolith at its centre is arguably the best known cursus complex in Britain and the large and presumed Neolithic round barrows such as Duggleby Howe, Willlie Howe, and Wold Newton have long been held as iconic sites in Neolithic studies (Kinnes 1979).

Despite the high academic profile that these sites have enjoyed and still command, little work has been undertaken on them either in terms of re-excavation, still re-analysis or the evaluation of their current condition. A notable exception is the review of Neolithic round barrows by Kinnes (1979) where the Yorkshire sites rank highly in his national corpus of such monuments. Résumés of the evidence have also been undertaken by Manby (1988) and Harding (1997) and Duggleby Howe has been "reconsidered" (Kinnes *et al.* 1983) and "revisited" (Loveday 2002). These papers, however, are all based on the reworking of old data albeit within new research (both empirical and theoretical) frameworks, and it remained true until the completion of the present project that the single radiocarbon date from any of these important Neolithic burial monuments was on the antler macehead associated with one of the secondary burials, Burial G, at Duggleby Howe (Loveday *et al.* 2007).

In 2006, the author embarked on an English Heritage-funded project to investigate and date the Neolithic barrows of the Upper Great Wold Valley (Figure 5.1). This project involved the topographical and geophysical survey of selected lesser-known sites such as the Wharram le Street double ring ditch known from the air but which had failed to show on earlier geophysical surveys (Rahtz *et al.* 1986), Esh's Barrow and Denby House long barrow, as well as some of the better-known surviving round barrows of the region such as Duggleby Howe, Wold Newton, and Willie Howe. In addition, the surviving archives from these and other possibly Neolithic sites were located and assessed to determine whether any material suitable for radiocarbon dating survived. The site archives proved to be of variable quality, and in some cases, such as for example, from Canon Greenwell's excavations, skeletal material appears not to have been retained at all. In others, such as John Mortimer's excavations at Wold Newton, only some of

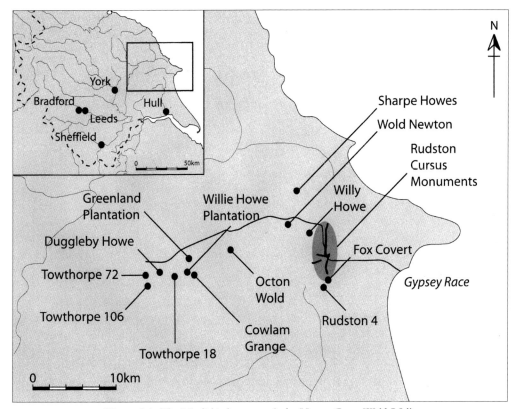

Figure 5.1: The Neolithic barrows of the Upper Great Wold Valley

the excavated material survives in the archive (and labelling is of variable utility). Nonetheless, samples were submitted for the putative Neolithic inhumations at Duggleby Howe, Wold Newton, Towthorpe 106, and Towthorpe 18 (all from the Mortimer archive at Hull and East Riding Museum), from Willie Howe (from the Brewster archive also at Hull and East Riding Museum) and from Fox Covert (Greenwell LXI) (archive at the British Museum). The long barrow surveys and the work at Duggleby Howe will form the bases of other reports, however it was considered timely to present here the results of the investigations at the Neolithic and other presumed Neolithic round barrow sites.

It must be stated at the outset that the relevant antiquarian archives have suffered a great degree of loss over the years. This depletion is no reflection on the current curators, rather a result of the gradual diminishing of the collections over time, not aided by wartime damage. No human skeletal material survives in the Greenwell archive and, whilst there are surviving bones (human and animal) in the Mortimer collection at Hull Museum, these have suffered from inaccurate labelling, detached labels and the one-time general lack of importance attached to skeletal remains (including by Mortimer himself).

The palaeoosteological report on the Duggleby Howe bones, for example, was undertaken by a Dr Garson and his report was published at the end of Mortimer's account of the excavation (Mortimer 1905, 30–40). Garson commented that even then, not all the bones recorded by Mortimer in his account of the excavation were present and available for study. Then in a telling statement, Mortimer responds:

> "*As a specialist, Dr Garson naturally attaches a greater importance to the collecting of osseous remains. But an ordinary archaeologist probably considers the collecting of other relics more important than securing the bones, for these are, except in the hands of a specialist, comparatively useless. I possess nearly two cartloads of crania and other portions of human skeletons (properly labelled and stored away) which have been collected at various periods from British Barrows.*" *(Mortimer 1905, 41).*

In other words, Mortimer did not see the full value of skeletal material beyond sexing, ageing and the occasional identification of disease or trauma. Archaeological science was in its infancy and Mortimer could not expect to have been aware of subsequent scientific developments and the tests to which skeletal remains may now be subjected or indeed the archaeological information that they can now provide. It is also untrue that the bones were properly labelled and stored away as Garson's comment about the missing bones makes clear. This is particularly true of the cremated remains.

WILLY HOWE (GREENWELL CCLII); [NGR: TA 063724]

Willy Howe lies just over 1km to the east of Wold Newton and was opened by Lord Londesborough in 1857 but no finds were recovered. It was re-opened 30 years later by Greenwell (Greenwell 1890, 22–4) who found a large central pit, 1.2m long, by 0.8m wide and 3.7m deep. The pit was filled with various chalky fills from which some animal bones were obtained. These bones and the "five chippings and a flake of flint" recorded by Greenwell have not been preserved.

Thurnham (1871, 522 footnote b) records a possible jet/lignite cup from "Willy Houe", perhaps similar to the Farway cups of Devon, that was found in the middle ages and reached the treasuries of Henry I, David I and Henry II. In this respect the folk-lore associated with the barrow may be of interest. Grinsell (quoting Harland, himself quoting the thirteenth century writer William of Newbridge) records that a travelling horseman heard merriment coming from the mound. He saw a door open in the side of the mound and, on looking inside, witnessed a feast in progress. On being offered a drink, the horseman took the cup, emptied its contents and rode off. He escaped his pursuers and brought the cup home (Grinsell 1936, 55).

This tantalising reference aside, there are no surviving finds from Willy Howe and its Neolithic date is assigned purely by virtue of its size and its proximity to Wold Newton and Duggleby Howe.

Topographical Survey

Though surrounded by arable, the mound itself is covered in trees and dense brambles making survey difficult (Figure 5.2). The ploughing extends to the base of the mound. The unfilled Greenwell (and Londsborough?) excavation is clearly visible as a deep trench in the centre of the mound with a large spoil heap to the northwest. The survey shows the mound on a gentle north-facing slope and there are slight traces of a shallow ditch some 10m wide around the base of the mound.

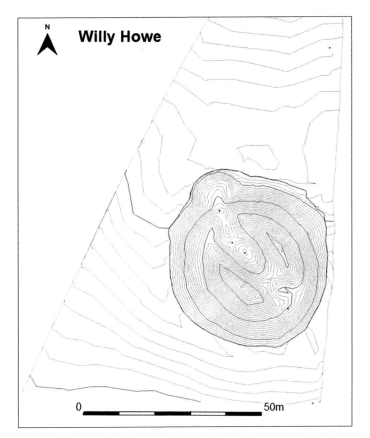

Figure 5.2: Topographical Survey of Willy Howe. (Contours at 10cm intervals)

Geophysical Survey
By Hannah Heard

The geophysical survey at Willy Howe covered an area 1ha in size centred on the barrow. It was carried out using resistivity and gradiometry soon after the harvest. The underlying geology is chalk and the overlying cover is Coombe 1 soil which is a typical brown calcareous earth consisting of well drained calcareous fine silty material.

Gradiometry

The gradiometer survey revealed a number of large positive anomalies situated around the round barrow (Figure 5.3 wi1–4). These may represent cut features associated with the construction of the mound. The variation in strength of the positive anomalies may indicate multiphase activity and be interpreted as phases of digging and subsequent filling, possibly adding to the barrow mound.

Situated in the southwest corner of the survey area are a number of faint positive linear anomalies (wi5) and an oval shaped positive linear anomaly (wi6). These may indicate further cut features of archaeological origin. A faint negative linear anomaly can be seen

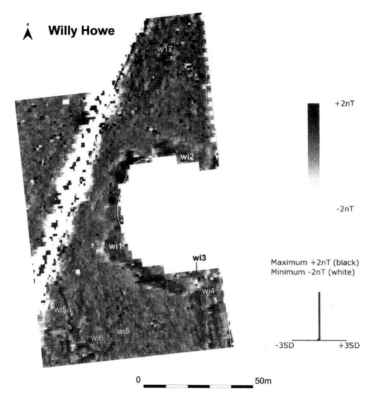

Figure 5.3: Gradiometer Survey of Willy Howe. (Source: Stratascan)

in the north of the survey (wi7). This may represent weak evidence of an earthen bank or structural remains of archaeological origin.

Resistivity

The resistivity survey contained readings of comparatively little variation. It required a relativity close plotting parameter to reveal potential archaeological anomalies. Similar cut feature responses can be seen surrounding the round barrow (Figure 5.4 wi11–14) although the shapes and extents vary slightly with those identified by the gradiometer survey. Further investigation would be needed to identify the nature and extents of these anomalies. Areas of high resistance can be seen close to the barrow mound (wi8–10). These may be associated with the limits of the mound's structure. Areas of high resistance have been identified across the survey area and may represent weak evidence for structural debris or compacted ground (wi15–17). A faint high resistance anomaly can be seen across the north of the survey area (wi6), its northern limit corresponding to the negative linear identified within the gradiometer survey. This area response may represent weak evidence for ground disturbance or slightly compacted ground. A faint low resistance linear anomaly has been identified along the western edge of the survey area (wi19–21), which corresponds to the positive linear anomaly (wi5a) seen in the gradiometer survey (Figure 5.3) and may represent a cut feature of archaeological origin.

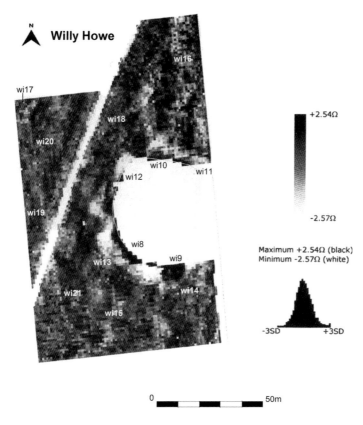

Figure 5.4: Resistivity Survey of Willy Howe. (Source: Stratascan)

Radiocarbon Dating

The absence of finds from this site meant that no samples could be submitted for radiocarbon dating to confirm the supposed Neolithic origins of the mound.

WOLD NEWTON (BALL HILL; MORTIMER 284); [NGR: TA 048726]

Wold Newton is a large mound lying some 18km to the northeast of Duggleby Howe. The game of "Throwl-egg" (rolling of dyed hard-boiled eggs) was apparently practiced at this site on Shrove Tuesdays (Grinsell 1936, 52). This site, also excavated by Mortimer (1905), covered multiple interments including an apparently primary multiple inhumation of at least six partly disarticulated skeletons. The barrow had a peat and turf primary mound in which were numerous deposits of animal bones. The primary interments lay on a layer of peat covering the chalk gravel subsoil. It appears from this stratigraphy and the proximity of the Gypsey Race, that there is a high probability that the surrounding ditch will contain important and environmentally rich deposits (possibly water-logged). The mound is also reported as having a "large surrounding causewayed ditch" (Loughlin & Miller, 1979, 141) visible on Ordnance Survey photographs however these photographs are not referenced and have not been traced at the National Monument Record or Ordnance Survey. The ditch does not appear on Stoertz's (1997) maps. Manby (pers. comm.) is of the opinion that the ditch was noted on RAF vertical photographs but no further information could be obtained. It is likely that this reference may have arisen from confusion with the causewayed ditch at Duggleby Howe.

Kinnes identifies this as a possible Neolithic barrow by virtue of a leaf-shaped point (arrowhead) associated with burial 7 and the disarticulated multiple burial. He interprets a length of segmented ditch uncovered by Mortimer as possibly representing a mortuary enclosure (Kinnes 1979).

Topographical Survey

The survey (Figure 5.5) shows that the barrow at Wold Newton still survives as a substantial oval, rather than truly circular, mound 40m southeast to northwest by 32m northeast to southwest on a slight north facing slope at the bottom of the Gypsey Race Valley. The irregularity of the mound, which still survives to 3m high, has been caused by comparatively recent animal scraping and rabbit activity. There are possible traces of a shallow ditch around the base of the mound, an observation that is supported by the results of the geophysical survey (see below).

Geophysical Survey
By Hannah Heard

The survey at Wold Newton consists of an area 1ha in size and was centred over the barrow. The area is currently used as pasture and is bounded by field boundaries to the east and west and a road to the north. A third field boundary crosses the south of the area. As with Willy Howe, the underlying geology is chalk and the overlying soils are known as Coombe 1.

Gradiometry

The gradiometer survey (Figure 5.6) has identified a number of features of archaeological origin. A positive linear anomaly has been identified just under the edge of the earthwork barrow (w1). This may represent a ditch that may have once surrounded the edge of the earthwork mound, but since covered due to erosion. A number of weak positive linear anomalies can be seen in the south of the survey area (w2), possibly representing two concentric curvilinear features. These may represent weak evidence for cut features of archaeological origin. Additional disjointed linear anomalies have been identified across the north of the survey area (w3–5), which may represent further cut features of archaeological origin, but could equally be of agricultural origin.

Three positive anomalies can be seen within the area of the round barrow which may represent cut features such as pits, or burials (w6, w6a and w7). A relatively strong positive anomaly can be seen along the western side of the survey area (w9) which may represent a cut feature or area of ground disturbance of possible archaeological origin. Additional positive anomalies situated in the north and south of the survey area may represent further cut features or areas of ground disturbance of possible archaeological origin (w10–11).

A weak negative linear anomaly around the positive feature w1 can be seen within the data. This may represent structural remains, such as a bank, or band of compacted ground

WOLD NEWTON

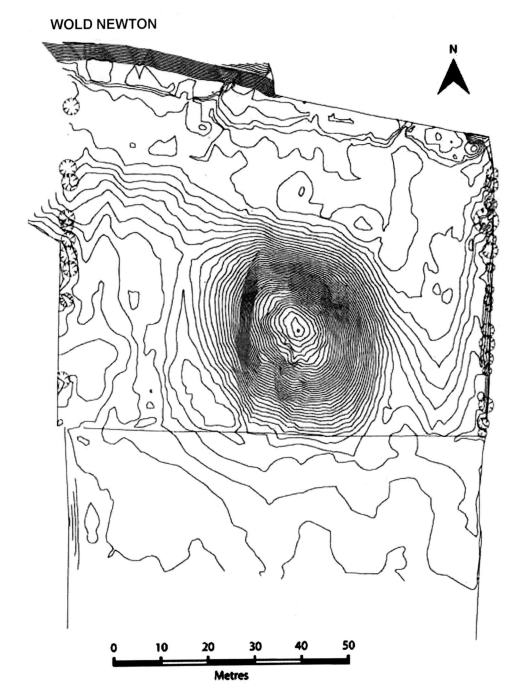

Figure 5.5: Topographical Survey of Wold Newton. (Contours at 10cm intervals)

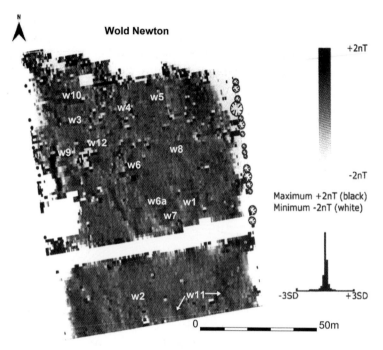

Figure 5.6: Gradiometer survey of Wold Newton. (Source: Stratascan)

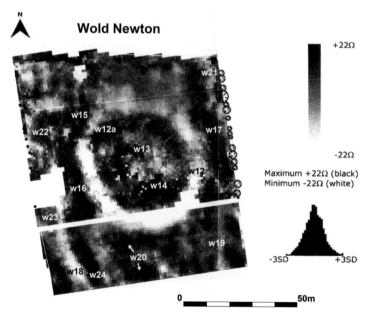

Figure 5.7: Resistivity Survey of Wold Newton. (Source: Stratascan)

associated with the barrow. An area of magnetic debris is situated to the northwest of the barrow (w12) which may indicate an area of ground disturbance of possible archaeological origin. Areas of magnetic disturbance have also been identified along the edges of the survey area. These are likely to be associated with the nearby road and field boundaries. A large number of positive anomalies with associated negative returns are present in the northern section of the survey area which are likely to represent near surface ferrous objects.

Resistivity

The resistivity survey (Figure 5.7) has proved successful in identifying ring ditch associated with the barrow (w12). Although, as a section of the ring ditch appears to be thinner and slightly disjointed it may be suggested that at a later date a section of the ditch was filled in (w12a). This large cut feature, surprisingly, was not identified by the gradiometer survey and surrounds the possible band of compacted ground (w8). A number of additional low resistance anomalies are present in the west and northeast parts of the survey area (w21–24), which may represent large cut features, areas of ground disturbance or features of pedological origin.

Two discrete areas of high resistance have been identified within the area of the barrow (w13 and w14) which correspond with the gradiometer anomalies w6 and w7. These anomalies may represent two discrete areas of structural remains or ground disturbance possibly associated with archaeological activity or burials associated with the barrow. Further areas of high resistance have been identified around the barrow (w15–18) which may represent structural debris of archaeological origin or areas of compacted ground. Further discrete areas of moderate high resistance can be seen throughout the southern section of the survey area (w19–20) and areas within the barrow. These may represent weak evidence for structural debris or areas of compacted ground. A band of high resistance can be seen in the north western edge of the survey area which is likely to be associated with the nearby field boundary and entrance.

Excavation Account

Excavated in 1894, Mortimer recorded the mound as 12ft (*c.*3.7m) high and 83ft (*c.*25.5m) in diameter and damaged by rabbit diggers. Starting on the west side, Mortimer's trench measured 60ft (*c.*18.5m) east to west by 30ft (*c.*9.2m) north to south. The barrow stood on a thin layer of peat overlying chalk gravel and the mound was composed of peat with a chalk gravel capping.

Mortimer recorded a child cremation 7ft (*c.*2.2m) southeast of the centre and 6ft (*c.*1.9m) deep into the mound. Two fragments of adult cranium were located 14ins (*c.*0.36m) north of the cremation. Some 18ft (*c.*5.5m) south-southeast of centre, were the remains of five skeletons (2–6) close together and crushed. These comprised three adults, one youth and one child. No. 2 (adult) was contracted on its right side with its head to the northwest. Thick skull fragments of an adult were also found: the fragments were dispersed. Associated with this multiple deposit were the skull and bones of a pig. Some fragments of "food vase" (*i.e.* prehistoric pottery) were found in the deposit.

Some 9ft (*c.*2.8m) east of centre and 8ft (*c.*2.5m) deep was burial 7 contracted on its right side with the head to the west and associated with a leaf-shaped point on the pelvis. "A little" to the east of centre and 9ft (*c.*2.8m) deep, burial 8 was contracted on its right side with its head to east-southeast. Mortimer also recorded abundant bones of small mammals and reptiles, flint, pottery and animal bone from the various unspecified parts of the mound.

The site was presumed to be Neolithic from the multiple inhumation on the old ground surface and from the presumed secondary burial higher up in the mound associated with a leaf-shaped flint point.

Human Osteology
By A. R. Ogden

(Full details can be found in the site archive)

Skeleton 2:17

This is a young female with gracile longbones, the left humerus of which has a powerful deltoid attachment (Figure 5.8). The skull has a sloping forehead. Also included with this skeleton were fragments of another adult cranium and the left angle of a child's mandible, aged 7–8 yrs.

Skeleton 7:18

This is a young male with a prominent occipital ridge, occipital bun, large glabellae and mastoids, supra-auricular crests and prominent chin. There is no gonial flare but prominent gonial projections and strong asymmetry: *i.e.* the left cerebellum is much larger than the right. There is some fusion of sutures and the premature closure of coronoid suture has led to Plageocephaly (long, thin skull). There is also in-vivo fracture of palatal cusp UR7 (Figure 5.9); this had occurred some time before death as the fracture edges have become

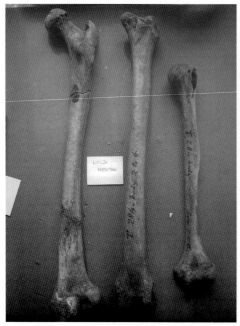

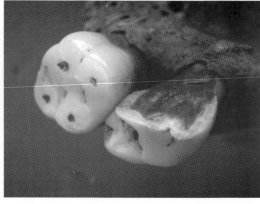

Figure 5.8 (left): Wold Newton 2.17. Left humerus with powerful deltoid attachment.

Figure 5.9 (above): Wold Newton 7.18 showing pre-mortem fracture of upper right molar.

rounded. Such fractures may be the result of biting on unexpected hard particles, or the result of violence causing the jaws to clash together. There is also evidence for advanced periodontitis. Fragments of a second adult skull along with bones of a child of 7–8 years were also included within 7:18.

The minimum number of individuals (MNI) is 3 adults and one child.

Animal Bone
By I Mainland (Full details are included in the site archive)

Four species were represented in the Wold Newton "nests" excavated by Mortimer (1905): field vole, bank vole, common frog and common toad. From the presence of large rodent post-cranial element, it can be suggested that rat (*Rattus* sp.) was probably also present, though no cranial material was recovered to support this identification. Unfortunately, all these species can be considered intrusive. During hibernation, frog and toad will tunnel down into earthen/stony mounds. They are indeed commonly found within barrows and cairns and where detailed taphonomical study of such deposits has been undertaken, they have almost always been found to be intrusive. Field voles and bank voles are both burrowing species, and hence may also have become incorporated into the barrow deposits at any time since its construction. These identifications thus suggest that the microfaunal assemblages would not prove reliable dating evidence.

Radiocarbon Dating
With Alex Bayliss

From the schematic section drawing published by Mortimer (Figure 5.10), it seems that the multiple deposit was earlier than Burial 7 which appears higher in the mound material. This inferred stratigraphic sequence has been included in the model shown in Figure 5.11, along with the interpretation that these burials result from a coherent period of Neolithic activity. This model has good overall agreement ($A_{overall} = 109.1\%$). The child from the multiple deposit died in 3910–3875 cal BC (5% probability) or 3805–3705 cal BC (90% probability;

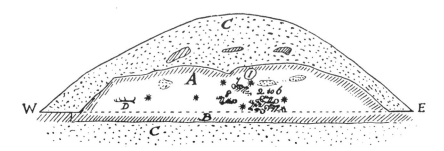

1---Cremated Interment.　　*A*—Peat soil.
B—Peat surface under the Barrow.　　*C*—Fine chalk gravel.
D—Antler of red deer.　　*—Nests of bones of frogs, &c.

Figure 5.10: Mortimer's schematic section through Wold Newton. (After Mortimer 1905, fig 1015)

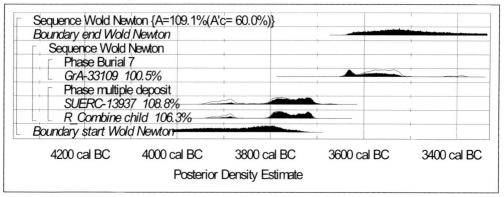

Figure 5.11: Probability distributions of dates from Wold Newton. Each distribution represents the relative probability that an event occurred at a particular time. For each of the dates two distributions have been plotted, one in outline which is the result produced by the scientific evidence alone, and a solid one which is based on the chronological model used. The other distributions correspond to aspects of the model. The large square brackets down the left-hand side of the figure, along with the OxCal keywords, define the overall model exactly

child; Figure 5.11), probably in 3800–3760 cal BC (39% probability) or 3745–3710 cal BC (29% probability). The surviving adult burial (Burial 2), died in 3920–3870 cal BC (7% probability) or 3820–3690 cal BC (87% probability) or 3680–3660 cal BC (1% probability; SUERC-13937; Figure 5.11), probably in 3795–3705 cal BC (68% probability). It seems that this collective mortuary deposit was made in the thirty-eighth century BC.

Burial 7 must have been inserted into the mound judging from the, albeit schematic, section drawing. This occurred rather later in 3645–3520 cal BC (95% probability; GrA-33109; Figure 5.11), probably in 3640–3620 cal BC (24% probability) or 3605–3545 cal BC (43% probability) or 3540–3535 cal BC (1% probability). There is insufficient surviving material from what is obviously a complex monument to estimate the period of use of this barrow reliably, although the site seems to have been used for at least a century.

TOWTHORPE 18; [NGR: SE 89816495]

Today there is no surface sign of the mound except, perhaps for a slightly increased density of chalk in the ploughsoil. Mortimer claims to have excavated the whole mound and therefore it was considered likely that topographical and geophysical survey would not be cost-effective. In view of the results obtained, however, and with the benefit of hindsight, this may have been an error. It is hoped to rectify this when the agricultural regime allows.

Excavation Account

When excavated by Mortimer in 1865, Towthorpe 18 survived to 3ft (*c.*0.9m) high by 75yds (*c.*69.2m) in circumference. Mortimer opened a trench 14ft (*c.*4.3m) square over the centre of the mound and located a central cremation "a few inches" below the surface as well as the detached teeth and bones from ox and pig in the mound material. A little to the southeast of the centre, 2ft (*c.*0.6m) from the apex, was a cache of bones of small dogs/foxes which

Figure 5.12: Finds from the central deposit of Towthorpe 18. (After Mortimer 1905, plates II & III. Not to scale)

appeared to Mortimer to have been deliberately arranged since in one case two leg bones were crossed over a skull. Southwest of the centre were the remains of six bodies in a deposit 5ft 6ins (*c*.1.7m) square and about level with the old ground surface. The bodies were close together and contracted with their faces upwards suggesting they had been placed on their backs. An undecorated hemispherical bowl (Towthorpe Bowl – Bowl 1) had been placed on the west side and a second similar bowl on northeast side (Figure 5.12). To the southwest of the first bowl was a lozenge-shaped flint arrowhead fixed into a human femoral bone. Four leaf-shaped arrowheads were found 12ins (*c*.0.3m) to the north of bowl 1 and a second lozenge/laurel flint point was found below the thigh of the second skeleton 1ft

Figure 5.13: Towthorpe 18. Fragment of child's occipital bone, showing severe porotic hyperostosis, most likely caused by some form of anaemia

Figure 5.14: Towthorpe 18. Squatting facet on right tibia (Schwartz 1995)

(*c.*0.3m) to the south of the first. Three deposits of flint flakes were located on the west, southwest, and southeast of the deposit and three pounder stones and an ox rib were also recovered from this context. 'Nests' of rats' bones (over twenty individuals) were found on the northeast and west sides of the burials. This multiple deposit appears to represent the primary burial activity and is associated with artefacts of undoubted Neolithic affinity. A second trench 7ft (*c.*2.2m) square to the north of the centre located only antler.

Mortimer resumed excavations in 1868 to investigate the whole mound. Twenty feet (*c.*6.2m) north of centre he encountered a conical hole 4ft 6ins (*c.*1.4m) deep, 3ft 6ins (*c.*1.1m) wide at top and 1ft (*c.*0.3m) wide at base. There were no finds in this feature other than charcoal and two pieces of decayed bone. Some 11ft (*c.*3.4m) northeast of the centre was an oval grave 12ins (*c.*0.3m) deep containing a contracted inhumation on its right side with its head to north-northwest. There were no artefacts and no visible cut in the mound for the grave. Some 15ft (*c.*4.6m) west of the centre was a plough disturbed burial with fragments of "food vase" and 12ft (*c.*3.7m) southwest of centre was a second plough-disturbed burial contracted on its left side, head to east, and associated with the base of another small vase. In addition, Mortimer located traces of a ditch encircling the barrow.

Human Osteology
By A R Ogden (Full report in the site archive)

Study of the human remains indicates that Towthorpe 18 contained a minimum number of six adults, and one subadult ?child. Pathologies recorded included a chronic abscess and severe porotic hyperostosis, the latter commonly associated with anaemia (Figure 5.13). Also recorded was a patent metopic suture, and a squatting facet, the latter of which suggests that long periods were spent crouching; this can be as comfortable, if not more comfortable, than standing (Figure 5.14).

Animal Bone
By I Mainland

Mortimer (1905, 9) describes how

> "*lower down, and in various places in the mound, detached teeth and bones of ox and pig were found. Probably some of these bones had been cast there by the barrow builders after they had eaten the flesh. A little to the south and east of the centre and about 2 feet from the apex were the skulls and part of the bones of three small dogs or foxes, probably placed there as food. The heads of these animals were of small size, though the canine teeth appeared larger than is usual with dogs of small size. From the positions of some of the bones in the three deposits, it seemed probable that the bodies of these animals had been cut to pieces before being placed in the barrow, as in one case two leg bones, crossing each other at right angles were on top of a skull*".

It is apparent that mammal bones were also found in proximity to the inhumations, "from the midst of the bodies the rib of an ox was taken" (Mortimer 1905, 10). Finally microfauna were recovered from within the body of the mound "on the north-east margin nests of rats' bones were found" (Mortimer 1905, 10).

When the mound was re-opened for the first (re-opening) and second times (second re-opening) further mammalian bone was recorded: "at a depth of about 2 foot, the upper portion of the antler of red deer bearing two tines occurred" (Mortimer 1905, 10); "a few splinters of flint and several bones of animals, were taken from various places in the barrow" (Mortimer 1905, 11).

The surviving faunal assemblage from Towthorpe 18
(Full details are included in the site archive)

FOX

A total of 15 bone fragments were identified as fox. A further 2 fragments of skull identified as canid are likely to derive from fox but lack sufficient diagnostic criteria to allow definite identification, as do the 4 skull, 7 vertebrae and 2 long bone shaft fragments which were recorded as small mammal. Bone condition was very good to excellent. A MNI of 2 is derived from the presence of two right humeri. The left femur, tibia and pelvis articulate with each other as do the RHS radius and ulna. It is probable from the presence of ribs, vertebrae, skull and at least some articulating limb bones that this assemblage represents the remnants of complete or at least partially articulated fox carcasses. Epiphysial fusion is complete in the tibia, femur, humerus, pelvis, metacarpal, metatarsal and ulna. There was no evidence for human modification on these bones.

COW

Six fragments of cattle bone were recovered from this assemblage: atlas (n=1), radius (n=1), loose upper molar (n=1), loose upper permanent premolars (n=4). Bone condition is excellent for the radius and loose teeth but the atlas exhibited some weathering of the surface. The atlas and the loose teeth are derived from (an) adult individual(s) while the radius has the appearance of a very young, probably foetal or neonatal individual. This indicates a MNI of two. The four large ungulate fragments identified are likely to derive from cow, though insufficient diagnostic criteria were presented to enable distinction from horse or red deer.

PIG

Pig is represented by thirteen fragments from very young and/or neonatal individuals. A couple of likely matches between left and right-hand-side elements are apparent (astragalus, humerus) indicating the possibility that partial burials are present. While it is not possible to "articulate" the limb bones recovered due to fusion and fragmentation, a consideration of bone size and state-of-fusion indicates that three individuals, two very young animals and a neonate, are potentially represented. Two deciduous teeth were identified but skull or vertebrae from pig or small ungulates were not apparent. Five small ungulate ribs were recovered and could derive either from pig or sheep/goat (see below). All fragments were in excellent condition.

SHEEP/GOAT

Sixteen fragments of sheep/goat were recovered none of which presented diagnostic criteria to enable distinction between sheep and goat. All fragments derived from neonatal or very young individuals and may reflect three partial burials comprising two neonatal lambs and one juvenile sheep (probably aged under six months). As with pig, no skull or vertebrae fragments were recovered, though the small ungulate ribs may derive from either pig or sheep/goat. All fragments were in excellent condition.

BIRD

Two unidentifiable bird fragments were recovered.

UNIDENTIFIED

A possible animal rib bone was found "lying among the six skeletons". This is a rib from a large ungulate, gnawed by canids at the proximal and distal ends but otherwise in excellent condition.

Discussion

A sizable assemblage of mammal bone has survived from Towthorpe 18. Once again, however, it is very difficult to securely provenance most of this material. Whilst Mortimer's excavation report presents a reasonably good indication of the location of mammalian bone, unfortunately, it was not generally archived with specific details of its derivation. There are two exceptions: (1) the large ungulate rib which has been archived along with a label indicating that it was recovered "lying among the six skeletons" and which must be the "rib of an ox" that Mortimer describes in his excavation report; (2) the partial fox skeletons which are probably those described by Mortimer (1905) as lying about "2 foot" from the apex of the mound.

Foxes will enlarge existing hollow/holes during den construction (Corbet & Southern 1977) and it is not inconceivable that the fox skeletons which were recovered from this barrow, and indeed others excavated by Mortimer (1905), derive from fox dens and are thus intrusive. Fur-bearing animals, including species such as foxes, pine martens, mustelids do, however, appear to have had some special significance during the Neolithic (Chiquet 2004; Fairnell & Barret in press) and it is not uncommon to find their remains placed within funerary contexts (Sharples 1984; Richard Thomas pers. comm.). It is interesting in this respect that beaver teeth are described by Mortimer (1905) in association with inhumation C at Duggleby Howe. The series of C14 dates from the fox bones is therefore of interest suggesting that they represent evidence for the special treatment of foxes during the Neolithic within the Wolds. Mortimer (1905, 41) draws attention to the high frequency with which fox occurs in the barrows and it would be interesting to explore further the nature of this association.

Radiocarbon Dating
With Alex Bayliss

Nine radiocarbon determinations are available from eight samples from Towthorpe 18 (Table 5.1). The two measurements on individual 3 from the primary burial deposit (OxA-17240 and SUERC-13930) produced statistically consistent measurements ($T'=0.0$, $T'(5\%)=3.8$, $v=1$; Ward & Wilson 1978) and have been combined before calibration and inclusion in the model (Figure 5.15).

The three dated individuals that seem to have derived from the primary mortuary deposit all fall in the mid-fourth millennium BC. The measurements on these skeletons are not statistically consistent, however ($T'=33.1$, $T'(5\%)=6.0$, $v=2$; Ward & Wilson 1978). Burials 6 and 4 are earlier. Dating suggests that these individuals died in the mid-fourth millennium BC, while burial 3 died rather later (see Table 5.1 and Figure 5.15). This suggests that the

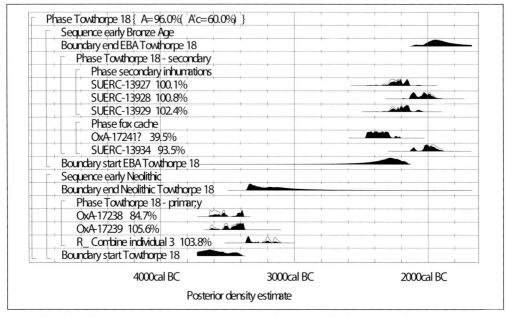

Phase Towthorpe 18 { A=96.0%(A'c=60.0%) }
  Sequence early Bronze Age
  Boundary end EBA Towthorpe 18
    Phase Towthorpe 18 - secondary
      Phase secondary inhumations
        SUERC-13927 100.1%
        SUERC-13928 100.8%
        SUERC-13929 102.4%
      Phase fox cache
        OxA-17241? 39.5%
        SUERC-13934 93.5%
  Boundary start EBA Towthorpe 18
  Sequence early Neolithic
  Boundary end Neolithic Towthorpe 18
    Phase Towthorpe 18 - primary
      OxA-17238 84.7%
      OxA-17239 105.6%
      R_Combine individual 3 103.8%
  Boundary start Towthorpe 18

4000cal BC   3000cal BC   2000cal BC

Posterior density estimate

Figure 5.15: Probability distributions of dates from Towthorpe 18. The format is identical to that of Figure 5.11. The large square brackets down the left-hand side of the figure, along with the OxCal keywords, define the overall model exactly

mortuary area may have been in use for some time and indeed some weathering has been noted on the surviving skeletal material, particularly burials 6 and 4, suggesting possible curation before final burial. This may mean that the deposit includes the remains of already ancient skeletal material and was deposited at the time or close to the time of the latest dated individual in the latter part of the fourth millennium BC (individual 3; Figure 5.15). Analogy might suggest that the mound was then erected over this primary deposit though we have no direct dating evidence for the mound construction itself.

Individuals 3A, 6A, and 5 date to the end of the third millennium and presumably represent the articulated secondary burials located in the mound material by Mortimer in his re-opening of the mound in 1868. The radiocarbon determinations on these three individuals are also not statistically consistent (T'=9.8, T'(5%)=6.0, v=2; Ward & Wilson 1978), which suggests that this activity consisted of a number of episodes, although in this case they may have spanned a relatively restricted period in the early Bronze Age (Figure 5.15).

It is not clear whether the fox bones relate to this episode of activity. The two measurements, one from each of the two foxes surviving in the archive, are not statistically consistent (T'=32.1, T'(5%)=3.8, v=1; Ward & Wilson 1978) which suggests that the foxes were not contemporary with each other (Table 5.1). This leaves us with a number of possibilities. Firstly, the deposit may have been made over a prolonged period of time broadly contemporary with the secondary interments, although Mortimer does not record any feature that might suggest an open pit or cavity in the mound material. Secondly, the remains may represent a natural earth in which the foxes died although, given the disparity of dates, this suggests that the earth would have been in use for a considerable

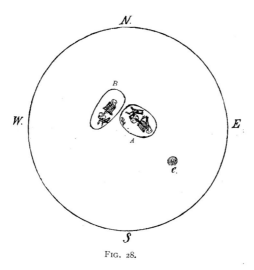

FIG. 28.

Figure 5.16: Schematic excavation plan of Towthorpe 106. (After Mortimer 1905, fig. 28)

period of time. Thirdly the deposit may represent a deliberate placing of fox bones, some curated, perhaps as a pelt or trophy. This was certainly Mortimer's interpretation given his observation that the humeri had been crossed over the skull and this is the interpretation preferred here and incorporated in the model. In this case, the deposit was made after the death of the later fox, in 2135–2085 cal BC (16% probability) or 2045–1895 (79% probability; SUERC-13934; Figure 5.15), probably in 2115–2100 cal BC (14% probability) or 2035–1945 cal BC (64% probability).

TOWTHORPE 106; [NGR: SE 87646394]

Towthorpe 106 survives as a slight mound in an area of arable. Opened in 1867, this already denuded barrow measured only 10ins (*c.*0.26m) high and Mortimer recorded that its circumference was "hardly traceable" (Mortimer 1905, 13). Having few remarkable recorded features, it was not selected for survey.

Excavation Account

On excavation an oval grave was located at the centre (Figure 5.16), this measured 5ft (*c.*1.5m) northwest to southeast, by 3ft 6ins (*c.*1.1m) and 16ins (*c.*0.4m) deep, with the crouched inhumation of a female at the base and with her head to the southeast. There were also the bones of an infant (contracted on its left side) 6ins (*c.*0.15m) behind the pelvis of the adult. Furthermore, there were also disarticulated child bones above the adult body and in the fill of the grave. A second grave lay 1ft (*c.*0.3m) to the northwest of the first. This measured 8ft (*c.*2.5m) southwest to northeast by 4ft 6ins (*c.*1.4m) and 3ft (*c.*0.9m) deep and contained a crouched female inhumation lying on her right side, with her head to the northeast. Finally, a small hearth was located on the old ground surface in the southeast quadrant. The disarticulated child and the multiple nature of the presumed primary burial suggested the possibility of a Neolithic date.

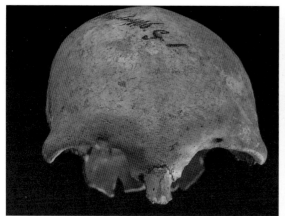

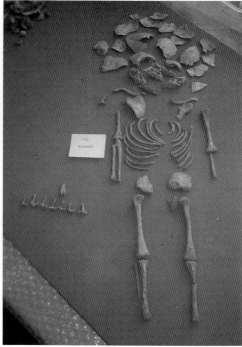

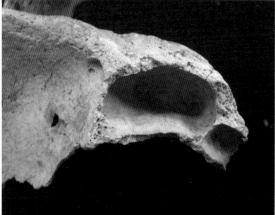

Figure 5.17 (top left): Towthorpe 106. Skull G1.

Figure 5.18 (middle left): Towthorpe 106 G2. Large frontal sinus, a common feature in many of these skulls.

Figure 5.19 (above): Towthorpe 106. One month-old infant.

Figure 5.20 (bottom left): Towthorpe 106. Fused cervical vertebrae from the month-old infant. A relatively high incidence of congenital and acquired abnormalities occur in this region of the vertebral column (cf. Scheuer & Black 2000, 197–8).

Human Osteology
By A. R. Ogden (Full report in site archive)

Towthorpe 106 has a minimum of three adults, an infant and a young child. G1 is the skull of a young adult (*c.*18-25 years) of uncertain sex. The morphology of the skull (Figure 5.17) included male supraorbital ridges, small mastoids, no suprameatal crests, and a female mandibular shape; wide sella turcica and Occipital bun. G2 is an old middle adult (*c.*36-45 years) with moderate periodontal disease on the molars. The skull and other bones of an old middle adult male with large glabellae and frontal sinuses are also present (Figure 5.18), along with a one month-old infant of which 75 per cent of the bones survive (Figures 5.19). This latter has two fused cervical vertebra (Figure 5.20) and probably suffered from Klippel-Feil syndrome (congenital shortened neck – commonly linked with cleft palate and spina bifida, either of which may have caused early death). Also present is a young child (*c.*eighteen-months) represented by fragments of skull and middle-order ribs.

Radiocarbon Dating
With Alex Bayliss

The chronological model for Towthorpe 106 is shown in Figure 5.21. This incorporates the interpretation that the disarticulated child was already in the grave and was dry bone and disturbed when the fully articulated burials were inserted. It is therefore earlier than the articulated adult and infant. We have also incorporated the assumption that this monument had a coherent period of use, however short. The radiocarbon dates (Table 5.1) are in good agreement with this reading of the sequence ($A_{overall}$ = 99.7%). The model suggests that the disarticulated child died in 2125–2085 cal BC (5% probability) or cal BC 2055–1925 (90% probability; SUERC-13936; Figure 5.21), probably in 2030–1960 cal BC (68% probability). The articulated adult female does not appear to have died at the same time as the articulated infant, as the weighted mean on the measurements from the adult is statistically inconsistent with the measurement on the infant (T'=4.7, T'(5%)=3.8, v=1; Ward & Wilson 1978). The infant was buried in 2035–1910 cal BC (95% probability; OxA-

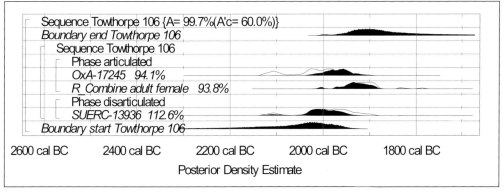

Figure 5.21: Probability distributions of dates from Towthorpe 106. The format is identical to that of Figure 5.11. The large square brackets down the left-hand side of the figure, along with the OxCal keywords, define the overall model exactly

17245; Figure 5.21), probably in 2000–1940 cal BC (68% probability). The adult female was buried in 2015-1995 cal BC (4% probability) or 1980–1880 cal BC (91% probability; adult female; Figure 5.21), probably in 1955–1895 cal BC (68% probability). Given the limited number of individuals dated, it is not possible to provide a reliable estimate for the period during which this barrow was in use although this may have been relatively short, perhaps just a few decades in the mid-twentieth century BC.

FOX COVERT ROUND BARROW (GREENWELL LXI); [NGR: TA 09846577]

Excavation Account

This round barrow measured some 50ft (*c.*15.4m) in diameter and 1ft 6ins (*c.*0.5m) high with traces of burning on the old ground surface. The following burials and features were located in the mound:

> Burial 1 – crouched inhumation of a child above the old ground surface
> Burial 2 – crouched inhumation of an adult male above the old ground surface associated with a jet button and shale/lignite ring
> Burial 3 – crouched inhumation of adult male on the old ground surface
> Burial 4 – disturbed bones of an adult male with burnt stones
> Burial 5 – crouched inhumation of an adult female in west end of an oval grave with a Beaker and antler pick
> Burial 6 – crouched inhumation of an adult female on the old ground surface with a bone pin and six flints
> Burial 7 – an adult cremation deposit in a pit with six flints
> Feature A – burnt earth deposit on the old ground surface with Neolithic bowl
> Feature B – Oval pit with a burnt fill, pottery and flints.
> Feature C – pit with earth and charcoal
> Feature D – pit with charcoal,

Surviving in the site archive are sherds from 128 Neolithic vessels and 6 flints from unspecified contexts though presumably relating to the Neolithic activity in features A–D.

Radiocarbon Dating
With Alex Bayliss

This barrow is apparently early Bronze Age in origin but covers a substantial amount of Neolithic activity associated with Carinated and Plain Bowls on or below the old ground surface (Newbigin 1937). None of the skeletal material from the burials survives in the Greenwell archive so no dates were obtained for the burial sequence and no palaeo-osteological work could be undertaken. However, three sherds preserved *in situ* had carbonised residues on the internal surfaces. There did not appear to be any obvious signs of contamination, such as the use of consolidants, on these sherds. Residues from three sherds were submitted for dating, one in duplicate. The two samples which were sent to the Scottish Universities Environment Research Centre (SUERC) failed, although results were reported for the two samples dated at Oxford. These results, however, appear to be anomalously young for the type of pottery concerned. The samples processed at

Oxford were pre-treated by an acid wash (1M HCl) at room temperature followed by fifteen minutes ultrasonication in a fresh solution of the same acid, rinsed in ultrapure water and the humic acids removed by ultrasonication in Milli-Q water. The total acid-insoluble fraction was dated. At SUERC, the samples were pre-treated using a standard acid-alkali-acid pre-treatment in an attempt to date the acid-insoluble and alkali-insoluble fraction. The samples dissolved in the alkali stage here and so it appears that they must have contained a significant component of younger humic acid contaminants. It is probably the incomplete removal of this contamination which has lead to the anomalous dates reported from Oxford. We therefore suggest that these results should not be regarded as accurate age-estimates for the pottery concerned and consequently this site remains undated by radiocarbon.

WILLIE HOWE PLANTATION; [NGR: SE 95506575]

Excavation Account

This site was excavated by Brewster in 1967 (Brewster & Finney unpublished) and is some 645m away from Mortimer 277 (see below). The dimensions of the mound prior to excavation are not given in the draft report but it is described as a "ghost mound" and the sections suggest that the mound was flat at the time of excavation. Brewster located graves and two ring-ditches, the inner measuring 21m and the outer 32m in diameter.

A robbed central grave, Grave 1, was interpreted as the primary burial. The grave measured 1.87m by 2.57m and was 1m deep. It had been robbed by an earlier undocumented excavation but some "*in situ* grave fill survived against the south and south-west side of the grave" (Brewster & Finney unpublished) and this fill contained bone representing the post cranial remains of at least three individuals. It was considered that these individuals might possibly have represented the remains of a primary multiple and disarticulated burial deposit.

Grave 2 contained a monoxylous oak coffin burial containing the contracted inhumation of an adult male associated with three flint flakes. A jet disc fragment was found in the fill. The femur of the skeleton produced a radiocarbon date of 2130–1690 cal BC (HAR-4995; Table 5.1). Grave 3 pre-dated the outer ditch and contained the crouched inhumation of an adult female associated with a long-necked Beaker and a bronze awl. Grave 4 was in the outer ditch and comprised the unaccompanied inhumation of a child. Grave 5, in the inner ditch comprised the partial remains of an adult female while Grave 6, within the area enclosed by the inner ditch and set in a natural hollow, comprised the remains of a child.

Radiocarbon Dating
(With Alex Bayliss)

Four individuals from Willie Howe have been dated (Table 5.1). The three individuals from the undisturbed deposits in Grave 1 were sampled as part of this project to test the hypothesis that they might represent a primary Neolithic multiple deposit. The individual from the oak coffin in Grave 2 had already been dated as part of Brewster's post-excavation analysis (see above). These four radiocarbon determinations are statistically

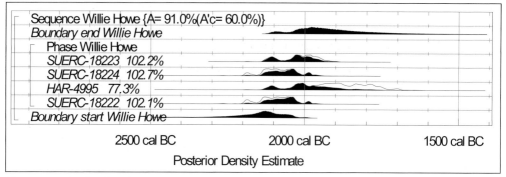

| Sequence Willie Howe {A= 91.0%(A'c= 60.0%)} |
| Boundary end Willie Howe |
| Phase Willie Howe |
| SUERC-18223 102.2% |
| SUERC-18224 102.7% |
| HAR-4995 77.3% |
| SUERC-18222 102.1% |
| Boundary start Willie Howe |

2500 cal BC   2000 cal BC   1500 cal BC

Posterior Density Estimate

Figure 5.22: Probability distributions of dates from Willie Howe. The format is identical to that of Figure 5.11. The large square brackets down the left-hand side of the figure, along with the OxCal keywords, define the overall model exactly

consistent (T'=4.5, T'(5%)=7.8, ν=3; Ward & Wilson 1978), and so have been modelled as representative of a single phase of use of the site. The other burials were not dated as part of this project given their obvious early Bronze Age affinity, but it would appear that the burial activity at this site actually took place over quite a short period of time, probably within a century of 2000 BC (Figure 5.22).

The late third millennium BC dates for the primary disarticulated deposits were unexpected. Clearly, in Yorkshire at least, multiple disarticulated deposits are not necessarily Neolithic (see below).

TOWTHORPE 72; (MORTIMER 72) [NGR: SE 87636393]

This round barrow was opened by Mortimer in 1866 measuring about 2ft (*c*.0.6m) high and 70ft (*c*.21.5m) in diameter, and near the centre were two oval pits each containing a contracted inhumation. To the northwest of the centre was an oval pit containing disarticulated and fragmentary human bone from adults and at least one child. It was considered that this deposit might be a Neolithic disarticulated deposit, however, below this mass of bone was a pile of cremated bone. One fragment of cremated bone indicated a cut made by a metal blade (identified by A. R. Ogden) so it is likely that the entire deposit dates to the Bronze Age. This site was not dated as part of the present project.

GREENLAND PLANTATION; (MORTIMER 276) [NGR: SE 91076541]

Opened by Mortimer in 1892, this mound had been used for comparatively recent dog burials. Near the centre was a grave measuring 5ft 6ins (*c*.1.7m) east to west by 5ft (*c*.1.5m) north to south and 5ft 6ins (*c*.1.7m) deep, which contained numerous disarticulated remains. Whilst these have been considered to represent Neolithic burials, they are loosely associated with Beaker fragments and, at the base of the pit was a cremation deposit with a stone battle axe. The Neolithic integrity of this deposit therefore seemed unlikely and was not dated as part of the present project.

COWLAM GRANGE; (WILLIE HOWE PLANTATION. MORTIMER 277) [SE95906635]

Opened by Mortimer in 1892, this mound was 4ft 6ins (*c*.1.4m) high by 55ft (*c*.16.9m) in diameter. The following burials were encountered:

> Burial 1 – an adult female crouched inhumation with a flint knife and jet ring;
> Burial 2 – an adult male crouched inhumation associated with a Food Vessel;
> Burial 3 – an oval grave dug into the old ground surface containing human bone fragments. Over the grave was an area of severe burning intermixed with charcoal and cremated human bone.

There is a reference to two Neolithic vessels from a hollow in the old ground surface, with animal bones (catalogue entry in Piggott 1931, 147); however, the animal bone associated with the Neolithic vessels could not be located, and the site was not dated as part of the present project.

SHARP HOWES; [NGR: TA 049777]

Despite an almost certain Neolithic presence in this barrow group, no organic material with certain Neolithic integrity could be identified in the archive, and therefore it was not dated as part of the present project. The two existing radiocarbon determinations (HAR-8518 and HAR-8519) obtained by A. Finney in 1986 provide Bronze Age dates for the construction of satellite barrows 2 and 4 (Table 5.1).

OCTON WOLD; (GREENWELL WEAVERTHORPE XLVII) [NGR: SE 99586869]

This round barrow was excavated first by Greenwell in 1867 who failed to find any burials and again by Brewster in 1966–8 (Brewster & Finney unpublished). Brewster identified a two phased mound, the later of which was associated with sherds of Beaker. Various stakeholes were sealed by the mound and two graves lay at the centre of the barrow. Grave 1 measured 2.52m by 2m at the top narrowing to 1.75 by 1m at the base and averaging 1.82m deep. A disturbed adult crouched inhumation lay at the base of the grave as well as some skull fragments.

Grave 2 measured 2.45m by 1.62m at the top narrowing to 2.3m by 1.5m at the base and was 1.5m deep. It contained at the base a contracted male inhumation constrained by chalk blocks and covered by a chalk and gravel mound which included some disarticulated human bone. The burial also included fragments of three other skulls from an adult male, adult female and a child as well as the scapula of a child. Redeposited human bone in the grave included bones from a robust adult male, adult female and new-born infant. A Beaker sherd was recovered from the fill. Two statistically consistent radiocarbon determinations (HAR-4250-1; T'=0.1, T'(5%)=3.8, ν=1) from human bone from the base of Grave 2 provide dates in the later third millennium BC (Table 5.1), in accordance with the long necked Beaker from the tertiary use of the shaft (Jordan *et al.* 1994, 127–8).

Graves 1 and 2 cut earlier graves 3 and 5. They contained the crouched inhumation of an adult female, the latter the crouched inhumation of an adolescent. Grave 4 contained two child inhumations with a fragment of Beaker from the grave fill.

The potential Neolithic origins of this mound stems from the recording of Neolithic ceramics from below the barrow. None, however, contained carbonised residues and this site was not dated as part of the present project.

RUDSTON 4; (GREENWELL LXII) [NGR: TA 09886583]

Excavations at this mound by Greenwell produced mainly burials of Beaker and Bronze Age affinity but Neolithic material was recovered from the mound. Pacitto (1972) records an old turfline below the turf mound of the barrow with Neolithic bowl (some decorated rims) pottery and artefacts in and below the old turfline as well as a hearth associated with charcoal and calcined bone. Three secondary burials were located. 1) a double inhumation, crouched with lower right leg bones missing: 2) on the northeast edge of a central pit was the crouched unaccompanied adult male inhumation: 3) a crouched unaccompanied male inhumation.

None of the material in the Greenwell Collection was suitable for dating. The Pacitto material is in the Grantham Collection and access to this was not made available.

DISCUSSION

Despite the importance of the Great Wold Valley to Neolithic and Bronze Age studies in Britain, little recent attention has been devoted to the iconic monuments of the area, with much of the discussion of the English and Welsh (and to an extent Scottish) Neolithic deriving largely from Wessex models (Harding 1997, 280; Barclay 2000). Duggleby Howe, for example, containing a well-documented burial sequence and nine different types of middle or late Neolithic prestige artefact had until recently (Loveday *et al.* 2007) not a single radiocarbon date to help chronologically bracket this sequence. Nor has, at least to the present writer's knowledge, the site ever been surveyed either topographically or geophysically. This would also be true of the other well-known and presumed Neolithic round mounds such as Wold Newton and Willy Howe: the former presumed to be Neolithic from its multiple disarticulated primary burial deposit and the association of a leaf-shaped flint point with a secondary burial, and the latter purely by its size and therefore similarity to Duggleby Howe.

The general aims of this project then, were to provide condition statements for some of the better known monuments, whether surviving as earthworks or not, and to provide an outline chronology for some of the presumed Neolithic burial monuments in the study area by utilising existing archives. The project has been remarkably successful, despite the limitations of the antiquarian archives. It has thrown up some unexpected results and the value of studying existing archives has been demonstrated. At the same time some obvious, and not so obvious, potential pitfalls in using such archives have been highlighted.

The surveys have provided a point-in-time record of the condition of the monuments and that at Duggleby Howe will be described elsewhere (Gibson in prep.). At Wold Newton, geophysical survey has revealed a large number of anomalies (Figures 5.5 & 5.6) and principally the large ditch around the mound. This suggests that the mound is slightly oval rather than strictly circular and there may be a causeway to the north-northeast. Some of the disturbances may be due to the activities of burrowing animals yet others are clearly archaeological. Below the mound and within the area enclosed by the ditch are two large anomalies suggesting dug features. The northern of the two is curved while the southern is more linear. While the exact nature of these features is uncertain, they call to mind the curved and straight façades at Callis Wold 275 (Coombs 1976; Kinnes 1979) at either end of a pavement containing multiple inhumations. There is a difference in scale here, however with the area occupied by the features at Wold Newton being in the region of 20m while at Callis Wold the distance between the palisades is only some 13m. It is tempting to think that these internal features at Wold Newton may represent the gullies south and west of centre identified by Mortimer, but the geophysical anomalies would appear to be too large for this interpretation to be valid. The complexity of the geophysical data, however, may suggest that the mound has had a complex history and is not a single-event monument.

Wold Newton has been described as having a large encircling ditch visible on aerial photographs (Loughlin & Miller 1979: Manby 1988) the implication being that it is comparable to the Duggleby enclosure (Harding 1997, 283). No trace of this ditch has been located during the present project. The "surrounding segmented ditch indicated by a grass mark" (Manby *et al.* 2003, 73) though unclear, would appear to refer to the ditch at the base of the mound. No aerial photographs supporting Loughlin and Miller's original claim have been located during the present project and no such ditch was recorded in Stoertz's comprehensive search of aerial photographs as part of the National Mapping Programme (Stoertz 1997). Until evidence can be produced to the contrary, the reality of this large outer ditch must remain very dubious, its existence only being perpetuated by secondary referencing.

A similar large ditch was located round the base of the mound at Willy Howe (Figures 5.2–5.4), which is of similar size to Wold Newton; unfortunately the overgrown nature of the mound prevented any exploration of the barrow itself.

The radiocarbon dating of Towthorpe 18 typifies some of the difficulties in working with antiquarian archives. Mortimer clearly reports that there was a primary multiple deposit with artefacts now known to be early Neolithic in date, and that there was a second phase of activity that has the hallmarks of early Bronze Age single contracted burials coming from within (rather than below) the mound. We expected that these skeletons would be numbered or labelled differently, and indeed it was the intention of this project only to date the Neolithic multiple deposit. It was a surprise, therefore, that burials 3 and 3A and burials 6 and 6A produced such widely differing dates. Burials 3A, 6A, 5 and the cache of fox bones have proved to be the early Bronze Age burials from the mound, whilst burials 3, 4 and 6 would appear to date the primary deposit.

As described above, the measurements from burials 3, 4 and 6 do not form a statistically consistent group and so it is unlikely that all these individuals died at the same time. It seems that, if this was a single deposit, then burial 3, being the most recent, dates its deposition, but that burials 4 and 6 may have been already skeletal and received secondary burial here (Figure 5.15; Table 5.1). It is interesting to note the weathering observed on the surviving fragments of Burials 4 and 6 (see above). According to the criteria of Buikstra and Ubelaker (1994) these burials exhibit severe weathering which indicates exposure for several years and probably also considerable movement. The exact length of time before final interment is, however, impossible to assess as it is heavily dependent on the local micro-environment for each bone. It is almost certain, however, that these bones were on or near the surface for years compared with the other skeletal material from this site (A. R. Ogden per. Comm.). The differences between the dates of burials 4 and 6 and that of burial 3 are shown in Figure 5.23. These distributions are strongly multi-modal, and

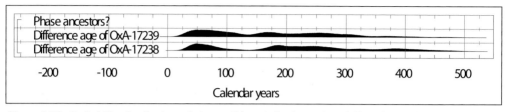

Figure 5.23: Probability distributions of the possible periods of curation of Burials 4 and 6 from Towthorpe 18, if they were deposited at the same time as Burial 3, derived from the model defined in Figure 5.15

are compatible either with the interpretation of a relatively restricted period of curation for the remains of known, recognised individuals such as is possible for disarticulated material from Hazleton North long cairn, Gloucestershire (Meadows *et al.* 2007, figs 17–18), or with the interpretation of a longer period of curation such as that discussed for some readings of the sequence at Fussell's Lodge long barrow, Wiltshire (Wysocki *et al.* 2007). Alternatively, of course, it is possible that these burials simply represent a deposit accumulating over a period of time, perhaps with distinct episodes of deposition as at Duggleby Howe (Gibson in prep). This would assume an exposure area open for some time, and presumably protected in some way from scavenging carnivores. Given the limitations of the record and archive of this excavation, it is not possible to decide between these scenarios on the evidence currently available.

Wold Newton posed none of these unexpected problems of labelling. Although the bones were not specifically labelled (those from the multiple deposit were only labelled "bodies 2 – 6") nevertheless it was clear from which deposit they derived. In the geophysical survey section above, it was concluded that this site was complex and had probably had several phases of activity. From the radiocarbon dates we can see two distinct episodes of Neolithic activity. The presumed primary, multiple and clearly at least partially disarticulated, deposit probably dates from the thirty-eighth century BC (Figure 5.11). Burial 7, associated with the leaf-shaped point and within the mound material, dates to 3645–3520 cal BC (95% probability; GrA-33109; Figure 5.11).

These dates from Wold Newton are amongst the earliest dates for Neolithic activity on the Yorkshire Wolds. The two measurements from Willerby Wold long barrow both have large margins of error and can only provide *Termini Post Quos* in the early fourth millennium BC for the construction of the monument, as the dated samples consisted of oak charcoal and may therefore suffer from the "old wood" effect (Table 5.1). A similar date is available for the Kilham Long Barrow but again this has a large margin of error, and is from unidentified charcoal from the bedding trench (Table 5.1). Old Wood has also had an effect on the four dates from the East Heslerton long barrow, the youngest date from which (HAR-7032) may be the closest in date to the actual construction and calibrates to 3640–3120 cal BC (Table 5.1). The dates from the Kemp Howe long barrow may be more reliable coming from both antler and an oak post from the façade trench. Both dates are consistent with a date in the first half of fourth millennium BC (Table 5.1).

A chronological model for the currency of early Neolithic burial in the Yorkshire Wolds is shown in Figure 5.24. All the dates on oak or unidentified charcoal have been incorporated in the model as *Termini Post Quos*, and the limited stratigraphic information available for Wold Newton has also been utilised. Otherwise, we have simply assumed

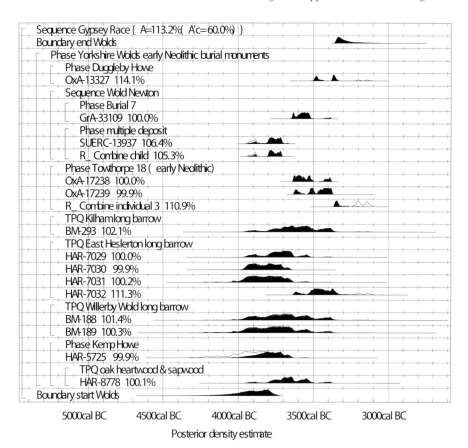

Figure 5.24: Probability distributions of dates from early Neolithic round and long barrows in the Yorkshire Wolds. The format is identical to that of Figure 5.11. The large square brackets down the left-hand side of the figure, along with the OxCal keywords, define the overall model exactly

that this practice of burial forms a coherent, and broadly constant, phase of activity and implemented a uniform distribution on the model to counteract the inevitable statistical scatter on the radiocarbon dates (Buck *et al.* 1992; Bayliss *et al.* 2007a). This model suggests that this type of burial in this area began in 4190–3725 cal BC (95% probability; start Wolds; Figure 5.24), probably in 3985–3775 cal BC (68% probability). The tradition ended in 3360–3115 cal BC (95% probability; end Wolds; Figure 5.24), probably in 3355–3265 cal BC (68% probability). These estimates are broadly in line with the more refined chronologies for the start of Neolithic practices which are emerging from recent work in southern Britain (Whittle *et al.* 2007; Bayliss *et al.* 2008), although much more work is required in this area before chronologies of a similar resolution will become available in Yorkshire. Here, the round barrows are broadly contemporary with the long barrows, although more dates on short-life material are needed particularly from the latter monuments. The paucity of burials between the later fourth millennium BC and the appearance of Beaker graves is not restricted to Yorkshire but is a national phenomenon.

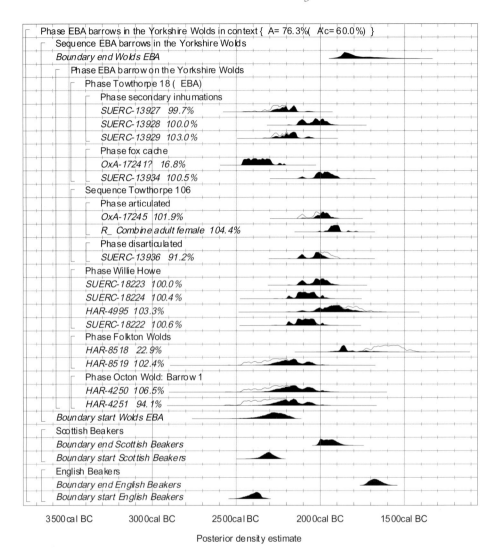

Figure 5.25: Probability distributions of dates from early Bronze Age barrows in the Yorkshire Wolds. The format is identical to that of Figure 5.11. The large square brackets down the left-hand side of the figure, along with the OxCal keywords, define the overall model exactly

A chronological model for the currency of early Bronze Age barrows in the Yorkshire Wolds is shown in Figure 5.25. The limited stratigraphic information available for Towthorpe 106 has been utilised in this model. Otherwise, we have simply assumed that this practice of burial forms a coherent, and broadly constant, phase of activity and implemented a uniform distribution on the model to counteract the inevitable statistical scatter on the radiocarbon dates (Buck *et al.* 1992; Bayliss *et al.* 2007a). This model suggests this type of burial in this area began in 2420–2150 cal BC (95% probability; start Wolds early Bronze Age; Figure 5.25), probably in 2330–2195 cal BC (68% probability). This tradition ended in

1925–1575 cal BC (95% probability; end Wolds EBA; Figure 5.25), probably in 1885–1750 cal BC (65% probability) or 1735–1710 cal BC (3% probability).

The dating of the multiple deposits from Towthorpe 106 and Brewster's Willie Howe proved to be early Bronze Age in date. In retrospect this was perhaps to be expected at Towthorpe 106 where sequential contracted inhumations could be envisaged. However the results were less expected at Willie Howe where the multiple disarticulated deposit came from a pit grave. This clearly supports Peterson's (1974) pertinent but often over-looked observations that multiple burials and disarticulated burials are far from exclusively Neolithic but that they extend well into the Beaker period and beyond. Indeed the present writer went so far as to suggest that given the complexity of and variation within Beaker burials in Britain, the idea that single contracted inhumations were the "Beaker norm" could no longer be upheld. It was also suggested that since the rite had already been in Britain since the early Neolithic, it was probably not a Beaker introduction (Gibson 2007). In the light of recent and current research, however, this needs refinement. A distinct "Beaker burial rite" associated with the ceramics and distinctive artefact package, often in pits, can be seen with early Beakers in Needham's primary Beaker period (Needham 2005) but "by the 23rd century…Beaker culture in Britain had insidiously inserted itself into broader culture" (Needham 2005, 207) and from this time, Needham's Fission Horizon, Beaker burials can be seen to be more varied and reflective of existing, indigenous (albeit old) burial traditions. Our dating for the appearance of this tradition in Yorkshire is consistent with the dating for the appearance of Beaker pottery in England and Scotland, as modelled by Bayliss *et al.* (2007b) using data from Needham (2005) and Sheridan (forthcoming).

ACKNOWLEDGEMENTS

In addition to the specialists whose names head the relevant sections, I am most grateful to the following individuals for their helpfulness during and support for this project: Martin Foreman and Paula Gentil of the Hull and East Riding Museum for their help and enthusiasm throughout. Gill Varndell facilitated access to the Greenwell Collection at the British Museum and the Trustees of the British Museum permitted the sampling of potsherds from Fox Covert. Paula Ware of MAP Archaeological Consultancy allowed access to the Brewster archive held in Malton, and Katy Whittaker assisted with the Brewster archive at the NMR, Swindon. Wendy Hart and Henriette Johansen took the 14C samples both in Hull and in Bradford. John McIlwaine, Rob Friell, Alex Harrison and Lisa McCaig undertook the topographic surveys. Figure 5.1 was drawn by Dan Bashford. Details of methods used in assessing osteology and radiocarbon dating lie in the site archive. Jim Leary oversaw the project for English Heritage and was supportive and sympathetic throughout.

I have also benefited greatly from discussions with Richard Bradley, Chris Gaffney, Ian Kinnes, Roy Loveday, Terry Manby, Janet Montgomery, Wolfgang Neubauer, and Alison Sheridan. To them all, I offer sincere thanks and offer the customary get-out clause, that any errors in this paper are not their responsibility.

Finally, my thanks to English Heritage for funding the project and to the various landowners and tenants for permitting the surveys and their interest in the archaeology of the Great Wold Valley.

Table 5.1. Radiocarbon Results from Presumed Neolithic Round Barrows from the Upper Gypsey Race Valley and Environs.

Lab ID	Sample ID	Material and context	13C (‰)	15N (‰)	C/N ratio	Radiocarbon Age (BP)	Calibrated Date (95% confidence)	Posterior density estimate (95% probability)
Duggleby Howe								
OxA-13327	Burial G	antler macehead associated with Burial G	-22.1			4597 ±35	3500–3130 cal BC	-
Towthorpe 18								
SUERC-13927	18.1 (3A)	human bone, left asc. ramus mandible; from individual 3A from primary burial deposit	-22.0	12.2	3.4	3800 ±35	23502130 cal BC	2340 – 2320 cal BC (1%) or 2310 – 3130 cal BC (92%) or 2085 – 2060 cal BC (2%)
OxA-17238	18.2 (6)	human bone, left asc. ramus mandible; from individual 6 from primary burial deposit	-20.2	10.6	3.3	4746 ±32	36403370 cal BC	3635- 3498 cal BC (52%) or 3435-3375 cal BC (43%)
SUERC-13928	18.3 (6A)	human bone, left coronoid process mandible; from individual 6A from primary burial deposit	-21.7	11.9	3.5	3655 ±35	21401920 cal BC	2140 – 1940 cal BC
SUERC-13929	18.4 (5)	human bone, right asc. ramus mandible; from individual 5 from primary burial deposit	-21.3	8.7	3.4	3775 ±35	23002040 cal BC	2295 – 2125 cal BC (86%) or 2090 – 2040 cal BC (9%)
OxA-17239	18.5 (4)	human bone, right asc. ramus mandible; from individual 4 from primary burial deposit	-20.1	10.0	3.3	4697 ±34	36303360 cal BC	3630 – 3585 cal BC (7%) or 3535 – 3480 cal BC (18%) or 3475 – 3365 cal BC (70%)
SUERC-13930	18.6 (3)	human bone, left asc. ramus mandible; from individual 3 from primary burial deposit	-21.6	10.6	3.5	4535 ±35	-	3365 – 3305 cal BC (54%) or 3300 – 3280 cal BC (2%) or 3275 – 3260 cal BC (2%) or
OxA-17240	18.7 (3.1)		-20.5	10.9	3.3	4541 ±31	-	3240 – 3115cal BC (37%)
mean of OxA-17240 and SUERC-13930: T'=0.0, T'(5%)=3.8, =1 (Ward and Wilson 1978)								
OxA-17241	18.8 (A)	animal bone, fox B, right humerus; from deposit in mound	-20.3	8.8	3.3	3877 ±30	24702200 cal BC	2470 – 2280 cal BC (93%) or 2250 – 2230 cal BC (2%)
SUERC-13934	18.9 (B)	animal bone, fox A, right humerus; from deposit in mound	-20.9			3615 ±35	21301880 cal BC	2131 – 2085 cal BC (16%) or 2045 – 1895 cal BC (79%)
Fox Covert								
OxA-17141	1	carbonised residue	-29.9			1627 ±29	cal AD 350540	-
OxA-17142	2 (A)	carbonised residue	-28.4			4466 ±37	33503010 cal BC	-
Wold Newton								
SUERC-13937	Burial 2	human bone, left femur; from primary multiple inhumation	-21.3	8.5	3.3	5000 ±35	39403690 cal BC	3920 – 3870 cal BC (7%) or 3820 – 3690 cal BC (87%) or 3675 – 3660 cal BC (1%)
OxA-17246	child	human bone, left angle of mandible; from primary multiple inhumation	-19.9	7.8	3.3	4968 ±33	-	3910 – 3875 cal BC (5%) or 3805 – 3705 cal BC (90%)
OxA-16752	child		-20.0	8.2	3.2	5038 ±33	-	
mean of OxA-17246 and OxA-16752 (child burial): T'=2.2, T'(5%)=3.8, =1 (Ward and Wilson 1978)						5003 ±23	3935 – 3705 cal BC	
GrA-33109	Burial 7	human bone, base of left mandible; from partially contracted inhumation with leaf-shaped arrowhead higher in the mound	-20.9	10.1		4780 ±35	36503380 cal BC	3645 – 3520 cal BC

Lab code	Sample	Material	δ13C			BP	cal date	cal date
Towthorpe 106								
OxA-17244	106.1	human bone, right tibia; from adult female	-20.4	10.1	3.3	3586 ±30	-	2015 – 1995 cal BC (4%) or 1980 – 1885 cal BC (91%)
SUERC-13935	106.2	in central grave	-20.5	9.8	3.5	3535 ±35	19801820 cal BC	
mean of OxA-17244 and SUERC-13935: T'=1.2, T'(5%)=3.8, =1 (Ward and Wilson 1978)						3565 ±23		
SUERC-13936	106.3	human bone, distal end of right femur; from disarticulated child skeleton in central grave	-21.2	12.0	3.5	3625 ±35	21301890 cal BC	2125 – 2085 cal BC (5%) or 2055 – 1925 cal BC (90%)
OxA-17245	106.4	human bone, right femur fragment; from contracted infant in central grave	-19.0	9.9	3.3	3645 ±29	21401930 cal BC	2035 – 1910 cal BC
Willie Howe								
HAR-4995	WILLHOWE	human bone (coffin burial)	-23.0			3550 ± 70	2130 – 1690 cal BC	2140 – 1815 cal BC
SUERC-18222	Willie Howe 1	human bone, adult clavicle, from the primary multiple disarticulated burial	-22.5	9.9	2.8	3700 ± 35	2200 – 1970 cal BC	2195 – 2175 cal BC (2%) or 2150 – 1975 cal BC (93%)
SUERC-18223	Willie Howe 2	human bone, adult clavicle, from the primary multiple disarticulated burial	-21.0	9.4	2.8	3645 ± 35	2140 – 1910 cal BC	2135 – 1940 cal BC
SUERC-18224	Willie Howe 3	human bone, adult clavicle, from the primary multiple disarticulated burial	-20.9	10.3	2.9	3690 ± 35	2200 – 1960 cal BC	2145 – 1960 cal BC
Folkton Wolds: Sharpe Howes 2								
HAR-8518	SHB2WQ	antler, Cervus elaphus	-24.6			3320 ± 70	1760 – 1430 cal BC	-
HAR-8519	SHB4G1	human bone, right tibia and femur	-22.5			3800 ± 70	2470 – 2020 cal BC	-
Octon Wold: Barrow 1								
HAR-4250	OWSG2A	human bone (burial 2 – secondary)	-21.5			3780 ± 80	2470 – 1970 cal BC	-
HAR-4251	OWSG2B	human bone (burial 2 – secondary)	-21.8			3820 ± 80	2480 – 2020 cal BC	-
East Heslerton								
HAR-7029	EHLB1	wood charcoal	-24.5			4920 ± 90	3950 – 3520 cal BC	-
HAR-7030	EHLB2	charcoal, Quercus spp., heartwood	-25.9			5020 ± 70	3970 – 3650 cal BC	-
HAR-7031	EHLB3	charcoal	-26.0			5020 ± 110	4050 – 3630 cal BC	-
HAR-7032	EHLB4	charcoal	-25.0			4640 ± 70	3640 – 3120 cal BC	-
Kemp Howe								
HAR-5725	KHT81248	antler	-22.0			5100 ± 120	4240 – 3640 cal BC	-
HAR-6205	KHG33618	human bone, right tibia and femur	-22.9			1380 ± 80	cal AD 540 – 780	-
HAR-8775	KHT9G5B5	human bone, right tibia and femur	-27.0			1290 ± 90	cal AD 590 – 970	-
HAR-8776	KHT6GIBI	human bone, right tibia and femur	-22.0			1310 ± 100	cal AD 550 – 970	-
HAR-8778	KHLBFBT3	Charcoal (mature oak)	-27.1			4870 ± 90	3920 – 3380 cal BC	-
HAR-8779	KHASGH62	Charcoal (unidentified)	-24.9			4330 ± 100	3340 – 2670 cal BC	-
HAR-8780	KHRBDE31	antler, Cervus elaphus	-22.6			3730 ± 70	2350 – 1930 cal BC	-
Kilham Long Barrow								
BM-293		Charcoal (unidentified)				4830±125	3950-3350 cal BC	
Willerby Wold Long Barrow								
BM-188		Base of crematorium trench (Quercus)				4900 ± 150	3990-3360 cal BC	
BM-189		Centre of façade trench (Quercus)				4960 ± 150	4050-3370 cal BC	

BIBLIOGRAPHY

Barclay, G. J. (2000) Between Orkney and Wessex: The search for the regional Neolithics of Britain. In A. Ritchie (ed.) *Neolithic Orkney in its European Context*, 275–285. Cambridge, McDonald Institute.

Bayliss, A., Bronk Ramsey, C., van der Plicht, J. and Whittle, A. (2007a) Bradshaw and Bayes: towards a timetable for the Neolithic. *Cambridge Archaeological Journal* 17(1) Supplement, 1–28.

Bayliss, A., McAvoy, F. and Whittle, A. (2007b) The world recreated: redating Silbury Hill in its monumental landscape. *Antiquity* 81, 26–53.

Bayliss, A., Whittle, A. and Healy, F. (2008) Timing, tempo and temporalities in the Early Neolithic of southern Britain. In H. Fokkens, B. J. Coles, A. L. van Gijn, J. P. Kleijne, H. H. Ponjee and C.G. Slappendel (eds.) *Between foraging and farming: an extended broad spectrum of papers presented to Leendert Louwe Kooijmans*, 26–42. Analecta Praehistorica Leidensia 40.

Brewster, T. C. M. and Finney, A. E. (Unpublished) Barrow Excavations in the East Riding of Yorkshire. Unpublished draft report held by Malton Archaeological Practice.

Buikstra, I. E. and Ubelaker, D. H. (1994) *Standards for Data Collection from Human Skeletal Remains*. Fayetteville, Arkansas Archaeological Survey (Research Series 44).

Chiquet, P. (2004) De l'usage de la martre au Néolithique moyen sur le site littoral de Concise-sous-Colachoz (Vaud, Suisse). In J.-P. Brugal and Desse, J. (eds.) *Petits Animaux et Sociétés Humaines. Du Complément Alimentaire aux Ressources Utilitaires*. Antibes, APDCA (XXIVe rencontres internationales d'archéologie et d'histoire d'Antibes).

Coombs, D. (1976) Callis Wold Round Barrow, Humberside. *Antiquity* 50, 130–131.

Corbet, G. B. and Southern, H. N. (1977) *The Handbook of British Mammals*. Oxford, Blackwell Publications.

Fairnell, E. and Barrett, J. (in press) Fur-bearing species and Scottish islands. *Journal of Archaeological Science*.

Gibson, A. M. (2007) A Beaker Veneer? Some evidence from the burial record. In M. Larsson and M. Parker Pearson (eds.), *From Stonehenge to the Baltic. Living with cultural diversity in the third millennium BC*, 47–64. Oxford, Archaeopress (BAR International Series 1692).

Gibson, A. M. (in prep) Recent research at Duggleby Howe.

Greenwell, W. (1877) *British Barrows. A record of the examination of sepulchral mounds in various parts of England*. Oxford, Clarendon Press.

Greenwell, W. (1890) Recent researches in barrows in Yorkshire, Wiltshire, Berkshire *etc. Archaeologia* 52, 1–72.

Grinsell, L. (1936) *The ancient burial mounds of England*. London, Methuen & Co.

Harding, J. (1997) Interpreting the Neolithic: the monuments of North Yorkshire. *Oxford Journal of Archaeology* 16(3), 279–95.

Jordan, D., Haddon-Reece, D. and Bayliss, A. (1994) *Radiocarbon dates from samples funded by English Heritage and dated before 1981*. London, English Heritage.

Kinnes, I. A. (1979) *Round barrows and ring-ditches in the British Neolithic*. London, British Museum (Occasional Paper 7).

Kinnes, I. A., Schadla-Hall T.; Chadwick P. and Dean, P. (1983) Duggleby Howe reconsidered. *Archaeological Journal* 140, 83–108.

Loughlin, N. and Miller, K. (1979) A survey of archaeological sites in Humberside. Hull, Humberside Archaeological Partnership.

Loveday, R. (2002) Duggleby Howe revisited. *Oxford Journal of Archaeology* 21(2), 135–46.

Loveday, R., Gibson, A. M., Marshall, P., Bayliss, A., Bronk Ramsay, C. and van der Plicht, H. (2007) The Antler Macehead Dating Project. *Proceedings of the Prehistoric Society* 73, 381–92.

Manby, T. G. (1988) The Neolithic period in eastern Yorkshire. In T. G. Manby (ed.) *Archaeology in eastern Yorkshire: essays in honour of T. C. M. Brewster FSA*, 35–88. Sheffield, Department of Archaeology and Prehistory.

Manby, T. G., King, A. and Vyner, B. E. (2003) The Neolithic and Bronze Ages: A time of early agriculture. In T. G. Manby, S. Moorhouse and P. Ottaway (eds.), *The archaeology of Yorkshire: an assessment at the end of the 21st century*, 35–116. Leeds, Yorkshire Archaeological Society (Occasional Paper 3).

Meadows, J., Barclay, A. and Bayliss, A. (2007) A short passage of time: the dating of the Hazleton long cairn revisited, 65–84. *Cambridge Archaeological Journal* 17(1) Supplement.

Mortimer, J. R. (1905) *Forty years' researches in British and Saxon burial mounds of East Yorkshire*. London, Hull and York, A. Brown & Sons.

Needham, S. P. (2005) Transforming Beaker culture in North-West Europe; processes of fusion and fission. *Proceedings of the Prehistoric Society* 71, 171–218.

Newbigin, N. (1937) The Neolithic pottery of Yorkshire. *Proceedings of the Prehistoric Society* 3(2), 189–216.

Pacitto, A. L. (1972) Rudston Barrow LXII: the 1968 excavations. *Yorkshire Archaeological Journal* 44, 1–22.

Peterson, F. (1974) Traditions of multiple burial in Neolithic and Bronze Age Britain. *Archaeological Journal* 129, 22–55.

Piggott, S. (1931) The Neolithic pottery of the British Isles. *Archaeological Journal* 88, 67–158.

Rahtz, P., Hayfield, C. and Bateman, J. (1986) *Two Roman villas at Wharram le Street*. York, York University (Archaeological Publications 2).

Scheuer, J. L. and Black, S. (2000) *Developmental juvenile osteology*. San Diego, Academic Press.

Schwartz, J. H. (1995) *Skeleton Keys. An introduction to human skeletal morphology, development and analysis*. Oxford, Oxford University Press.

Sharples, N. (1984) Excavations at Pierowall Quarry, Orkney. *Proceedings of the Society of Antiquaries of Scotland*, 114, 75–126.

Sheridan, J. A. (forthcoming) Scottish Beaker chronology: an assessment of the currently-available radiocarbon dating evidence. In J. Turek and M. Krutova (eds.), *Beaker days in Bohemia and Moravia*. Prague, Archaeologica.

Stoertz, C. (1997) *Ancient landscapes of the Yorkshire Wolds*. Swindon, RCHME.

Thurnham, J. (1871) On ancient British barrows, especially those of Wiltshire and the adjoining counties (Part II. Round barrows). *Archaeologia* 43, 283–552.

Ward, G. K. and Wilson, S. R. (1978) Procedures for comparing and combining radiocarbon age determinations: a critique. *Archaeometry* 20(1), 19–31.

Whittle, A., Barclay, A., Bayliss, A., McFadyen, L., Schulting, R. and Wysocki, M. (2007) Building for the dead: events, processes and changing worldviews from the thirty-eighth to the thirty-fourth centuries cal BC in southern Britain. *Cambridge Archaeological Journal* 17(1) Supplement, 123–47.

Wysocki, M., Bayliss, A. and Whittle, A. (2007) Serious mortality: the date of the Fussell's Lodge long barrow. *Cambridge Archaeological Journal* 17(1) Supplement, 65–84.

Chapter 6

"One of the Most Interesting Barrows Ever Examined" – Liffs Low Revisited

Roy Loveday and Alistair Barclay

On 14 July 1843 Thomas Bateman (Figure 6.1) opened a barrow on a ridge known as the Liffs south of the village of Biggin in the Derbyshire Peak District. He was not presumably optimistic since he recorded: "… the mound was sadly mutilated, at least one-third of it having been removed." Working from the best preserved section, he – or rather his workmen – dug down finding various human and animal bones and two small pieces of "very thick cinerary urn" before they reached the heart of the mound. There they encountered an open topped octagonal cist of "thin flat limestones". Within lay a flexed male skeleton, head to the south, with an antler macehead behind its bent knees and a remarkable array of items placed together behind its head and shoulders (Figure 6.2). "Upon the summit of the little heap, formed by the accumulation of relics, lay a small drinking or incense cup of novel and unprecedented shape, which was unfortunately broken and crushed but has been since restored" (1848). The items forming this "little heap" are striking. In addition to the "small drinking cup" they comprised:

- Two boar's tusks
- Two long, kite shaped arrowheads
- Two long, partially polished flint axes
- Two lozenge shaped "spearheads"
- Two edge polished flint knives (one serrated on the back)
- "Numerous other pieces of flint of indescribable form"
- Three pieces of red ochre

Even without the antler macehead placed behind the knees (Figure 6.2), this represents the largest array of grave goods to certainly accompany a single Neolithic burial in Britain (Table 6.1) (Figures 6.3–6.4, selected grave goods); the sixteen very similar items found on the crest of a round cairn at Ayton East Field., North Yorkshire seem not to have accompanied a burial (Manby 1974; Kinnes 1979), while those from Duggleby Howe, East Yorkshire were divided between three burials (C, D, & G: Mortimer 1905, 23–42). The Liffs Low concentration is made all the more remarkable by its isolation: Duggleby Howe is one of thirteen Neolithic round barrows covering individual or paired burials with grave goods in eastern Yorkshire; Liffs Low finds only two convincing companions in the Peak District.

Previously, explanation for the remarkable array of grave goods at Liffs Low was sought in its suggested and widely accepted very late Neolithic date. John Barnatt, faced with evidence from an unauthorized excavation in the 1930s of a disturbed inhumation from an early

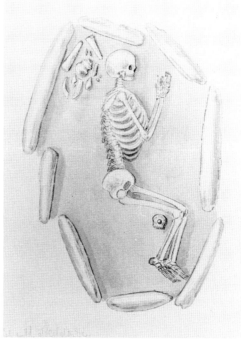

Figure 6.1 (left): Portrait of Thomas Bateman (1821–1861) by unknown artist. (Copyright National Portrait Gallery, London RN48150); Figure 6.2 (right): Bateman's plan of the Liffs Low burial cist. (Bateman archive copyright Sheffield City Museum).

phase of the barrow, possibly, but not certainly, associated with a Beaker, has suggested that the corded decoration on the small cup relates to AOC Beakers (1996a, 113). If this were so Bateman's burial would sit comfortably, if still somewhat extravagantly, in a milieu of accompanied burial. Such a horizon has now, however, been called into question by a range of dates returned by antler maceheads that place them almost exclusively between 3600 and 2900 BC (Loveday *et al.* 2007). Unfortunately, the date returned by the Liffs Low macehead had to be withdrawn and could not subsequently be re-run, but its range lay within that of the other maceheads re-dated for the same reason. It seems virtually certain, therefore, that the artefact belongs within the same horizon, well in advance of Beakers (2450–1750 BC), and even southern Grooved Ware (2900–2200 BC). It remains possible that it was a curated item, but the other artefacts in the grave heap point clearly to a middle Neolithic horizon.

Throughout this paper we use the term middle Neolithic to cover the period from 3500–2800 BC, 600–700 years that followed on from the abandonment of causewayed enclosures and preceded the uptake of Grooved Ware; an episode when cursus monuments became the dominant monument form (Barclay & Bayliss 1999; Loveday 2006) and Peterborough ware the ceramic of choice (Barclay 2002, 90; Gibson & Kinnes 1997; Barclay 2007, 343–4 and tables 15.1, 3 and 4). Selective single burial, perhaps reserved for special and/or significant individuals marks the beginning of this period and was replaced by cremation burials at its close. The chronology for the single barrow burial rite and how it developed during

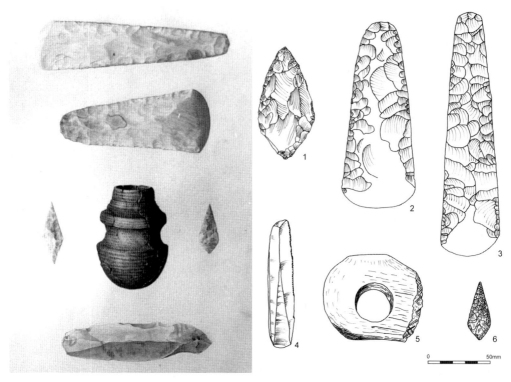

Figure 6.3 (left): Bateman's drawing of the grave goods. (Bateman archive copyright Sheffield City Museum);
Figure 6.4 (right): Grave finds. (After Kinnes 1979)

the later fourth millennium BC is an area for further research and one in which new work at Duggleby Howe is likely to make a significant contribution (Alex Gibson, this volume Chapter 5; and in prep.). Where the Liffs Low burial precisely sits within this sequence is uncertain, although our re-analysis of some of the finds suggests that it is unlikely to be amongst the earliest burials of this type and may well belong to somewhere in the middle (3300–3000 BC) (see appendices).

THE BURIAL AND BARROW IN CONTEXT

Local context

Although the Peak District limestone plateau is noted for its barrows, there are relatively few in the immediate environs of Liffs Low (Figure 6.5). Far greater densities are evident in areas some 4–6km distant. As Barnatt's invaluable maps (1996b, 1.5, 1.18) make clear, this cannot be explained in terms of differential destruction: very high densities to the southwest occur in an area where only small islands were unaffected by cultivation, whereas near Liffs Low the pre-enclosure fields of Biggin were of limited size (*c.*1km square in a basin some 4km square) and left the adjacent upper plateau wholly untouched. On this, only in the vicinity of Arbor Low (6km away), does barrow density increase significantly. Within the dispersed distribution virtually every barrow is hilltop sited for maximum visibility. Liffs Low is different. It lies near the base of a saddle on a ridge and, despite being skyline-sited across some 2km of the Biggin basin to the north, would have been visible for only about 200m on the opposing side and obscured totally from west and east by adjoining hills. Its siting imperative appears to have been quite different to that of the later hill top barrows. It was clearly intended to be seen primarily from the Biggin basin – the stone fan recorded by Barnatt covering just the northern surface of the final phase barrow would have aided that visibility (1996a).

The purpose of such siting remains obscure. The medieval fields of Biggin, limited though they were, may have obscured a short cursus-type monument. Certainly today through their provision of good pasturage, they effectively mask potential evidence of settlement akin to that recovered beneath Liffs Low itself and, following ploughing, on the higher land of the upper plateau near Aleck Low just 2km away (Barnatt 1996a, 121; Hart 1981, 42–6). The fact that the medieval village of Biggin appears to have been a late secondary settlement from Hartington (its earliest record is as Neubigging in 1244), and that it shared the basin with more than one monastic grange (Featherstone 1998), suggests that this was not ideal land for permanent occupation; absence of a ready source of water was an obvious obstacle. These arguments, however, apply with even greater force to the Neolithic settlement locales recorded near Aleck Low. It is worth recalling, therefore, that water was available from adjacent dales to which transhumant pastoralists might daily drive their animals or to the north where Dove Dale widened sufficiently for permanent settlement (Barnatt 1996b, 63–9). Liffs Low could then record an early stage of landscape niche acquisition.

It remains possible, due to the poor locational details furnished by Bateman, that the barrow under discussion normally identified as Liffs Low, was not in fact the one dug by him. A very badly robbed mound on the top of the adjacent hill recorded by Barnatt could as well fit Bateman's descriptions of Liffs Low's situation "... on the southwest extremity of Biggin Township" and "… upon a ridge of high land, near the village of Biggin, which goes by the name of the 'Liffs'" (Barnatt 1996a, 96–8). The name Liffs appears on the 1884 Ordnance Survey map on the slope between the two barrows and the heavily robbed nature of the upper site might seem to better accord with Bateman's statement that a third of the mound he excavated had been removed; more perhaps subsequently for adjacent wall building. Barnatt was at pains to explain the lack of clear evidence for this removal during his examination of the lower barrow, and the strange circumstance there of other burials, one possibly associated with a Beaker, being found at apparently primary levels within it (Barnatt 1996a, 98). The upper barrow would also accord with the common local pattern of hill top siting. Against this re-identification though stands the fact that only the lower of the two barrows was marked on the 1884 map, surveyed 40 years after Bateman's excavation.

Regional context

Belief that the barrow now termed Liffs Low was indeed the one excavated by Bateman is supported by the siting of the other two securely identified later Neolithic round barrow burials in the region: Stonesteads and Grub Low near Waterhouses. They, like it, are both placed on slopes where they would have been visible principally from adjacent valleys, whilst neighbouring barrows are hilltop sited for maximum impact.

Table 6.1.

Graves and simple burials (principal artefacts)	Leaf arrowheads	Lozenge arrowheads	Transverse arrowheads	Leaf/lozenge point	Edge polished axe	Edge polished adze	Stone axe	Edge polished knife	Fully polished knife	Plano-convex knife	Boar tusk blade	Beaver incisor	Antler macehead	Jet slider	Skewer pin	Fabricator	Towthorpe ware	Peterborough Ware
Liffs Low		2		2	2			2			2		1					1
Stonesteads	1										1							
Grub Low	2																	
Yorkshire series																		
Duggleby Howe K																	1	
G					1								1					
D									1									
C			5								12	2			1			
Ayton East Field		5		2	3	1		1		1	2		1					
Whitegrounds				1										1				
Aldro 88	1										1						1	
Aldro 94								1									1	
Aldro C75 (1)								1										
(2)									1									
Painsthorpe 99	2			1													2	
Painsthorpe 118														1				
Cowlam LVII											1	1						
Garton Slack 112															?3			
Huggate Wold 230				2														
Riggs 16														1				
Pickering						1				1								
Crosby G. CLXXIV 1											2				1			
2														1		1		
Southern series																		
Mount Fm. Dorchester								1										
Radley oval barrow 1	?1													1				
2								1										
Linch Hill, S. Harcourt								1						1				
Five Knolls, 5, Beds								1										
Charlecote, Warwicks.		1																
Cop Heap, Wilts								?2						1				
W.Stoke 35a, Wilts.			4															
Handley 26, Dorset														1				1

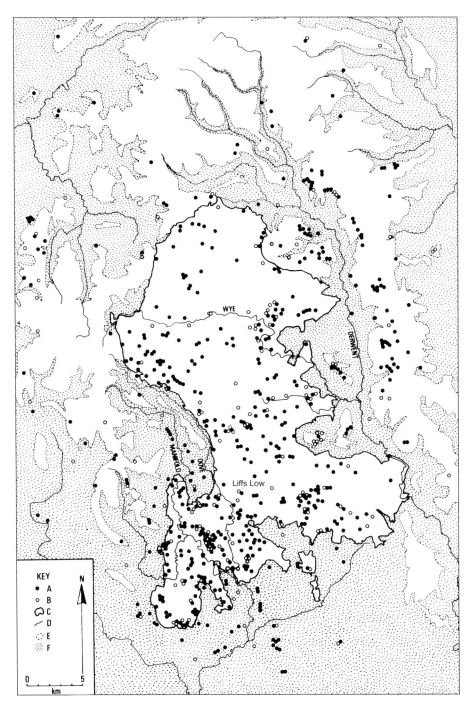

Figure 6.5: Location of Liffs Low and the overall distribution of barrows in the Peak District (After Barnatt 1996b, fig. 1.3, reproduced courtesy of John Barnatt)

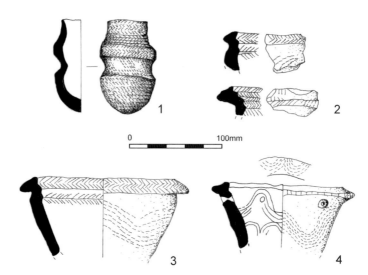

Figure 6.6: Detail of the flask (after Vine 1982 and Bateman 1848) and other sherds (after Manby 1975)

Unlike Liffs Low, the single contracted inhumations under these round barrows were accompanied by only the simplest of artefacts: a boar's tusk blade at the feet and a leaf-shaped arrowhead, a scraper, flint flakes and small bone "ring" near the shoulder at Stonesteads and two leaf-shaped arrowheads at Grub Low (Kinnes 1979; Barnatt 1996a, 133). Barnatt has noted as possible Neolithic burials examples on stone pavements conceivably akin to that at Stonesteads but these may as readily be paralleled by collective burial arrangements such as that at Long Low, Wetton. A significant number of others include Beakers. Even the well-attested Neolithic cave burials in the area fail to extend the grave good inventory significantly – besides pottery (Mortlake sherds at Calling Low Dale, Rains Cave and Fox Hole Cave), this comprises simply leaf-shaped arrowheads, a petit-tranchet derivative arrowhead and, at Treak Cliff fissure, a greenstone axe, flint flakes and an antler tine accompanying three or four disturbed inhumations (Barnatt 1996a, 135–6).

The Liffs Low vessel (Figures 6.3 and 6.6), or flask, has no close parallel within the Peak either for elements of its form or decorative motifs (Vine 1982, 21–2 and figs. 266–84). In fact, the decorative design of the flask stands out from all other Peak assemblages, including the large predominantly Ebbsfleet Ware one from Wigber Low (Manby 1983, 53). The small almost cup-like Mortlake Ware bowl with impressed bird bone decoration recovered from the cist within the cave at Calling Low Dale (Gilks 1971 fig. 1 and pl. 1) is also very different from the flask despite its burial context, as, further afield, is the so-called Mortlake ware sherd accompanying a burial at Elf Howe, eastern Yorkshire that looks as if it actually derives from a collared vessel (Kinnes 1979, fig. 18.8). Mention should also be made of the two vessels recovered from a cist burial at Arbor Low that have been considered to have Peterborough Ware affinities (Piggott 1931, 128 and fig. 18.3) but almost certainly belong within the Food Vessel tradition as Manby clearly states (1957).

Closed chambered mounds (Long Low and possibly Stanhope, Bostern, and Pea Low) appear to dominate the south western zone of the limestone plateau where Liffs Low lies to the exclusion of long barrows. The great bank barrow of Long Low is the only certain representative of the latter class and seems to have been superimposed upon a closed chambered site at its northern end (Barnatt 1996b, fig. 1.17). This stands in marked contrast to the striking density of later round barrows that survive in the zone despite very extensive medieval agricultural encroachment (Barnatt 1996b, 11, fig. 1.5). Long mounds were either sited on lower ground here and have been destroyed or represented a "foreign" element excluded in favour of "traditional" closed chambers. The latter explanation might account for the probably late addition of a novel bank barrow at Long Low and the presence at Liffs Low of a cist somewhat in the closed chamber tradition (Barnatt 1996b, 126).

National context

The principal grave goods from Liffs Low find an immediate echo in those accompanying individual burials under round barrows in eastern Yorkshire rather than in the limited edge-polished flint knife – jet slider repertoire of southern middle Neolithic burials (Table 6.1).

Antler maceheads are found almost exclusively in this burial context in northern Britain (Duggleby Howe G; Ayton East Field; Crosby Garrett CLXXIV and, less certainly contemporary at Cowlam LVII and Aldro C76: Kinnes 1979; Simpson 1996). Boars' tusks, absent in the south, are also common grave goods. Yet within this Yorkshire elaborate artefact milieu the Liffs Low material presents distinct areas of divergence that demand attention. Axes, for instance, were not common grave goods (Kinnes 1979; Pitts 1996, app. 4). The provision of two is unparalleled unless the Ayton East Field "hoard" is included on the assumption that the bone recorded with it from the crest of the mound represented an interment. This is all the more striking in view of the relative regional rarity of flint axes in the Peak, there being no source there (Moore 1979). Nor is it at all likely that the axes were manufactured from the nearest available source – small glacially derived flint in the Trent Valley (Henson 1989, 17). A Yorkshire source seems most plausible yet the form of the Liffs Low axes was significantly different to axes accompanying burials there. Unlike the specialized waisted types selected at Duggleby (burial G), Whitegrounds and East Ayton (two of the four), they were of simple edge-polished type. Duggleby and Seamer axes were, it seems, moving along the eastern seaboard (*e.g.* to Biggar Lanarkshire: Sheridan 1992, 206-7) but not inland to the southwest; although well recorded as surface finds from the Yorkshire Wolds, they are entirely missing in similarly substantial collections from the Peak District (Manby 1974, fig. 40) (Figure 6.7).

Despite the lack of specialized shaping the Liffs Low axes are superb examples (Figures 6.3–6.4). Amongst grave goods, the larger of the two is second only to the adze from Duggleby in length (188mm as against 236mm), and longer than the finest examples from the York hoard and the Thames (Clarke *et al.* 1985, 252–3; Adkins & Jackson 1978). The smaller of the two axes, although lying within the upper end of the size range of edge-polished specimens from the Thames, is exceeded in length as a grave good only by the two previously mentioned axes and that from Greenbrae, Aberdeenshire (Kenworthy 1977). The Ayton East Field axes are all shorter. Liffs Low axe forms are echoed by examples from the latter "hoard" but perhaps more closely by specimens from the Thames in London (*e.g.* Adkins & Jackson 1978, nos. 1, 2, 8 and 10), mostly deriving from localities also noted for the recovery of antler maceheads. The smaller Liffs Low axe has been specifically compared by Manby and Hayfield (1996) both to an example of marked triangular form found during fieldwalking over the barrow C77 at Aldro in eastern Yorkshire (a mound that also produced a jet slider: Mortimer 1905, fig. 75, fig. 154), and to that from Greenbrae, Aberdeenshire found with amber and jet beads (Kenworthy 1977). The longer Liffs Low axe of slender, pointed butt type is a familiar edge-polished variety (*e.g.* Moore's class 2: 1979) yet its extremely attenuated, chisel-like form appears to have more in common with fine, fully polished examples such as that from Helpingham, Lincolnshire (Moore 1979, fig. 2; Pitts 1996, 342, Crudwell type). These fine widespread specimens have been explained as ceremonial artefacts.

The "two flint knives polished on the edge, one of them serrated on the back" (Bateman 1848) (Figure 6.4) at Liffs Low recall the polished-edge knife and serrated blade found with one of the burials at Aldro C75 and similar knives from the East Ayton "hoard". Such knives – unlike the fine all-over-polished broad flake type (Manby 1974, type 1: 1974) placed with the other interment at Aldro C75, and with burial D at Duggleby Howe – have been found as often with burials in the south as in the north. There they seem particularly associated with jet sliders (Table 6.1), an artefact type closely sourced to eastern Yorkshire yet absent from the Peak District region. While the presence of kite-shaped arrowheads

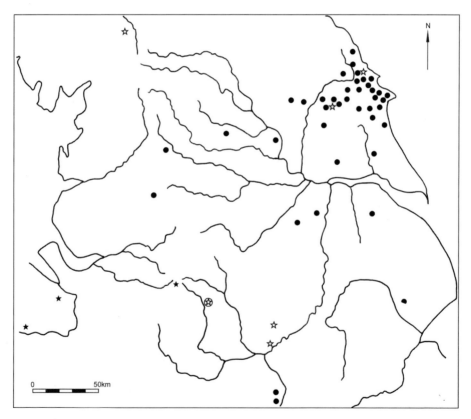

Figure 6.7: Regional distribution of antler maceheads (white stars; Liffs Low: star in circle), Maesmore maceheads (black stars), and waisted flint axes (black circles). After Simpson 1996, Roe 1968 and Manby 1974.

(Figures 6.3–6.4) and boar-tusks at Liffs Low serve to link it with other northern burials, the absence of specifically crafted Yorkshire prestige artefacts (waisted axes, fully polished broad flake flint knives and jet sliders) both from the burial and the region as a whole raises questions regarding the degree of association (temporal or cultural) of Yorkshire Wolds and Peak District elites in the middle Neolithic (see Figure 6.7).

The unique pottery vessel (Figure 6.6) without doubt belongs to the Peterborough Ware style as its key attributes – round base, neck-fillet, cavetto zone, stepped rim, decoration and fabric (use of quartzite) – can all be paralleled (*e.g.* Carnaby Top Site 19: Manby 1975, fig. 14: nos. 1–2, 5 and 7). It is typical of the Peterborough style in that it is decorated all-over with various motifs created by aplastic finger-nail impressions and arranged in horizontal rows. These include rows of oblique and herringbone impressions, oblique bands of end-to-end marks and "false cord". One important point is that most recent depictions of the vessel lack one significant detail, that the neck had originally carried oblique bands of end-to-end finger-nail impressions. This detail was recorded by Bateman (see Figure 6.3; Bateman 1848, 43; compare with Piggott 1931, fig. 20; Kinnes 1979, 18.7; Vine 1982, 322) but may have been partially lost during the various reconstructions of the vessel. This detail is important as it provides a possible link with Fengate and Rudston vessels from East Yorkshire (Manby 1975, fig. 13 nos. 3, 4, 5 and 10).

Peterborough Ware from funerary contexts in the Peak has been mentioned above. To date this is the only known region where the practice of placing pottery vessels within the grave occurs. Elsewhere pottery is notable by its absence, despite the occurrence of a range of small bowls and cups with Peterborough Ware affinities. The same is generally true of the early Neolithic period, although rare examples of cups deposited within long barrows are known (*e.g.* Hazleton North, Gloucestershire – Saville 1990, 105). In the Midlands and Thames Valley, ring ditch enclosures and barrows tend to have only limited grave associations, which never included pottery (see Table 6.1). However, fragmentary bowls were occasionally deposited within the ditches and internal features of these sites. At Horton (Berkshire) part of a Fengate Ware bowl was placed in the outer oval ditch (Ford & Pine 2003, 22 and fig. 2.6), while at Barford (Warwickshire) and at Dorchester-on-Thames (Site I) fragments of Ebbsfleet Ware bowls were placed in the ditches or internal features (Atkinson *et al.* 1951, pl. X; Oswald 1969). At Staines Road, Shepperton fragments from at least five bowls and other more fragmentary vessels were recovered from the ditch fill together with various placed deposits of animal bone and the remains of at least two individual inhumation burials (Jones 2008).

DISCUSSION

Liffs Low appears to be positioned so that it is strikingly visible from just a small basin area on the edge of the upper limestone plateau connected by Biggin Dale to the dissected region of the southwest. This area lacks the scattering of small chambered cairns and long barrows that characterises the Peak District as a whole but does possess a remarkable bank barrow – Long Low – set near its centre. The affinities of this monument are decidedly middle Neolithic and probably related to social group coalescence and increased centralization of power (Loveday 2006, 88–102). It is noteworthy therefore that the region has produced the only three certain Neolithic individual burials under round barrows (Liffs Low, Stonesteads, and Grub Low) and that it later came to possess the densest concentration of round barrows on the entire Peak. Its dales and shelves undoubtedly represented the most attractive, and perhaps contested, "home ranges" for occupation, just as they did in the medieval period (Barnatt 1996b, 11). Here, near the head of river systems running south to the Trent from whence workaday flint for the Peak communities almost certainly came, the Liffs Low burial may have staked early proprietorial rights. In such a context, particular importance attaches to the antler macehead.

The antler macehead

The macehead alone is given prominence in the burial by being placed apart from the other grave goods (Figure 6.2). Like the other classic examples found with burials (Duggleby Howe; Ayton East Field; Crosby Garrett CLXXIV: Simpson 1996), it lacks immediate local mortuary parallels. Rather than fitting into localized traditions (conceivable only in the Duggleby area if we accept the cruder specimens from Cowlam 57 and Aldro C76) these items were, it seems, regionally highly distinctive as grave goods. A symbolic role therefore seems likely.

Interestingly the Liffs Low macehead, unlike the others with burials in northern England, has distinct points of similarity with the London – Thames Valley concentration. It alone can be linked to a regional grouping (albeit small) that includes riverside/riverine activity (Attenborough on the Trent near the Derwent confluence: Posnansky 1958) and it alone bears lattice decoration (Simpson 1996). Equally significantly, a stone macehead with cut facet lattice decoration closely comparable to that on antler maceheads from Brentford and Teddington (Simpson 1996, nos. 47 and 50) comes from near the headwaters of the Dove at Quarnford just 15km from Liffs Low (Roe 1968, fig. 38). Such maceheads, known as the Maesmore type after the exquisite example found near Maerdy in Clwyd, are extremely rare and with the exception of an example found at the entrance to the right hand recess of the eastern tomb at the great mound at Knowth in Ireland, lack context (Eogan & Richardson 1982). Unfortunately, even that example lacks temporal clarity since it could represent a later insertion into the accessible chamber; certainly the spiral motifs that uniquely accompanies the characteristic lattice decoration on this artefact suggests post-3000 BC horizons, possibly associated with Grooved Ware related activity around the tomb (Eogan & Roche 1997; Loveday *et al.* 2007). Recent dating of a lattice decorated antler macehead from Brentford to 3630–3360 cal BC (OxA-13440: 4684±37 BP. Loveday *et al.* 2007) leaves little doubt that the antler forms are prototypes for these fine Maesmore specimens. The example from Quarnford may possibly represent an early example of the type since it lacks the quality of the Maesmore and Knowth specimens.

Significantly, these rare stone maceheads (comprising just five decorated and four undecorated examples) are almost wholly concentrated in two equally spread regional groupings: from Quarnford, Staffordshire to Maesmore, Clwyd, either side of the Cheshire Plain, and from Aidens, Sutherland to Urquart, Moray around the Moray Firth (Roe 1968, fig. 34). The former alone includes a find spot of a decorated antler macehead that could be advanced as a prototype – that at Liffs Low (Figure 6.7).

The relatively blank zone of the Cheshire Plain has understandably discouraged notions of a western link from the Peak District in favour of more obviously productive northern and easterly ones. The northeasterly flowing Trent, into which the Dove and Derwent drain, dominates our perception of the natural orientation of the area so totally that the fact is often overlooked that the rivers Bollin and Dane flowing into the Mersey, rise less than a kilometre from the sources of the Manifold and Dove, on the other side of Axe Edge. The source of the River Dane is actually in Quarnford where the Maesmore style macehead was found and where the watershed crossing is easy. The Mersey estuary lies only some 30km from the western upland edge and no more than 50–60km from the edge of the limestone plateau. Evidence of Neolithic – early Bronze Age activity across this area, including the remarkably productive site at Oversley Farm, Wilmslow, points to the influence of valleys such as the Bollin and Weaver-Dane, both as areas of settlement and as corridors into the Pennines (Timberlake 2005, 10–11). It should also be noted that settlement adjacent to the rivers Dove and Manifold would have been effectively restricted to their northern, upper reaches where significantly the motte and bailey castle at Pilsbury was constructed in the early medieval period as the centre of the De Ferriers estates (Barnatt & Smith 2004, 90): south of Hartington and Biggin the valleys are too narrow and gorge-like for settlement until the rivers leave the limestone plateau near Ashbourne fifteen winding kilometres away.

Significantly perhaps the eponymous macehead from Maesmore was recovered only a short distance along the Alwen Valley from its confluence with the Dee, which is marked out by the presence of probable cursus sites (Gibson 1999). These two rivers furnish an obvious corridor into the northern Welsh uplands from both the Cheshire Plain and the coast. The predominantly northern and coastal clustering of Group VII axes in Wales (McKClough & Cummins 1988, map 7), most significantly roughouts (Chappel 1987, fig. 9.27), leaves little doubt that these were their primary distribution routes. Chappell notes, however, that the main concentration of Group VII axes lies neither here nor around the source but in the Peak District (Chappell 1987, 252, n.1). Whilst ease of modern collecting on the limestone plateau as opposed to Graig Llwyd, and the focusing effect of the henge at Arbor Low, must be given due account when assessing the figures, the possibility that the area acted as a secondary distribution centre, akin to the Yorkshire Wolds (Bradley & Edmonds 1993), deserves consideration; an axe roughout from the Trent at Holme Pierrepoint (Moore 1979) indicates that preforms were being transported to the region. The limestone plateau certainly appears to have been the principal centre for the consumption, and probably distribution, of Group XX axes deriving from a Charnwood Forest source 55km south (Loveday 2004). The presence of axe fragments sourced to Groups VI,VII, and XX along with Peterborough style pottery on the old land surface sealed by the cairn at Wigber Low near Kniverton (Collis 1983) could indicate their contemporary circulation in the middle Neolithic but recovery of two Group XX axes from a Grooved Ware pit at Rothley, Leicestershire, albeit deliberately "undressed" (Cooper & Hunt 2005), and a high register of Group VII axes from such pits nationally (F. Roe pers. comm.) advises caution. Other hints of a western rather than eastern orientation to Peak District communities in the middle Neolithic include the fact that kite-shaped arrowheads are far more common as stray finds there, in the northwest, and in Wales than in eastern Yorkshire, despite very intensive collecting in the latter area (Green 1980, 74–5, 97, fig. 35). Closely comparable cave burials associated with Peterborough Ware have been found at Calling Low Dale, Monyash and Gop, Flintshire (Barnatt 1996a, 135–6; Sheridan & Davis 1998, 150.) and Manby (1983) has drawn attention to incised lattice decoration akin to that on the Liffs

Low antler macehead on Peterborough Ware sherds from Rains Cave and from Gawthorpe, Cheshire. The fact that the closest parallel for Peak District chambered tombs lie in the simple box-like chambers of Anglesey (Barnatt 1999b, 24) could point to an earlier origin for this western "axis".

"The little heap"

Other items in the Liffs Low grave raise a number of questions, not least by their placement. Bateman was at pains to emphasise that they were deposited "in a cluster behind the shoulders" (Figure 6.2). He details their discovery in order: "... almost the first observed articles were a pair of enormous tusks of the wild boar... next came two arrowheads of flint ...; two flint celts or chisels; two spearheads ...; two flint knives; ... numerous other pieces of flint ...; with these were found three pieces of red ochre ..." and then adds that "Upon the summit of the little heap formed by this accumulation of relics lay a small drinking or incense cup of a novel and unprecedented shape" (1848).

This is quite unlike the normal provision of grave goods. The items were clearly piled up, or perhaps placed within a bag, and the small pot placed on top. The fact that with the exception of the latter, they were all placed as pairs encourages the suspicion that they were symbolic, rather than personal, articles. Such consistent duality occurs in no other mid–late Neolithic burial (Kinnes 1979, figs. 3.2-3) (see Table 6.1).

Practical explanations are possible for the pairs of boar tusks, that also occur at Ayton East Field and Crosby Garrett (with six pairs at Duggleby Howe), and for the pairs of leaf points also noted at Ayton East Field, Towthorpe 18, Huggate Wold 230 (with four at Winterbourne Stoke 3a, Wiltshire). The tusks almost certainly came from single animals and could represent trophies, albeit with possible symbolic as well as personal value, while the pairing of leaf points – assuming their use as spearheads – may represent the standard weaponry of a single person. But there are no other burials with two axes – a particular extravagance in the Peak District, devoid as it is of a flint source – nor two knives. The closest approximation is to be found in the deposit found on the top of the mound at Ayton East Field. Like the Liffs Low "heap" this may have been contained in a bag and interestingly included only a token bone deposit (Kinnes 1979, 17). The four axes there could, with the two "spearheads" and two boar tusks, represent deliberate pairing; as at Liffs Low there seems no question of the items being hafted when deposited as might be expected of grave goods.

Such duplication could, of course, simply reference pairs of boar tusks: a desire to maintain numerical and probably symbolic equality. But its extravagant expression at Liffs Low seems to indicate more, particularly in view of the apparent offering nature of the "little heap". Cosmological notions of duality may underlie this highly structured deposit, related either to the "others" or to contemporary social structuring. Anthropology attests the not uncommon division of social groupings of tribal size into moieties, often with different claims of descent or arenas of action. On occasions this finds political expression in dual rulership. It is not without interest, therefore, that double burials appear to be a marked feature of the Neolithic "individual" burial tradition. They appear to be recorded in the north at Crosby Garrett CLXXIV, Aldro C75, Cowlam LVII (and Duggleby Howe if burials G and D are separated from burial C: Kinnes *et al.* 1983; but see Loveday 2002; and Gibson in prep.), and in the south at Handley 26, Dorset and the oval barrow at Radley,

Oxfordshire (Kinnes 1979; Bradley 1992; Barclay & Halpin 1999). In the latter case – a modern excavation unlike the others – we can securely associate the two burials. Their legs were crossed in a manner that the excavator considered impossible had the interments been separated by a long interval. We also know they were male and female, the former having a jet slider on his hip, the latter an edge-polished flint knife by her head (Bradley 1992). If the others were also cases of contemporary double burial, questions must arise over the nature of this coincident mortality. At Liffs Low, however, duality seems only to have been symbolically rendered unless the burial excavated in the 1930s proves to have been contemporary rather than a feature of the barrow extension (Barnatt 1996a).

A further possible explanation for the duplication of grave goods/symbols lies not in joint rulership but a single ruler uniting joint polities (*e.g.* Upper and Lower Egypt). Working from this hypothesis a range of possible combined "realms" could be conceived: the Peak District and the middle Trent Valley, or the Cheshire Plain, North Wales or the Yorkshire Wolds. Of these the latter would appear the most obvious in view of the common early adoption of individual burial and the later close connections attested by early Bronze Age grave goods, most notably jet. But as we have seen there are significant differences of middle Neolithic prestige artefact style that separate the two regions. Close connection appears to be heralded only by artefacts associated with later Grooved Ware: polished discoidal flint knives, stone maceheads and chisels (Manby 1974 figs. 35, 38 and 40). In fact, were it not for the Liffs Low burial itself, the question of inter-regional identity during the middle Neolithic would hardly arise. Cases are better made for the middle Trent Valley and Cheshire Plain, across both of which axes passed to the Peak District. A long-lived connection with the latter is hinted at by the northerly distribution of jet artefacts of mid-late Neolithic date in Wales (Sheridan & Davis 1998), the material or the fabricated items almost certainly arriving via the Peak that later had a particular association with the material (Bateman 1861, 46-8; Machin 1971; Radley 1969).

Wider contacts?

The most enigmatic feature of the Liffs Low burial is undoubtedly the miniature pot that had been placed on top of the "heap". Possible parallels for the various elements making up its unique form have been considered above. In view of its Peterborough Ware (Mortlake) decorative affinities it is not without interest that Gibson, in a discussion of Bronze Age miniature vessels, advances a diminutive (40mm) vessel in this tradition from the Dublin area as perhaps the earliest manifestation of the type (2004, 274 and fig. 91), although possible early Neolithic thumb pots are also known. The Liffs Low vessel is more than twice this size (103mm) and cannot strictly be classed as miniature but is uncharacteristically small. Abercromby suggested a connection with TRB collared flasks as long ago as 1906, and although this idea has been ignored or dismissed since (*e.g.* Childe in Piggott 1931, 132; Kinnes 2004, 109), it is worth noting that these vessels similarly belong at the lowest end of their local ceramic size range (*e.g.* Midgley 1992, fig. 31).

That a copy of a TRB collared flask might be made – however poorly – and placed with a middle Neolithic burial in central England might reasonably be doubted. But what marks it out from other vessels is its flask form. This is currently without precise parallel in Britain, although it can be noted that a range of vessels, including cups and dishes, are known (Barclay 2000; Barclay & Edwards forthcoming). The flask would have fitted comfortably into the palm of a hand and may have been designed to contain a precious liquid, perhaps a medicinal, narcotic, or ritualized substance. Certainly, the cylindrical neck and closed form may have been designed to hold a stopper. Andrew Sherratt (1991) noted that the typologically similar TRB flasks could have been for consuming certain types of narcotic substances such as opium and cannabis, which at the time were infused. He also noted that the form of such vessels, when, inverted, resembled the head of the opium poppy, although this would be harder to argue for the Liffs Low flask. Nonetheless, the form of the Liffs Low vessel is perhaps more likely to have signalled its unusual contents than to have resulted from ceramic experimentation or random long distance cultural copying.

There is another feature of the grave assemblage that suggests external, possibly North European, influence – the three pieces of ochre. This material has been found with a small number of early Bronze Age burials in Britain, including that at Garton Slack 40, eastern Yorkshire, where a miniature biconical pot containing bones of "some small animal" had been placed in the mouth of the deceased after its mandible had been removed and placed on its chest (Mortimer 1905, 229; Gibson 2004, 277). It is also recorded from stone circles in Cumbria (Gretigate and Druid's Temple), at The Sanctuary in Wiltshire (Burl 1981, 152), and as an exotic element at the village of Skara Brae, Orkney. All are late Neolithic (Grooved Ware) or early Bronze Age contexts. Earlier than this it was a rarity. A small lump of ochre has, however, been found at the bottom of the re-cut ring-ditch at Shepperton, Middlesex, in a section that also produced a wolf skull. Mortlake Ware sherds were recovered from the same level at many points around the ditch (Jones 2008, 13–14, 28–32) and a date of 3500–3130 cal BC (OxA-4059: 4595± 85 BP) was obtained from animal bone in a level above the ochre (Jones 2008, 10). Pieces of ochre also came from the Cotswold chambered tombs of Nympsfield and Rodmarton, but their accessible chambers could have permitted later deposition associated with Peterborough Ware. Significantly, the ochre recovered from Nympsfield is recorded as coming from the ante-chamber *directly beneath* a sherd of an ovoid necked jar (Clifford 1938, 196, 198 and 204). This unusual ceramic form with close TRB affinities has been noted only in Ebbsfleet assemblages, both in the south (Piggott 1962, 32–8) and north (Manby 1988, 52 and fig. 4.8). There seems little doubt that the ochre was a placed deposit associated with Ebbsfleet style Peterborough Ware activity on the site. That found in the northern passage at Rodmarton can probably be similarly explained (Clifford & Daniel 1940, 143), while pieces of haematite recovered from Mendip long barrows at Orchardleigh and Priddy are not certainly of Neolithic date (Lewis 2005, 65–6).

It seems then that the first appearance of ochre in England and Wales correlates with the advent of Peterborough Ware (*c.*3500 BC), significantly, perhaps, in the Ebbsfleet style, since this simplest manifestation of the tradition bears the closest similarity to elements of TRB and Vlaardingen ceramics. Along with the echoes of collared flasks in the Liffs Low pot, this strongly suggests a need to seek parallels outwith the British Isles in northwestern Europe. Ochre had figured prominently in cemeteries of Mesolithic date and most LBK graves reveal evidence of its use but this dropped dramatically with the advent of long barrow burial (Midgley 2005, 66, 110). It was still occasionally used however (Strassburg 2000, 357–8), and most strikingly for our context here, was found adhering to the lower interior of a small (100mm) funnel-necked beaker at the Lindebjerg long barrow, in northwest Zealand. The pot had probably been placed on the stump of a façade post of the first phase barrow; a sherd of another somewhat larger beaker (150mm across) bearing similar traces came from the base of the posthole (Liversage 1980, 97, 117–8). Although of beaker, not collared flask form, the small vessel was almost identical in size to that from Liffs Low and the fact that small pots containing ochre have been recorded elsewhere (examples displayed at the National Museum, Budapest from Bodrogkevesztur and Jaszladany) hints at a wider European tradition. The position of the little pot at Liffs Low on top of the heap or bag certainly suggests a final magico-ritual offering like that at Lindebjerg. The three small pieces of ochre with rubbed down surfaces may have been placed beside it; they alone were provenanced rather vaguely in the heap and could have rolled from the top when the cist was infilled.

If we insist upon viewing British middle Neolithic individual burials as a purely insular phenomenon we are at some difficulty to explain a range of novel features: sudden acceptance of ochre as a burial accompaniment (in addition to Liffs Low, Mortimer refers to "several thin patches of ferruginous matter (not the residue of oxidizing iron implements) in contact with the body (K), over and under it at the base of the shaft" at Duggleby Howe (1905, 29)); the shape of the Liffs Low pot, and new forms like necked jars; the sudden popularity of boars tusks; and the inclusion of arrowheads and axes with burials. Clearly there are no precise parallels as sought by archaeologists in the past working within simplistic concepts of invasion and cultural imposition. If, however, we take stock of developments in our understanding of northwest European littoral and wetland communities it can be seen that their capacity to adopt or reject elements of the material culture of neighbouring upland groups, and to participate in medium and long-distance exchange networks, furnishes precisely the fluid situation that might lead incomers to sow the seeds of the Peterborough Ware phenomenon in the Thames estuary area (Loveday 2009). As Louwe Kooijmans has succinctly stated: "As far as material culture is concerned 'Vlaardingen' is one element of a wide culture complex between Trichterbecher (TRB) and Seine-Oise-Marne (SOM)" (1993, 76). From such a melting pot might European traditions of grave goods (*e.g.* axes, arrowheads, boar tusks *etc.* Midgley 2005, 112 and 125) make their appearance in Britain.

The leap from the riverine aspect of Peterborough Ware to the emphatically upland, high status burial at Liffs Low demands explanation. That could partly lie in the local circumstances that permitted Trent Valley communities, marked out by their use of antler maceheads, or less visible Cheshire Plain groups, to develop and control summer grazing on the Peak District limestone plateau. It may also lie in the nodal advantage that this territory furnished and hence the ability to control the movement of axes of Groups VII and XX. And it may have been bolstered, or even achieved, through ritual dominance of the region. The major cursuses at Aston upon Trent and Potlock (the ditches of the latter producing Peterborough Ware) are significantly located close to the Derwent and Dove confluences respectively, while a sinuous double section of wall lying askew within the medieval field walls of Biggin poses the possibility that a cursus lies obscured there (Loveday 2006, 112–3).

It is abundantly clear that the Liffs Low burial is in many ways distinct from those on the Yorkshire Wolds. Not only is it richer in terms of individual items placed with a single body, the manner in which these were placed suggests something quite different to the individual grave goods placed with burials G, C and D at Duggleby Howe. Coupled with the lack of classic Yorkshire "prestige" artefacts and the apparent lack of successor burials, this could point to a short lived, more ceremonially structured, phenomenon temporally or politically isolated from developments around Rudston but drawing on a common Peterborough-antler macehead associated background.

Perhaps the greatest contrast, however, lies in barrow size: Duggleby Howe is 6.5m in height and appears to belong to a tradition of great barrows of presumptively later Neolithic date (Manby 1988, 64–6); Liffs Low is only some 1.5m in height and apparently quite separate from the scattering of large round mounds covering collective interments in the Peak (Barnatt 1996b, 63–7). That contrast may, however, be illusory. The earth mound that at Duggleby covered all the prestige burials (completed at the opening of the third millennium BC – Gibson in prep.) stood no higher than 1.67m, closely comparable not only to Liffs Low but to almost all middle Neolithic round mounds covering individual accompanied inhumations (Kinnes 1979). Even with the covering of "small chalk grit", that contained most of the cremations, and the capping of 0.3m of Kimmeridge Clay, the Duggleby mound stood no higher than 3.4m and was only some 23m in diameter (Mortimer 1905). Comparably sized barrows in eastern Yorkshire are Wold Newton 284, Garton Slack 79, and South Side Mount (Manby 1988, 64–6), and in Derbyshire, Gib Hill and the Round Hill – the former beside the henge at Arbor Low and the latter, placed centrally inside the cropmarks of a henge on the Trent gravels (Harding & Lee 1987, 116–9). The final near doubling of Duggleby Howe to a height of 6.5m and a diameter of 40m – comparable only to Willie Howe (Gibson, this volume Chapter 5) and the great mounds of Wessex (Knowlton Great Barrow, Hatfield, and Conquer, see Barber *et al.*, this volume Chapter 9) – remains undated but by virtue of its great size, and position, is most unlikely to have resulted from medieval mill base construction as sometimes suggested. Rather, it seems, both it and Willie Howe represent late Neolithic monumental statements.

It seems probable then that we are looking at two late fourth–early third millennium BC traditions: one of middle Neolithic individual burials under modestly sized round barrows and the other of great, and apparently empty, late Neolithic mounds that, away from eastern Yorkshire, are the ideological adjuncts to henges and rooted in Grooved Ware cosmology. Duggleby Howe by apparently uniquely combining the two appears to have falsely raised our expectations of middle Neolithic round mounds. In the Peak District the two traditions remained separate and are represented by Liffs Low and just 6km away, the substantial mound of Gib Hill.

ACKNOWLEDGEMENTS

We would like to thank Fiona Roe, John Barnatt, Emma Butterfield, Ian Ritchie and Julien Parsons for their help and advice. Julien Parsons kindly made the Bateman archive and finds available for study. We would also like to thank David Field and Jim Leary for inviting us to speak at the conference and for their encouragement during the writing of this paper. Pippa Bradley kindly read through the text and Linda Coleman helped with the illustrations.

BIBLIOGRAPHY

Adkins, R. and Jackson, R. (1978) *Neolithic stone and flint axes from the River Thames*. London, British Museum (Occasional Paper 1).

Atkinson, R. J. C., Piggott, C. M., and Sandars, N. K. (1951) *Excavations at Dorchester, Oxon*. Oxford, Department of Antiquities, Ashmolean Museum.

Barclay, A. (2000) *Spatial histories of the Neolithic: a study of the material culture of central southern England*. Reading, Department of Archaeology University of Reading (Unpublished PhD thesis).

Barclay, A. (2002) Ceramic lives. In A. Woodward and J. D. Hill (eds.) *Prehistoric Britain. The ceramic basis*, 85-95. Oxford, Oxbow Books (Prehistoric Ceramics Research Group, Occasional Publication 3).

Barclay, A. (2007) Connections and networks: a wider world and other places. In D. Benson and A. Whittle (eds.) *Building memories. The Neolithic Cotswold long barrow at Ascott-Under-Wychwood, Oxfordshire*, 331-344. Oxford, Oxbow Books (Cardiff Studies in Archaeology).

Barclay, A. and Bayliss, A. (1999) The chronological development of cursus and related monuments. In A. Barclay and J. Harding (eds.) *Pathways and ceremonies: The cursus monuments of Britain and Ireland*. Oxford, Oxbow Books.

Barclay, A. and Edwards, E. (forthcoming) The Prehistoric pottery. In G. Hey, C. Dennis and C. Bell (eds.) *Yarnton: Neolithic and Bronze Age settlement and landscape*. Oxford, Oxford Archaeology (Thames Valley Landscapes Monograph).

Barclay, A. and Halpin, C. (1999) *Excavations at Barrow Hills, Radley: prehistoric volume 1*. Oxford, Oxford Archaeology (Thames Valley Landscapes Monograph).

Barnatt, J. (1996a) A multiphased barrow at Liffs Low, near Biggin, Derbyshire. In J. Barnatt, and J. Collis (eds.) *Barrows in the Peak District. Recent Research*, 95–136. Sheffield, Collis.

Barnatt, J. (1996b) Review and interpretation of extant sites and past excavations. In J. Barnatt, & J. Collis (eds.) *Barrows in the Peak District. Recent research*, 1–94. Sheffield, Collis.

Barnatt, J. & Smith, K. (2004) *The Peak District. Landscapes through Time*. Macclesfield, Windgather Press.

Bateman, T. (1848) *Vestiges of the antiquities of Derbyshire*. London.

Bateman, T. (1861) *Ten Years' digging in the Celtic and Saxon grave hills in the counties of derby, Stafford and York from 1848 to 1858*. London.

Bradley, R. (1992) The excavation of an oval barrow beside the Abingdon causewayed enclosure, Oxfordshire. *Proceedings of the Prehistoric Society* 58, 127–42.

Bradley, R. and Edmonds, M. (1993) *Interpreting the axe trade: production and exchange in Neolithic Britain*. Cambridge, Cambridge University Press.

Burl, A. (1981) *Rites of the Gods*. London, Dent

Chappell, S. (1987) *Stone axe morphology and distribution in Neolithic Britain*. Oxford, British Archaeological Reports (BAR British Series 177).

Clarke, D. V., Cowie, T. G. and Foxon, A. (1985) *Symbols of power at the time of Stonehenge*. Edinburgh, HMSO.

Clifford, E. M. (1938) The excavation of the Nympsfield long barrow, Gloucestershire. *Proceedings of the Prehistoric Society* 4, 188–213.

Clifford, E. M. and Daniels, G. E. (1940) The Rodmarton and Avening portholes. *Proceedings of the Prehistoric Society* 6, 133–65.

Collis, J. (1983) *Wigber Low, Derbyshire: a Bronze Age and Anglian burial site in the White Peak*. Sheffield, University of Sheffield, Department of Prehistory and Archaeology.

Cooper, L. and Hunt, L. (2005) An engraved Neolithic plaque with Grooved Ware associations. *PAST* 50, 14–15.

Eogan, G. and Richardson, H. (1982) Two maceheads from Knowth, Co. Meath. *Journal of the Royal Society of Antiquaries of Ireland* 112, 123–38.

Eogan, G. and Roche, H. (1997) *Excavations at Knowth (2)*. Dublin, Royal Irish Academy & Department of Arts, Culture and the Gaeltacht.

Featherstone, P. (1998) *Biggin and Hartington Nether Quarter*. Biggin: Featherstone.

Ford, S. and Pine, J. (2003) Neolithic ring-ditches and Roman landscape features at Horton (1989 to 1996). In S. Preston (ed.) *Prehistoric, Roman and Saxon sites in eastern Berkshire. Excavations 1989–1997*, 13–85. Reading, Thames Valley Archaeological Services Ltd (Monograph 2).

Gibson, A. M. (1999) Cursus monuments and possible cursus monuments in Wales: avenues for research (or roads to nowhere?). In A. Barclay, and J. Harding (eds.) *Pathways and ceremonies. The cursus monuments of Britain and Ireland*, 130–40. Oxford, Oxbow Books (Neolithic Studies Group Seminar Papers 4).

Gibson, A. M. (2004) Small but perfectly formed? Some observations on the Bronze Age cups of Scotland. In A. Gibson, and J. A. Sheridan (eds.) *From sickles to circles. Britain and Ireland at the time of Stonehenge*, 244–70. Stroud, Tempus.

Gibson, A. M. (in prep) Recent research at Duggleby Howe.

Gibson, A. M. and Kinnes, I. (1997) On the urns of a dilemma: radiocarbon and the Peterborough problem. *Oxford Journal of Archaeology* 16(1), 65–72.

Gilks, J.A. (1971) The Peterborough Ware bowl from Calling Low Dale, Derbyshire. *Derbyshire Archaeological Journal* 91, 37–39.

Green, H. S. (1980) *The flint arrowheads of the British Isles*. Oxford, British Archaeological Reports (BAR British Series 75).

Harding, A. F. and Lee, G. E. (1987) *Henge monuments and related sites of Great Britain*. Oxford, British Archaeological Reports (BAR British Series 175).

Hart, C. R. (1981) *The North Derbyshire Archaeological Survey to AD 1500*. Chesterfield, North Derbyshire Archaeological Trust.

Henson, D. (1989) Away from the core? A northerner's view of flint exploitation. In I. Brookes, and P. Phillips (eds.) *Breaking the Stony Silence. Papers from the Sheffield Lithics Conference 1988*, 5–31. Oxford, British Archaeological Reports (BAR British Series 213).

Jones, P. (2008) *A Neolithic ring-ditch and later prehistoric features at Staines Road Farm, Shepperton*. Woking, SpoilHeap Publications.

Kenworthy, J. B. (1977) A reconsideration of the "Ardiffery" finds, Cruden, Aberdeenshire. *Proceedings of the Society of Antiquaries of Scotland* 108, 80–93.

Kinnes, I. (1979) *Round barrows and ring-ditches in the British Neolithic*. London, British Museum (Occasional Paper 7).

Kinnes, I. (2004) "A truth universally acknowledged": some more thoughts on Neolithic round barrows. In A. Gibson, and J. A. Sheridan (eds.) *From sickles to circles. Britain and Ireland at the time of Stonehenge*, 106–15. Stroud, Tempus.

Kinnes, I. A., Schadla-Hall T.; Chadwick P. and Dean, P. (1983) Duggleby Howe reconsidered. *Archaeological Journal* 140, 83 – 108.

Lewis, J. (2005) *Monuments, ritual and regionality: The Neolithic of northern Somerset*. Oxford, British Archaeological Reports (BAR British Series 401).

Liversage, D. (1980) Neolithic monuments at Lindebjerg, northwest Zealand. *Acta Archaeologica* 51, 85–152.

Louwe Kooijmans, L. P. (1993) Wetland exploitation and upland relations of prehistoric communities in the Netherlands. *East Anglian Archaeology* 50, 71–116.

Loveday, R. (2002) Duggleby Howe revisited. *Oxford Journal of Archaeology* 21(2), 135–46.

Loveday, R. (2004) Contextualizing monuments: the exceptional potential of the middle Trent Valley. *Derbyshire Archaeological Journal* 124, 1–12.

Loveday, R. (2006) *Inscribed across the landscape. The cursus enigma*. Stroud, Tempus.

Loveday, R. (2009) From Ritual to Riches – the route to individual power in Later Neolithic Eastern

Yorkshire? In K. Brophy and G. Barclay (eds.) *Defining a Regional Neolithic: The Evidence from Britain and Ireland*, 35-52. Oxford, Oxbow Books.

Loveday, R., Gibson, A., Marshall, P., Bayliss, A., Bronk Ramsey, C., and van der Plicht, H. (2007) The Antler Maceheads Dating Project. *Proceedings of the Prehistoric Society* 73, 381–92.

Machin, M. L. (1971) Further excavations of the enclosure at Swine Sty, Big Moor, Baslow. *Transactions of the Hunterian Archaeological Society* 10, 5–13.

Manby, T. R. (1957) Food Vessels of the Peak District. *Derbyshire Archaeological Journal* 77, 1–29.

Manby, T. G. (1974) *Grooved Ware sites in Yorkshire and the north of England.* Oxford, British Archaeological Reports (BAR British Series 9).

Manby, T. G. (1975) Neolithic Occupation Sites on the Yorkshire Wolds. *Yorkshire Archaeological Journal* 47, 23–59

Manby, T. G. (1983) Prehistoric pottery. In J. Collis, *Wigber Low, Derbyshire: A Bronze Age and Anglian burial site in the White Peak*, 53–58. Sheffield, University of Sheffield.

Manby, T. G. (1988) *Archaeology in eastern Yorkshire: essays in honour of T. C. M. Brewster FSA.* Sheffield, Department of Archaeology and Prehistory.

Manby, T. G. and Hayfield, C. (1996) A flint axe from Aldro, East Yorkshire. *Yorkshire Archaeological Journal* 68, 235-9.

McKClough, T. H. and Cummins, W. A. (1988) *Stone axe studies: volume 2.* London, Council for British Archaeology (Research Report 67).

Midgley, M. S. (1992) *TRB Culture. The First farmers of the North European Plain.* Edinburgh, Edinburgh University Press.

Midgley, M. S. (2005) *The monumental cemeteries of prehistoric Europe.* Stroud, Tempus.

Moore, C. N. (1979) Stone axes from the East Midlands. In T. H. McKClough, and W. A Cummins (eds.) *Stone Axe Studies*, 45–8. London, Council for British Archaeology (Research Report 23).

Mortimer, J. R. (1905) *Forty years' researches in British and Saxon burial mounds of East Yorkshire.* London, Hull and York, A. Brown & Sons.

Oswald, A. (1969) Excavations for the Avon/Severn Research Committee at Barford, Warwickshire, 1966-7. *Birmingham Archaeological Society Transactions and Proceedings* 83, 3-64.

Piggott, S. (1931) The Neolithic Pottery of the British Isles. *The Archaeological Journal* 88, 67–158

Piggott, S. (1962) *The West Kennet long barrow. Excavations 1955-6.* London, HMSO.

Pitts, M. (1996) The stone axe in Neolithic Britain. *Proceedings of the Prehistoric Society* 62, 311–72.

Posnansky, M. (1958) Neolithic finds from Attenborough near Nottingham. *Antiquaries Journal* 38, 87–8.

Radley, J. (1969) A shale bracelet industry from Totley Moor, near Sheffield, *Transactions of the Hunterian Archaeological Society* 9 264–8.

Roe, F. E. S. (1968) Stone maceheads and the latest Neolithic cultures of the British Isles. In J. M. Coles, and D. D. A. Simpson (eds.) *Studies in ancient Europe*, 145–72. Edinburgh, Edinburgh University Press.

Saville, A., 1990, *Hazleton North, Gloucestershire, 1979-82. The excavation of a Neolithic long cairn of the Cotswold-Severn group.* London, English Heritage Archaeological Report 13.

Sheridan, J. A. (1992) Scottish stone axeheads; some new work and recent discoveries. In N. Sharples, and J. A. Sheridan (eds.) *Vessels for the ancestors. Essays on the Neolithic of Britain and Ireland in honour of Audrey Henshall*, 194–212. Edinburgh, Edinburgh University Press.

Sheridan, J. A. and Davis, M. (1998) The Welsh "Jet Set" in prehistory: a case of keeping up with the Joneses? In A. Gibson, and D. Simpson (eds.) *Prehistoric ritual and religion. Essays in honour of Aubrey Burl, 148–62.* Stroud, Sutton.

Sherratt, A. (1991) Sacred and profane substances: the ritual use of narcotics in later Neolithic Europe, 50-64. In P. Garwood, D. Jennings, R. Skeates and J. Toms (eds.) *Sacred and Profane.*

Proceedings of a conference on archaeology, ritual and religion, Oxford, 1989. Oxford, Oxford University Committee for Archaeology (Monograph 32).

Simpson, D. D. A. (1996) "Crown" antler maceheads and the later Neolithic in Britain. *Proceedings of the Prehistoric Society* 62, 293–309.

Strassburg, J. (2000) *Shamanic Shadows. One hundred generations of undead subversion in Southern Scandinavia, 7000–4000 BC*. Stockholm, Stockholm Studies in Archaeology 20.

Timberlake, S. (2005) The archaeology of Alderley Edge and the northeast Cheshire Hinterland – A Review. In S. Timberlake, and A. J. N. W Prag, (eds.), *The archaeology of Alderley Edge. Survey, excavation and experiment in an ancient mining landscape*, 6–19. Oxford, British Archaeological Reports (BAR British Series 396).

Vine, P. M. (1982) *The Neolithic and Bronze Age Cultures of the Middle and Upper Trent Basin*. Oxford, British Archaeological Reports (BAR British Series 105).

APPENDICES

Appendix A – Liffs Low radiocarbon date footnote

Mandy Jay, Mike Richards, Mike Parker Pearson & Stuart Needham

The Liffs Low skeleton excavated by Thomas Bateman in July of 1843 (associated with a collared flask in the Peterborough tradition and a shaft-hole antler mace-head, along with other objects) was radiocarbon dated as part of the Beaker People Project. The sample used was from the zygomatic of the skull, and the collagen used for dating was extracted by Mandy Jay at Mike Richards' laboratories at the Max Planck Institute for Evolutionary Anthropology in Leipzig, and submitted to SUERC for dating as a pre-prepared sample. The date obtained is:

SUERC-26173 (GU-19925): 4510 ± 30 BP

Using OxCal 4.0 (IntCal 04) (Bronk Ramsey 1995, 2001; Reimer *et al.* 2004), this calibrates to:

3340 to 3110 BC (68.2% probability); 3350 to 3100 BC (95.4% probability)

The $\delta^{13}C$ value obtained in Leipzig as part of the Beaker People Project is –21.6‰, whilst that obtained as part of the radiocarbon dating process at SUERC is –21.5‰.

The museum accession reference data for this skull at the Weston Park Museum, Sheffield, are:

J93.931 (P22), Bateman Collection, Box ARC 479, 14.7.1843

Whilst it was expected that this sample would confirm a date which was earlier than the Beaker period on which the project is focusing, this and some other later Neolithic samples are providing invaluable background, comparative data for the pre-Beaker cultural period with which to investigate the transitional position.

Acknowledgements

The Beaker People Project is an inter-disciplinary and multi-institutional project, funded by the Arts and Humanities Research Council, looking particularly at mobility, diet and environment through the isotopic analysis of approximately 250 Late Neolithic and Early Bronze Age burials from across Britain, including a Peak District group from the Bateman Collection at Sheffield's Weston Park Museum.

Principal Investigator: Mike Parker Pearson

Co-PI (isotope research): Mike Richards

Co-PI (osteology): Andrew Chamberlain

Research Associate for this date: Mandy Jay

References

Bronk Ramsey, C. 1995. Radiocarbon calibration and analysis of stratigraphy: the OxCal program. *Radiocarbon*, 37 (2): 425–430.

Bronk Ramsey, C. 2001. Development of the radiocarbon program OxCal. *Radiocarbon*, 43 (2A): 355–363.

Reimer, P. J., Baillie, M. G. L., Bard, E., Bayliss, A., Beck, J. W., Bertrand, C. J. H., Blackwell, P. G., Buck, C. E., Burr, G. S., Cutler, K. B., Damon, P. E., Edwards, R. L., Fairbanks, R. G., Friedrich, M., Guilderson, T. P., Hogg, A. G., Hughen, K. A., Kromer, B., McCormac, G., Manning, S., Ramsey, C. B., Reimer, R. W., Remmele, S., Southon, J. R., Stuiver, M., Talamo, S., Taylor, F. W., van der Plicht, J. & Weyhenmeyer, C. E. 2004. Intcal04 terrestrial radiocarbon age calibration, 0–26 cal kyr BP. *Radiocarbon*, 46 (3): 1029–1058.

Appendix B

Roy Loveday and Alastair Barclay

This date confirms our reading of the Liffs Low burial. The fact that it is statistically indistinguishable from those obtained from the Attenborough macehead (Loveday et al 2007) and the principal prestige burial (G) at Duggleby Howe (Gibson forthcoming) points to a broadly contemporary northern phenomenon encompassing riverine and burial activity, although the 2–3 century date ranges across a plateau in the calibration curve could mask short term developments hinted at by differences of axe morphology.

It seems we might now justifiably begin to employ the terms 'Earlier Middle Neolithic' (covering the period 3500–3300 cal BC associated with cursus construction) and 'Later Middle Neolithic' (covering the period 3300–2900 cal BC associated with individual burial) as short hands to ease and clarify discussion of the southern British evidence.

We are very grateful to Mandy Jay and the members of the Beaker Peoples Project for sharing this date with us.

Chapter 7

Neolithic Round Barrows on the Cotswolds

Timothy Darvill

The rolling limestone uplands of the Cotswold Hills of eastern Gloucestershire and adjacent parts of Oxfordshire in the mid-west of England provided the geographical context for one of the eleven regional groupings of Neolithic round barrows identified by Ian Kinnes in his seminal study of these monuments (Kinnes 1979; 1992a, figure 1A.2). Like most of the other regional groupings identified, the Cotswold Hills are rich in long barrows of the fourth millennium BC (Darvill 2004) and round barrows conventionally dated to the second millennium BC and later (Drinkwater & Saville 1984). Starting from the systematic tabulated listings and descriptions published by Helen O'Neil and Leslie Grinsell (1960), Kinnes recognized five sites: Notgrove, Hungerfield, Dry Heathfield, The Waste, and The Soldier's Grave. Reviews of these structures, further fieldwork, and the results of commercial archaeology has expanded knowledge of some of the known examples and revealed a handful of further possible examples (Darvill & Grinsell 1989; Darvill 2006, 20–22). This short review provides an update of the Cotswold Neolithic round barrows thirty years on from their recognition as a distinct regional group. Figure 7.1 shows the distribution of certain and probable examples, emphasizing the clustering of sites in the north Cotswolds and along the west-facing Cotswold escarpment.

SITES RECOGNIZED TO 1979

The existence of a small round barrow or "rotunda" stratigraphically pre-dating the construction of the classic long barrow at Notgrove (NGR: SP 09592119. GLO 4) with a transcepted terminal chamber was recognized by Elsie Clifford during her excavation of the site in 1934–5 (Clifford 1936, 125) although it was John Corcoran who highlighted its significance as part of his consideration of multi-phase megalithic monuments (1969, 83). Ian Kinnes includes the site as a Stage AC round barrow with stone chamber noting its diameter as 7m and height of 2.1m, its construction using limestone blocks and the kerb of dry-stone walling (Kinnes 1979, 20–1). The chamber in the centre of the barrow is polygonal in shape with overlapped and doubled orthostats and a corbelled roof structurally integral to the cairn. Following the original excavation report he notes that the cist contained the fragmentary and disarticulated remains of one adult male associated with struck flint flakes. A re-examination of the skeletal remains by Martin Smith and Megan Brickley (2006, 344) concluded that although the remains from the cist

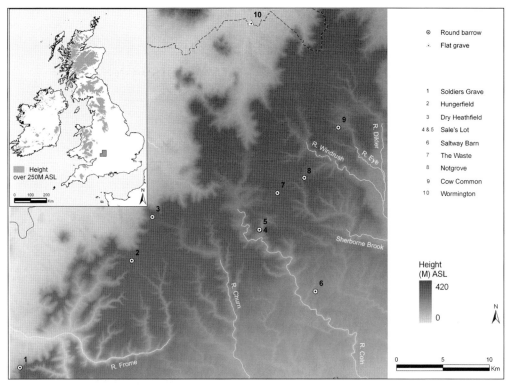

Figure 7.1: Map of the Cotswold showing the distribution of certain and probable Neolithic round barrows discussed in the text. (Sources: various. Illustration by Vanessa Constant)

were those of an adult aged between 20 and 30 at death it was not possible to determine the sex. Moreover, the condition of the bones and the presence of carnivore tooth-pits suggested a degree of exposure prior to burial. A radiocarbon determination on a single sample from the cist produced a date of 3696–3518 cal BC (WK-17179: 4816±43 BP). On the top of the rotunda Clifford found a scatter of human bones (1936, 143), which analysis by Smith and Brickley reassessed as the partial fragmented remains of an adult; a child aged 5–7 years; and an infant. A radiocarbon determination on one of the child's bones produced a date of 3520–3118 cal BC (WK-17181: 4607±43 BP) which overlaps with a series of four determinations from human and animal bones recovered from the chamber and passage of the overlying long barrow which ranged from 3649–3384 cal BC (WK-17182: 4784±38 BP) through to 3329–2921 cal BC (WK-17184: 4427±38 BP). Clearly, the dating evidence supports the stratigraphic evidence for the primacy of the round barrow and places the burial within the cist in the second quarter of the fourth millennium BC. Equally, it shows that the time-gap between the use of the round barrow and the construction of the long barrow is rather short, almost certainly less than a century; a conclusion that conforms well with the accumulating evidence for "short-chronology" models for the construction, use and abandonment of long barrow sites in southern Britain (Whittle *et al.* 2007).

Figure 7.2A (top) and 7.2B (bottom): Neolithic round barrows on the Gloucestershire Cotswolds. A: Soldier's Grave, Frocester. B: Hungerfield, Cranham. (Photographs: Timothy Darvill)

The Hungerfield Barrow, Cranham (NGR: SO 91317 12603) has been taken out of cultivation (Figure 7.2B) and in Spring 2009 was subject to detailed topographic survey and geophysical surveys (Roberts 2010). This work confirmed that the barrow was about 30m across with no encircling ditch. In the centre was an area of disturbance. Magnetic anomalies in the central area support Kinner's interpretation of the site as a crematorium (1979, 9). None of the other round barrow sites listed by Kinnes in the Cotswold group have undergone further investigation, although The Soldier's Grave at Frocester (NGR: SO 794015) has been partially cleared of trees (Figure 7.2A). Dry Heathfield in Barrow Piece Plantation, Coberley (NGR: SO 93531712) stands between the causewayed enclosures on Crickley Hill and the Crippets long barrow (GLO 7) but is now invisible on the surface, while The Waste at Hawling (SP 056217) was destroyed in the nineteenth century when the area was quarried for roadstone.

ADDITIONAL SITES

Since 1979 a handful of possible Neolithic round barrow sites in the Cotswolds have been proposed, of which four can be accepted as reasonably certain or probable.

Sale's Lot, Withington (NGR: SP 04881576. GLO 94) was excavated by Helen O'Neil in 1963–5 following and during clearance of the site as part of agricultural improvements that were never completed (O'Neil 1966). Damage from bulldozing was extensive and the structure complicated, but O'Neil's own analysis and subsequent reviews by the present author (Darvill 1982, 60–1; Darvill & Grinsell 1989, 52) suggested three phases to the site: a small-scale settlement with a timber house; a pair of round barrows; and finally the construction of a long barrow incorporating the earlier round barrows with a single lateral chamber towards the western end (Figure 7.3). The eastern round barrow was about 11m in diameter and comprised a stone cairn with a dry-stone outer kerb and some evidence of an internal revetment wall. The chamber area was heavily disturbed but appeared to comprise a narrow passage opening from the east side of the mound with an irregular chamber at its western end. The overall appearance is close to the "trench chamber" round barrows defined by Kinnes and exemplified by Whitegrounds, North Yorkshire, and Black Beck, Cumbria (1979, 63), although it is a form that blurs into the more widely recognized category of simple passage grave (Boujot & Cassen 1993, 478) and might better be classified as such. Four pieces of human bone recovered from the eastern round barrow at Sale's Lot have been dated (Smith & Brickley 2006, table 4). Two pieces of cremated bone fairly well associated with the pre-barrow occupation were dated to 3907–3651 cal BC and 3634–3374 cal BC (WK-17192: 4958±40 BP and WK-17187: 4716±38 BP respectively) while pieces of unburnt long bone and temporal bone reasonably interpreted as relating to the use of the round barrow / passage grave returned dates of 3656–3385 cal BC (WK-17193: 4799±39 BP) and 3516–3103 cal BC (WK-17188: 4589±49 BP) respectively. The presence of human remains in pre-barrow contexts associated with occupation debris is attested at other sites in the Cotswolds (*cf.* Saville 1990, 21) and should occasion no surprise. Here at Sale's Lot occupation dating to *c.*3600 BC followed by a round barrow/simple passage grave at *c.*3500 BC accords with the available dated samples, and like Notgrove supports a short chronology model for a succession of activities at the site.

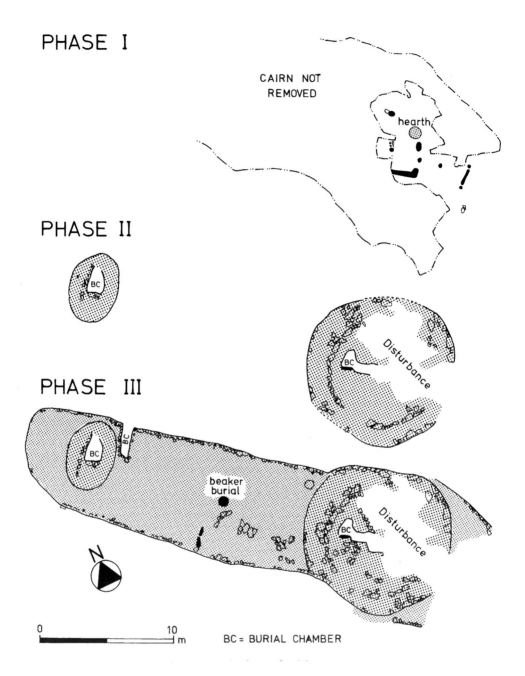

Figure 7.3: Provisional phasing for Sale's Lot long barrow, Gloucestershire (GLO 94). (After Darvill & Grinsell 1989)

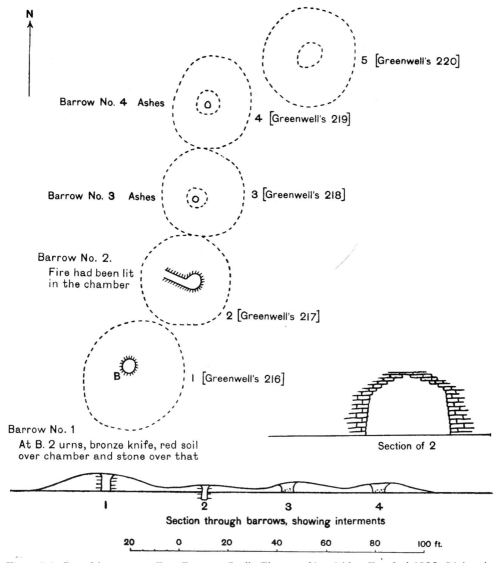

Figure 7.4: Round barrows on Cow Common, Swell, Gloucestershire. (After Crawford 1925, 91 based on surveys by Sir Henry Dryden, 13 October 1874)

The western round barrow, O'Neil's Grave 2 (1966, 20), was even more heavily disturbed than the eastern end, but appears to comprise a slightly ovoid mound about 4m east to west by 5m north to south. More or less in the centre was a slightly boat-shaped cist defined by drystone walling reminiscent of the central chamber in the better-preserved and somewhat larger Soldier's Grave at Frocester mentioned above (Clifford 1938; Kinnes 1979, 21). A few human teeth and a flint leaf-shaped arrowhead were found within Grave 2 at Sale's Lot; a single radiocarbon determination on a piece of long bone shaft gave a date of 3346–3026 cal BC (WK-17190: 4476±39 BP).

Cow Common Round, Swell (NGR: SP 1362633. GLO 23) was excavated by William Greenwell in 1874 and is one of a conjoined row of five barrows (Figure 7.4). Barrow 2 (Greenwell's 217) comprised a round mound *c*.12m in diameter with a partly subterranean central "beehive" chamber approached via a narrow passage leading into the mound from the northwest (Greenwell 1877, 447–52; Crawford 1925, 90–2). Heavily disturbed even before Greenwell's work the site may tentatively be classified as a "trench-chambered" round barrow (*cf*. Kinnes 1979, 63) or a simple passage grave.

Rather similar is Saltway Barn, Bibury (NGR: SP11510906. GLO 92) excavated by W. F. Grimes in 1939–40 in advance of works to build a war-time airfield (Grimes 1960, 5–40). The round barrow was constructed around a central rock-cut pit in which was a round chamber *c*.1.6m in diameter approached via a short passage opening from the south side of a rather irregular cairn *c*.11m east to west by 7m north to south that was constructed as a series of cells delimited by a rough kerb of drystone walling. The site had certainly been used by shepherds or farmers in the eighteenth century, but flint flakes and a few sherds of pottery in the floor of the chamber suggest the re-use of a much earlier construction. Like Cow Common, this site fits tolerably well into the "trench-chamber" type round barrows, especially as the chamber at Saltway Barn is partly subterranean.

A number of so-called "beehive chambers" in the Cotswolds have been suggested as possible Neolithic round barrows or simple passage graves, but none are very convincing and following comments made by Samuel Lysons (1865, 319–20) probably represent fairly modern shelters. The example at Ablington, Bibury, for example, is almost entirely subterranean (Passmore 1934), while those Cow Common long (Grimes 1960, 31) and Bevan's Quarry, Temple Guiting (O'Neil 1967, 27–8 and 39–40) are recent reuses of earlier monuments. Another possible early round barrow at Belas Knap long barrow (GLO 1) suggested by the present author (Darvill 1984, 87) on the basis of a "broken circle of stones" about 2.2m in diameter revealed by excavations in 1865 (Lawrence 1866) has been dismissed by Ian Kinnes (1992b, 97–8) citing unpublished drawings in the British Museum and must now be discounted.

DISCUSSION

Since 1979 the number of recognizably Neolithic round barrows in the Cotswolds has doubled to eight sites. These concentrate in the north Cotswolds and along the escarpment edge. Although three examples have associated radiocarbon dates placing them in the middle and later fourth millennium BC, the overall chronology of these monuments is weak. It is clear that some pre-date the construction of long barrows, although seemingly only by a short period best measured in decades rather than centuries. Significantly, however, the overall tradition of building round barrows in the Cotswolds is much longer-lived than the fashion for constructing and using long barrows that must now be seen as compressed within the four centuries following 3800 BC (Whittle *et al.* 2007), although some were probably re-opened later. By implication, round barrows must be seen as variously earlier than, contemporary with, and later than a series of other monument forms and burial traditions in the region, among them the long barrows already mentioned, portal dolmens, and oval barrows (Darvill 2004, 46–66). Some of these classes of monument may have an enduring currency like the round barrows themselves; others such as the long barrows were a short-lived fashion. Moreover, flat graves must increasingly be recognized as part of the overall mélange of burial traditions represented in the area and while the list of recorded examples presented by Kinnes (1979, 126–7) includes none from the Cotswolds that too has now changed. Excavations in advance of pipeline construction between Wormington and Tirley in 2000 revealed a pit-grave at Wormington Farm, Worcestershire (NGR: SO 372039). The grave was 2m long by 0.49m wide and 0.49m deep. It contained the fairly well-preserved skeleton of a female aged between 25 and 40 years, placed in a flexed position on her left side. The remains were radiocarbon dated to 3640–3376 cal BC (WK-15335: 4747±48 BP). Examination of the skeleton revealed that she had suffered from degenerative joint disease and had an oblique fracture to the right ulna. No grave goods were found, but there was a flint flake in the fill of the grave (Coleman *et al.* 2006, 29).

ACKNOWLEDGEMENTS

All radiocarbon dates cited in the text of this paper have been calibrated using OxCal v.4.0, using calibration curve Intcal04, and are expressed as age ranges at *c.*95% confidence limits (2σ) in calendar years BC. General dates are given as calendar years, centuries or millennia BC. Long barrows are referred to by their County Numbers (*e.g.* GLO 00) listed by Corcoran (1969, 277–88) with later additions listed by Darvill (2004, 244–9). Thanks to Martin Smith for comments concerning the human remains for these sites and Vanessa Constant for the preparation of the accompanying figures.

BIBLIOGRAPHY

Boujot, C. and Cassen, S. (1993) A pattern of evolution for the Neolithic funerary monuments of the west of France. *Antiquity* 67, 477–91.

Clifford, E. (1936) Notgrove long barrow, Gloucestershire. *Archaeologia* 86, 119–61.

Clifford, E. (1938) The Soldier's Grave, Frocester, Gloucestershire. *Proceedings of the Prehistoric Society* 4, 214-18.

Coleman, L., Hancocks, A. and Watts, M. (2006) *Excavations on the Wormington to Tirley Pipeline, 2000.* Cirencester, Cotswold Archaeology (Monograph 3).

Corcoran, J. X. W. P. (1969) The Cotswold-Severn Group. In T. G. E. Powell, J. X. W. P. Corcoran, F. Lynch and J. G. Scott, *Megalithic enquiries in the west of Britain,* 13–106 and 273–95. Liverpool, Liverpool University Press.

Crawford, O. G. S. (1925) *The long barrows of the Cotswolds.* Gloucester, John Bellows.

Darvill, T. (1982) *The megalithic chambered tombs of the Cotswold-Severn region.* Highworth, Vorda.

Darvill, T. (1984) Neolithic Gloucestershire. In A. Saville (ed.), *Archaeology in Gloucestershire: from the earliest hunters to the Industrial Age,* 80–112. Cheltenham, Cheltenham Art Gallery and Museums and the Bristol and Gloucestershire Archaeological Society.

Darvill, T. (2004) *Long barrows of the Cotswolds and surrounding areas.* Stroud, Tempus.

Darvill, T. (2006) Early prehistory. In N. Holbrook and J. Juřica (eds.), *Twenty-five years of archaeology in Gloucestershire. A review of new discoveries and new thinking in Gloucestershire, South Gloucestershire and Bristol 1979–2004.* 5–60. Kemble, Cotswold Archaeology (Bristol and Gloucestershire Archaeological Report 3).

Darvill, T. and Grinsell L. V. (1989) Gloucestershire barrows: supplement 1961–1988. *Transactions of the Bristol and Gloucestershire Archaeological Society* 107, 39–105.

Drinkwater, J. and Saville, A. (1984) The Bronze Age round barrows of Gloucestershire: a brief review. In A. Saville (ed.), *Archaeology in Gloucestershire: from the earliest hunters to the Industrial* Age, 128–39. Cheltenham, Cheltenham Art Gallery and Museums and the Bristol and Gloucestershire Archaeological Society.

Greenwell, W. (1877) *British Barrows. A record of the examination of sepulchral mounds in various parts of England.* Oxford, Clarendon Press.

Grimes, W. F. (1960) *Excavations on Defence Sites, 1939-45. Mainly Neolithic and Bronze Age.* London, HMSO Ministry of Works Archaeological Reports 3.

Kinnes, I. (1979) *Round barrows and ring-ditches in the British Neolithic.* London, British Museum (Occasional Paper 7).

Kinnes, I. (1992a) *Non-megalithic long barrows and allied structures in the British Neolithic.* London, British Museum (Occasional Paper 52).

Kinnes, I. (1992b) Balnagowan and after: the context of non-megalithic mortuary sites in Scotland. In N. Sharples and J. A. Sheridan (eds.), *Vessels for the ancestors: essays on the Neolithic of Britain and Ireland in honour of Audrey Henshall,* 83–103. Edinburgh, Edinburgh University Press.

Lawrence, W. L. (1866) Examination of a long barrow in Gloucestershire. *Proceedings of the Society of Antiquaries of London* (Series 2) 3, 275–82.

Lysons, S. (1865) *Our British ancestors.* Oxford, J & H Parker.

O'Neil, H. (1966) Sale's Lot long barrow, Withington, Gloucestershire 1962–1965. *Transactions of the Bristol and Gloucestershire Archaeological Society* 85, 5–35.

O'Neil, H. (1967) Bevan's Quarry round barrow, temple Guiting, Gloucestershire, 1964. *Transactions of the Bristol and Gloucestershire Archaeological Society* 86, 16–40.

O'Neil, H. and Grinsell, L. V. (1960) Gloucestershire Barrows. *Transactions of the Bristol and Gloucestershire Archaeological Society* 79, 3–149.

Passmore, A. D. (1934) A bee-hive chamber at Ablington, Gloucestershire. *Transactions of the Bristol and Gloucestershire Archaeological Society* 56, 95–8.

Roberts, A.J. (2010) A geophysical summary of Bucks Head Barrow, Cranham. *Glevensis* 42, 11–16.

Saville, A. (1990) *Hazleton North, Gloucestershire, 1979-82. The excavation of a Neolithic long cairn of the Cotswold-Severn group.* London, English Heritage Archaeological Report 13.

Smith, M. and Brickley, M. (2006) The date and sequence of use of Neolithic funerary monuments: new AMS dating evidence form the Cotswold-Severn region. *Oxford Journal of Archaeology* 25(4), 335–55.

Whittle, A., Barclay, A., Bayliss, A., McFadyen, L., Schulting, R. and Wysocki, M. (2007) Building for the dead: events, processes and changing worldviews from the thirty-eighth to the thirty-fourth centuries cal BC in southern Britain. *Cambridge Archaeological Journal* 17(1) Supplement, 123–47.

Chapter 8

Silbury Hill: A Monument in Motion

Jim Leary

INTRODUCTION

On the 29 May 2000 a hole 2.25m wide and 13m deep appeared on the top of Silbury Hill, the enormous earthen mound situated in the heart of the Marlborough Downs in Wiltshire and part of the Stonehenge, Avebury and Associated Sites World Heritage Site (Figure 8.1). Following a further collapse in the December of that year, the resulting crater was filled with polystyrene blocks as a temporary measure and a seismic survey undertaken in order to determine the overall condition of the hill. As part of these investigations a number of boreholes were drilled from the summit. Two of these boreholes encountered the tunnel that had been driven horizontally from the side of the mound to the centre in the 1960s, revealing that it had not been completely backfilled. After much public debate and scrutiny, a scheme for permanent remedial works was agreed; this involved re-opening the horizontal tunnel and filling it (as well as all other known voids) with chalk, to ensure the long term integrity of the monument.

This provided archaeologists with an opportunity to re-enter the mound and record and sample the various phases of construction in detail, and therefore an intensive programme of archaeological works was built into the overall conservation project. The main part of this work began in May 2007 and, inclusive of a small excavation on the summit as well as a watching brief during remedial work on the hillside, finished a year almost to the day later in May 2008. The majority of the 2007/8 work was directed by the present author and therefore this paper will focus on the internal structure of the mound; the new information about the construction process, as will be seen, has clearly influenced the interpretations outlined below. David Field undertook an earthwork survey of the mound in 2002, revealing much about its external shape and development, which is not discussed here (see Field, this volume Chapter 1); nor is the intensive environmental sampling programme managed by Gill Campbell. A monograph is currently in preparation which will set out all these works in full. A full dating programme is also in progress and the results are eagerly awaited; radiocarbon dates processed prior to the work described here and based on archived material as well as an antler fragment recovered from the summit in 2001 suggest that the mound was initially raised in the twenty-fourth century BC (Bayliss *et al.* 2007).

The hole that had opened up on the summit appeared to be a remnant of the earliest known major investigation into the mound; the sinking of a shaft, recorded as being about 2.5m square and 30m deep, from the top to the centre of the hill, and which was effected

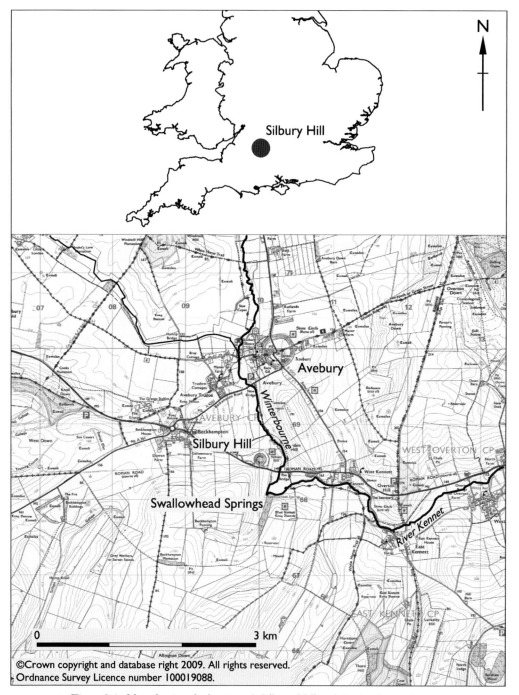

Figure 8.1: Map showing the location of Silbury Hill and the Swallowhead springs

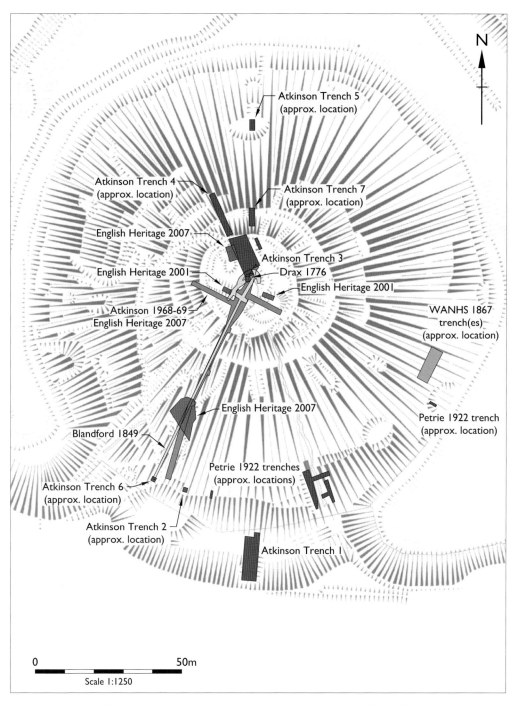

N

Atkinson Trench 5
(approx. location)

Atkinson Trench 4
(approx. location)

Atkinson Trench 7
(approx. location)

English Heritage 2007

Atkinson Trench 3
Drax 1776

English Heritage 2001

English Heritage 2001

WANHS 1867
trench(es)
(approx. location)

Atkinson 1968-69
English Heritage 2007

English Heritage 2007

Petrie 1922 trench
(approx. location)

Blandford 1849

Petrie 1922 trenches
(approx. locations)

Atkinson Trench 6
(approx. location)

Atkinson Trench 2
(approx. location)

Atkinson Trench 1

0　　　　　　　　　50m

Scale 1:1250

Figure 8.2: Location plan of the main investigations into Silbury Hill

by Edward Drax in 1776 (Figure 8.2). Little of this event was reported, although two letters written by Drax during his time at Silbury have recently been discovered and, once fully transcribed and analysed, may shed some light on this investigation (Edwards 2010). Intriguingly one of the letters alludes to (although is by no means explicit about) the presence of a central post represented by a vertical void, any evidence of which would have been removed by the shaft. It is unknown whether this shaft was ever backfilled. This investigation was followed in the summer of 1849 when Henry Blandford (assisted by Richard Falkner) drove a horizontal tunnel from the south side to the centre of the mound (Figure 8.2). This work was arranged by the Central Committee of the Archaeological Institute to coincide with the annual meeting arranged that particular year in Salisbury. Having reached the centre of the mound Blandford considered his work done, whereupon John Merewether, Dean of Hereford, decided the exploration should continue, but eventually he too abandoned the search, which continued even then under the Reverend John Bathurst Deane. This work was later commented on by Merewether and Charles Tucker (Merewether 1851; Tucker 1851). The tunnel, which was just under 1m wide and 2m high, was begun on the southwest side of the mound next to the westernmost causeway across the ditch. It was initially dug through natural solid chalk; however it inclined upwards and after 30m broke through the old ground surface. Thereafter the tunnel followed the old ground surface, keeping it about half a metre below the roof so that any grave cut could easily be seen (Field 2002; Whittle 1997). Towards the centre of the tunnel they encountered a conical heap of earth, chalk rubble, sarsen boulders and black soil, with preserved mosses. Also at this point the tunnel roof was raised by another 2m in order to investigate a hollow-sounding area; however the hollow sound disappeared on investigation (Merewether 1851). Side cuttings were made after Merewether decided to extend the tunnelling, as well as a semi-circular gallery on the western side which curved back to rejoin the Main Tunnel. A drawing of this event was made by William Lukis, which shows the line of the tunnel on a cross-section of the mound (Edwards 2002). The tunnel was closed in September 1849 but evidently not backfilled and Tucker recorded that where possible supports and props were withdrawn; he also reported that a wall of bricks was constructed over the entrance and the mound made good around it (Tucker 1851).

Other investigations followed, but the third major intervention was between 1968 and 1970, when Richard Atkinson, then professor at Cardiff University, supervised the excavation of a tunnel that followed a similar line to the 1849 tunnel, subsuming it for most of its length, and including two short lateral tunnels to the east and west (Figure 8.2). (It was this tunnel, including both laterals, that was re-opened in 2007). Atkinson also opened a number of trenches on the summit and sides of the hill, as well as the main ditch around Silbury. This work was instigated and sponsored by the BBC, overseen by David Attenborough, the then controller of BBC2, and televised as part of the BBC's Chronicle series. Despite thorough recording and sampling, the detail of this work was not published (although summaries can be found in Atkinson 1967; 1968; 1969a; 1969b; 1970; 1978) and much of the archive was subsequently lost. The fragmentary archive was, however, later published by Alasdair Whittle (Whittle 1997).

Just as he did at Stonehenge, Atkinson identified three main phases to the site: Silbury I: an organic mound with a low bank against it; Silbury II: a chalk mound with another low bank, and a quarry ditch; and Silbury III: the final mound that can be seen today, which

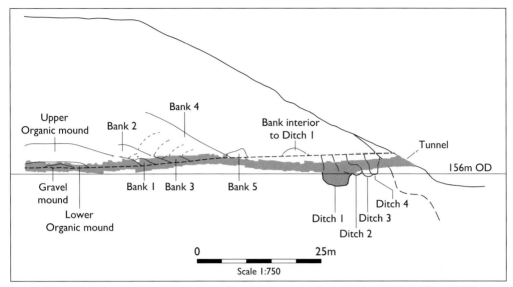

Figure 8.3: Schematic section of the prehistoric phases visible within the tunnel at Silbury Hill

buried the earlier ditch and was itself quarried from the surrounding ditch. As pointed out by Whittle (1997) (who identified at least eleven phases of activity from Atkinson's section drawings), this is a very simplistic model of the mound and the recent work, as outlined below, has shown it to be far more complex with numerous phases: the mound seemingly growing through many small events, rather than a few grand constructions (Figure 8.3).

THE ARCHAEOLOGICAL SEQUENCE

Although the geology of the region is chalk, a mantle of clay-with-flints (possibly eroded from upslope at some stage in the past) directly underlies Silbury Hill and was recorded in the tunnel sides. This clay deposit appears to be restricted to the footprint of the mound (discussed later).

The old ground surface

Evident throughout the majority of the tunnel sides, and sloping down to the north, is the old ground surface, which appears to extend under the entire mound (Colour Plate 1). Examination of local soils on clay-with-flints shows that this layer clearly does not represent a full soil profile, and some of the topsoil must have been removed at some stage prior to or during construction. This process could have been part of a deliberate act of ground preparation before monument construction began or could have simply occurredd as a natural part of the construction process.

Within the central part of the mound, a concentration of charcoal, charred hazel nutshell fragments and other charred plant remains, as well as two pig or wild boar teeth were recorded within a small, defined area of the upper part of the old ground surface, and may well indicate the fragmentary remains of a hearth. Small quantities of flint micro-debitage across the old ground surface indicate some, but not extensive, knapping had occurred prior to or during the initial phases of the monument (Barry Bishop pers. comm.).

The Gravel Mound

The first clear evidence for construction activity is a low, fairly unimpressive, gravel mound overlying the old ground surface in the centre; it measured just less than a metre high and nearly 10 metres in diameter (Figure 8.3 and Colour Plate 1). The material used for this mound was Pleistocene gravels, suggesting that people would have had to quarry the material or found it exposed in a river valley, for example the side of the River Kennet; either way, it was clearly very deliberately imported and used here. Environmental evidence suggests that the material was extracted from an open grassland environment. As became abundantly clear to us in the tunnel, once the loose Gravel Mound was exposed, it collapsed fairly rapidly – this was clearly not lost on the people constructing the mound, and they may have strengthened the sides with thin deposits of topsoil and subsoil.

The Lower Organic Mound

Subsequently, a series of layers of topsoil, subsoil and turf, perhaps representing basket loads of material, were dumped over the Gravel Mound, forming a larger mound (just over a metre high, and over 16 metres in diameter), although it would have still been relatively inconspicuous in the landscape (Figure 8.3 and Colour Plate 1). A stakehole recorded on the edge of these deposits can be included with the stakeholes recorded during Atkinson's work, which are likely to be part of a sequence of stakes demarcating the edge of this Lower Organic Mound. The majority of material for this mound had probably derived from the immediate locality, as it had been removed from above a clay-with-flints geology, and perhaps even represented the material stripped away prior to construction of the Gravel Mound. This phase of activity is likely to have occurred soon after the Gravel Mound had been constructed, as indicated by the freshness of the snail shells recovered from the Gravel Mound, which suggests that they had been rapidly buried (Paul Davies, pers. comm.).

A few metres away from this central mound and overlying the old ground surface were two further, much smaller, organic mounds. They stood only half a metre high, but were clearly purposefully constructed, and one was even separated from the Lower Organic Mound by a feature interpreted as a small, possibly interrupted, gully. Environmental samples from this mini-mound recovered plant remains associated with woodland or scrub, such as yew berries, sloe stones, uncharred hazel nutshell fragments and bramble seeds (Gill Campbell pers. comm.). Well-preserved insect remains were recovered in abundance from this feature, and they suggest that it may contain a component of gathered organic material. It is clear, therefore, that the earliest phases of Silbury Hill do not simply consist of one mound – but a number of mounds, becoming consolidated into a single monument only later.

Pits

At this point mound creation stopped, albeit perhaps only briefly, since two pits were recorded cutting into the top of the Lower Organic Mound (Colour Plate 2). Both were around a metre in diameter and over half a metre deep, and were largely devoid of finds; a few small pieces of animal bone and some evidence for flint knapping, with one pit producing a number of larger flakes and the other a relatively large collection of micro-debitage. If these collections of flint were deliberately dumped into the pits, they could indicate a degree of selection in what was being deposited. One pit also contained an army of worker ants, signifying the inclusion, perhaps inadvertently, of a turf containing an ant nest during backfilling (Mark Robinson pers. comm.).

Upper Organic Mound

Mound building continued, and the pits and Lower Organic Mound became sealed under a series of interleaved layers of different material, comprising a mix of topsoil and subsoil chiefly from soils that had developed over chalk (and therefore distinct from the Lower Organic Mound), as well as basket loads of chalk, clay, gravel and turf (Figure 8.3 and Colour Plate 3). Together these layers formed a mound perhaps as high as 5m or 6m (continuing above the tunnel) with an estimated diameter of 35m (continuing beyond the end of the tunnel). Also included within the Upper Organic Mound were a number of naturally rounded and unmodified sarsen stones which had clearly been deliberately incorporated within the mound as part of the mound construction, rather than as any sort of setting on top or around it.

Ditch and banks

The Upper Organic Mound was then surrounded by at least five chalk banks that presumably formed rings around it; each new ring expanding the monument outward by a few more metres (Figure 8.3). The tops of two of the banks (Bank 2 and Bank 4) were not seen and therefore could have continued over the Upper Organic Mound, covering it entirely; Banks 1, 3, and 5, however, were much smaller (*c.*1.5m high).

Surrounding all this activity, at some 36m from the edge of the Upper Organic Mound, and recorded just inside the tunnel entrance, was a large ditch and internal bank; the ditch perhaps the quarry for the banks (Figure 8.3). By excavating a narrow slot through the tunnel floor a section through the lower fills of this ditch, down to the base, was visible. This ditch was large; over 6.5m deep and 6m in width and assuming it was circular in plan, it would have formed an enclosure a little over 100m in diameter. It is not clear whether this was dug before or after the Upper Organic Mound, although presumably, if the chalk was used to build the banks, afterwards. The ditch may not have been continuous since the base of it sloped up on the western side of the area investigated, as if coming to an abrupt end. This can be interpreted either as an entrance corresponding to a similar break in the external ditch (the causeway) or, as with other Neolithic enclosures on chalk, a continuous ditch that had been cut in small, connected sections. The parallels that spring immediately to mind are Stonehenge and Flagstones (but also see others in the discussion on formative henges by Burrow, this volume Chapter 11). This buried ditch and internal bank are important features and we should think of at least some of the earlier phases of Silbury as an enclosure – an open, accessible and perhaps public arena; the antithesis of our classic understanding of the monument as a closed and exclusive space (Colour Plate 4).

Activity at the site continued – however the tunnel dips down through these later phases of activity, below the old ground level, and as such, we no longer see the mound in the tunnel sides. What is clear, however, is that it is not simply one single, homogenous phase, but a series of complex phases; the mound growing in size incrementally. Examination of the buried ditch section would seem to support this: as the hill expanded outwards,

that it had a function, or even that the Neolithic inhabitants drew a distinction between it and other features in the landscape.

By focussing on this process of creation (the formation process), we can see the mutability of the mound as important; the final form being secondary to that process: perhaps nothing more than the frozen state it was left in after that activity stopped (of course when later generations exapted and adapted the hill, its appearance changed again: a process that continues to happen right up to the modern day). In this way we see Silbury as a monument that grew; it developed out of a series of ceremonies over time but not to any pre-conceived plan. It emerged, like a living organism, from within the landscape, rather than a cultural artefact that was grafted on to it (Ingold, this volume Chapter 15). It materialised, developed, and grew into maturity; it had a past, a present and a future.

It is true that much of the material that made up Silbury could be found from the general locality, but there does seem to have been a degree of deliberate selection of materials. For example the material used to construct the Gravel Mound had been imported on to the site, whilst the majority of soil that made up the Lower Organic Mound was derived from over the clay-with-flints geology, whereas the Upper Organic Mound comprised, amongst other material, topsoil and subsoil largely derived from over chalk. Further, the soil used in one of the mini-mounds seems to have come from a woodland setting, contrasting with the grassland setting from which the Lower and Upper Organic Mound material was derived. In terms of visual perception these dark organic mounds all contrast starkly with the underlying yellow gravels used in the Gravel Mound, as well as the overlying chalk phases. Large, heavy sarsen boulders had also been incorporated into the Upper Organic Mound as well as the final chalk phases recorded on the summit, where they were also associated with fragments of antler pick. Given their weight the inclusion of sarsen boulders implies a certain motivation for their use. They were not on display in any way; indeed one would have had to be present during the construction to know that they had been used at all.

Silbury Hill was made out of the very stuff the inhabitants walked on and were surrounded by – chalk, clay, topsoil, turf, even sarsen boulders; a variety of local materials, each deliberately selected and used in a particular context. However, it was not made by people transforming this material into a monument (*contra.* Cummings 2002); it was not imposed upon the landscape, and its form was not given in advance. The form of the monument was generated by the pattern of movements of the people and the local material, and perhaps it was the rhythmic repetition of that movement that gave rise to the regularity of form – the roundness of it. To put it another way: the regularity of Silbury's form embodies the regularity of the movements (the ceremonies) that created it (James 2003; Whittle 2005). This is, incidentally, the exact opposite of the static, disinterested museum artefact that it is preserved as today: our constant attempts to cleanse it of its recent past and maintain it in some sort of idealised Neolithic state ignore the fact that it always has been a monument in motion.

It is worth also considering here the enclosure ditch buried under the final phases: there is a tacit acknowledgement in the literature that ditches around mounds represent quarry ditches and are therefore secondary in importance to the mounds; by-products of the main activity (although see Ashbee 2004; Nowakowski 2007). However at Silbury the ditch recorded in the tunnel was anything but functional (at least in a practical sense):

the chalk removed during the initial cut may have been used in the construction, but after that it was rapidly (as indicated by the unweathered sides) backfilled using as much chalk again (a deliberate process as shown by the use of small revetting walls to assist the backfilling), and then re-cut, not just once but another three times (the new profile cutting through the backfill of the previous cut). This highlights that the ditch had greater significance than usually ascribed to it. Whilst the external ditch, if one could imagine it empty of four and a half millennia of infill, is every bit as monumental as the mound itself. In a similar but inverted way, Neolithic flint mine shafts are considered the focus of activity at flint mine sites; whereas the mounds alongside them are described in functional terms as spoil heaps, a by-product of the main activity. By suggesting that we should hold ditches (below-ground world) in similar esteem to their associated mounds (above-ground world), perhaps we should also value flint mine mounds (above-ground world) alongside the shafts (below-ground world), or perhaps it is the combination of the two that was important.

LOCATION

It is important to remember that Silbury was set in a landscape saturated with the past; overlooked by the earlier Neolithic monuments of Windmill Hill and West Kennet long barrow, whilst also set within a complex of contemporary and near contemporary monuments. As we have seen, a considerable amount of activity may also have taken place on the site prior to the development of the monument. In other words it was already a special place.

Silbury Hill sits on the toe of a spur of chalk protruding from the southern slope of the Kennet Valley onto the valley floor of the River Kennet, set low within a natural bowl. The low-lying position of the monument and the fact it is surrounded by high areas precludes the desire for height as the main interpretation. It clearly occupies a liminal zone; the chalk spur it sits on representing the edge of the dry chalk upland penetrating into the wetter lowland area. Further, the geology is unusual in the immediate area of Silbury: overlying the chalk is a mantle of clay-with-flints, which is normally found on higher areas of the chalk (usually capping interfluves), but in this locality may have been eroded downslope in the distant past (Canti 2009). This unusual geological setting is unlikely to have been lost on the Neolithic inhabitants and may have been of some significance for the siting of the activity that created the mound.

To the south of Silbury Hill are the Swallowhead springs, and at this point the small and seasonal Winterbourne, which flows north to south just to the east of the monument, changes direction and size and becomes the River Kennet. The monument was positioned at a low point in the landscape adjacent to rivers and springs, and, therefore, clearly associated with water. Indeed, the so-called ditch extension with its large square end may even have been a monumentalised spring head (Barry Bishop pers. comm.). In such a setting, the huge external ditch must surely have been filled with standing water for much or all of the year, reflecting the inverted image of the mound (Colour Plate 7). The economic impact of water is, of course, implicit, and its life-giving properties must undoubtedly have had enormous importance. But the special qualities of water may also have had cosmological significance. As Colin Richards has pointed out (Richards 1996a and 1996b), water represents a potent metaphor – a metaphor for movement and journeying, as well as carrying notions of purity. Richards has also pointed out that rivers, streams and lakes create physical boundaries, and divide the world. In this sense, the standing water in the ditch around the monument could be seen as a boundary or a transition, perhaps embodying aspects of purification.

It may be useful to pursue this connection to water further. Silbury is situated at the very head of the River Kennet and although the post-glacial hydrology of the upper Kennet Valley is far from clear, it could be that this fact is of considerable importance. Today we describe the River Kennet as a tributary of the River Thames; the latter a river we believe from the artefacts and remains recovered from it to have had significant ritual importance throughout much of the prehistoric period (Bradley & Gordon 1988; Bradley 1990; Ehrenberg 1980; Field 1989; York 2002). One could argue however that rather than being a tributary flowing into another river, the River Kennet may have been part of the main river (Figure 8.5). It is far more logical to see the River Kennet, which flows west to east, and the similarly aligned part of the Thames as one river; the north-south part of the Thames, the section that flows through Oxford, is a more likely candidate as the tributary (Barry Bishop pers. comm.). Silbury Hill is arguably therefore located at the very point this sacred river first flows from the ground; the place that later became Silbury Hill marked this point, and over time, as the mound developed, it would have became an important visual point of reference.

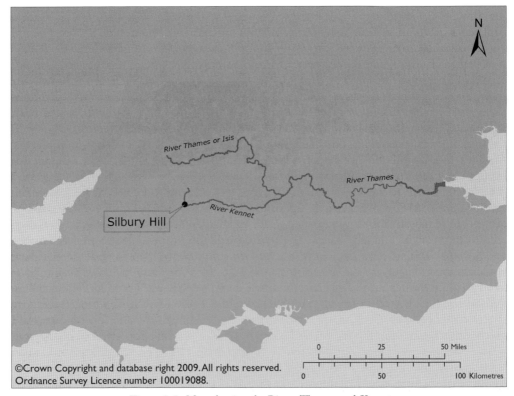

Figure 8.5: Map showing the Rivers Thames and Kennet

CONCLUSIONS

This paper has set out a summary of the sequence recorded during the 2007/8 investigations at Silbury Hill. It has identified numerous phases of the mound, suggesting that the archaeological stratigraphic sequence is considerably more complex than previously thought; the mound growing through many small events, rather than a few grand statements, and that it is no longer appropriate to use the terms Silbury I, II or III. This paper has also highlighted that previous interpretations have focussed on the final form of the mound, which implies that it was constructed to a particular size and shape. However, in the above discussion I suggest that the various phases of Silbury emphasise the protean nature of the monument, and I therefore propose that discussions should now focus on the formation process rather than the final form. This paper has also considered the location of Silbury, concluding that there is a clear association with the rivers and springs it lies alongside.

ACKNOWLEDGEMENTS

I am very grateful to all my colleagues involved in the successful completion of the fieldwork, with special thanks to the archaeologists, miners and engineers who worked in uniquely difficult conditions within the tunnel. I would also like to take this opportunity to thank my colleagues for their continued assistance throughout the post-excavation work. The environmental elements of the project are being managed by Gill Campbell who is also analysing the plant remains, whilst the finds are being managed by Nicola Hembrey and Kayt Brown. Matt Canti is analysing the old ground surface, Paul Davies the land snails, Mark Robinson the insects, Barry Bishop the flint work, Fay Worley and Ian Riddler the antler, and Josh Pollard the sarsen stones; and I thank each and every one of them for allowing me to use their unpublished work here. I would also like to thank Brian Edwards for sharing research on the antiquarian background to the mound and particularly the discovery of the Drax letters. Fachtna McAvoy managed the project between 2000 and 2007, including the first few weeks of fieldwork in 2007. I am very grateful to Barry Bishop for discussions about the rivers Kennet and Thames; he alone made the connection between the two as discussed here. Many thanks to Dave Field, Tim Darvill, Jonathan Last, Fay Worley, Gill Campbell, Matt Canti and Josh Pollard for reading and commenting on this paper. Eddie Lyons produced Figures 8.1–8.4; Andrew Lowerre produced Figure 8.5; James Davies took Colour Plate 7; and Judith Dobie produced Colour plate 4.

BIBLIOGRAPHY

Ashbee, P. (2004) Early ditches: their forms and infills. In R. Cleal and J. Pollard (eds.) *Monuments and Material Culture. Papers in honour of Avebury archaeologists: Isobel Smith*. Salisbury, Hobnob Press.
Atkinson, R. J. C. (1967) Silbury Hill. *Antiquity* 41, 259–62
Atkinson, R. J. C. (1968) *Silbury Hill*. London, BBC.
Atkinson, R. J. C. (1969a) A season at Silbury. *The Listener*, 16 January.
Atkinson, R. J. C. (1969b) The date of Silbury Hill. *Antiquity* 43, 216.
Atkinson, R. J. C. (1970) Silbury Hill, 1969–70. *Antiquity* 44, 313–4.
Atkinson, R. J. C. (1978) Silbury Hill. In R. Sutcliffe (ed.), *Chronicle*, 159–73. London, BBC.
Barrett, J. (1994) *Fragments from antiquity. An archaeology of social life in Britain, 2900–1200 BC*. Oxford, Blackwell Publishers.

Bayliss, A., McAvoy, F. and Whittle, A. (2007) The world recreated: redating Silbury Hill in its monumental landscape. *Antiquity* 81, 26–53.

Bradley, R. (1990) *The passage of arms. An archaeological analysis of prehistoric hoards and votive deposits.* Cambridge, Cambridge University Press.

Bradley, R., and Gordon, K. (1988) Human skulls from the River Thames, their dating and significance. *Antiquity* 62, 503–509.

Canti, M. G. (2009) Geoarchaeological studies associated with remedial measures at Silbury Hill, Wiltshire, UK. *Catena*, DOI:10.1016/j.catena.2009.02.008Canti.

Cummings, V. (2002) Experiencing texture and transformation in the British Neolithic. *Oxford Journal of Archaeology* 21(3), 249–261.

Edwards, B. (2002) A missing drawing and an overlooked text: Silbury Hill archive finds. *Wiltshire Archaeological and Natural History Magazine* 95, 89–92.

Edwards, B. (2010) Silbury Hill: Edward Drax and the Excavations of 1776. *Wiltshire Archaeological and Natural History Magazine* 103, 257–68.

Ehrenberg, M. (1980) The occurrence of Bronze Age metalwork in the Thames: an investigation. *Transactions of the London and Middlesex Archaeological Society* 31, 1–15.

Field, D. (2002) *The investigation and analytical survey of Silbury Hill.* Archaeological Investigation Report Series, AI/22/2002, London, English Heritage (unpublished report).

Field, D. (1989) Tranchet axes and Thames picks: Mesolithic core-tools from the West London Thames. *Transactions of the London and Middlesex Archaeological Society* 40, 1–46.

Ingold, T. (2000) *The perception of the environment. Essays in livelihood, dwelling and skill.* London, Routledge.

James, W. (2003) *The ceremonial animal. A new portrait of anthropology.* Oxford, Oxford University Press.

Keiller, A. (1939) Avebury. Summary of excavations, 1937 and 1938. *Antiquity*, June.

Merewether, J. (1851) *The examination of Silbury Hill in July and August 1849.* Memoirs Illustrative of the History and Antiquities of Wiltshire and the City of Salisbury, 73–81. London, Archaeological Institute of Great Britain and Ireland.

Nowakowski, J., A. (2007) Digging deeper into barrow ditches: investigating the making of early Bronze Age memories in Cornwall. In J. Last (ed.) *Beyond the grave: new perspectives on barrows*, 92–113. Oxford, Oxbow Books.

Renfrew, C. (1973) Monuments, Mobilization and Social Organization in Neolithic Wessex. In C. Renfrew (ed.), *The Explanation of Culture Change: Models in Prehistory*, 539–58. London, Duckworth.

Richards C. (1996a) Monuments as landscape: creating the centre of the world in Late Neolithic Orkney. *World Archaeology* 28(2), 190–208.

Richards C. (1996b) Henges and water: towards an elemental understanding of monumentality and landscape in late Neolithic Britain. *Journal of Material Culture* 1(3), 313–36.

Tucker, C. (1851) *Report of the examination of Silbury Hill. Memoirs Illustrative of the History and Antiquities of Wiltshire and the City of Salisbury.* Proceedings of the Meeting of the Archaeological Institute at Salisbury 1849, Archaeological Institute of Great Britain and Ireland.

Wainwright, G. (1971) The Excavation of a Late Neolithic Enclosure at Marden, Wiltshire. *The Antiquaries Journal* 57, 177–239.

Whittle, A. (1997) *Sacred mound, holy rings. Silbury Hill and the West Kennet palisade enclosures: a later Neolithic complex in north Wiltshire.* Oxford, Oxbow Books (Monograph 74).

Whittle, A. (2005) Lived experience in the early Neolithic of the Great Hungarian Plain. In D. Bailey, A. Whittle and V. Cummings (eds.), *Unsettling the Neolithic.* Oxford, Oxbow Books.

York, J. (2002) The life cycle of Bronze Age metalwork from the Thames. *Oxford Journal of Archaeology* 21(1), 77–92.

Chapter 9

The Brood of Silbury? A Remote Look at Some Other Sizeable Wessex Mounds

Martyn Barber, Helen Winton, Cathy Stoertz, Ed Carpenter and Louise Martin

As the recent work at both Silbury Hill and Durrington Walls has shown, renewed investigation of apparently well-known sites has the potential to throw up plenty of surprises, something always worth bearing in mind when seeking to understand individual monuments or even areas of landscape on the basis of past excavations, no matter how recent they may seem. It is not unusual to find, for example, that those excavations were small in scale, while the choice of where to dig may have been determined by research questions very different to those that might be posed today. Meanwhile, systematic survey of the broader environs of a site is a relatively recent phenomenon.

This paper is concerned with three substantial round mounds of definite or possible Neolithic date – the Great Barrow at Knowlton, and Conquer Barrow at Mount Pleasant, both in Dorset, plus the Hatfield Barrow, Marden, Wiltshire – how the analysis of aerial photographs can assist in understanding them, and in the case of the latter how geophysical prospection can add to the picture. Each of these mounds is also associated with one or more henges. This is, of course, a category of monument that is itself beset with difficulties, something that is not explored here. The use of the term "henge" in this paper is not intended to imply anything beyond the fact that the enclosures concerned each possesses a bank with internal ditch, and a date of construction and initial use somewhere in the middle centuries of the third millennium BC (probably).

It may seem odd to talk of analysing large round barrows from the air, but in none of the cases discussed here was the mound itself the main focus of attention. In fact, each of the three mapping projects had rather different origins. The Knowlton landscape was mapped at the request of Bournemouth University's archaeology department in order to help provide a broader landscape context for the excavations they were undertaking within the Knowlton complex (Gale in prep.). Mount Pleasant and, by default, Conquer Barrow, attracted attention following the recognition of previously unrecognised cropmark features photographed as part of English Heritage's annual reconnaissance programme. The Marden survey, meanwhile – still in progress at the time of writing – is part of a multi-disciplinary assault on the henge and its environs, stimulated initially by conservation and management concerns.

An important matter that is still all too often overlooked when dealing with aerial photographs is the need to examine every available and accessible photograph. In England, for example, any survey that ignores the collections of the National Monuments Record in Swindon, or the Unit for Landscape Modelling (formerly CUCAP), Cambridge, is of limited value. The same applies to any survey that concentrates on those two archives to the exclusion of relevant local collections, such as those held by or accessible through the relevant Historic Environment Record or local authority planning department. These points should be more than evident from the cases discussed here. For example, the Hatfield Barrow at Marden only appears clearly on aerial photographs taken in the summer of 1976, while important detail at Mount Pleasant has only appeared on obliques taken by Dorset-based photographer Francesca Radcliffe during the 1990s. There is no such thing as a "representative sample" of aerial photographs (*contra.* Challis *et al.* 2008).

Similarly, there is never one single photograph that captures everything. Single images packed with cropmarks tend to be favoured for illustration, but there will always be something missing. The maps produced in the course of projects such as that focused on Marden represent the compilation of archaeological detail identified on hundreds, and more usually thousands, of vertical and oblique photographs taken since the early decades of the twentieth century. As much detail, if not more, comes from analysis of historic photographs as is recorded from new reconnaissance coverage, although the latter continues to make significant contributions.

Lidar is discussed only under Marden. Although its archaeological potential had been recognised by the time of the Knowlton and Mount Pleasant surveys, it was not practicable to make use of it for either project. For Marden, as is the case for a number of other current survey projects undertaken within or on behalf of English Heritage, lidar data is used alongside the aerial photographs. Aerial photography is, of course, essential to the interpretation of potential features identified through analysis of lidar data. Lidar is proving an invaluable tool, but its value lies in complementing rather than replacing aerial photography. Much that can be recorded by lidar has already been captured on easily accessible aerial photographs, while there is also much that is simply beyond the reach of lidar – too many cropmark sites lack sufficient residual height or depth to be captured by the technique, while too many sites recorded from historic aerial photographs are no longer around for lidar to find.

THE MOUNDS

Apart from proximity to henges, the one thing that these three examples – Great Barrow, Hatfield Barrow and Conquer Barrow – have in common is size. None of them approaches the scale of the final phase of Silbury Hill, of course, although all are comparable with earlier phases of that monument. In addition, all three of the mounds have acquired, over the years, an association with the late Neolithic – although only Conquer Barrow has produced dating evidence – and the amount of exploration at each has been minimal. Hatfield Barrow was last dug into over two hundred years ago, after which it collapsed, and its exact position has only recently been re-established (see below). Some brief examination of the outer ditch of the Great Barrow at Knowlton occurred in 1958, but nothing datable was found, nor was a complete section obtained (Field 1962). The ditch around Conquer Barrow was briefly examined in 1971 by Geoffrey Wainwright. A few years earlier at Marden, Wainwright displayed little interest in the Hatfield Barrow beyond relocating it, something he felt had been achieved by Tony Clark's geophysical survey. Conquer Barrow was clearly not on the agenda when the Mount Pleasant campaign began, the limited trenching only happening because a ditch terminal turned up in one of the trenches dug to examine the henge earthworks. One conclusion that could be drawn from a reading of Wainwright's Mount Pleasant report is that the presence of a ditch around the Conquer Barrow mound was unexpected. Indeed, as we shall see, arguing that the mound was built onto the henge bank is a fair enough hypothesis, but is also one that runs into trouble when trying to account for the surrounding ditch.

In all three cases, other round barrows are present in the immediate vicinity, usually in plough-levelled form and visible solely as cropmark ring-ditches. There is, of course, no reason to presume that none of these had late Neolithic (or even earlier) origins, but that is something that could be determined only by excavation, and only then if the relevant deposits have survived centuries, and perhaps millennia, of ploughing. Distinguishing a Neolithic barrow from a Bronze Age one is not possible on cropmark evidence alone.

THE GREAT BARROW, KNOWLTON, DORSET

By Cathy Stoertz

The Great Barrow at Knowlton is one of the few surviving earthworks within a large multi-period monument complex – comprising four henges and over 170 round barrows – which occupies west- and northwest-facing slopes overlooking the River Allen on the eastern fringes of Cranborne Chase (Colour Plate 8). It may be the largest round barrow in Dorset (Gale 2003, 60), although this depends on the assumption that Conquer Barrow was built on to the bank of the Mount Pleasant henge (see below). The Great Barrow survives as a tree-covered mound about 135ft (*c.*41m) in diameter and about 21ft (*c.*6.4m) high (RCHME 1975, 116) (Colour Plate 9). The barrow's size and its similarity to other large mounds associated with henges in Wessex suggest that it may be later Neolithic in origin (Barrett *et al.* 1991, 108), although this proposed date has not been demonstrated by excavation. If it were later Neolithic, the Great Barrow could be seen as a link between the henge group and the extensive Bronze Age barrow cemeteries, occupying a place at the end of one tradition and the beginning of another (Barrett *et al.* 1991, 108).

The Great Barrow is enclosed by two filled-in ditches, the outermost of which is 120m in diameter and segmented or causewayed in a manner strongly reminiscent of a henge. It is remarkably similar in appearance and size to the surviving earthwork of the Church Circle henge, which lies immediately to the west. The relationship between the barrow mound, its outer ditch and the henges poses unresolved questions, but it seems possible that at least one phase of the Great Barrow is Neolithic.

The Church Circle, at the centre of the henge complex, is the best preserved of the group. The other henges, the South Circle, the North Circle and the Old Churchyard, have been severely abraded by ploughing, leaving aerial photographs to provide the best visual evidence for once substantial features.

Near the henge group are several small features which may also have belonged to the Neolithic ritual landscape. A possible long barrow has been recorded within a circular ditch. This feature is similar to a site at Huggate, on the Yorkshire Wolds (SE 871576), which the Ordnance Survey map depicted as a round barrow. When the mound was eroded by ploughing, the cropmark which formed over its remains revealed a pair of parallel ditches, suggesting that a long barrow lay beneath, or had been converted into, the round barrow (Stoertz 1997, 23 and fig. 8).

Two oval enclosures which resemble mortuary enclosures (Malim 1999; Loveday & Petchey 1982) are located to the north and northeast of the Knowlton henge group; a subrectangular enclosure, also to the northeast of the henges, has been interpreted as a third possible mortuary enclosure. The aerial photographic evidence does not indicate whether any of these enclosures was ever covered by a mound or associated with an external or internal bank.

The Bronze Age at Knowlton is represented by round barrows – over 170 were recorded by aerial photographic survey (including the Great Barrow and the round barrow with internal ditch pair described above), and it is likely that there were more in antiquity. The most recent aerial photographic evidence suggests that, although the round barrows are commonly discussed in terms of Northern, Central, and Southern cemeteries, their distribution along the slopes above the River Allen more nearly represents a single large group. Very few of the round barrows exhibit any surface relief – the vast majority have been identified on aerial photographs by the characteristic ring-ditches which form when overlying vegetation responds to higher soil moisture in a barrow's perimeter ditch. Occasionally, differential soil moisture has also made it possible to detect vestiges of the mounds themselves.

At the edges of the round barrow cemeteries are several clusters of roughly circular "positive" cropmarks (*maculae* or splodges) which, normally, would be interpreted as excavated features or circular hollows possibly representing pond barrows. Although pond barrows are known on Cranborne Chase, and one has been excavated 5.5km to the north at Down Farm (Barrett *et al.* 1991, 128-38), it seems unusual to find so many in one place. One possible explanation for the *maculae* is that some form of reversal of the cropmark has taken place, and either the features represent solidly packed mound material, or barrow ditches and platforms have reacted to drought stress in the same way. However, a more likely interpretation of the solid circles has emerged at High Lea Farm, less than 4km to the southwest along the River Allen. There, as at Knowlton, aerial photographs taken in 1989 recorded both solid circular features and open ring-ditches showing as positive cropmarks. Geophysical survey and trial excavation by Bournemouth University's School of Conservation Sciences in 2002–3 has indicated that, while the open ring-ditches represent the remains of round barrows, the *maculae* are most likely to have been caused by natural features, known as dolines or sinkholes, in the underlying chalk (Gale *et al.* 2004, 162–3 and fig. 21).

Among the round barrows are seventy-six ring-ditches or mounds with diameters of 15m or less. Most appear in two main clusters, within the Northern and Southern barrow cemeteries, while a third, smaller, group lies adjacent to the main henge complex. In the Northern and Southern cemeteries, the small barrows are arranged in tightly spaced groups and, particularly in the Southern cemetery, they appear to have been inserted into spaces between larger round barrows, suggesting a later date than the larger barrows. Similar very small round barrows have been recorded elsewhere in England in Bronze Age, Iron Age, Roman and early medieval contexts. Support for post-Bronze Age date at Knowlton may perhaps be derived from the presence in the vicinity of possible Iron Age square barrows – in one of the square barrow cemeteries at Garton Slack, on the Yorkshire Wolds, very small round barrows represented a very late phase of the burial rite (Stead 1991, 17; Stoertz 1997, 39).

During the Iron Age and Roman periods, the monumental landscape of Neolithic and Bronze Age Knowlton appears to have given way to one of primarily agricultural and domestic use. Several long linear features form a rough grid pattern probably representing a series of land divisions or boundaries, elements of which appear to have been aligned on the henges. At several points, the course of a linear feature crosses over a round barrow, suggesting that construction of the boundaries post-dates that of the barrows and larger monuments. A compact group of rectangular fields lies immediately to the south of, and is apparently bounded by, a linear feature which abuts the South Circle. The field system appears to fit broadly within the grid pattern of the presumed Iron Age or Roman boundaries, and to respect the positions of several large round barrows. To the southeast is a group of fragmentary rectilinear enclosures or fields, associated with a trackway and two possible square barrows.

Much later, in the twelfth century AD, a church was constructed at the centre of the Church Circle. Its ruins stand within a sub-rectangular enclosure defined by a slight bank which fits closely within the inner ditch of the henge. This enclosure appears to be a churchyard boundary, and is probably medieval in date, but could be later.

A DIFFICULT RELATIONSHIP: CONQUER BARROW AND MOUNT PLEASANT

By Martyn Barber

Conquer Barrow sits immediately outside and to the west of the large "henge enclosure" known as Mount Pleasant, which is located on the eastern edge of modern Dorchester, Dorset (Figure 9.1). The mound's flat summit, 7m in diameter, stands approximately 8m above the surrounding ground surface. The base of the mound is around 30m in diameter (RCHME 1970, 504). The mound has an interesting relationship with the henge. As Mike Pitts put it, "Conquer Barrow at first sight appears to stand on the henge bank" (Pitts 2000, 280). In fact, the general consensus until quite recently has been that the mound was indeed built onto the enclosure's outer bank, although their relationship has never been explored below the turf.

Mount Pleasant was the focus of limited excavations led by Geoffrey Wainwright in 1970–71, part of a programme of work that also took in the contemporary earthwork henge enclosures at Marden and Durrington Walls, both in Wiltshire. The investigation of Conquer Barrow and its relationship to the earthwork enclosure was not among Wainwright's initial objectives (Wainwright 1979, 5). Like others before him, he saw the mound as having been built onto the enclosure bank. Indeed, it was this apparent relationship which had led to O. G. S. Crawford suggesting the possibility of a Neolithic date for Mount Pleasant in the first place (Piggott & Piggott 1939, 158; Crawford 1953, 169). Judging by the lack of discussion in his final report, Wainwright presumably saw Conquer Barrow as a fairly unproblematic, albeit larger than normal, Bronze Age round barrow.

While examining the henge's western entrance in 1970, one of Wainwright's trenches unexpectedly encountered a ditch terminal in the gap between the enclosure's inner ditch and outer bank. Auguring and limited trenching led to further ditch segments being examined, resulting in the conclusion that the Conquer Barrow mound was surrounded by a

Figure 9.1: An RAF oblique view, looking south, of Mount Pleasant and its environs. Mount Pleasant itself lies just above and left of centre, though little of it can be seen here. In the foreground are flooded water meadows associated with the Frome, while further flooding can be seen to the south (top) including water meadows associated with the South Winterbourne. Conquer Barrow is partially visible beneath trees just above the centre of the photograph. (RAF Photograph: 58/RAF/2687/0413 24th January 1959 © Crown Copyright)

broadly circular ditch interrupted by at least two causeways. Unfortunately, after confirming the existence of the ditch and obtaining some dating evidence, no further examination of the ditch and none at all of the mound was undertaken.

Wainwright's belief that the mound post-dated the enclosure led him to dismiss the one radiocarbon date obtained from the barrow ditch. An antler pick was recovered from

Cutting XLVI, dug across the middle of the barrow ditch segment closest to the henge's western entrance. It came from either the primary fills (Wainwright 1979, 67) or from the actual base of the ditch (Wainwright 1979, 175). The radiocarbon date it produced, 2880-2480 cal BC (BM-795: 4077±52 BP), was indistinguishable from those obtained on oak charcoal samples associated with the "pre-enclosure settlement" traces recovered from beneath the henge bank, 2890-2460 cal BC (BM-644: 4072±73 BP), and from more oak charcoal within the primary fills of the henge ditch at the northern entrance 2880–2460 cal BC (BM-792: 4058±71 BP) and 2870-2470 cal BC (BM-793: 4048±54 BP).

In theory this should have presented few problems. Although the dates were all very similar, the ranges associated with them provided plenty of scope for the barrow to have been built after the henge bank. However, there was an additional difficulty. The western entrance to the henge had been considerably reduced in width some centuries after the initial construction phase (dated by antler from primary fills to 2290–2035 cal BC (BM-645: 3734±55 BP) and 2300–1970 cal BC (BM-646: 3728±59 BP)). Conquer Barrow lies at the point where the henge bank and ditch were extended southwards. Therefore if Conquer Barrow post-dated the bank, then the early radiocarbon date could not be accepted. The alternative scenario – that the date was accurate – and its implications were not explored. Instead, Wainwright suggested that the antler pick "must be derived from an earlier context" (Wainwright 1979, 67), pointing to the traces of "pre-enclosure settlement" a short distance to the south of the barrow ditch.

Aside from the antler pick, the barrow ditch segments produced little in the way of datable evidence. Most promising were eight potsherds recovered from the aforementioned Cutting XLVI and from Cutting XLVIII, the latter being a very narrow trench dug into the terminal of the next barrow ditch segment to the west. However, these sherds have proved problematic.

A single sherd described as being of "Bronze Age fabric" was said to have come from Cutting XLVI's layer 8, a mix of chalk silt and finer humic material that overlay the primary rubble (Wainwright 1979, 83). The same cutting apparently yielded a Beaker sherd from layer 4, the nature and extent of which was not described. Neither of these sherds was discussed or illustrated in Ian Longworth's pottery report. Indeed, no Beaker sherd was attributed to Cutting XLVI in the tabulated list of pottery finds (Wainwright 1979, 82). Instead, that list features the sherd of "Bronze Age fabric" in Cutting XLVI – though not in layer 8 but in layer 7, described as a buried soil covering the primary layers – plus a further seven sherds from the primary fills of Cuttings XLVI and XLVIII. None of them could be assigned at the time to any recognisable class of pottery, and none of them came from Cutting XLVI layer 4, thus creating an element of mystery around the Beaker sherd. Clearly, the pottery from Conquer Barrow's ditch might repay further attention.

Re-evaluation

The relationship of Conquer Barrow to the Mount Pleasant enclosure has attracted comment since Wainwright's excavations were published, although for the most part his general sequence of events has been accepted. This sees the barrow mound being built on to the enclosure bank at a relatively late stage in the enclosure's development. However, Wainwright's rejection of the radiocarbon date from the barrow ditch has attracted criticism. Peter Woodward (1991, 136) argued for accepting the date and placing Conquer Barrow in

The new archaeological aerial survey, carried out to English Heritage National Mapping Programme (NMP) standards, includes interpretation, mapping and analysis of all archaeological features visible on aerial photographs and lidar images, ranging in date from the Neolithic to the twentieth century. This component of the Marden project has examined 75sq km in the Vale of Pewsey between Manningford Abbots and Potterne. The areas to the immediate north, south and east of this were surveyed from aerial photographs as part of the Avebury World Heritage Site NMP Project (Small 1999; Crutchley 2005) and Salisbury Plain Training Area NMP Project (McOmish *et al.* 2002) respectively.

Previous work

A common theme throughout the published literature is the condition of Marden henge and its barrows. In 1768, a letter from the Reverend Mayo to the Society of Antiquaries described the levelling of parts of the henge (Wainwright 1971, 182), while Cunnington's 1807 excavation of Hatfield Barrow, described by Colt Hoare, culminated in the spectacular collapse of the "Giant of Marden" (Hoare 1821, 6; Wainwright 1971, 183; Pitts 2000, 62–4). Contemporary concern for the monument is evident in a letter written, presumably after the 1807 excavation, to the lords of the manor – the Chapter of Winchester Cathedral – requesting that they take action to prevent the mound being levelled (Bowles 1828, 80). However, subsequent ploughing in the mid-nineteenth century ensured there was apparently no trace left of the barrow by the 1860s when the Reverend John Wilkinson compiled the notes for the parish history (Wainwright 1971, 183). Wainwright, in his role at the Ministry of Works, arranged for the whole henge to go into permanent pasture in the 1960s (Wainwright 1971, 226; Pitts 2000, 64).

The tentative and doubtful classification of the Marden enclosure as a henge began with Grahame Clark (1936), although O. G. S. Crawford had already compared the earthworks at Durrington with both Avebury and Marden (Crawford 1929), and had included Marden on the Ordnance Survey's *Map of Neolithic Wessex*, published in 1932. Marden had long attracted attention prior to this, of course, and Antiquarian researchers had already recognised possible comparisons for the enclosure. The Reverend Mayo compared it to Avebury in 1768 (Wainwright 1971, 182) and a little later Richard Colt Hoare suggested that "Wiltshire claims justly the pre-eminence over every other province; for it possesses an Abury, a Marden and a Stonehenge" (Hoare 1821, 116).

The antiquarian interest in Marden was concerned as much with the Hatfield Barrow as with the henge enclosure. Andrews and Dury's 1773 map of Wiltshire depicted the barrow but not the henge (WANHS 1952, No. 11). In 1798 a local naturalist, James Norris, described a visit to Marden, at an unknown date, and it was the situation of the barrow within a "moat-like" enclosure which seemed to strike him as significant. He described the Hatfield Barrow as "above usual size, and nearly hemispherical; it is surrounded by a broad intrenchment, which, from being constantly supplied with water from innate springs, forms a sort of moat, which does not become dry even in the midst of summer; a circumstance I have never found attending any other barrow" (Withering Junior 1822, 236). The size of the barrow is consistently mentioned. For example, in 1768 the Reverend John Mayo suggested Hatfield Barrow was "the largest barrow in these parts, except Silbury" (Wainwright 1971, 182).

The morphological characteristics, broadly similar to Durrington Walls, and the position of the Marden enclosure on the River Avon drew the attention of Geoffrey Wainwright in the 1960s (Pitts 2000, 62–4). Wainwright excavated part of the south entrance and a pit defined structure at Marden in 1969 (Wainwright 1971) and confirmed the Neolithic date of the enclosure. The Ancient Monuments Laboratory carried out geophysical survey as part of Wainwright's investigations and located the site of the Hatfield Barrow (see below). Wainwright summarised the antiquarian interest in Hatfield Barrow, and noted its location on his site plan, but did not discuss the significance of the lost large mound in relation to his excavations of the henge at Marden or to possible parallels elsewhere.

New evidence from old aerial photographs

The site has been photographed from the air, often for non-archaeological purposes, at relatively regular intervals since the 1940s, and the NMR collection includes aerial photographs taken before the construction of housing over the southwest side of the henge. Among the features recorded are former field boundaries which appear to overlie parts of the barrow ditch. However, despite the repeated photography it was only during the dry summer of 1976 that the parchmarks of the Hatfield Barrow itself were captured. Those aerial photographs indicate that parts of the barrow almost certainly survive as sub-surface remains and possibly as very slight earthworks. The recent English Heritage geophysical survey also indicates that some of these sub-surface remains still survive.

As far as the barrow is concerned, the evidence on aerial photographs suggests an asymmetric site about 75m across, comprising a mound *c.*55m across enclosed by a broad ditch or hollow (Figure 9.2). When viewed in stereo, the vertical photographs taken in August 1976 show the barrow as a very low mound sitting in a shallow scoop, which extends farther on the eastern side and is – possibly – partially surrounded by a ditch. The aerial photographs, and recent Environment Agency lidar data, suggest a disturbed area of ground at the location of the barrow. Ground-based analytical field survey may be able to determine whether there is still any coherence to these remains. The shape of the apparent hollow around the barrow is reminiscent of the scoop which extends to the west of Silbury Hill. However, the validity of such comparisons remains to be tested and further exploration is required to understand the nature of the Hatfield Barrow.

The recent survey has once again underlined the value of proper evaluation of material held in archives. The aerial photographs have been part of the open access collection at the NMR for decades but, as little attention has been paid to Marden, their significance for the lost barrow has not been recognised. The mapping from those aerial photographs provides the first measured plan of the barrow since the early nineteenth century (Hoare 1821, plate 1, no. 2).

The aerial survey of Marden environs therefore provides valuable archaeological data on the henge, Hatfield Barrow and possible contemporary monuments in the Vale of Pewsey (Colour Plate 11). Mapping and assessing monuments and landscapes from all periods, including the twentieth century, allows us to understand possible gaps and biases in the information from aerial photographs. The survey also provides information for the "missing link" between other similar projects collected using a consistent methodology (Avebury World Heritage Site and environs: Small 1999; Salisbury Plain Training Area: McOmish *et al.* 2002). This provides seamless contextual archaeological data for the three major henge monuments in Wiltshire.

Figure 9.2: Extract from an Ordnance Survey aerial photograph taken in 1976. The Hatfield Barrow shows as a parchmark in grass to the right of the buildings in the centre of the henge. North is to the top of the photograph. (OS Photograph: OS76183 Frame 43 21st August 1976 © Crown Copyright. All rights reserved. Licence number 100017771)

Geophysics 1969 and 2008

Marden henge was first targeted by geophysical survey by Tony Clark of the Ancient Monuments Laboratory ahead of the 1969 excavations. Though the surviving records of the survey are sketchy, in the excavation report it was noted that the eastern entrance of the henge and the remains of a large ditch, 28m wide and 105m in diameter, believed to relate to the Hatfield Barrow were successfully located (Wainwright 1971, 182). Wainwright suggested that magnetometry revealed all these features (Wainwright 1969, 154) but it would appear that in fact transects of earth resistance were actually responsible for locating the Hatfield Barrow ditch.

In April 2008 a new survey was undertaken at Marden as a preliminary study to assess the response at the site to recorded survey prior to more detailed coverage (Martin 2008). The field purported to contain the Hatfield Barrow was surveyed with recorded area magnetometry and earth resistance survey. The magnetic survey revealed no significant anomalies either in the location recorded by the ordnance Survey (who have consistently recorded the position of Hatfield barrow 70m west of the location suggested by Wainwright) or on the plan published in the excavation report (Wainwright 1971). However, as seems to have been the case forty years previously, an earth resistance survey was far more successful.

The survey was undertaken with a Geoscan MSP40 wheeled resistance square array over an area 200m by 60m. Time constraints meant that a fuller area could not be covered, but nonetheless interesting results were obtained.

The survey revealed a large area of low resistance, approximately annular in shape with a protrusion to the northeast of the anomaly. The location and dimensions of this compare incredibly favourably with the southeast third of the large ditch recorded in 1969. Despite only covering one-third of the ditch the current results, including the protrusion, correlate well with the 1976 aerial photographs and suggest that at the centre of the encircled area there exists higher resistance material and so perhaps remnants of the mound. At the time of writing, further work is planned for 2009, and it is hoped that more information about this feature will be forthcoming.

Does size really matter?

As noted above, the aerial photographs suggest a diameter for the Hatfield Barrow of around 55m. This isn't too far from Wainwright's estimate – based on the 1969 earth resistance transects, and clearly assuming a regular circular ditch around the mound, he offered approximate measurements for the latter of 105m external diameter, the ditch itself being 28m wide. This leaves around 49m for the mound. There is clearly a discrepancy to resolve here, with the aerial photographs suggesting 75m rather than 105m for the overall size of the monument, and the recent geophysics seeming to support the latter. There are also significant differences to be found among the measurements made in the eighteenth and nineteenth centuries.

These measurements related to different aspects of the barrow (area, height, diameter, and circumference) and were recorded in various units (chains, yards, feet *etc.*). There is little clue to the methods used, and an obvious explanation for the discrepancies is that these early investigations produced inaccurate results. Looking only at height, John Mayo's description of the barrow in 1768 gave this as 50ft (15.2m), while his son Charles Mayo (1750–1829) recorded it as 40ft (12m), though this has been dismissed as a guess (Cunnington 1955, 8). Philip Crocker, the surveyor employed by Richard Colt Hoare, described the barrow as "*about* 4 chains over" (Cunnington 1955, 8: our italics), while Cunnington and Colt Hoare themselves recorded a height for the mound of 22.5ft (6.8m) in 1807. If the 15.2m and 6.8m heights are accepted then it is perfectly possible that Charles Mayo really did measure the mound at 12m during his lifetime. However, if we accept these measurements, then we have to accept a massive reduction in height – 8.4m in only 40 years.

Whatever the exact dimensions of the barrow were, three different visitors were clearly struck by the mound's exceptional size. James Norris in 1798 wrote of a "remarkable tumulus … above the usual size" (Withering Junior 1822, 235–6). Richard Colt Hoare, under whose auspices the mound was excavated in 1807, uses a number of phrases: "huge pile", "enormous tumulus", "large round barrow" and "gigantic barrow" (Hoare 1821, 4–6). The excavator, William Cunnington, referred to the mound as "the Giant of Marden" (letter to Hoare, in Cunnington 1955, 10). In Camden's *Britannia*, it was described as "the largest barrow in these parts, except Silbury" (Camden 1806, 159).

The extent of the surviving parts of the mound visible on aerial photographs, plus the antiquarian accounts, suggest an original monument which would be large by Wiltshire standards. The loss of most of the mound, and the limited evidence from the antiquarian excavations, mean that we may never know of the original height or composition of the mound and whether it was the result of one or more phases of construction. After their excavation in 1807 Cunnington and Colt Hoare could not agree on whether the mound was for burial or not (Hoare 1821, 6), and it is impossible to draw any conclusions from their records. Therefore it is difficult to draw direct comparisons with other large Neolithic or Bronze Age mounds in Wiltshire. However, the Hatfield Barrow was obviously a striking feature and we can explore possible associations with broadly contemporary monuments and the natural landscape.

Location, location, location

The location of the monuments in the Vale of Pewsey has puzzled some archaeologists through the twentieth century. In her *Introduction to the archaeology of Wiltshire* (1934), Maud Cunnington was dismissive of the potential for prehistoric remains in the Vale of Pewsey and went as far as to suggest that the earthworks at Marden were the remains of a Norman motte and bailey. Stuart Piggott, writing about the Bronze Age in Wessex, described the vale as a "distinct barrier" dividing "the chalk into two archaeological provinces", reflecting the archaeological emphasis on the chalk downland (Piggott 1938, 53). Leslie Grinsell writing in 1958 accepted a Neolithic date for Marden, in part due to the number of small finds made there in the 1950s, but claimed that "the most remarkable feature of the site is its position – on the Upper Greensand" (Grinsell 1958, 59). Whether the non-chalk or chalk edge location is of significance to anyone but recent archaeologists remains to be seen. The relative lack of monuments could be related to the fertile soils in much of the Vale, but it is likely to be the result of intensive medieval and post medieval farming, and consequent ploughing-out of earlier man-made features, rather than a genuine reflection of a preference for the chalk in the Neolithic and later prehistoric periods.

On the chalk escarpment overlooking the Vale of Pewsey, about 6km to the north and northeast of Marden, there are causewayed enclosures at Rybury and Knap Hill, and long barrows including Adam's Grave. In contrast the edge of the chalk escarpment to the south seems to have no Neolithic monuments (McOmish *et al.* 2002, fig. 2.3). The setting and relationship between the possible contemporary monuments around Marden, if there is one, is almost certainly more complex than, for example, inter-visibility (Oswald *et al.* 2001, 99–102). It is also likely that natural features, such as Woodborough Hill, the river, and what may have been waterlogged marshy ground to the northwest, are also significant.

The relevance of water to Neolithic and Bronze Age monuments has been much discussed (for example Richards 1996; Cleggett 1999; Harding 2003). The significance of the location of the henge enclosure at Marden on the river Avon is also noted in most published discussions of the site. The river could form a "south side", or the enclosure could be described as embracing part of the river. The henge ditch is described as waterlogged by antiquarians, something noted by Wainwright in his excavations (Wainwright 1971, 187). This possibly has interesting implications for the relationship of the henge to the river and for the archaeological potential for waterlogged deposits in the ditch fills. The scoop or broad ditch around the Hatfield Barrow could also have significance in this context.

Another example of the possible significance of water can be seen a little farther downstream from Marden, just beyond Wilsford, where a large barrow cemetery is situated on the valley floor partly obscured by the post medieval water meadows. This large group is clustered together in the flood plain perhaps suggesting this was seen as premium space. The flood pattern of this stretch of river may have been slightly different in prehistory but the valley floor is relatively narrow and so the barrows will almost certainly have been seasonally flooded in the lifetime of the barrow builders and their ancestors. Aerial photographs have recorded a similar pattern of Neolithic and Bronze Age funerary monuments appearing as cropmarks below the post-medieval water meadows in the lower Avon Valley at Fordingbridge and elsewhere in Hampshire (Young 2008, 33–35, figures 17 and 18).

Further work

The air photo analysis and mapping of Marden and environs is one of the early stages of the English Heritage project, and the "rediscovery" of the Hatfield Barrow is a significant result. The results of the aerial survey of Marden and the Vale of Pewsey will be presented as an English Heritage Research Department Report. Analytical field survey will address the full extent, nature and condition of the earthworks and what this tells us about the origins and development of the site. Further geophysical survey may be able to determine the extent of the surviving sub-surface remains and could pick up other features not visible on the aerial photographs. Reassessment of the excavation archive and selected further excavation could provide answers to some very basic questions, for example whether the Hatfield Barrow is Neolithic or Bronze Age. The final combined results of the various investigation techniques should also help us to begin to assess the Marden monuments' chronological place in the local and regional late Neolithic, both within the immediate environs of the Vale of Pewsey and in relation to the Avebury and Stonehenge areas.

FINAL THOUGHTS ON THE BROOD

The Great Barrow, the Hatfield Barrow and the Conquer Barrow have all, at times, featured together in discussions of Neolithic barrows. More recently, Ann Woodward has included them in discussions of "aggrandised barrows", a category that seems to comprise barrows of unusually great size (*e.g.* Woodward 2000, 139–42; Needham & Woodward 2008, 5–6). Woodward, following John Barrett (*e.g.* Barrett *et al.* 1991, 128; Barrett 1994, 31, 126-7) has suggested that some of these exceptionally large mounds may have served as raised platforms for the performance of ceremonies or rituals. She has also drawn attention to the extensive views both from these mounds and of the mounds from the surrounding landscape. It seems implicit from her discussions that many of these "aggrandised" mounds are regarded as the product of a lengthy, episodic process of enlargement. It is equally clear that an origin in the Neolithic is not necessary for inclusion in the category, with most barrows mentioned either originating in the early Bronze Age or not reaching their aggrandised height until then.

Neither the Great Barrow at Knowlton, nor the Hatfield Barrow has produced any dating evidence whatsoever. The assumption that they may have origins in the Neolithic, ahead of the main period of round barrow building, seems to rest entirely on (i) their great size and (ii) their proximity to henges, although of course the latter relationship was not available to the earliest observers. Underlying this is a vague sense of connection between these barrows and Silbury Hill. Indeed, this possible relationship is more explicit among earlier discussions, and is firmly linked to the idea that all of these mounds were first and foremost burial mounds, comparable with the greater body of Bronze Age round barrows, but differing in their great size and earlier origins. Thus for H. J. Massingham, who as a keen adherent of Grafton Elliot Smith saw the origins of Silbury Hill in the Egyptian pyramids, "Silbury … was the patriarch and these deviations from the orthodox type of round barrow were its progeny" (Massingham 1926, 115). Silbury was the memory of a pyramid; other lesser but still sizeable mounds were its brood.

Many henges – definite and possible – feature round barrows or ring-ditches in close proximity. Few are out of the ordinary in terms of diameter of ring ditch or height of mound. At the same time, few round barrows of definite Neolithic date are of unusual size. Furthermore, many sizeable round barrows seem to exist independently of henges. Just a kilometre or so west-southwest of Conquer Barrow is the Lanceborough King Barrow, which today comprises a mound 7m high and 56m in diameter, surrounded by a ditch 76m in diameter. Nearby is a horseshoe-shaped earthwork regarded by some as one form or another of "fancy barrow", and more recently as a hengiform (Woodward 2000, 140). Even if it were some form of henge, with an enclosed area measuring 27m by 31m it is hardly of Mount Pleasant proportions, and is dwarfed by the King Barrow. A further 4km to the southwest is the Clandon Barrow, 5.5m high and 30m in diameter, but apparently lacking a ditch (Needham & Woodward 2008). No henge of any form has been claimed here. Neither Clandon nor Lanceborough have seen sufficient excavation to indicate whether they originated before the advent of metal.

Obviously, aerial photographs alone cannot provide dating evidence, but placing individual sites or monuments within a broader landscape context allows some discussion of possible relationships with neighbouring monuments, especially where there is additional evidence in the form of earthwork survey, geophysical survey or excavation. The case for a Neolithic origin for Conquer Barrow arose from an attempt to relate recently-mapped cropmark and soilmark information to Wainwright's published excavations at Mount Pleasant. The other two mounds are a little more problematic.

There is clearly a sequence, and perhaps a lengthy one, to be unravelled at Knowlton. At the very least, there is a need to account for the mound and the two surrounding ditches. Excavation would undoubtedly unravel a far more complex sequence. The resemblance of the outer ditch to the ditch associated with some henge monuments has been remarked on, but are we looking at a mound and ditch that were subsequently surrounded by a henge-like ditch? Or a henge that was subsequently occupied by a substantial barrow, which itself may have risen and expanded in numerous stages?

Recent work at Silbury Hill has emphasized the degree to which a single monument can be the end product of numerous episodes of activity, most of them probably unforeseen at the very start of the process (Leary, this volume Chapter 8). Silbury is not the product of a single blueprint. The same is likely to be true of the Hatfield Barrow, although its collapse and the removal of mound material mean that much detail has been lost. However, the aerial photographic evidence appears to show something far more irregular than is evident at either Knowlton or the Conquer Barrow, and the general resemblance to the situation at Silbury has been pointed out above. It is disappointing that Wainwright's investigations at Marden, contemporary with Atkinson's tunnelling at Silbury Hill, only included the rediscovery of Hatfield Barrow's location and not its examination, so we have no real clues as to when it may have originated. Was the mound – or a mound – in existence before the henge? However, Wainwright's priorities were the search for timber settings and the examination of ditch terminals which "at the entrances to enclosures of any type and date are normally productive in finds on account of the tendency to discard rubbish into them on entering or leaving the enclosure" (Wainwright 1971, 184).

Ultimately, all that the three barrows discussed here definitely have in common is great size and proximity to a henge, while there are sufficient differences to question suggestions of a coherent group of monuments. We cannot really be sure that any of the mounds had Neolithic origins, something that depends, of course, on one's own opinion of when the Bronze Age emerged from the Neolithic. Aerial photography and geophysical survey can provide considerable detail, sometimes allowing existing interpretations to be challenged, as well as placing sites within a broader landscape context. However, questions of chronology, sequence and purpose can really only be addressed through excavation, which makes it ironic that in the case of Conquer Barrow, relatively recent excavation seems to have thrown up questions rather than answers.

BIBLIOGRAPHY

Barber, M. (2004) Mount Pleasant from the air. Cropmarks old and new at the henge enclosure near Dorchester, Dorset. *Proceedings of the Dorset Natural History and Archaeological Society* 126, 7–14.
Barber, M. (forthcoming) *Mount Pleasant, Dorset: a survey of the Neolithic henge and associated features seen on aerial photographs*. Swindon, English Heritage (Research Department Report Series).
Barrett, J. C. (1994) *Fragments from antiquity. An archaeology of social life in Britain, 2900–1200 BC*. Oxford, Blackwell Publishers.
Barrett, J. C., Bradley, R., and Green, M. (1991) *Landscape, monuments and society: the prehistory of Cranborne Chase*. Cambridge, Cambridge University Press.
Bowles, W. (1828) *Hermes Britannicus*. London, J. B. Nichols & Son.
Camden, W. (1806) *Britannia* (Trans. R. Gough) Vol 1. London, J. Stockdale & J. Nichols.
Challis, K., Kokalj, Z., Kincey, M., Moscrop, D., and Howard. A. J. (2008) Airborne lidar and historic environment records. *Antiquity* 82, 1055–1064.
Clark, J. G. D. (1936) The timber monument at Arminghall and its affinities. *Proceedings of the Prehistoric Society* 2, 1–51.
Cleggett, S. I. (1999) The River Avon: real time realm of the ancestors. *Proceedings of the Dorset Natural History and Archaeological Society* vol 121, 49–52.
Crawford, O. G. S. (1929) Durrington Walls. *Antiquity* 3, 49–59.
Crawford, O. G. S. (1953) *Archaeology in the field*. London, JM Dent & Sons Ltd.
Crutchley, S. (2005) Recent aerial survey work in the Marlborough Downs region. In G. Brown, D. Field and D. McOmish (eds.) *The Avebury landscape: aspects of the field archaeology of the Marlborough Downs*, 34–42. Oxford, Oxbow Books.
Cunnington, M. (1934) *The archaeology of Wiltshire*. Devizes, Charles Henry Woodward.
Cunnington, R. H. (1955) Marden and the Cunnington manuscripts. *Wiltshire Archaeological and Natural History Magazine* 56, 4–11.

Field, N. H. (1962) Discoveries at the Knowlton Circles, Woodlands, Dorset. *Proceedings of the Dorset Natural History and Archaeological Society* 84, 117–124.

Gale, J. (2003) *Prehistoric Dorset*. Stroud, Tempus.

Gale, J., Cheetham, P., Laver, J., and Randall, C. (2004) Excavations at High Lea Farm, Hinton Martell, Dorset: an interim report on fieldwork undertaken in 2002–3. *Proceedings of the Dorset Natural History and Archaeological Society* 126, 160–6.

Gale, J. (ed.) (in prep.) *Archaeological investigations in the environs of the Knowlton Henge Complex, Dorset, 1993–7.*

Grinsell, L. V. (1958) *The archaeology of Wessex*. London, Methuen.

Harding, J. (2003) *Henge monuments of the British Isles*. Stroud, Tempus.

Hoare, R. C. (1821) *The ancient history of Wiltshire Vol. 2*. London, Luckington [Facsimile edition 1975: Wakefield, EP Publishing].

Linford, P 2008 *Geophysical survey in the shadow of the hill*. English Heritage Research News 10, 10–13 ISSN 1750–2446

Loveday, R. and Petchey, M. (1982) Oblong ditches: a discussion and some new evidence. *Aerial Archaeology* 8, 17 –24.

Malim, T. (1999) Cursuses and related monuments of the Cambridgeshire Ouse. In A. Barclay and J. Harding (eds.) *Pathways and ceremonies: The cursus monuments of Britain and Ireland*, 77–85. Oxford, Oxbow Books (Neolithic Studies Group Seminar Papers 4).

Martin, L. (2008) *Marden Henge, Wiltshire: Report on Geophysical Survey, April 2008*. Portsmouth, English Heritage. (Research Department Report Series 70/2008Report available online at http://research. english-heritage.org.uk/report/?14691).

Massingham H. J. (1926) *Downland Man*. London, Jonathan Cape Ltd.

McOmish, D., Field, D. and Brown, G. (2002) *The field archaeology of the Salisbury Plain Training Area*. Swindon, English Heritage.

Needham, S., Parfitt, K., Varndell, G. (eds.). (2006) *The Ringlemere Cup. Precious cups and the beginning of the Channel Bronze Age*. London, British Museum (Research Publication 163).

Needham, S. and Woodward, A. (2008) The Clandon Barrow: a synopsis of success in an early Bronze Age world. *Proceedings of the Prehistoric Society* 74, 1–52.

Oswald, A., Dyer, C., Barber, M. (2001) *The creation of monuments. Neolithic causewayed enclosures in the British Isles*. Swindon, English Heritage.

Piggott, S. (1938) The early Bronze Age in Wessex. *Proceedings of the Prehistoric Society* 4, 52–106.

Piggott, S. and Piggott, C. M. (1939) Stone and earth circles in Dorset. *Antiquity* 13, 138–58.

Pitts, M. (2000) *Hengeworld*. London, Century.

RCHME (1970) *An Inventory of Historical Monuments in the County of Dorset. Volume 2: The South East (part 3)*. London, HMSO.

RCHME (1975) *An Inventory of Historical Monuments in the County of Dorset. Volume 5: East Dorset*. London, HMSO.

Richards C. (1996) Henges and water: towards an elemental understanding of monumentality and landscape in late Neolithic Britain. *Journal of Material Culture* 1(3), 313–36.

Small, F. (1999) *The Avebury World Heritage Site Mapping Project*. Swindon, English Heritage (unpublished Report).

Smith, R. J. C., Healy, F., Allen, M. J., Morris, E. L., Barnes, I., Woodward, P. J. (1997) *Excavations along the route of the Dorchester by-pass, Dorset, 1986–8*. Salisbury, Wessex Archaeology (Wessex Archaeology Report No 11).

Sparey-Green, C. (1994) Observations on the site of the "Two Barrows", Fordington Farm, Dorchester; with a note on the "Conquer Barrow". *Dorset Natural History and Archaeological Society Proceedings* 116, 45–54.

Stead, I. M. (1991) *Iron Age Cemeteries in East Yorkshire*. London, English Heritage (English Heritage

Archaeological Report 22).

Stoertz, C. (1997) *Ancient landscapes of the Yorkshire Wolds*. Swindon, RCHME.

Wainwright, G. (1969) Marden. *Current Archaeology* 2(6), 152–155.

Wainwright, G. (1971) The excavation of a late Neolithic enclosure at Marden, Wiltshire. *Antiquaries Journal* 51, 177–239.

Wainwright, G. (1979) *Mount Pleasant, Dorset: excavations 1970–1971*. London, Society of Antiquaries (Reports of the Research Committee 37).

WANHS (1952) [1773] *Andrews' and Dury's Map of Wiltshire, 1773: A Reduced Facsimile*. Devizes, Wiltshire Archaeological and Natural History Society.

Withering, W. (Junior) (1822) *The Miscellaneous Tracts of the Late William Withering, Volume 1*. Longman, Hurst, Rees, Orme and Brown, London.

Woodward, A. (2000) *British Barrows: a matter of life and death*. Stroud, Tempus.

Woodward, P. (1991) *The South Dorset Ridgeway: survey and excavations 1977–84*. Dorchester, Dorset Natural History and Archaeological Society Monograph Series 8.

Young, A. (2008) The aggregate landscape of Hampshire: results of the NMP Mapping. Truro, Cornwall County Council Heritage Environment Service (Report available online at: http://ads.ahds.ac.uk/catalogue/archive/hantsagg_eh_2008/

Chapter 10

The Mystery of the Hill

Jonathan Last

INTRODUCTION: THE SEARCH FOR CLARITY

Perhaps more than any other prehistoric monument, Silbury Hill has always been associated with the mysterious, even the paranormal. Folktales describe how the Devil was planning to empty a huge sack of earth on Marlborough but was forced to drop it at Silbury (because of either the magic of the priests from Avebury or the cunning of a local cobbler, depending which version one prefers). More recently, the "appearances" of crop circles near the monument might be placed in the same category. Read another way, however, those circles could be seen as a vernacular expression of British "Neo-Romantic" art – which has a longstanding connection with the monument. Whereas Stonehenge appealed more to the Romantic painters of the early nineteenth century, most notably Turner and Constable, its subsequent commercialisation meant that Silbury and Avebury (at least prior to Keiller's restorations) attracted more attention from twentieth century artists interested in the "archaic modernism" of the prehistoric landscape; a kind of home-grown version of the discovery by European Modernists of "primitive" art elsewhere in the world (Hauser 2007, 14–15, 189–90). Paul Nash, who painted Silbury Hill in 1936, found in the monument "an image of geometric mass in the landscape, amplified by a mystical rather than historical resonance" (Hauser 2007, 128–9), while John Piper described Silbury in equally sculptural terms as "dark and wonderfully shaped, like an inverted hand-turned wooden bowl" (Ingrams 1983, 123). A generation later, in the 1970s, another British Neo-Romantic, Richard Long, exhibited a chalk spiral entitled *A line the same length as a straight walk from the bottom to the top of Silbury Hill* (the nostalgic and ritual aspects of land art are often expressly associated with Neolithic monuments: Lippard 1983; Cardinal 2004, 190), while the modernist composer Harrison Birtwistle wrote the "non-romantic" ensemble piece *Silbury Air* (Birtwistle 2009). It seems that the combined formal and enigmatic qualities of Silbury appealed to a variety of twentieth century artistic sensibilities.

Those mysterious qualities have also ensnared, though less productively, archaeologists trying to understand what the monument was for. Antiquarian certainty that Silbury Hill was a barrow covering a burial inspired Romantic poets to express their own sense of nostalgia (Pitts 2008), but John Lubbock (1865, 86) already doubted whether it was sepulchral, and by the mid-twentieth century one notes an air of frustration: "It remains as much a mystery as ever" (Clark 1945, 110); "Its purpose and its age remain a riddle" (Hawkes & Hawkes 1947, 59). The difference between the archaeological and artistic approach is neatly characterised by Smiles (2004, 148) in describing Paul Nash's relationship with Alexander Keiller: "Keiller wanted clarity where Nash wanted mystery". With clarity lacking, Silbury became something of a footnote in academic textbooks; the impoverished archaeological narratives failed to engage the public and allowed fringe theories to flourish (see Dames 1976 for a critique of archaeological approaches – and the development of one of those theories). Although the lack of interpretative engagement with Silbury has been overcome, especially since Atkinson's excavation in the late 1960s, I believe there are still problems with the nature of a discourse that seeks to understand the monument in terms of its function; meanwhile, the idea that Silbury is an intractable mystery recurs unhelpfully in material produced for public consumption. In this brief paper I wish to suggest that in both academic and popular accounts of Silbury Hill and related sites we need to better mediate the opposed desires of Keiller and Nash.

MONUMENTAL TRADITIONS

One facet of archaeologists' search for clarity is the urge to classify; prehistoric barrows and mounds have been classified to death ever since Stukeley. But unique sites which do not fit in these schemes then become very difficult to account for, particularly "ritual" monuments, since ritual is frequently defined as formalised behaviour that should fit some kind of pattern (Brück 1999, 314). While round mounds clearly were constructed in the British Neolithic, as demonstrated by Ian Kinnes's pioneering synthesis (Kinnes 1979), now being updated, that tradition seems to be variable and fragmented.

There are few monuments which really bear comparison to Silbury. Other large prehistoric mounds are very different in scale: the now-destroyed Hatfield barrow at Marden, for example, is estimated at only some four per cent of the volume of Silbury (Whittle 1997, 149). Ongoing debate over sites like the Marlborough Mound (Brown *et al.* 2005, 9–10), Castle Hills in Catterick (Hale & Platell 2004) and Droughduil Mote at Dunragit (Thomas 2004) suggest there may be other "medieval" mounds that would bear reinspection. But in the absence of confirmed dates for these, the need for parallels has led to Silbury being seen as a reflection of more distant monuments like Newgrange, Maeshowe or even the Pyramids (Whittle 1997, 150; Thomas 1999, 217). Even though we are more open to the idea that individuals could travel long distances in prehistory, any resemblances between these sites are vague at best and (since they are all chambered tombs) add little to our understanding of Silbury as a structure.

In terms of date, too, the availability of better chronologies now makes the Neolithic round mound "tradition" look rather less coherent (Bradley 2007, 80). While Silbury has recently been dated to the second half of the third millennium BC (though the duration of its construction remains uncertain: Bayliss *et al.* 2007), the primary mound of Duggleby Howe was in place by about 2900 BC and the other Yorkshire "Great Barrows" seem to span an extended period from the mid-fourth to the early second millennia BC (Gibson, this volume Chapter 5). There no longer seems to be any reason to see Silbury as part of any particular horizon or tradition of Neolithic mound building.

Instead of formal comparisons we need to look at these places in another way. Just as there is an overlapping variety of Neolithic linear monuments (long barrows, long mounds, bank barrows, long mortuary enclosures and cursus enclosures; see Last 1999) so circular principles and particular materials (timber, turf, soil, chalk/stone, even human remains) may have been combined in different ways at different times and places throughout the period. And just as sites like Duggleby or Newgrange (Eriksen 2008) are now seen to have their own complex and extended sequences, so the evidence that Silbury did not have a few discrete phases, as previously envisaged, but was a continuous project with a large number of stages (Leary, this volume Chapter 8) suggests that comparing the final forms of monuments is misleading. On the other hand, if we are looking for similarities in architectural practices, and set aside the much greater scale of Silbury, there is a whole series of potentially comparable monuments not too far away.

These include the multi-phase round barrows recently discussed as a group by Garwood (2007, 34), who argues for a relatively narrow chronological range within the early Bronze Age (*c.*2100–1750 BC) for most practices of architectural elaboration and mound enlargement in southern Britain. Could Silbury be seen as a similar monument to sites like Amesbury 71, albeit elaborated and enlarged on a grand scale? Leaving the absence of burials aside for a moment (see below), possible links with the later round barrows of Wessex and beyond are complicated by the present uncertainty over the duration of Silbury and the general lack of detailed understanding of the chronology of construction at multi-phase barrows. For instance, many late third millennium BC Beaker burials underlie substantial barrow mounds, but frequent evidence for the reopening of graves and the removal and insertion of human remains (Gibson 2007) implies that substantial mounds were not present till late in the sequence, and may even have been associated with the "closure" of the monument (Last 2007). The presence of Beaker "flat" graves (they were presumably marked in some way) in the landscapes around later barrow cemeteries, as at Radley Barrow Hills (Barclay 1999, 324), further supports the view that large barrow mounds are generally a second millennium BC phenomenon. Thus in terms of considering its relationship to a round barrow "tradition" it makes a difference whether Silbury reached its final form in 2300 or 2000 BC. Was it already a long-abandoned monument when the construction of large round barrows began, or was it still an active project? More dates are keenly awaited.

BARROW ARCHITECTURES

Nevertheless, the study of multi-phase round barrows has something to add to our understanding of Silbury, whatever its duration. Eschewing formal comparisons, it is clear firstly that many barrows were not solely (or even primarily) about disposal of the dead (see *e.g.* Jones 2005); and secondly that their construction was often a complex process of manipulating socially and symbolically charged materials and substances. For instance, Mary Ann Owoc has written about the way some Somerset barrows can be seen as "technological performances", with unique constructional sequences emerging "from a dialectic of material engagement in which site creation and the use of elements at each locale was at once a product of their physical nature, the universe of ideas and values placed upon them, and their social contexts of production" (Owoc 2007, 125). The idea that barrows were the outcomes of sequences of actions where relationships between the participants, and the qualities of the materials being manipulated, were more important than the overall form of the monuments can be illustrated in numerous ways. An example not far from Silbury is West Overton G6b, where soil, turf, clay, sarsen, flint and chalk were utilised in very specific ways in the construction of a complex round barrow over a primary Beaker grave (Smith & Simpson 1966).

The location of this site was not insignificant: it already had a history when the grave was dug, marked by the presence of Neolithic sherds beneath and incorporated within the barrow mound. Numerous frog bones on the base of the grave indicate that it was open for some time before being backfilled with clean chalk rubble. Irregularly arranged groups of sarsen boulders around the grave sealed a group of child burials, while a circular bank of flint nodules and burnt sarsens surrounded the boulders and graves (the bank sealed two more child burials and seems to have been contemporary with at least one of them, since bank material rested directly on the skeleton). The area defined by the sarsen boulders was then covered by a layer of grey clay, of a clean composition that did not seem to occur naturally in the local area. The mound which sealed all of these structures comprised a central turf stack over the clay layer, followed by a covering deposit of chalk-free humic soil.

Leaving aside possible specific parallels with Silbury in the form of the sarsen boulders and basal clay layer, it is clear that a very precise, sequential manipulation of deliberately chosen, "pure" substances was undertaken by the builders, as the site was gradually transformed from pit to surface to ring-cairn to mound. At different times it would have presented different colours and textures, evoking different parts of the landscape. Simply labelling the monument a round barrow fails to capture this story and overlooks the substances and performances embedded in its final form (see Leary, this volume Chapter 8).

This kind of practice has similarities to and differences from the *bricolage*-like process of building long barrows in the earlier Neolithic, characterised by McFadyen (2007) as "quick architecture". The deliberate and evocative manipulation of natural and transformed substances of various kinds (not just the timber/stone dualism often discussed in this context: *e.g.* Parker Pearson and Ramilisonina 1998) is common to both, but the Neolithic monuments emphasise the division, arrangement and inter-relationship of deposits, with materials partitioned and propped, sometimes in rather precarious ways (as at Ascott-under-Wychwood: McFadyen *et al.* 2007, 132–6). In contrast the Bronze Age architecture seems to be periodic or phased and cumulative, the sequential reworking at particular times of a series of more stable states. Construction through the accumulation of layers recalls the sequence being interrogated at Silbury. This is architecture without architects in the modern sense, but plane surfaces, rings, and mounds may be the logical shapes of the "periodic architecture" of multi-phase barrows, just as linear forms, bays and divisions made up the skeleton of the quick architecture of the fourth millennium BC.

PRESENTING SILBURY

Central to our understanding of Neolithic and Bronze Age monumentality, these practices also recall the activities of artists who, as outlined above, have engaged with the materials, forms and textures of prehistoric sites – though it is important to understand the work of contemporary artists as "more a matter of working in parallel than simple imitation" (Gayford 2007). In this way the artistic response to the "mystery" of sites like Silbury Hill can indeed aid archaeologists' hunt for clarity, albeit in relation to understanding the making of sites rather than their function. Like recent artistic practice, which represents an engagement with the world rather than being "about" anything, barrow construction can be seen as a materialisation of people's ideas about the landscape and their relationship with their environment, rather than being "for" a specific purpose. Moreover, a narrative that stresses the nature of architectural practice in the Neolithic and Bronze Age as well as the qualities of materials may be one way to overcome the problems of conveying academic interpretations of prehistoric monuments to the public – problems which, for the reasons outlined above, Silbury particularly exemplifies. While much remains to be learnt about Neolithic round mounds there is, as the present volume shows, a body of knowledge that can be made sense of within interpretative narratives, despite such sites continuing to resist classification and functional labels. Unfortunately, the headline information provided to visitors by archaeologists and heritage managers often continues to emphasise our ignorance; and headlines are important when visitors rarely read texts in their entirety (Toolis & Ellis 2004).

In terms of language this material returns us to the riddles and mysteries of the 1940s. For example, the English Heritage website (checked in March 2009) calls Silbury Hill "huge and mysterious" and states that "we do not know its purpose or meaning". Similarly, the teachers' information sheet begins by saying that "no one knows why it was built" – although a companion sheet on the history of the Avebury monuments ventures a suggestion that Silbury was "possibly a territorial marker". Meanwhile the pupils' sheet asks schoolchildren to guess what they think the hill was for (though "territorial marker" is not one of the options!). These quotations and the confusion over function exemplify an approach to public interpretation that goes well beyond Silbury: for Avebury in general we are told by the English Heritage website that the use and purpose of this sacred landscape "can still only be guessed at"; while the introduction to the Stonehenge page states in a similar fashion that: "Mystery surrounds this 5,000 year old monument [... the stones'] ultimate purpose remains a fascinating and enduring mystery".

In printed publications too, we find regular appearances of the "m"-word. It crops up in various editions of the official Avebury guidebook: while there are several pages on Silbury for those who read the whole text, the Introduction declares simply that "the purpose of the largest man-made mound in Europe remains a mystery" (Malone 1995, 4). Similarly the *Heritage Unlocked* guide concludes a brief history of Silbury with the statement that "The exact purpose of the site [...] remains a mystery" (Endacott & Kelleher 2004, 86).

I believe this substitution of mystery for interpretation highlights a problem with our desire to provide functional explanations of prehistoric monuments in popular accounts. While academic narratives, attuned to the histories, settings and practices associated with these sites, can make sense without asserting a single purpose or function for them, as the recent work on round barrows shows, in outputs aimed at a wider audience what is presented is our lack of understanding. In the absence of a function we are given a prehistoric mystery, but rather than the creative sense of mystery invoked by the artists discussed above, it tends to obscure appreciation of the site.

The mystery is emphasised despite the fact there is often plenty of information available. Indeed the popular publications and teaching sheets about Silbury (along with all the other monuments around Avebury and Stonehenge) are full of facts and figures about its size, date and sequence. But the way such information is presented is also old-fashioned, drawing on some of the archaeology of the 1960s and 1970s, which was more interested in calculating the labour represented in prehistoric monuments (*e.g.* Startin 1982) than the social aspects of construction (*cf.* Richards forthcoming). As the quotations above demonstrate, Silbury's mystery is invariably coupled with its size. Moreover the gendered nature of the discourse of efficiency is also sometimes reproduced today: "It is assumed that at least 1,000 men were involved" in the construction of Silbury (Endacott & Kelleher 2004, 85). Emphasising its scale without humanising the construction process inevitably leads to an impoverished interpretation of the monument, just as asking what it was for not only presupposes a single "function" but also privileges the final form of the monument over its components (Leary, this volume Chapter 8) – then all we can say is that it is "huge and apparently useless" (Malone 1995, 25).

How have we got ourselves into the position of selling prehistoric sites to the public on the basis of our lack of knowledge about them, rather than the research that is continually advancing understanding? Is it a feeling that academic narratives are too demanding, or the sense that people love a good mystery? In either case it looks like a failure of archaeologists to address their narratives to audiences beyond the academy. For Paul Nash, the mysterious qualities of Silbury Hill augmented his response to its materiality: "art offered a viable alternative to archaeological research, a vital engagement with the past as opposed to the sterility Nash associated with empirical method" (Smiles 2004, 151); "He liked landscapes that had a look of strangeness, that could be thought to connect with distant history but left the reconstruction of it to the imagination" (Causey 2001, 24). Unfortunately, unlike Nash's imaginative engagement, the "mystery" in archaeological publicity is as intellectually sterile as any empirical method, in effect a refusal to interpret. Descriptions then fall back on facts and figures as a substitute for narrative, and it is unsurprising that fringe interpretations have flourished instead, from the pseudo-archaeological (Dames 1976) to the science-fictional (Cowie 2002).

As archaeologists interested in promoting prehistory, we need to present to visitors a more imaginative engagement with aspects of the materiality of these monuments – the qualities of the substances available to the builders, the ways that practices of making (re) produced social relations, and the means by which monuments shaped and were shaped by their landscape setting. The discussion of different kinds of architectural practice, as outlined above for West Overton G6b, is one possible academic narrative that could be rewritten effectively for popular accounts; Tim Ingold's "earth-sky world" (this volume Chapter 15) provides another example. Just as academic archaeology is finding more affective ways to discuss prehistoric monuments, so we owe visitors to Silbury more appealing stories which challenge the folktales and fringe theories by humanising the mystery of the hill.

BIBLIOGRAPHY

Barclay, A. (1999) The monument complex in its regional context. In A. Barclay and C. Halpin, *Excavations at Barrow Hills, Radley, Oxfordshire. Volume 1: the Neolithic and Bronze Age monument complex*, 320–5. Oxford, Oxford Archaeological Unit (Thames Valley Landscapes 11).

Bayliss, A., McAvoy, F. and Whittle, A. (2007) The world recreated: redating Silbury Hill in its monumental landscape. *Antiquity* 81, 26–53.

Birtwistle, H. (2009) Mystery, but without the romance. *British Archaeology* 105, 66.

Bradley, R. (2007) *The prehistory of Britain and Ireland*. Cambridge, Cambridge University Press.

Brown, G., Field, D. and McOmish, D. (2005) Some observations on change, consolidation and perception in a stone landscape. In G. Brown, D. Field and D. McOmish (eds.), *The Avebury landscape: aspects of the field archaeology of the Marlborough Downs*, 1–11. Oxford, Oxbow Books.

Brück, J. (1999) Ritual and rationality: some problems of interpretation in European archaeology. *European Journal of Archaeology* 2(3), 313–44.

Cardinal, R. (2004) European modernism and the arts of prehistory. In G. Berghaus (ed.), *New perspectives on prehistoric art*, 179–96. Westport, Praeger.

Causey, A. (2001) Introduction. In A. Causey (ed.), *Paul Nash: Writings on Art*, 1–33. Oxford, Oxford University Press.

Clark, G. (1945) *Prehistoric England* (Third edition.). London, Batsford.

Cowie, J. (2002) *Silbury dawning: the alien visitor gene theory*. Edinburgh, The Media Shack.

Dames, M. (1976) *The Silbury treasure*. London, Thames & Hudson.

Endacott, A. and Kelleher, S. (2004) *Heritage unlocked: guide to free sites in Bristol, Gloucestershire and Wiltshire*. London, English Heritage.

Eriksen, P. (2008) The great mound of Newgrange: an Irish multi-period mound spanning from the Megalithic Tomb period to the early Bronze Age. *Acta Archaeologica* 79, 250–273.

Garwood, P. (2007) Before the hills in order stood: chronology, time and history in the interpretation of early Bronze Age round barrows. In J. Last (ed.), *Beyond the grave: new perspectives on barrows*, 30–52. Oxford, Oxbow Books.

Gayford, M. (2007) Ancient and modernism: prehistoric art often prompts the remark, "it looks so modern" – but do contemporary artists agree? *Apollo* 546 (on-line at: http://www.apollo-magazine.com/archive/)

Gibson, A. (2007) A Beaker veneer? Some evidence from the burial record. In M. Larsson and M. Parker Pearson (eds.), *From Stonehenge to the Baltic. Living with cultural diversity in the third millennium BC*, 47–64. Oxford, Archaeopress (BAR International Series 1692).

Hale, D. and Platell, A. (2004) A grandstand view. *Current Archaeology* 209, 43–7.

Hauser, K. (2007) *Shadow Sites: photography, archaeology, and the British landscape, 1927–1955*. Oxford, Oxford University Press.

Hawkes, J. and Hawkes, C. (1947) *Prehistoric Britain*. London, Chatto and Windus.

Ingrams, R. (1983) *Piper's places: John Piper in England and Wales*. London, Chatto and Windus.

Jones, A. M. (2005) *Cornish Bronze Age ceremonial landscapes c.2500–1500 BC*. Oxford, Archaeopress (BAR British Series 394).

Kinnes, I. (1979) *Round Barrows and ring-ditches in the British Neolithic*. London, British Museum (British Museum Occasional Paper 7).

Last, J. (1999) Out of line: cursuses and monument typology in eastern England. In A. Barclay and J. Harding (eds.), *Pathways and ceremonies: the cursus monuments of Britain and Ireland*, 86–97. Oxford, Oxbow Books (Neolithic Studies Group Seminar Papers 4).

Last, J. (2007) Covering old ground: barrows as closures. In J. Last (ed.), *Beyond the grave: new perspectives on barrows*, 160–80. Oxford, Oxbow Books.

Lippard, L. (1983) *Overlay: contemporary art and the art of prehistory*. New York, Pantheon Books.

Lubbock, J. (1865) *Pre-historic Times, as illustrated by ancient remains, and the manners and customs of modern savages*: London, Williams and Norgate.

Malone, C. (1995) *The Prehistoric monuments of Avebury*. London, English Heritage.

McFadyen, L. (2007) Neolithic architecture and participation: practices of making at barrow sites in southern Britain. In J. Last (ed.), *Beyond the grave: new perspectives on barrows*, 22–9. Oxford, Oxbow Books.

McFadyen, L., Benson, D. and Whittle, A. (2007) The long barrow. In D. Benson and A. Whittle (eds.), *Building memories: The Neolithic Cotswold long barrow at Ascott-under-Wychwood, Oxfordshire*, 79–136. Oxford, Oxbow Books.

Owoc, M. (2007) To build or not to build: Bronze Age monument construction as technological practice.

In J. Last (ed.), *Beyond the grave: new perspectives on barrows*, 114–28. Oxford, Oxbow Books.

Parker Pearson, M. and Ramilisonina (1998) Stonehenge for the ancestors: the stones pass on the message. *Antiquity* 72, 308–26.

Pitts, M. (2008) A Victorian time capsule and Emmeline Fisher's poem on Silbury Hill. *British Archaeology* 98, 9.

Richards, C. (forthcoming) Building the great stone circles of northern Britain: questions of materiality, identity and social practices. In J. Chapman, G. Cooney and B. O'Connor (eds.) *Materialitas: Working stone, carving identity*. London, Prehistoric Society (Research Papers).

Smiles, S. (2004) Thomas Guest and Paul Nash in Wiltshire: two episodes in the artistic approach to British antiquity. In S. Smiles and S. Moser (eds.), *Envisioning the past: Archaeology and the image*, 133–57. Oxford, Wiley.

Smith, I. and Simpson, D. (1966) Excavation of a round barrow on Overton Hill, north Wiltshire. *Proceedings of the Prehistoric Society* 32, 122–55.

Startin, D. (1982) Prehistoric earthmoving. In H. Case and A. Whittle (eds.), *Settlement patterns in the Oxford region: excavations at the Abingdon causewayed enclosure and other sites*, 153–6. London, Council for British Archaeology (Research Report 44).

Thomas, J. (1999) *Understanding the Neolithic*. London, Routledge.

Thomas, J. (2004) The later Neolithic architectural repertoire: the case of the Dunragit complex. In R. Cleal and J. Pollard (eds) *Monuments and material culture. Papers in honour of an Avebury archaeologist: Isobel Smith*, 98–108. Salisbury, Hobnob Press.

Toolis, R. and Ellis, C. (2004) Changing interpretations. Public access and interpretation on a developer-funded excavation at Brachead, Glasgow. In P. Frodsham (ed.), *Interpreting the ambiguous: archaeology and interpretation in early 21st century Britain*, 67–74. Oxford, Archaeopress (BAR British Series 362).

Whittle, A. (1997) *Sacred mound, holy rings. Silbury Hill and the West Kennet palisade enclosures: a later Neolithic complex in north Wiltshire*. Oxford, Oxbow Books (Monograph 74).

Chapter 11

The Formative Henge: Speculations Drawn from the Circular Traditions of Wales and Adjacent Counties

Steve Burrow

INTRODUCTION

Monuments with round mounds are well known in the Welsh Neolithic, with many megalithic tombs exhibiting this form of external casing. For example at Dyffryn Ardudwy in Gwynedd a portal dolmen set within a round mound was later encased within an extension of the site resulting in a rectangular monument (Powell 1973). Similarly at Ty-Isaf in Powys, a burial chamber surrounded by a round mound was extended until a classic Cotswold-Severn form was achieved (Grimes 1939). In other parts of Wales, notably in the southwest and Anglesey, megalithic tombs set within round mounds are well known if largely undated, and these have been the subject of comprehensive study (Barker 1992; Lynch 1969). In contrast, non-megalithic round mounds have proved elusive, a few examples are known and these are discussed below, but excavations at scores of round mounds across the country have proved the vast majority to be Bronze Age.

But, if one removes the "mounds" from the title of this volume, Wales has a lot to offer. Two other types of Neolithic round monument are known: the causewayed enclosure – only recently identified in Glamorgan, Pembrokeshire, Powys and possibly Anglesey; and the henge – examples of which have been known for many years. Furthermore, several other Neolithic round monuments have been excavated, surveyed, and photographed over the years which do not fit into these well known types, but which all could be grouped as formative henges.

This paper summarises the evidence for this nascent site-type in Wales and neighbouring areas of England, and considers their relationship to other contemporary monuments in this broad region. But by way of introduction it begins with an overview of the formative henge as it has been discussed to date.

THE STONEHENGE EARTHWORK

Stonehenge in Wiltshire, best known for its sarsen and bluestone circles, is also surrounded by an earthwork. This encircling bank and ditch has been recognised as an integral part of the monument since at least the sixteenth century AD, when William Camden mentioned it in the first edition of his *Britannia* (1586, 119). And illustrations of this earthwork began to appear in the seventeenth century AD, for example in Camden's 1610 edition of *Britannia*; in the plan generated by Inigo Jones's study of the site in 1620, and in a plan drawn by John Aubrey in 1666. In all these representations, the earthwork serves as an artistic frame, aiding the appreciation of the stones within rather than as an object of study in its own right. This could be said to be a fair reflection of its function for many of those who visit the stones today.

The earthwork became a focus in its own right as a result of excavation by William Hawley between 1919 and 1926, with further sections being dug and redug by Richard Atkinson in 1954 and by John Evans in 1978. The results of their work, supported by topographic and geophysical survey, show the earthwork to consist of a chalk-cut ditch 107m in diameter formed by the joining of a number of short, fairly straight, ditch segments, on average 1.68m deep (Cleal *et al.* 1995, 24, 67). The circumference of the ditch is notable for its pronounced circularity, in contrast to the sub-circular form of many other prehistoric monuments. The bank inside this ditch is over 5m wide and survives to around 0.6m high (Cleal *et al.* 1995, 94), but Atkinson (1956, 10), extrapolating from the volume of ditch material, believed that it may originally have been 1.8m high. Another bank encircled the outer face of this ditch and, although this appears to have been as wide as the inner bank, it was probably not as high (Cleal *et al.* 1995, 501).

The Stonehenge earthwork may originally have possessed three entrances. There is an 11m wide gap in bank and ditch on the northeast side, a 3m wide gap in the south side (although there is some debate about whether this is original), and the possibility of a 2m wide gap on the south-southwest side (Cleal *et al.* 1995, 110). This last "entrance" appears to have been blocked by the digging of a single pit across its centre, although when this event occurred is not known, and the possibility remains that the pit may have been part of the original design of the monument, making this entrance illusory.

SEPARATING STONEHENGE FROM HENGES

In 1932, T. D. Kendrick and C. F. C. Hawkes defined a new class of monuments, the henge, deriving the name from Stonehenge and the nearby Woodhenge. Their original description of this class saw them as "prehistoric 'sacred places'" but the looseness of this definition led the authors to note "we are not agreed that all these [henge] monuments are of about the same age and are ceremonial sites" (Kendrick & Hawkes 1932, 83). J. G. D. Clark focused the definition a little more with the recognition that "as general rule [at henges] the ditch is placed within the bank" (Clark 1936, 23). This aspect of the definition was central to S. and C. M. Piggott's understanding of the henge (Piggott & Piggott 1939, 138) and has remained so ever since (*e.g.* Atkinson 1951, 82), but by the 1980s it was recognised that this emphasis on the external bank created problems for the position of Stonehenge within the henge category since its main bank was inside the ditch (Harding & Lee 1987, 41).

Radiocarbon dating provided a partial answer to this anomalous situation. The growing body of dates for henges has shown that the classic, bank outside ditch, form, became current from around 2800 BC (Harding 2003, 12). But antlers from the base of the Stonehenge ditch, which were presumably used in its digging, returned dates of between 3020 and 2910 BC (Cleal *et al.* 1995, 531). This has allowed Stonehenge to be separated out as an earlier form, and has encouraged the use of terms like "protohenges" (Cleal *et al.* 1995, 114), or "formative henges" (Harding 2003, 13) to describe this and other similar sites. The latter term is preferred here, although doubts are expressed at the end of this article about its long-term value.

EXCAVATED "FORMATIVE HENGES"

Having separated the Stonehenge earthwork from other henges on chronological grounds, Cleal *et al.* (1995, 113) identified two likely parallels: Flagstones in Dorset, and Llandegai A in Gwynedd.

Only half of the Flagstones enclosure survived, the rest being lost beneath development (Table 11.1). But, extrapolating from the site plan, it is likely that the monument was originally a regular circle, 100m in diameter, formed by a circuit of unevenly spaced chalk-cut pits (Smith *et al.* 1997, 30). The construction technique left many gaps in the circuit, with especially large ones being present in the northwest (7.4m wide) and northern sections (3m wide), suggesting entrances at these points. No trace of any banks survived, but fill seemed to have entered the ditch equally from both sides, raising the possibility that the enclosure had both internal and external banks, as at Stonehenge. The date of the Flagstones enclosure is problematic as antlers from the base of the ditch produced non-overlapping results of 3361–2911 cal BC (OxA-2322: 4450±90 BP) and 2878–2299 cal BC (HAR-8578: 4030±100BP), although the presence of a "jumble of bones" belonging to a child buried in the ditch, around 3367–2931 cal BC (HAR-9158: 4490±70 BP) suggest that the former construction date is the more likely.

Llandegai A forms part of a group of monuments, which included a cursus and classic henge, all of which were excavated as a rescue project in 1966 and 1967 (Lynch & Musson 2001). This enclosure's markedly circular gravel-cut ditch was 80m in diameter, with a 1.3m wide entrance in the west-southwest side, and a 7m wide internal bank. More gravel would have come from the ditch than was necessary to produce this bank, raising the possibility that an external bank was also present, although if this was the case, it was set too far out to have contributed to the ditch fills (Lynch & Musson 2001, 41). Dating is also uncertain at Llandegai A since no dates are available for the ditch's primary fills. Instead a scatter of charcoal from a later stabilisation layer returned a date of 3518–2680 cal BC (NPL-221: 4420±140 BP), with a 1σ standard deviation calibration refining this to 3332–2915 cal BC. Pits inside the enclosure have also been dated to 3339–2932 cal BC and 3360–3013 cal BC (GrN-27192 4450±40 BP and GrN-22954: 4480±50 BP respectively) and, although these cannot be directly related to the earthwork, in combination the evidence suggests a construction date in the last three centuries of the fourth millennium BC.

These three sites – Stonehenge, Flagstones, and Llandegai A – are often linked in discussion and could be said to form the type sites for formative henges. With this in mind it is worth reiterating the features they share:

- Construction probably between 3350 and 2900 BC.
- A markedly circular form between 80–107m in diameter.
- Bank set within ditch, but with the possibility of another ?smaller bank outside this.
- ?narrow entrances.

On the other hand, the distances which separate these three sites – over 300km from Llandegai A to Flagstones – appears to count against their being a unified phenomenon. But other sites which share some or all of these characteristics can be recognised in the spaces between, all of which are to some extent speculative, but which in combination raise the possibility that formative henges might once have been built in some numbers between Anglesey and Wessex, and beyond (see Figure 11.1 and Table 11.1).

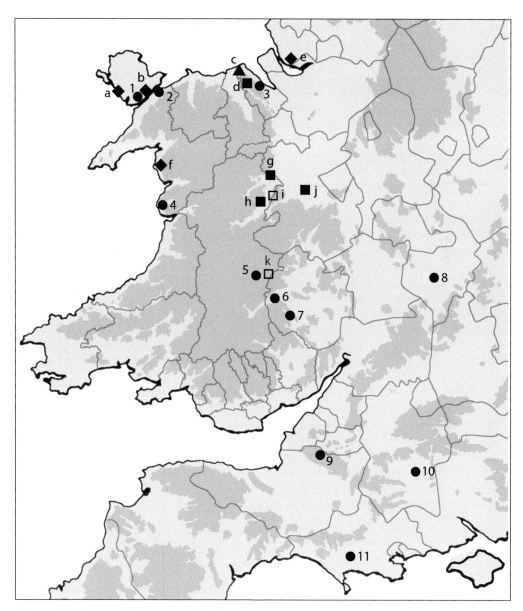

Figure 11.1: Location of sites mentioned in the text. Circles = circular enclosures; squares = graves enclosed by circles; open circles = ?houses; diamonds = passage tombs; triangle = large mound. 1. Castell Bryn Gwyn; 2. Llandegai A; 3. Ysceifiog; 4. Gwyddelfynydd, Bryn Crug; 5. Walton 'gyrus'; 6. Whitney-on-Wye; 7. Golden Valley; 8. Wasperton; 9. Priddy Circles; 10. Stonehenge; 11. Flagstones. a. Barclodiad y Gawres; b. Bryn Celli Ddu; c. Gop Hill; d. Ysceifiog; e. The Calderstones; f. Llandbedr; g. Four Crosses; h. Sarn-y-bryn-caled; i. Trelystyan; j. Meole Brace; k. Upper Ninepence

Table 11.1

Site (NGR)	Diam. of ditch (m)	% of circumference visible
Stonehenge (SU120421)	115	100% visible, 50% of ditch excavated
Flagstones (SY704900)	102	50% visible, all of available ditch excavated
Llandegai A (SH593710)	80	100% visible, 1 wide trench across ditch
Castell Bryn Gwyn (SH465670)	80	75% visible, 2 trenches across ditch
Wasperton (SP260583)	100	50% visible, 25% of ditch excavated
Priddy 1 (ST539525)	168	75% visible, 4 trenches across ditch
Priddy 2 (ST540528)	168	100% visible
Priddy 3 (ST540530)	166	100% visible
Priddy 4 (ST541535)	180	50% visible, ditch sampled with boreholes
Ysceifiog (SJ152752)	88–101	100% visible, 2 trenches across ditch
Gwyddelfynydd, Bryn Crug (SH608037)	75	50% visible on aerial photographs, 100% visible on geophysics
Golden Valley (SO368359)	100–107	100% visible on aerial photographs
Walton gyrus (SO251599)	97	80% visible on aerial photographs
Whitney-on-Wye (SO283471)	130	75% visible on aerial photographs

Beginning at the north end of this distribution, Darvill (2006, 97) has recognised an enclosure at Castell Bryn Gwyn on Anglesey, which fits well within this group. This multi-phase site began as an earthwork consisting of a 9m wide flat-bottomed ditch, with an internal stone bank 4.8m wide. A single cobbled entranceway 1.8m wide cut the west side of this enclosure, and excavation revealed other areas of cobbling in the interior (Wainwright 1962). Peterborough pottery contained in this cobbling and from contexts above the footings of the bank, suggest a construction date between 3400 BC and 2500 BC (Gibson & Kinnes 1997). The only evidence contradicting this is a bronze awl found below this stone bank, although since the overlying Peterborough Ware seemed unweathered (Wainwright 1962, 53) this was probably intrusive.

The precise form of this monument is uncertain since the bank and ditch were reused and enlarged in the Romano-British period, and the site was only subject to limited excavation. But if the form of the later enclosure followed the earlier monument around its entire circumference, as it appears to do at excavated points, then the ditch would have been *c.*80m in diameter. The similarity between the size, form, entrance arrangement and dating of this monument and Llandegai A is apparent (see Figure 11.2).

The sub-circular 100m diameter enclosure at Wasperton in Warwickshire can be dated to this period on similar grounds. Here, Peterborough Ware was found in the primary fills of the ditch, adjacent to the larger of the two excavated entrances (Hughes & Crawford 1995). Unfortunately, with only half of the assumed ditch circuit identified it is hard to be certain how "regular" this circle might have been.

Lynch (2003, 26) has also argued that the sub-circular enclosure at Ysceifiog may be an atypical henge. This 88–101m diameter enclosure is within the size range of formative henges and only its irregular circumference counts against its inclusion in this class. The Whitford Dyke butts the earthwork to north and south confirming that it is pre-medieval, although this does not help efforts to date it more precisely. This relationship led Cyril Fox to excavate both dyke and circle in 1925, but unfortunately his two trenches did not produce datable material (Fox 1926). Even so his excavation of an early Bronze Age burial mound

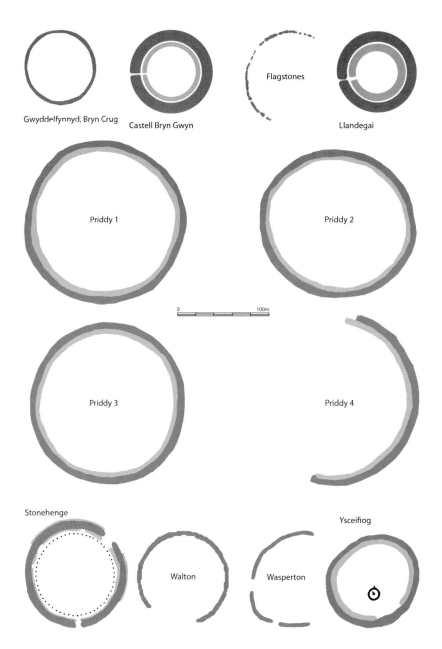

Figure 11.2: Plans of potential formative henges. (Sources of illustrations given in the acknowledgements)

within the enclosure produced one strand of evidence which would support an early date: below this mound was found a probable middle Neolithic pit grave, which is discussed in more detail below. This discovery adds weight, but not certainty, to the suggestion that Ysceifiog is a formative henge, asymmetrical or not.

It has also been suggested that the line of four circles at Priddy in Somerset may be linked to this group. E. K. Tratman (1967, 98 and 120) believed them to be henges, with the closest parallel he could provide being Stonehenge, because the banks at Priddy were built inside the ditches. Lewis (2005, 87) supports a Neolithic date for these monuments and ties them closer to the formative henges described above through parallels with Llandegai A and Castell Bryn Gwyn, among others.

It is unfortunate that while Taylor and Tratman's excavations in the 1950s provided good information on the structure of the Priddy Circles, no artefactual evidence was found, and the charcoal deposits which were present were either too small or unsuitable for dating (Tratman 1967, 105). At the time of writing the results of radiocarbon dates from a new series of excavation at these circles by Jodie Lewis and Mike Allen are still awaited (Mahon 2008, 4; Allen & Lewis pers. comm.). Until these dates become available, in favour of the Priddy Circles' classification as formative henges is their arrangement of bank inside ditch (although this is the normal arrangement of these two elements across all periods), and their pronounced circularity. Against, is their size: the smallest is about 162m in diameter, the biggest 173m – all are much larger than any other potential member of this group.

UNEXCAVATED, POTENTIAL, "FORMATIVE HENGES"

Using the morphological criteria presented above several other sites which are as yet only known from aerial photographs, can be proposed as candidate formative henges.

A circular enclosure, 75m in diameter was discovered during aerial reconnaissance by J. K. S. St Joseph at Gwyddelfynydd, Bryn Crug in the 1970s, and geophysical survey by Gwynedd Archaeological Trust makes clear its pronounced circularity (Smith & Hopewell 2007). The form and size of this cropmark suggests parallels with Llandegai A, as does its possible pairing with another, slightly less regular 55–60m diameter enclosure 440m to the southwest which Crew and Musson (1996, 12) have compared with the Llandegai henge (Llandegai B).

The Walton Basin, an area rich with Neolithic monuments (Gibson 1999; Jones 2009), contains another potential formative henge. This cropmark circle is sometimes called the Walton Gyrus, an interpretation of its function which rests on its size, circularity and proximity to Roman marching camps in the basin. But it could equally be argued that the marked circularity of this 97m diameter enclosure, and its proximity to the Walton palisaded enclosure, just 80m to the east, would support a Neolithic date.

Two other candidates have been revealed by aerial reconnaissance 13km and 26km to the south in Herefordshire. The first at Whitney-on-Wye has been described by Barber (2007, 92) as a 130m diameter sub-circular enclosure defined by a narrow ditch. The second in the Golden Valley (Musson, pers. comm.) is between 100–107m in diameter and appears to survive as an earthwork, although Keith Ray (pers. comm.) indicates that there is some doubt as to its antiquity. Another example has also been argued for at Stanton Drew's Great Circle in north Somerset (Lawson 2007). Here geophysical survey by David *et al.* (2004, 347) has revealed a 127m diameter circular ditch, with a wide entrance on the northeast side. This morphology is indeed similar to the other formative henges proposed above, but the presence of nine pit and stone circles within its interior suggests closer comparison with later Neolithic sites like Woodhenge in Wiltshire (Cunnington 1929). Since the primary ditch fills of this latter monument have been dated to between 2477 BC and 1980 BC (Pollard & Robinson 2007, 159) the Stanton Drew circle is not considered to be a formative henge in this review. Other formative henges could doubtless be proposed in regions beyond those covered by this paper, and with this in mind, the crop-circle described by Harding and Healy (2007, 120), near Stanwick in Northamptonshire, is worthy of note.

Without excavation and the recovery of datable material it is impossible to prove the age of these enclosures, raising the risk that a phantom site type will be created where all roughly circular enclosures of requisite size are pronounced to be middle Neolithic. Similarly, there is the danger that other potentially middle Neolithic enclosures will be overlooked if they do not meet the criteria outlined above. Nonetheless, the possibility that formative henges may have been widespread and well-defined in the Neolithic mind is worth pursuing.

CONTEMPORARY CIRCULAR TRADITIONS IN WALES AND ADJACENT COUNTIES

The origin of formative henges has been sought in the early Neolithic, with causewayed enclosures being listed as a likely inspiration (*e.g.* Cleal *et al.* 1995, 113–4). Those examples found in the chalklands (Flagstones and Stonehenge) support this hypothesis, since they were built with segmented ditches, as are causewayed enclosures, albeit with those segments being joined at Stonehenge. It is possible that similar techniques were employed elsewhere – certainly causewayed enclosures are known in Wales and the borders – but segmented construction has not been recognised off the chalk, perhaps because it wasn't used, perhaps because such traces wouldn't survive in gravel, or possibly because the trenches dug across most other sites have been too narrow to identify such details.

But attempts to link formative henges back to causewayed enclosures seem, at one level, to be unnecessary since there are other middle Neolithic sites which could have provided a contemporary inspiration for these monuments. In Wales, such inspirations can be grouped under three broad headings: domestic structures, pit graves and passage tombs.

Domestic structures

Middle Neolithic domestic structures are rare, and Wales can only boast one from the years after 3000 BC: a 6m diameter circle of stakeholes with a hearth at its centre, built at Upper Ninepence in Powys, around 3021–2620 cal BC, with the most likely date being around 2900 cal BC (SWAN-24: 4240±70 BP) (Gibson 1999, 36). If this round house is representative of domestic structures in Wales at the turn of the millennium, then it is likely that the builders of formative henges were constantly reminded in their daily life of the possibilities of the circular form. Whether round houses in Wales were used before 3000 BC is not known, but certainly the form persisted into the late Neolithic, with two further examples being built at Trelystan around 2900–2500 BC (Britnell 1982, 139; Gibson 1994, 134).

Another structure which may be relevant here is a 6m diameter penannular ditched enclosure at Sarn-y-bryn-caled. A cremation was placed in one of the ditch terminals beside the entrance, and the ditch was cleared out before 2900–2670 cal BC (BM-2819:

Table 11.2

	Pit grave	Burial rite	Mound	Ditch
Four Crosses	Y	3 inhumations	Reuse in the BA, suggests pit grave was marked	20
Meole Brace	Y	Not known	Not known	15
Trelystan	Y	1 inhumation 1 cremation	Y	None
Ysceifiog	Y	1 inhumation	Y	11

4220±40 BP) with further cremations being added (Gibson 1994, 159-61). The scale of this monument and the presence of two large postholes at the entrance, suggest that a structure once stood in the enclosure's interior; and it is tempting to envisage a round house, the plan of which could easily have been removed by later ploughing (see Figure 11.3).

Pit graves

While middle Neolithic domestic architecture remains scarce in Wales and its nature largely speculative, there is little doubt that circular burial monuments were being built at the same time as formative henges, notably in the upper Severn Valley (Table 11.2).

The multi-phase site at Four Crosses 5 began as a 3.8 to 4.5m diameter pit grave, dug 1.4m deep into gravel around 3333–2889 cal BC (CAR-670: 4380±70 BP) (Warrilow *et al.* 1986, 64). An adult was buried in the grave, crouched on their left side and accompanied by a calf's jaw bone, and a pear-shaped stone. Two smaller slots cut into the base of this grave, contained further burials, and the grave was encircled by a 20m diameter ditch. This encircling ditch can be paralleled at another likely pit grave, the poorly preserved site of Meole Brace in Shropshire (Hughes & Woodward 1995), where a shallow grave was surrounded by a ditch 15m in diameter. Radiocarbon dating of charcoal from a primary fill produced a date of 3518– 2927 cal BC for this site (OxA-4204: 4535±100 BP), although it is possible that this is intrusive to the context.

The possible pit grave at Ysceifiog provides a third example and is of particular interest in the present context since it sits off-centre within the possible formative henge of the same name, described above. The grave was 2m by 3m by 1.5m deep, with an entrance "ramp" on the northwest side, and it contained a single inhumation probably buried in a wooden coffin. The grave was covered by a cairn, 2.4–3m in diameter and 0.75m high, and was encircled by a ditch 11m in diameter, which also had an entrance ramp (Fox 1926). Fox believed that this grave was the primary burial of an early Bronze Age mound, and it was only in 1994 that Musson noted its similarities to pit graves at Four Crosses and Trelystan. These similarities argue strongly for a middle Neolithic date for the pit grave, even though the grave itself is indeed overlain by an early Bronze Age mound (Musson 1994, 103).

The similarity of these three burial monuments (four if you include a ditchless pit grave at Trelystan, 12km from Four Crosses (see Britnell 1982)) and their proximity to one another is striking. They suggest a regional tradition entailing the digging of an out-size grave, a burial rite centred on inhumation, the marking of the grave with a mound, and the defining of the burial monument by an encircling ditch, 11m to 20m in diameter. Elements of this tradition are found in other areas to east and south (see Kinnes 1979),

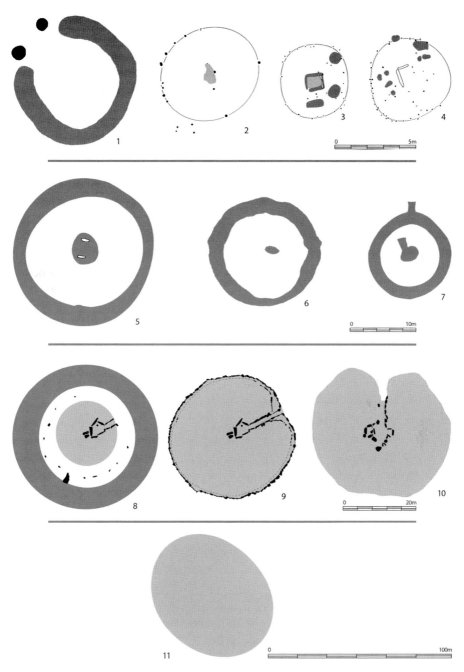

Figure 11.3: Plans of other circular structures discussed text, c. 3000 BC. 1. Sarn-y-bryn-caled; 2. Upper Ninepence; 3 and 4. Trelystan B and A; 5. Four Crosses; 6. Meole Brace; 7. Ysceifiog; 8 and 9. Bryn Celli Ddu, phase 1 and final monument; 10. Barclodiad y Gawres; 11. Gop Hill. (Sources of illustrations given in acknowledgements)

but their consistency in this part of Wales is notable. Since these burial sites overlap both geographically and chronologically with formative henges it is likely that the morphology of one influenced the design of the other.

Passage tombs

While pit graves are found in northeast and central Wales, passage tombs extend to east and west the distribution of circular burial traditions contemporary with formative henges. Best preserved are Barclodiad y Gawres and Bryn Celli Ddu on Anglesey, with carved stones at Llanbedr in Gwynedd and the Calderstones in Liverpool suggesting that other examples once existed to the south and east. It has also been argued that the massive, 67–99m diameter and 13.8m high cairn on Gop Hill might also cover a passage tomb (Lynch 2003, 24), but no structures were found at its centre when a shaft was dug in the 1880s (Boyd Dawkins 1902), and the site remains undated.

At Barclodiad y Gawres the mound consisted of large stones piled against the orthostats of the passage and chamber, bulked out with peat turves, probably cut from an adjacent marshy area (Powell & Daniel 1956, 23). As a result there was no need for ditch digging, and the mound provided a visible circular motif on its own. The same could be said of Bryn Celli Ddu in its final form, but excavation in the 1920s also revealed a circular ditch, 25m in diameter (Hemp 1930, fig 1), below the final passage tomb. It has been argued that this is the remains of an earlier henge destroyed by the construction of the passage tomb (O'Kelly 1969), but a radiocarbon dating programme and reassessment of Hemp's archive undermines the assumptions upon which this hypothesis is based (Burrow forthcoming). Instead, it seems that the ditch was dug to define a sacred space and to provide spoil for the construction of a primary mound around the passage tomb's chamber. Construction probably took place over just a few years between 3050 and 2900 BC.

Parallels for Bryn Celli Ddu's encircling ditch can be found in Ireland at the passage tomb Newgrange K (Eogan 1983), and at the complex cairn at Fourknocks 2 (Hartnett 1971). But in the context of the present discussion it can be noted that the scale of the ditch is broadly comparable to those which surround the pit graves at Four Crosses and Ysceifiog, raising the possibility that the form of Bryn Celli Ddu represents a fusion of indigenous Welsh and intrusive Irish influences. It can also be pointed out that at the time that Bryn Celli Ddu was being built, the formative henges of Castell Bryn Gwyn and Llandegai A may well have been in existence, just 5km and 8km away respectively.

DEATH AND THE FORMATIVE HENGE

The discussion above has shown that a number of potential formative henges exist within Wales and the Borders and that these were built alongside a range of other circular monument traditions belonging to the domestic and mortuary spheres of middle Neolithic life. Returning to the original definition of the henge, it seems likely that these structures were built to service a need for sacred spaces or communal meeting places which would otherwise be absent from the Neolithic around 3000 BC. But moving beyond this statement towards a clearer view of the function of these sites is more difficult. While pottery and flint has been found at several potential formative henges, it is often difficult to prove that these are contemporary with the enclosures rather than pre- or post-dating their main phase of use. Even so, stratigraphy and radiocarbon dates do make it possible to discern a link between some of these sites and death, for example at Stonehenge, Flagstones, and Llandegai A.

At Stonehenge, the fifty-six Aubrey Holes are thought to be contemporary with the ditch (Cleal *et al.* 1995, 575). While debate continues as to the primary function of these holes – sacred pits, postholes for timbers, or postholes for bluestones – the secondary fills of twenty-four out of thirty-four excavated examples contained cremated bone. A cremation from Aubrey Hole 32, has returned a date of 3079–2891 cal BC (OxA-18036: 4332±35 BP) suggesting that the enclosure may have been associated with death since its initial construction, and other dates indicate a continued relationship (Parker Pearson 2008). At Flagstones the cremated remains of an adult and the articulated and disarticulated remains of children were found on the base of the ditch (Smith *et al.* 1997, 37). And within the enclosure at Llandegai was found a pit containing cremated bone from an adult, dated to 3360–3013 cal BC (see above), as well as pottery and stone flakes, covered by an axe polishing slab (Lynch & Musson 2001, 45). Just outside the enclosure's entrance a 9m diameter pit circle contained multiple cremations, and produced dates of 3328–2918 cal BC and 3015–2891 cal BC (GrN-26818: 4420±40 BP and GrN-26817: 4320±30 BP respectively). The presence of the pit grave inside the Ysceifiog enclosure could also be taken as evidence of a relationship between the formative henge and the dead.

This is not to suggest that these enclosures were primarily burial places – this seems unlikely given the comparatively few burials found in comparison to their scale – more likely the inclusion of human bone, sometimes just token deposits, may have served to validate the other activities which took place within their interiors. Quite what these activities were remains difficult to grasp, as is also the case for the activities carried out within classic henges.

THE FUTURE FOR FORMATIVE HENGES

Much of the data presented in this paper is speculative, and individually each case could be argued against if one wished to dismiss this version of the formative henge. But given the existence of clear, large-scale meeting places in both the early and late Neolithic, it seems a reasonable hypothesis that a similar type of site should be present in the gap between; whether future research will find that this tradition has the coherency suggested in this paper is another matter.

But to indulge the speculation for a little longer, if research into middle Neolithic enclosures is to become as coherent as that for the periods before and after, one useful step might be to move on from the name they have acquired, "formative henges", which is itself derived from attempts to explain a late Neolithic phenomenon rather than to make sense of the middle Neolithic.

The builders of these circular enclosures were not experimenting with forms *en route* to their destination: the henge. Similarly, they were not built as debased causewayed enclosures, by people who had lost the design plans for this early Neolithic monument type. These middle Neolithic enclosures were designed as monuments of their time, built alongside other contemporary domestic and burial monuments, and for their study to proceed, it seems appropriate that they should have a name of their own. Perhaps the next example to be proven by excavation should supply it.

Mahon, J. (2008) Prehistory of Mendip, weekend study tour 15-17 August 2008. *PAST* 60, 4–5.

Musson, C. R. (1994) *Wales from the air: patterns of past and present*. Aberystwyth: Royal Commission on the Ancient and Historical Monuments of Wales.

O'Kelly, C. (1969) Bryn Celli Ddu, Anglesey. *Archaeologia Cambrensis* 118, 17–48.

Parker Pearson, M. (2008) *The dead of Stonehenge: cremation and inhumation practices in context*. Dublin, World Archaeology Congress (Pre-circulated papers).

Piggott, S. and Piggott, C. M. (1939) Stone and earth circles in Dorset. *Antiquity* 13, 138–58.

Pollard, J. and Robinson, D. (2007) A return to Woodhenge: the results and implications of the 2006 excavations. In M. Larsson and M. Parker Pearson (eds.) *From Stonehenge to the Baltic. Living with cultural diversity in the third millennium BC*, 159–168. Oxford, Archaeopress (BAR International Series 1692).

Powell, T. G. E. (1973) Excavation of the megalithic chambered cairn at Dyffryn Ardudwy, Merioneth, Wales. *Archaeologia* 104, 1–50.

Powell, T. G. E. and Daniel, G. E. (1956) *Barclodiad y Gawres: the excavation of a megalithic chamber tomb in Anglesey, 1952–1953*. Liverpool, Liverpool University Press.

Smith, R. J. C., Healy, F., Allen, M. J., Morris, E. L., Barnes, I. and Woodward, P. J. (1997) *Excavations along the route of the Dorchester by-pass, Dorset, 1986-8*. Salisbury, Wessex Archaeology.

Smith, G. and Hopewell, D. (2007) *Assessment of monuments at risk in an agricultural landscape – ceremonial monuments: henges and stone circles in north-west Wales*. Bangor, Gwynedd Archaeological Trust (Unpublished report).

Tratman, E. K. (1967) The Priddy Circles, Mendip, Somerset. Henge monuments. *Proceedings of the University of Bristol Spelaeological Society* 11, 97–125.

Wainwright, G. J. (1962) The excavation of an earthwork at Castell Bryn-Gwyn, Llanidan parish, Anglesey. *Archaeologia Cambrensis* 111, 25–58.

Warrilow, W., Owen, G. and Britnell, W. J. (1986) Eight ring-ditches at Four Crosses, Llandysilio, Powys. *Proceedings of the Prehistoric Society* 52, 53–87.

Chapter 12

Monumentality and Inclusion in the Boyne Valley, County Meath, Ireland

Geraldine Stout

INTRODUCTION

Every winter for many years I have joined the masses attending the solstice "event" at Newgrange in County Meath. Over that time certain rituals have evolved; "Here comes the sun" by the Beatles always plays in the car as I travel at dawn across the Meath countryside. In the misty haze, familiar faces emerge at Newgrange car-park, many not seen since the previous solstice. People move in unison towards the boundary gate; they hug, laugh, and chat. As we stamp our feet and wait in the bitter cold to be allowed access to the monument, inevitably, there is talk about who the dignitaries will be this year. There is heightened expectation that can only be compared with a Hollywood premier as a coach pulls up at the gate and well dressed, personalities are swiftly ushered in; Government ministers; foreign ambassadors; businessmen; the "golden circle" of Ireland. Eventually, the gates are open and we charge up the hill to the front of the mound anxious not to miss any of this amazing miracle of engineering unfold. We turn our backs on the dignitaries; our eyes are peeled on Redmountain as we wait for the sun to ascend above the ridge. Policemen, "guardians of the tomb", ask the crowds to kindly move back so the sun can shine in! Suddenly the valley beneath us transforms into a sea of pastels and the rays of the morning sun light up the opening of the roof box elevated above us. An emotional link is forged with prehistoric communities who are remembered on that day and the past reaches seamlessly into the present.

Social distinction between those who enter the inner sanctum of Newgrange and those who remain outside continues to be an issue 5,000 years after it was first constructed. Ireland's premier was recently criticised in the National Press for inviting his "cronies" to the Solstice in an article that was headed "Solstice places reserved for Ahern's Drumcondra Mafia" (*Irish Independent*, 6 May 2008). This paper focuses on the social engineering by the original builders of the Neolithic passage tombs of Ireland and the efforts that they made to cater for the needs of the greater public who remained on the periphery of religious ceremonies. It considers the "inclusive" features that were added to the exterior of these mounds to enhance and extend the religious experience of prehistoric visitors. It builds on the work of Richard Bradley (1998, 101–15; 2007, 103–6) and Alison Sheridan (1986, 17–31) who first developed theories on the elaboration of the exterior of these round mounds. Initially, this paper presents a brief overview of the monumental nature of the burial mounds at Brú na Bóinne World Heritage Site. Secondly, it examines excavation and field evidence and traces the development of inclusive monumentality within a group of passage tomb

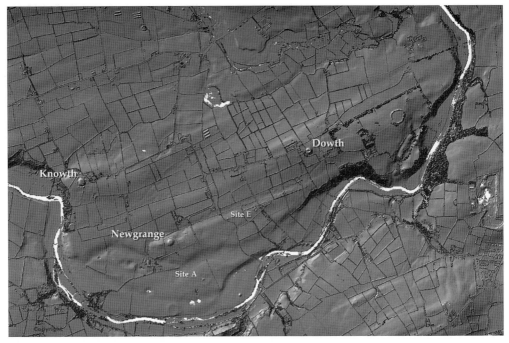

Figure 12.1: Lidar view of Brú na Bóinne World Heritage Site (2008).

cemeteries that witnessed a transformation from burial mounds to public monuments. This paper then examines evidence of similar developments in the final tradition of passage tomb building around Ireland and elsewhere. Finally, it explores the implications of such developments for the subsequent construction of late Neolithic/early Bronze Age henge monuments in the area.

MONUMENTALITY AT BRÚ NA BÓINNE

Newgrange and the many other burial mounds in the Boyne Valley are in every sense monumental. They meet all the criteria for "monumentality"; their grand scale, their design quality, their ability to inspire communities 5,000 years on. Within the Brú na Bóinne World Heritage Site (Figure 12.1) there are forty-one known passage tombs (Eogan 1986, 30–89; Stout 2002, 22–32). The round mounds which cover these burial chambers appear in three main cemeteries, which mark out three prominent knolls, enclosed by this dramatic bend in the River Boyne. Every effort was made to enhance the visibility of the mounds. Smaller mounds are arranged around the three largest sites, a circular pattern exists at Knowth, a linear one at Newgrange a dispersed one at Dowth. The linear arrangement of the mounds at Newgrange reflects the natural form of the hog-backed ridge upon which they were built, and it extends one kilometre eastwards to Ballincrad where there are two smaller mounds close to a large elongated mound associated with impressive megalithic art.

Newgrange holds a central and domineering position with the other two cemeteries lying to its east and west. It sits majestically at the top of a natural staircase and occupies the most prominent (albeit not the loftiest) seat in an island of land enclosed by the River Boyne. At its feet the sea tide ebbed and flowed and streams and rivers ran down from Redmountain into the Boyne creating a swirling cauldron rich in the fruits of the sea, field and forest. Below Newgrange the satellite tombs occupy the terraces that make their descent to the bank of the river. This arrangement is reminiscent of the tombs on the descending ledges at Carrowkeel, in County Sligo. The mound nearest the river at Newgrange was formerly on an island within the River Boyne. All the mounds have a round profile with the exception of the larger mounds at Knowth and Newgrange, which are flat-topped. They are usually delimited by a series of kerbstones, set end to end. However, kerbstones are not apparent at Newgrange A and Dowth H. When we look at the size of these mounds we see that they can range from as small as 12m in diameter at Knowth site 3 to 36m at Newgrange Site B which, for purposes of comparison, is about the same size as Maeshowe in Orkney.

Extensive excavations within the passage tomb cemeteries of the Boyne Valley have provided a significant number of radiocarbon dates. Archaeological evidence from Brú na Bóinne indicates that burial mound construction did not start before 3345 BC with the main building phase lasting until around 2900 BC. The passage tombs represent a remarkably close-knit group and it has been postulated that the period of construction could be as little as 180 years (between 3260 BC and 3080 BC) (Grogan 1991, 129). It is clear that monument building in the Boyne Valley involved a careful choice of location and sensitivity to the natural formation of its landscape. There is a sense of order and symmetry, a formality in their arrangement not just within the cemeteries but within the landscape itself suggesting an overall vision or grand plan for monument building in this sacred place. Their great visibility sends out a strong message of the power possessed by the tomb builders (Bergh 1995, 130).

DEVELOPMENT OF INCLUSIVE MONUMENTALITY

A long history of field survey and excavation in the Boyne Valley allows a detailed insight into the architecture of these burial mounds and more minute constructional detail is available for the twenty-five excavated sites at Newgrange, Knowth and Townleyhall. It allows the identification of "inclusive" features that provided a larger audience with access to the tombs ceremonial features: a flattened entrance façade, which would have formed a stage area; a distinctive entrance stone or settings used as a depository for votive offerings and exotic stones; preponderance of symbolic art on the external kerbstones which acted as architectural pointers to certain actions during religious ceremonies. External platforms would have accommodated a larger audience than the confined burials chambers and their presence represents a change from a focus on the enclosed space of a tomb to the creation of open arenas (Bradley 1998, 101).

Knowth cemetery

At Knowth cemetery there is the main mound (which covers two burial chambers back to back) and seventeen smaller tombs (Figure 12.2) (Eogan 1986, 30–89). The building sequence is not clear for all the tombs but at least two of the burial mounds Site 13 and Site 16 are earlier than the main mound as part of their mounds were removed and the outer passage of Site 16 was re-aligned during the construction of Site 1. In contrast, Site 17

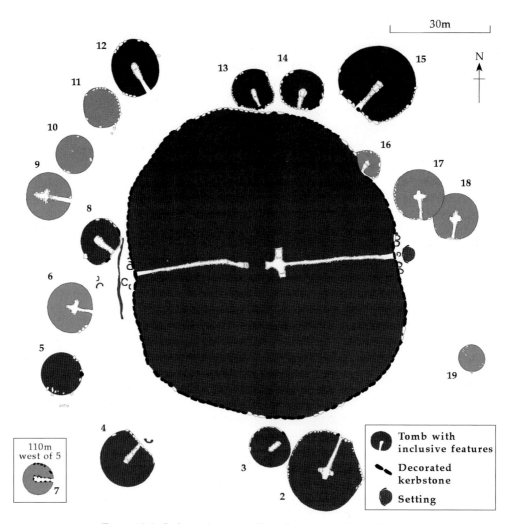

Figure 12.2: Inclusive features at Knowth cemetery, County Meath

and Site 18 are thought to be stratigraphically later than the main mound. There may have also have been an earlier tomb or "sub-Knowth" under the main mound like Newgrange. Some of the decorated stones from Knowth were re-cycled from an earlier tomb. These were used in the construction of the western and eastern tomb (Eogan 1998, 162–71).

At Knowth at least nine of the smaller mounds have "inclusive" features in their exterior (Figure 12.2); many of these have undifferentiated passage chambers, which are thought to be the earliest in the building sequence. A kerbstone at the entrance of Site 2 was decorated and there were votive deposits of flint found in that area. At Site 3 a back kerbstone was decorated. Amongst the most impressive of the smaller mounds is Site 4, which has a flattened entrance façade and a circular setting in front with quartz paving and two concentric rings. There is a generous amount of space in this area between this satellite tomb and the main mound allowing plenty of room for people to circulate around a particularly fine concentration of kerbstone art on the main mound. Site 5 was badly damaged but had one decorated kerbstone. At Site 8 there is a recessed entrance with two decorated kerbstones in the front of the mound. Site 12 has one decorated kerbstone along its eastern perimeter. Site 13 has four decorated kerbstones including three at the entrance. Site 14 has three decorated kerbstones at the front. The kerbstones are largest at the entrance of Knowth 15, which also has a flattened façade with a decorated entrance stone and another along the eastern perimeter of the mound. As Site 13 is earlier than Site 1 it is clear that these special external features were an early development in the tomb architecture of Knowth.

The main mound at Knowth Site 1 is flat-topped. On both sides of Site 1, there are various features in the recessed areas of the burial chamber entrances including settings, standing stones and spreads of exotic stones. Seven of the settings on the eastern side are all quite similar in make-up. In the west a standing stone was placed directly opposite the entrance and it had been artificially smoothed. Quartz is found at both entrances. Near the entrance to the eastern tomb is a timber circle or "Woodhenge". The main mound has the greatest concentration and most continuous display of megalithic art on kerbstones in the Boyne Valley (or indeed in all of Europe), bounded by a kerb of 123 stones. Ninety kerbstones are decorated and decoration is found on the backs of eleven (Eogan 1986, 150). The only real gaps are in the north and northeast where Site 1 incorporated two of the earlier tombs and there is little room to view the external art. One of the fundamental differences of Knowth Site 1 kerb art and the other cemeteries is the large size of individual motifs. Claire O'Kelly (1973, 379) was of the impression that the desire was to make the ornament "larger than life" and visible to the large crowds who gathered around the exterior of the monument. The audience had changed from the few individuals who were permitted to see the art of the interior to a larger group that remained outside (Bradley 1998, 110).

Newgrange cemetery

The main mound at Newgrange is part of a cemetery of four satellite tombs that extend to its east and west (Figure 12.3). There are two further isolated tombs on the river terraces beneath it. Excavations at Newgrange provide evidence that at least some of the smaller mounds predate the larger tombs but probably not to any great extent given that the art is similar to the main mound and there are also traces of elaboration in the exterior of the tombs. A smaller mound of turf under the main site at Newgrange has been revealed in excavations by M. J. O'Kelly and Anne Lynch and is apparent in the noticeable bulge in the rear of the mound (Stout & Stout 2008, 12). Within the Newgrange cemetery, Kelly argued that Site K was the earliest because of its simplest form, and Site Z stratigraphically the latest (O'Kelly *et al.* 1978, 249–352). Site L appears to be later than Site K as it was flattened on the west side where it is closest to Site K.

Newgrange Site K is a multi-period site, the primary phase consisting of a short passage leading into an undifferentiated chamber, which was covered by a circular mound held by a kerb of low contiguous boulders. One of the boulders to the west of the entrance was decorated. This was enclosed by a ditch with an opening on the same axis as the passage. The passage was extended and the mound enlarged to cover the passage. There was a fragment of a decorated stone in the front (Stone A) and a curiously-shaped concoid

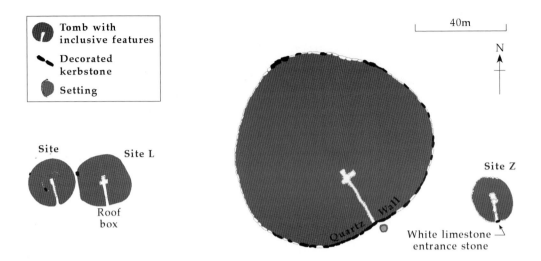

Figure 12.3: Inclusive features at Newgrange cemetery, County Meath.

stone in front of the entrance (O'Kelly *et al.* 1978). Beside it is Newgrange L'a cruciform tomb with one decorated kerbstone west of the entrance, which is quite distinctive. The passage tomb is thought to have had a roof slot below the lintel-which was a less elaborate version or forerunner of the Newgrange main mound (Lynch 1973, 147–61). Frances Lynch suggests that revisits would have been for something unconnected with funerals; to leave offerings for the dead such as at Danish mortuary houses or pottery like that placed in the chamber of West Kennet.

Newgrange 1 is the largest of the tombs on the summit and has an array of exterior "inclusive" features; a flattened façade, quartz and granite boulder revetment, an elevated highly decorated roof box, decorated kerbstones and "dish-like" settings at the entrance. The mound is flat-topped; the large level area on the top measures approximately 45m in diameter and is large enough to have functioned as a sacred platform for ritual fires or the enactment of ceremonies at important times of the year. Two antiquarian reports from the early eighteenth century record a standing stone at the top (Stout 2002, 40). A survey of the mound in 1776 shows that this standing stone had been removed by that date, but it also shows a triangular stone located just outside the entrance to the passage. Excavation in front of the tomb did not reveal this triangular stone but there was a broad shallow trench precisely where the stone is depicted in the antiquarian drawing (Stout 1993).

There are thirty-nine decorated kerbstones around the main mound at Newgrange. The decorated stones are arranged in three distinct locations; at the front façade of the tomb either side of the entrance, coinciding with the limits of the quartz, around the highly decorated "back" stone in the northwest sector of the mound (K52), and near the third highly decorated stone in the east (K67). The concentrations would have acted as architectural pointers to ceremonial practice. Elsewhere the art can be difficult to see but visibility improves at particular times of the year, depending on the position of the sun shining on the stones. Some may be mere graffiti built up over many years of public ceremonies during the Neolithic. They show little sign of being executed by the hands of craftsmen and many people seem to have been involved. This is in marked contrast to the quality of the kerbstone art at Site 1 at Knowth.

Deposition of non-local exotic stones clearly played some part in the outdoor ceremonies at Newgrange. Five types of non-local "collectable cobbles" and quartz were used to embellish the tombs at Newgrange (Mitchell 1992, 128–45). Quartz, because of its whiteness, is regarded as a symbol of purity and light in many different societies. In Ireland it is traditionally associated with burials and remembrance. Even today quartz pebbles are placed on modern graves. The cobbles at Newgrange are small enough to have been brought to the tomb by hand. Possibly pilgrims from far afield came to these public ceremonies and left behind a symbolic token of their own place.

Here we are witnessing the development of a hierarchy of pilgrimage sites in Neolithic Ireland. The exotic cobbles at Newgrange provide the clue to the broad spread of the congregation served by the Boyne Valley monuments (Figure 12.4). The stone used to embellish the mounds at Newgrange was white quartz from the Wicklow Mountains which lies over 60km south of the Boyne Valley; dark granite from the Mourne Mountains at least 50km to the north; and gabbro cobbles from Carlingford mountains, the most likely source being a stretch of shore at Dundalk Bay. Communities in these areas shared similar religious beliefs with those in the Boyne Valley and built passage tombs in large numbers. It is possible that these communities made their own pilgrimage to this religious centre during significant solar events bringing with them cobbles from their own area. Such communities were drawn to the "Vatican" of these great centres of Neolithic religion.

Excavations at Newgrange exposed a number of "inclusive" features near the entrance that could be linked to ceremonies associated with burial. An oval setting was found in front of the kerbstone immediately to the right of the entrance stone. A low mound of quartz pebbles and rounded boulders of grey granite covered it. In this dish-like setting a flint blade, knife and a highly polished phallic stone were found.

The periphery of Newgrange continued to be a focus for intense outdoor ritual activity into the late Neolithic/Beaker period. Remains of great fires were revealed around the entrance of Newgrange. Deep pits were dug to receive votive offerings of burnt animals. The stones of the Great stone circle act as a calendar casting a shadow on the decorated entrance stone during the winter and summer solstices, equinoxes and other key astronomical events (Prendergast 1991, 22–5). A massive timber circle was placed near the entrance at Newgrange which enclosed passage tomb Site Z (Sweetman 1985, 283–98). An earthen henge enclosed the passage tomb Newgrange Site A on the terrace below (Stout 1991). The range of calibrated dates for the late Neolithic/Beaker activity extends from 2855 BC to 2140 BC. A pre-Beaker/late Neolithic phase could have begun as early as 2850 BC (Grogan 1991, 126–32).

At Newgrange cemetery a building sequence is postulated which sees the tombs getting larger, the exteriors becoming more important and elaborate with the addition of quartz, and granite boulders, decorated kerbstones and stone settings. As Site K is earlier than Site 1 we can, nonetheless, say that these "inclusive" features were an early development in the tomb architecture of the Newgrange cemetery. If, as is likely, Site 1 and Site Z come at the end of the tomb building sequence it makes sense that these are the sites which become incorporated into the later "henge" monuments (the Great Stone Circle and the

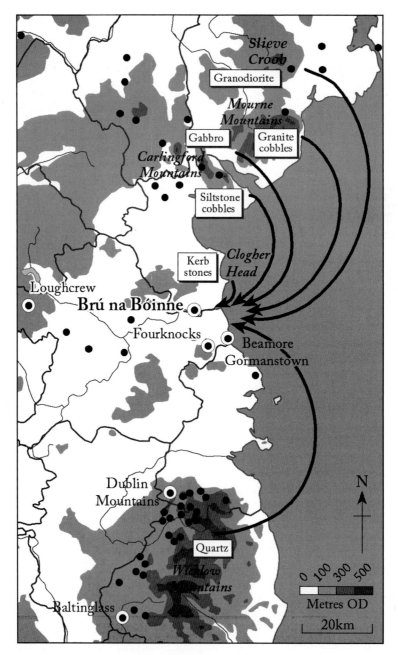

Figure 12.4: Comparative distribution map of Passage Tomb building communities in eastern Ireland and the origin of exotic stones at Newgrange, County Meath

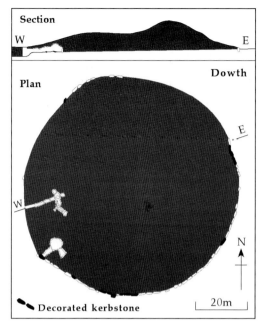

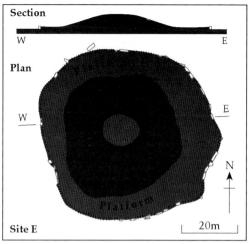

Figure 12.5 (left): Inclusive features at Dowth cemetery, County Meath; Figure 12.6 (right): Ground Plan and elevation of Dowth Site E, County Meath

"Woodhenge"). The main mound at Newgrange is the most elaborate with its winter solstice alignment. By the time Site Z was built the builders were using the same quarry for the greywacke structural stones, but they have added a distinctive entrance stone and quartz and granite boulders were being ritually placed at the entrance. This is the site that becomes enclosed by the pit-circle. Closer to the river is the large burial mound known as Newgrange Site A, a flat-topped mound, *c.*30m in diameter, with no visible kerbstones. It too became enclosed by a henge.

Dowth cemetery

The cemetery at Dowth comprises the main mound with at least two satellite mounds on the ridge immediately to the east of Dowth but there may have been at least three more in the vicinity (Figure 12.5). The main mound compares in size and situation with Knowth and Newgrange yet has remained virtually unexplored in modern times (O'Kelly & O'Kelly 1983, 136–90). Unfortunately, the lack of modern scientific examination means that there is not the kind of detailed architectural evidence that we have for Knowth and Newgrange. But we can make some basic observations. Like Newgrange and Knowth three of the surviving tombs mark out the summit of the ridge. There are few "inclusive" features associated with these mounds with the exception of Dowth Site E and Dowth Site H. One of the largest of the satellite tombs, Site H, may have had a decorated kerbstone. A decorated kerbstone was found in a ditch very close to Site H and it is was re-erected south of Newgrange near the perimeter fence. Dowth Site E is situated on the same ridge as Newgrange and is a round mound, *c.*22m in diameter and 4m high. Around the foot is a low, broad platform, which may have been used to accommodate pilgrims during religious ceremonies (Figure 12.6). This is defined by a kerb, which gives the site an overall diameter of *c.*31m.

What is clearly monumental about the main mound at Dowth is the small area that is taken up by the burial chambers, relative to the great extent of the cairn. The mound at Dowth covers two burial chambers both in the western periphery of the mound. At sunset on the shortest day of the year the rays of the setting sun illuminates the southern passage and circular chamber in a manner similar to the winter solstice event at Newgrange (Moroney 1999). Quartz is also visible around the front of the mound. Dowth has fifteen known decorated kerbstones, but much of the kerb at Dowth has never been exposed. Their arrangement around the mound is quite similar to Newgrange except for the rarity of art around the entrances. There is one decorated entrance stone at the southern burial chamber and a cluster on the right hand side of the mound in the south and again diametrically opposite the entrance to the southern burial chamber in the east of the mound. There is a single example of kerbstone art in the northwest. The emphasis on the dextra echoes the presence of the right-hand recess in the southern burial chamber and extension to the right-hand recess in the northern chamber. Within the Dowth cemetery, therefore, external elaboration is apparent at the main mound with its decorated kerbstones and the presence of a platform at Site E. There is also the association of henge monuments and a stone circle in close proximity to the cemetery at Dowth Demesne (Stout 2002, 35–7).

Monknewtown cemetery

The single mound at Monknewtown lies south of the Mattock River in the northern boundary of Brú na Bóinne World Heritage Site. It is the same size as Newgrange Site B with a chamber and southeast oriented passage and irregular kerbing. There does appear to be a platform encircling the mound. An earthen henge monument is located close by. One of the burials found inside the henge was a cremation of a child, which was contained in a Carrowkeel bowl; a style of pottery usually found in passage tombs and highlighted the overlapping of two cultural traditions (Sweetman 1976, 70).

INCLUSIVE MONUMENTALITY ELSEWHERE IN IRELAND

In this survey of the cemeteries in the Boyne Valley we have seen the move towards inclusivity becoming apparent from the earliest stages of mound construction through to the final stages represented by the mounds of Knowth, Dowth and Newgrange. Amongst the suite of "inclusive" architectural features the most apparent is the profusion of decorated kerbstones. There is an abundance of kerbstone art in the Boyne Valley, but outside of the Boyne it occurs relatively rarely and, where it does occur, it is in the larger tombs; Loughcrew, County Meath, Baltinglass, County Wicklow, Knockroe, County Kilkenny. There are only two other passage tombs that might have megalithic art on the exterior; Carnavaghan, County Armagh and Millin Bay, County Down (Shee-Twohig 1981, 93–121). Megalithic art on kerbstones is often associated with "inclusive" features such as flattened façades, quartz embellishment and dish-like settings. For example, Loughcrew in County Meath is an important group of decorated passage tombs but there are only two occurrences of decorated kerbstones and these are at the largest of the passage graves. Cairn T is the principal passage grave with central position on Carnbane East (Figure 12.7A). This site has a flattened façade and evidence for circular settings at the entrance. There is a very tall kerbstone again to the right

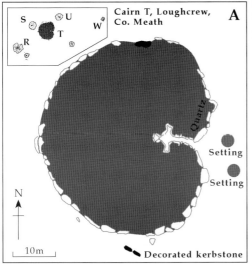

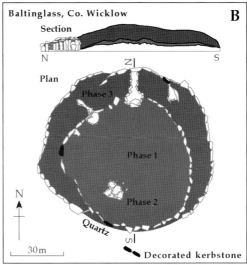

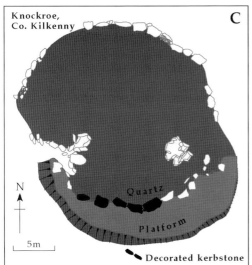

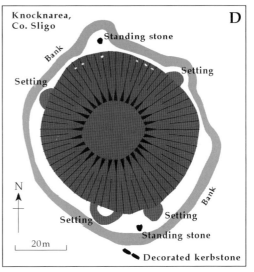

Figure 12.7: Inclusive features at (A) Cairn T, Loughcrew, County Meath; (B) Baltinglass, County Wicklow; (C) Knockroe, County Kilkenny; (D) Knocknarea, County Sligo

of the entrance known as the Hag's Chair with decoration on the back and front (K29). At Cairn T a layer of quartz also extended around the cairn behind the kerbstones. At the entrance to Cairn T are circular settings (McMann 1993, 17). The large passage tomb at Baltinglass, in County Wicklow (Figure 12.7B) is another site outside the Boyne Valley where there is evidence for multi-period construction evident with three successive structures built on the one site. But there is a flattening of the façade in the latest phase associated with an abundance of quartz and decorated kerbstones in both phases (Walsh 1946, 221–36).

In southeast Ireland, at Knockroe, County Kilkenny, there is a passage grave (Figure 12.7C) located above a bend in the river which shows remarkable similarities to the tombs in the Boyne Valley, particularly Knowth (O'Sullivan 2004, 44–50). Megalithic art has been found on seven kerbstones on the southern side of the cairn where there is also a platform (O'Sullivan 1987, 84–95). A great deal of quartz, which was part of the cairn façade and not deliberately lain on the ground, was concentrated around the kerbstones that flanked the entrance. There were also rounded cobbles. The decorated kerbstones are concentrated behind this quartz platform. The western chamber in this tomb is aligned on the winter solstice, when the setting sun shines along the axis of the passage and into the chamber (O'Sullivan 1993, 5–18).

In the west of Ireland stands the spectacular mound at Knocknarea in County Sligo (Figure 12.7D). Traditionally known as Maeve's cairn it represents an investment of time and resources on the part of its prehistoric builders, equivalent to the sum of investment of all other cairns in the region (Bergh 1995, 93). The flat top of Knocknarea is large enough to have functioned as a sacred platform, for ritual fires or the enactment of ceremonies. There are complex exterior features including circular settings (Bergh 1995, 89–90). Here they marked cardinal points with two large slabs that may have associations with different positions of the moon and sun (Bergh 1995, 94). Bergh (1995, 86) has identified a series of platforms built around the flanks of several passage tombs in county Sligo near Knocknarea. At Listoghil, for example, there is an 8m wide platform immediately outside the kerb that runs along the perimeter of the cairn. These were associated with an outer stone circle (Bergh 1995, 85). At Cairns Hill West, south of the cairn and adjoining its edge is a 9m wide platform.

Outside Ireland there is also evidence that the external spaces of these monuments were transformed for public gatherings. In the final tradition of passage-tomb architecture on Orkney, the Maeshowe types of cairn incorporated platforms into the monuments and platforms were also added to some of the older monuments (Noble 2006, 131), Maeshowe itself is built on an earthwork platform enclosed by a ditch and possibly a wall. At Quoyness and Taversoe Tuick these platforms became the focus of ritual deposits (Bradley 1998. 111–2). The cruciform tomb at Barclodiad y Gawres in North Wales was enclosed by a low cairn (Bergh 1995). Breton tombs have also produced evidence for outdoor ceremonial activity at the entrance to the tombs. Many of the cairns such as Gavrinis, Lle Carn, and Barnenez reveal monumental stepped façades which sometimes acted as depositories for votive offerings (Briard 1997, 88).

DISCUSSION

From this survey of round mounds in the Boyne Valley it is clear that from the earliest stages of construction the builders were incorporating architectural detail to enhance the experience of those members of the community who remained outside the monument during religious events. This probably began with the flattening of the entrance façade which created a formal stage area in front of the entrance used for the performance of various rituals that would have been observed by large congregations gathered there. They also began to carve religious symbols on some of the outside kerbstones although most of the religious icons were placed in the interior. It appears that as time went on and as congregations grew the tombs grew in size and decoration on the kerbstones became more visually pronounced. Decorated kerbstones were also arranged in a particular pattern with emphasis on the entrance and right hand side of the mound probably influenced by the movement of the sun from east to west. Priests or priestesses may have accompanied worshippers around the stones, interpreting the symbols and performing rituals in front of them. Stone dishes were placed at the entrance to the tombs to contain votive offerings that included flint tools, phallic stone and exotic cobbles carried to the site by pilgrims.

Perhaps a modern analogy for this type of sea change in ritual practices can be found in the approach to Catholic mass before and after Vatican II. Before, the priest stood with his back to the worshippers and the mysteries of the altar ceremony were obscured, while the language of the ceremony further veiled the nature of the rite. After Vatican II the altar rail was removed and worshippers had a full view of the altar and of the celebrant. The language used was that of the local congregation and the numbers involved in the sacred rites were expanded to include lay members of the population. Within a few centuries of the final building phases of passage tombs there was a renewed phase of monument building in the Boyne Valley. In the late Neolithic, peripheries of the larger passage tombs, in particular their entrances became a focus for intense outdoor ritual activity. Large henges of standing stones, timber and earth were constructed (Stout 1991, 245-84). Building these timber, stone circles and earthen henges clearly continued a process of ever increasing inclusion that was already well advanced during the Neolithic (Bradley 2007, 116).

In Ireland outside of the Boyne Valley there are large, heavily "accessorized" passage tombs that must have formed regional pilgrimage centres like the mounds in Brú na Bóinne. These are also the sites that have significant solar alignments; Loughcrew at the spring equinox; Knockroe at the winter solstice and Knocknarea throughout the year. While earlier mounds in Europe also have inclusive features such as terraces, it is in Ireland and in Irish influenced tombs abroad that inclusive ceremonial practice became a key element of Neolithic worship.

ACKNOWLEDGEMENTS

I am grateful to David Field and the Neolithic Studies Group for an opportunity to give this paper at their Conference on Round Mounds and Monumentality in November 2008 and for their invitation to contribute to this volume. I would like to thank my colleagues Paul Walsh and Eamon Cody for sharing their wide knowledge of Irish megalithic tombs with me; Russell Ó Riagáin for helpful discussion; Emma Fahey, Colin Byrne, Russel Ó Riagáin and Matthew Stout for assisting in the field survey of Dowth Site E; Anthony Cairns, Loreto Guinan and Louise Mc Keever for access to the Lidar survey. Clare Tuffy for help with illustrations and lastly Matthew Stout who very kindly read the text and prepared all the drawings.

BIBLIOGRAPHY

Bergh, S. (1995) *Landscape of the monuments*. Stockholm, Riksantikvarieambet Arkeologiska Undersoknigar.
Bradley, R. (1998) *The significance of monuments*. London, Routledge.
Bradley, R. (2007) *The prehistory of Britain and Ireland*. Cambridge, Cambridge University Press.
Briard, J. (1997) *The megaliths of Brittany*. Locon, Editions Gisserot.

Eogan, G. (1986) *Knowth and the passage-tombs of Ireland.* London, Thames & Hudson.

Eogan, G. (1998) Knowth before Knowth. *Antiquity* 72, 162–71.

Grogan, E. (1991) Appendix: Radiocarbon dates from Brúgh na Bóinne. In G. Eogan, Prehistoric and Early Historic culture change at Brúgh na Bóinne. *Proceedings of the Royal Irish Academy* 91C, 126–32.

Lynch. F. (1973) The use of the passage in certain passage graves as a means of communication rather than access. In G. E. Daniel, and P. Kjærum, (eds.) *Megalithic graves and ritual: papers presented at the 3rd Atlantic Colloquium 1969*, 147–61. Moesgard, Jutland Archaeological Society (Publication 11).

McMann, J. (1993) *Loughcrew: The Cairns.* Oldcastle, Co. Meath, After Hours Books.

Mitchell, G. F. (1992) Notes on some non-local cobbles at the entrance to the passage-graves at Newgrange and Knowth, County Meath. *Journal of the Royal Society of Antiquaries of Ireland* 122, 128–45.

Moroney, A. (1999) *Dowth: Winter Sunsets.* Drogheda, Flax Mill Publications.

Noble G. (2006) *Neolithic Scotland: timber, stone, earth and fire.* Edinburgh, Edinburgh University Press.

O'Kelly, C. (1973) Passage-grave art in the Boyne Valley. *Proceedings of the Prehistoric Society* 39, 354–82.

O'Kelly, M. J., Lynch, F. and O'Kelly, C. (1978) Three passage-graves at Newgrange, Co. Meath. *Proceedings of the Royal Irish Academy* 78C, 249–351.

O'Kelly, M. J. and O'Kelly, C. (1983) The tumulus at Dowth. *Proceedings of the Royal Irish Academy* 83C, 135–90.

O'Sullivan, M. (1987) The art of the passage tomb at Knockroe, County Kilkenny. *Journal of the Royal Society of Antiquaries of Ireland* 117, 84–95.

O'Sullivan, M. (1993) Recent investigations at Knockroe passage tomb. *Journal of the Royal Society of Antiquaries of Ireland* 123, 5–18.

O'Sullivan, M. (2004) Little and large: Comparing Knockroe with Knowth. In H. Roche, E. Grogan, J. Bradley, J. Coles and B. Raftery (eds.) *From megaliths to metals*, 44–50. Oxford, Oxbow Books.

Prendergast, F. (1991) New data on Newgrange. *Technology Ireland* 22, 22–5.

Shee-Twohig, E. (1981) *The megalithic art of western Europe.* Oxford, Clarendon Press.

Sheridan, J. A. (1986) Megaliths and megalomania: An account and interpretation of the development of passage tombs in Ireland. *Journal of Irish Archaeology* 3, 17–30.

Stout, G. (1991) Embanked enclosures of the Boyne Region. *Proceedings of the Royal Irish Academy* 91C, 245–84.

Stout, G. (1993) The Vallency Triangle. *Archaeology Ireland* 7, 8–9.

Stout, G. (2002) *Newgrange and the Bend of the Boyne.* Cork, Cork University Press.

Stout, G. and Stout, M. (2008) *Newgrange.* Cork, Cork University Press.

Sweetman, P. D. (1976) An earthen enclosure at Monknewtown, Slane, county Meath. *Proceedings of the Royal Irish Academy* 85C, 195–221.

Sweetman, P. D. (1985) Excavation of a Late Neolithic/Early Bronze Age pit cicle at Newgrange, Co. Meath. *Proceedings of the Royal Irish Academy* 870, 293–98.

Walsh, P. T. (1941) The excavation of a burial cairn on Baltinglass Hill, Co. Wicklow. *Proceedings of the Royal Irish Academy* 46, 221–36.

Chapter 13

Round Mounds Containing Portal Tombs

Tatjana Kytmannow

INTRODUCTION

Portal tombs usually have a small rectangular chamber, flanking portal stones, and comprise the megalith class with some of the largest capstones in Europe, some weighing up to 150 tons. In Ireland especially they have been the subject of extensive discussion and description for more than a century (Wakeman 1891; Borlase 1897; Cody 2002; De Valera & Ó Nualláin 1964; 1972; Ó Nualláin 1989; Kytmannow 2007; 2008). Most portal tombs had a mound or cairn during their construction phase to give the orthostats stability and to provide a ramp to drag, push, roll, or lift the capstone onto the structure. Afterwards, the inside of the chamber would have been cleared of stones, soil or scaffolding and the cairn or mound modelled to the shape and height desired by the builders. Obviously this is not the only function or meaning of a cairn or mound. They delineate and emphasize open spaces; they can give a megalith greater visual presence; they can restrict and control access; and they can link several, possibly multi-period chambers, integrating them into the same structure. The form of a mound is therefore meaningful.

MORPHOLOGY

Mounds and cairns of portal tombs have not received much discussion. However, *c.*50 per cent of the 217 portal dolmens in Ireland, Wales, and Cornwall have some form of mound or cairn (Kytmannow 2007, 84). All possible forms have been attested: rectangular, trapezoidal, round, and oval. Cairns, *i.e.* stone built mounds, are more common, but this statistical bias could be due to the much better survival rate of such a morphological element in mountainous and rocky areas than in low-lying arable regions. Earthen mounds surrounding portal tombs do exist, for example at Clonlum, Co. Armagh.

Cairn sizes of portal tombs vary considerably, from sparse plinths or the last remnants of a much larger original cairn such as at Clogher, Co. Clare (2m by 3m by 0.3m = 1.8 cubic metres); and the tiny round mound at Errarooey Beg, Co. Donegal (3.46 cubic metres); to huge, high, long cairns of composite monuments in upland areas, the largest being Carneddau Hengwm South (2750.80 cubic metres). The largest cairns all surround multi-chambered tombs. The average cairn size is 213.39 cubic metres representing more than 500 tons of stone. Not one cairn is higher than the portal tomb it surrounds so the capstone would always be visible in these monuments. Whittle (2004, 85) argues for the likelihood of low platforms and less of a mounding and enclosing pile of stones. In areas such as the fertile valleys of southeastern Ireland, the Dublin area, and in some parts of Tyrone and Cavan, cairns are rare. The cairns there have probably been cleared away either as a source of stone and/or to increase available arable land. Because portal tomb cairns have usually no kerbstones (exceptions include: Corleanamaddy, Co. Monaghan; and Cleenrah, Co. Longford), the removal of a cairn is relatively easy. In some instances the stones which would have originally constituted a cairn are still present in an adjoining field wall: Ballyknock A, Co. Mayo, has a much larger wall close-by and parallel to the tomb; Ticloy, Co. Antrim, has some structural stones and most of the cairn stones in the next field wall; Ardabrone, Co. Sligo had some large stones and all of the former cairn were bulldozed towards the wall around sixty years ago when the present owner was a child; Mayo, Co. Cavan, was partly bulldozed and turned into a wall forty years ago by the uncle of the present owner; and at Pawton, Cornwall, the cairn seems to have changed its shape during the last 150 years from round to oval, either through field clearance or ploughing. Cairns and clay-rich mounds make handy building material for road metal, wall building, and house construction, and in many cases the destruction of the cairn or mound would have happened without witnesses or documentary evidence.

Stones for the cairns were most likely sourced in the locality, similar to the actual megalithic stones for the chamber construction. There is no evidence that stones for portal tombs were transported from any great distance; they all occur in the immediate area. The vast majority of portal tombs are placed parallel to a small stream and in some cases it can be argued that the cairn stones came from the stream beds. However, cairn stones picked from the stream bed and ancient field clearance stones look very similar and some cairns were obviously used to deposit later field clearance stones, *e.g.* Malin More D, Co. Donegal (Kytmannow 2007, 48). There is no evidence for quarry pits to source the cairn stones or the megalithic stones. A recent thorough survey and investigation of the stone technology employed in the Burren, Co. Cavan, revealed that the stones for the megaliths were drawn from large erratic sandstone boulders, while the cairns were mainly built from local limestone (Kytmannow *et al.* forthcoming). This is especially interesting because one of the largest and best examples of a round mound or cairn with a portal tomb is located here, Burren A South (Figures 13.1 and 13.2).

Round mounds or cairns vary in size, but the largest are *c.*20m in diameter and *c.*2m high and therefore reach the scale and proportions of passage tombs. Several of the tombs here discussed are located in dense bogs in the north of Ireland (Keerin, Co. Tyrone; Ballyvennaght C, Co. Antrim; Knocknalower, Co. Mayo) so their cairns are covered with bog and turf and their exact size cannot be determined. However, these portal tombs never required a supporting cairn during construction as their chambers are diminutive; tiny examples of a common blueprint. Furthermore, they rest on top of the cairn and are imbedded in the material (see Figures 13.1 and 13.2). The orthostats do not reach the ground below. This implies that the construction of the mound or cairn was either at the same time as the portal tomb chamber, or could even predate it. There are some round mounds or cairns with larger portal tombs, but they normally do not reach the large proportions of the mounds here discussed and the orthostats are imbedded in the ground below the cairn.

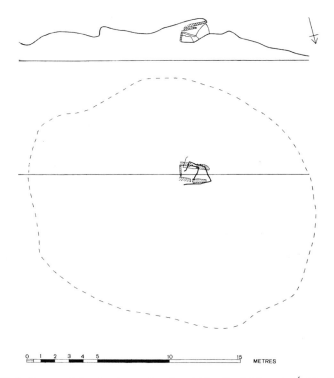

Figure 13.1: Burren A South, plan and section. (After De Valera & Ó Nualláin 1972)

Figure 13.2: Burren A south, Co. Cavan, the small portal tomb inside the cairn

EXCAVATIONS

Excavations have revealed that several portal tombs started out with a round cairn which was later enlarged. In west Wales the site of Dyffryn Ardudwy, Merioneth, was initially a small portal tomb in a round cairn, before it was enlarged as a long barrow to accommodate a second tomb (Powell 1973), and Aghnaskeagh A was also changed from a small oval cairn to a large elongated one (Evans 1935; Brindley 1988). In southwest Wales Pentre Ifan, Pembrokeshire, was substantially enlarged during its lifetime (Grimes 1949; Barker 1992, 23–26). That a long cairn can be part of the original design was suggested by Cooney (1997) who found evidence for a revetment at the multi-chambered tomb at Melkagh, Co. Longford. A development through different stages is also testified for other tomb types, for example at Mid Gleniron I, Dumfries and Galloway, two small burial chambers, each in its own oval cairn, were incorporated into one large long cairn when a subsidiary chamber was added (Scarre 2007, 32).

There is a strong aspect of regionality for a distinct group of tiny, miniature portal tombs with portal stones under 1.5m high, often in very large round cairns, the chamber imbedded into the cairn. They are restricted to the geographical north of Ireland. In these cases the cairn is not needed to support the chamber structure. There is certainly no practical reason to use such small slabs for the construction of the chamber and then to build it into a very large mound. Most of these tombs are in locations where there is no shortage of very large slabs and stones for tomb construction, with suitable slabs sometimes only metres away as at Kilclooney More A (see Kytmannow 2007, 58-60). The cairn gives the small portal tomb more visual presence, raising it to the top of an artificial hill, but more visually striking features could have been equally achieved by using larger orthostats and capstones from the outset.

The few miniature portal tombs which are not in a large cairn are instead set on a natural hillock which resembles a cairn (Templemoyle, Co. Donegal), or set beside a natural outcrop (Altdrumman, Co. Tyrone) or large erratic boulders (Carrickacroy, Co. Cavan). Such locations ensured that the portal tomb could be found relatively easily despite its small size. The monument would have also been linked to an important natural place giving it more visual presence and more significance, a role that would have otherwise been fulfilled by the round cairn.

SUB-TYPES

Four main sub-types of portal tomb have been recognized and classified A through to D (Figure 13.3) (Kytmannow 2008). Sub-type A comprises multi-chambered examples and the eighteen recorded examples are largely confined to the northern part of Ireland with a few examples in Wales and Cornwall but none in the southern part of Ireland (Figure 13.3). Sub-type B, very small tombs in large round cairns, is the smallest group with around fifteen to seventeen examples spread over a wide territory (Figures 13.3 and 13.4). Sub-type C includes the regular portal tombs with seventy-three recognized examples across all areas in which portal tombs are known (Figure 13.3). Sub-type D are the especially large ones, sometimes of enormous proportions, with massive capstones, for which fifty-four examples are known in all regions which have portal tombs but are over-represented in the southern part of Ireland and in Cornwall (Figure 13.3).

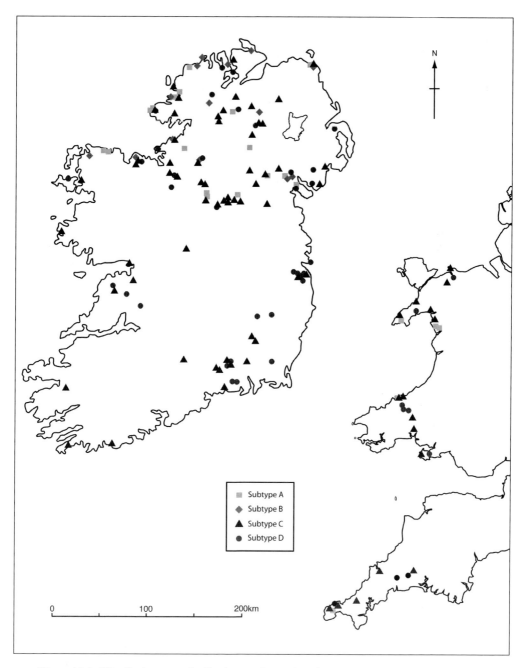

Figure 13.3: Distribution map of all subtypes of portal tombs. (After Kytmannow 2007, 151–2)

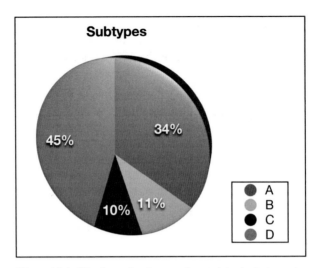

Figure 13.4: Pie-chart of subtypes of portal tombs in percentage

Amongst the more recent discoveries of portal tombs are five of sub-type B, two of which were discovered in 2008-09. Portal tomb studies experienced a bit of a revival in recent years, sparked by new publications (Bradley 1998; Cummings 2001; 2002a; 2002b; 2003; Cummings & Whittle 2003; 2004; Kytmannow 2008; Tilley & Bennett 2003; Whittle 2004) and the efforts of active field workers. Because sub-type B can blend into the landscape if the cairn is overgrown with peat and bog or does not exist, there are possibly even more to be found through further fieldwork.

Four of the portal tombs of sub-type B are found in one of the eight clusters of portal tombs. In these clusters the portal tombs represented are diverse in form and size. The question arises whether there was a taboo to replicate the same morphological type in the same cluster. It could have possibly offended the members of the group who had erected one tomb if another one looked very similar. This implies that the different styles or variants were of social significance and one group of society identified with one tomb, especially in a macro-region which shared the same landscape.

DISCUSSION

To build an artificial hill and to place a miniature portal tomb on top of it, or within it, changes the access to the ritual significantly; it would be visible for all. Most portal tombs are located in a valley, parallel to a stream, best seen from the side and with a view obscured from at least one direction. They are also never built on top of the highest point in the immediate locality. In contrast, any ritual at miniature portal tombs would be visible for a large group. It may be that a different function was associated with this type. Only limited physical strength was needed to erect these small structures and it could be argued that a different stratum or social group built these tombs, for example, women, children, and/or older persons. Even the physically weakest could have been involved in the building of the cairn into which the small portal tomb was then set. There is no space for any activity inside the tomb, and any celebrations, depositions, and ritual actions could have been observed by the whole group. The equal access to the ritual is mirrored by the round shape of the cairn; it is not easy to determine the front or the back of a round structure.

CONCLUSION

Very large round cairns with diminutive portal tombs inserted are a phenomenon of the geographically northern part of Ireland. They are not cists, but chambers clearly placed above the natural soil and secondary to the mound. The capstones are normally larger than would be required to cover the chamber, but they still weigh as little as one to two tons and could be lifted by two to four people. In contrast, the material from some of the round or oval cairns weighs up to 600 tons. Many hundreds of hours of work would have to go into construction, but the whole tomb could have been exclusively built by women, children, and older people. The round cairn and the equal access to the ritual make these tombs symbols of equality.

ACKNOWLEDGEMENTS

Thanks are due to Libby Mulqueeny and Thorsten Kahlert for providing maps and graphics. Stephen Clarke and Jim Mallory proof-read this text.

BIBLIOGRAPHY

Barker, C. T. (1992) *The chambered tombs of south-west Wales. A re-assessment of the Neolithic burial monuments of Carmarthenshire and Pembrokeshire*. Oxford, Oxbow Books (Monograph 14).

Borlase, W. C. (1897) *The dolmens of Ireland*. London, Chapman and Hall.

Bradley, R. (1998) Ruined buildings, ruined stones: enclosures, tombs and natural places in the Neolithic of south-west England. *World Archaeology* 30(1), 13–22.

Brindley, A. L. (1988) Aghnaskeagh A, County Louth: the portal dolmen and the cemetery cairn. *Journal of the County Louth Historical and Archaeological Society* 11(4), 394–97.

Cody, E. (2002) *Survey of the megalithic tombs of Ireland. Volume VI. County Donegal*. Dublin, Stationery Office.

Cooney, G. (1997) Excavation of the portal tomb site at Melkagh, Co. Longford. *Proceedings of the Royal Irish Academy* 97C, 195–244.

Cummings, V. (2001) *Landscapes in transition? Exploring the origins of monumentality in south-west Wales and south-west Scotland*. Cardiff, Cardiff University (Unpublished PhD thesis).

Cummings, V. (2002a) All cultural things: actual and conceptual monuments in the Neolithic of western Britain. In C. Scarre (ed.) *Monuments and landscape in Atlantic Europe. Perception and society during the Neolithic and early Bronze Age*, 107–121. London, Routledge.

Cummings, V. (2002b) Experiencing texture and transformation in the British Neolithic. *Oxford Journal of Archaeology* 21(3), 249–61.

Cummings, V. (2003) The origins of monumentality? Mesolithic world-views of the landscape in western Britain. In L. Larson, H. Kindgren, K. Knutsson, D. Loeffler, and A. Åkerlund (eds.) *The Mesolithic on the move: proceedings of the Mesolithic 2000 Conference*, 75–81. Oxford, Oxbow Books.

Cummings, V. and Whittle, A. (2003) Tombs with a view: landscape, monuments and trees. *Antiquity* 77, 255-266.

Cummings, V. and Whittle, A. (2004) *Places of special virtue: megaliths in the Neolithic landscapes of Wales*. Oxford, Oxbow Books.

De Valera, R. and Ó Nualláin, S. (1964) *Survey of the megalithic tombs of Ireland: Volume 2, Co. Mayo*. Dublin, Stationery Office.

De Valera, R. and Ó Nualláin, S. (1972) *Survey of the megalithic tombs of Ireland: Volume 3, Cos Galway and Cavan*. Dublin, Stationery Office.

Evans, E. E. (1935) Excavations at Aghnaskeagh, Co Louth, Cairn A. *County Louth Archaeological Journal* 8, 235–55.

Grimes, W. F. (1949) Pentre-Ifan Burial Chamber, Pembrokeshire. *Archaeologia Cambrensis* 100, 3–23.

Kytmannow, T. (2007) *Portal tombs in the landscape. The chronology, morphology and landscape setting of the portal tombs of Ireland, Wales and Cornwall*. Belfast, Queen's University School of Geography, Archaeology and Palaeoecology (Unpublished PhD thesis. Two volumes).

Kytmannow, T. (2008) *Portal tombs in the landscape. The chronology, morphology and landscape setting of the portal tombs of Ireland, Wales and Cornwall*. Oxford, Archaeopress (BAR British Series 455).

Kytmannow, T., Mens, E., Gunn, J. and Kahlert, T. (forthcoming) Art imitating nature – the relationship between worked pedestal rocks and megaliths in the Burren area, Co. Cavan, Ireland. In E. Mens and J. N. Guyodo (eds.), *Actes du colloque international, Technologie des premières architectures en pierres en Europe occidentale, Nantes, Musée Dobrée, 2,3 et 4 octobre 2008*. Rennes, Presses Universitaires de Rennes.

Ó Nualláin, S. (1989) *Survey of the Megalithic Tombs of Ireland: Volume V, Co. Sligo*. Dublin, Stationery Office.

Powell, T. G. E. (1973) Excavation of the Megalithic Chambered Cairn at Dyffryn Ardudwy, Merioneth, Wales. *Archaeologia* 104, 1–50.

Scarre, C. (2007) *The megalithic monuments of Britain and Ireland*. London, Thames & Hudson.

Tilley, C. and Bennett, W. (2001) An archaeology of supernatural places: the case of West Penwith. *Journal of the Royal Anthropological Institute* 7, 335–62.

Wakeman, W. F. (1891) [1848]. *Handbook of Irish antiquities*. Dublin, Hodges, Figgis and Co.

Whittle, A. (2004) Stones that float to the sky: portal dolmens and their landscapes of memory and myth. In V. Cummings and C. Fowler (eds.) *The Neolithic of the Irish Sea: materiality and traditions of practice*, 81–90. Oxford: Oxbow Books.

Chapter 14

Native American Mound Building Traditions

Peter Topping

Native American mound building encompasses some 7000 years of tradition, ranging from the shell rings of the Archaic Period to the platform mounds of the Contact Period when communities such as the Calusa on the Gulf Coast of Florida first encountered Europeans. The major complexes such as Cahokia, or those of the Ohio/Illinois Hopewell, were constructed by small-scale agriculturalists who were sufficiently organised to build major, communal monuments. This tradition encompassed a variety of mound types, ranging from conical forms to platform mounds and at their most eccentric the effigy mounds and their doppelgangers, the inverse "intaglios". This paper will present a broadly chronological survey of the major mound building traditions in North America and attempt to sketch something of the social context of these sites; the restrictions of word length prevent a comprehensive survey.

ARCHAIC MOUNDS *c.*5000 BC–700 BC

The southeast appears to have the earliest record of mound building from the evidence of the earth and shell midden-like mounds constructed by early hunter-gatherers from roughly 5000 BC. Many of these early mounds are complex entities which embody "capping events" that coincided with the abandonment of settlements; some featured cemeteries, and mounds could be built at locations without burial or settlement associations. At *c.*3000 BC a sub-tradition of conical mound building appeared, which was then followed some 500 years later by a new tradition of larger mounds comprising linear shell ridges which were then re-configured into U-shaped "amphitheatres" – which coincided with the first appearance of pottery at these southeastern sites. The shell rings of the Atlantic and Gulf Coasts range from small individual examples to complex, concentric sets of rings and the above mentioned U-shaped monuments. Detectable mound building "events" are evidenced by discrete dumps of clean shell, which may also demonstrate ceremonial feasting, thus physically embedding ceremony into the structure of the mound. Domestic activity is also present, suggesting that such sites might have influenced the development of the circular Archaic villages of the middle Savannah River in Georgia as part of the Shell Mound Archaic culture concept. At Stallings Island a peak in shell fish gathering coincided with the appearance of pottery, which led to the development of a circular village, plaza and a cemetery. These events were underpinned by certain innovations to increase the subsistence base, some possibly stimulated by a "ritual intensification", but by roughly 1,500 BC the complex had been abandoned, perhaps as a result of a population-resource imbalance (Sassaman *et al.* 2006).

At Watson Brake in the Lower Mississippi Valley of northeast Louisiana, lies one of the earliest mound complexes which effectively demonstrates that mound building developed well before the appearance of the Poverty Point complex (see below). The site is located upon a low river terrace overlooking a swamp which provided the inhabitants with many of their resources. Watson Brake comprised a setting of eleven mounds inter-connected by a low ridge 1m high forming an oval "enclosure" roughly 280m in diameter. The mounds range between 1.0m to 4.5m in height, with one exceptional mound standing 7.5m high. However, the intriguing feature of this site is its very early construction date of 3400 BC, placing it some 2400 years earlier than Poverty Point (Saunders 1997). Watson Brake may have functioned as an aggregation point, where scattered groups came together on a seasonal basis to reaffirm shared cultural beliefs and maintain group dynamics. The close proximity of the adjacent wetlands will have provided many natural resources to create the subsistence base for these social or ceremonial gatherings. The enclosed sub-circular space created by the mounds and linking ridge would have formed an earthen amphitheatre where ceremonial events could be enacted and overseen by the surrounding community. Such periodic or seasonal gatherings would create a forum for group debate about seasonal activities, and provide the platform for the exchange of raw materials or finished artefacts, presaging the situation which developed – or continued – at Poverty Point. The exchange of culturally-significant artefacts may also have underpinned the ceremonialism undertaken at these complexes.

Between 5300 BC and 2700 BC, the Preceramic Archaic Mount Taylor Period in the Southeast, the primary deposits in many mounds record evidence for intensive freshwater shell fishing by hunter-gatherer communities. These early mounds are then overlain by the culturally distinctive deposits of the fibre-tempered pottery users during the Ceramic Archaic Orange Period *c.*2700 BC to1600 BC. The final episodes of mound building at these sites was performed by the post-Archaic St Johns Tradition horticulturalists between *c.*1600 BC and AD 1500, demonstrating that many shell mounds were the result of long-term processes where periodic social interaction was founded upon the communal harvesting of shell fish. Little settlement evidence exists amongst these mounds, although at the Hontoon Dead Creek Complex, the southern shell midden produced "multiple crushed shell surfaces" which may have been evidence of house foundations or communal middening stretching over many generations of use (Randall 2008, 13–14).

Mortuary features were developed at certain mound sites. At the Harris Creek Mound excavations discovered a sequence of two mortuaries which contained a minimum of 175 individuals, demonstrating the potential longevity of use. The data from the Hontoon Dead Creek Complex recorded a ridged, domestic shell midden which was overlain by smaller mounds of clean shell. Following this phase, burials were inserted into deposits of white sand or in pits located upon the shell ridge. Recent stable isotope analysis demonstrated a demographic which included individuals from the local St Johns Valley in Florida, but also others from further afield in southern Florida, Virginia and Tennessee (Randall 2008, 14). This suggests that both local and distant communities came together periodically at these aggregation sites, which were special places in the cultural landscape, to reinforce their shared social and political agendas and cement kinship links and alliances through the medium of monumentalised burial practices.

A number of trajectories influenced mound building at roughly 4000 BC, including hydrographic events which determined potential locations for settlement and mound construction, and arguably the most culturally significant – long distance exchange. In Florida non-local artefacts appeared from South Carolina and Georgia, particularly bannerstones (a polished, bilaterally symmetrical stone with a central perforation; often considered to be an atlatl [spear thrower] weight). These pieces were deposited as grave goods or in caches, demonstrating both the extensive nature of the exchange network and the long-distance connections of widely dispersed groups and communities. Such a melange of cultural influences, including local innovation, led to "ongoing and non-directional transformations in structure and practice that register merging social complexities through time and space" (Randall & Sassaman, lecture, SAA Annual Meeting, 27 April 2007). The long-distance movement of bannerstones, whether through exchange or journeying as part of cultural renewal, may also have enabled the introduction of pottery, and through a "coalescence of once-separated coastal and interior populations" ultimately led to the development of new settlement patterns and mound building (Randall 2008, 15). Of particular interest are the large U-shaped shell mounds which may have been constructed as a venue for community ceremony and periodic gatherings. For example, at the Silver Glen Complex in Florida, the U-shaped earthwork was constructed upon a pre-existing shell ridge which may contain a mortuary facility, thus sedimenting the past into a monument for the present. Ceremonial or ritual activity may lie behind the presence of abundant deposits of decorated pottery submerged near the shoreline, and the discovery that different forms of pottery predominate in different parts of the mound complex (Randall 2008, 15–16).

It would appear that the different forms of shell mounds became pivotal to the social histories of Archaic hunter-gatherer groups, and became the catalysts to affirm, maintain, and renew community dynamics (*e.g.* kinship and alliances) but *also* provide the stimulus to initiate new trajectories for social transformations through the mechanism of periodic gatherings. However, some Late Archaic shell mounds were primarily functional – even if they had accumulated as the result of feasting or seasonal events. In Maine, the Moorehead phase shell middens were relatively unstructured, had little evidence for ritualised deposition, but do record a heavy reliance on swordfish and coastal fishing, thus demonstrating specialised subsistence strategies (Robinson 2008, 24).

During the Late Archaic (*c.*3000 BC – 1000 BC) shell middens were also formed into rings along the coastal areas of South Carolina, Georgia and Florida, suggesting the presence of at least eight separate cultures which appeared to be more socially complex than adjacent contemporary hunter-gatherers (Russo 2008, 18). The Rollins shell ring, for example, appears to emerge from rising ground in the east to create a sub-circular, erratic enclosure with an entrance break of some 100m wide located in the southern side and a series of twelve irregular sub-enclosures appended around the northern and western perimeters. The enclosed plaza is roughly 120m in diameter. Most shell rings provide little evidence of permanent habitation, they produce a limited range of pottery types amongst their assemblages, and other forms of artefacts are rare (*i.e.* bone tools, lithics and shell tools). The limited size of the assemblages prevents the identification of patterning, although the presence of decorated ceramics and serving bowls suggests that the shell rings were special places, an observation lent weight by the lack of *in situ* burials. The plaza, partly or totally enclosed by the shell ring, was clearly the social stage for special activities. Analysis of the shells forming the rings has discovered a variation in the size and quality of the harvested shells themselves, suggesting social distinctions may be recorded in certain parts of these arenas, possibly linked to social status – or simply demonstrating the locations of the most successful shell fishers in the extended community. Consequently, shell rings can be viewed as monuments which were "built to endure, they defined the plaza as communal and ceremonial space, presenting it to supernature, the greater world, and posterity." (Russo 2008, 18).

The classic Late Archaic mound complex is Poverty Point in northeast Louisiana, constructed between *c*.1000 BC and 700 BC. The site is located in the Lower Mississippi Valley overlooking the floodplain from a 7.6m high bluff and covers an area of over 200ha, although contemporary occupation extends over some 5km of the floodplain; at the foot of the bluff lies the Bayou Maçon. Poverty Point is the second largest mound complex in the United States after Cahokia, and was constructed from some 750,000–1,000,000 cubic metres of earth. The site comprises a series of six concentric, semi-circular earthen ridges 20m to 40m wide and standing 1m to 3m high, which together create a C-shaped setting opening onto the floodplain and the bayou. The ridges are cut by a series of five "aisles" between 10m to 49m wide and radiating inwards towards a roughly semi-circular plaza with an area of *c*.15ha. Within the confines of the plaza lay two platform mounds, the Dunbar Mound in the north and Sarah's Mount in the south. The Dunbar Mound appears to have been the foundation for a series of wooden buildings as the mound was periodically enlarged. On the western side of the plaza lay a series of large, deep pits which may have held substantial posts that functioned as calendrical or seasonal markers.

On the western (outer) side of the ridges lies the large, imposing Mound A, aligned on the central aisle through the ridges, and considered by many commentators as representing the effigy of a flying bird. The mound achieves a height of over 21m, its wings have a span of 195m and the body and head total 216m in length. The mound rises in stages towards the shoulder/head of the effigy. A possible astronomical alignment exists between Mound A and the central aisle through the ridges, which sights the spring and autumn equinoxes. Two further mounds lie a little distance from Mound A but are in alignment together creating a north to south axis through Mound A. The northern mound is the domed Mound B which is some 6m high and 55m in diameter, and that to the south of A is a platform mound known as the Ballcourt Mound – which was not a ballcourt – and is 30m square. Roughly 2.4km to the north of Poverty Point is the Motley Mound which is slightly smaller than Mound A and thought to be an unfinished bird effigy. Equidistant but to the south of Mound A lies the Lower Jackson Mound which is considered to pre-date Poverty Point by up to a millennium, but its location was subsequently integrated into the north to south alignment to legitimise links to an earlier ancestral presence.

Poverty Point lies near the confluence of six rivers, thus was in an important strategic location and well placed to have a pivotal role in riverine trade networks, particularly concerning lithics. The Poverty Point exchange network drew in both lithic raw material and finished artefacts derived from over ten sources in the Southeast and Midwest, some travelling distances of up to 1000km. However, this exchange network, and whatever socio-political system underpinned it, collapsed after some 2–300 years, thus bringing to an end a regionalised centre for trade and exchange which also had a clear role in the seasonal ceremonial cycle from the evidence of the various astronomical alignments apparently embedded into the structure of the Poverty Point complex.

THE ADENA (EARLY WOODLAND) *c.*450 BC–AD 200

The Adena emerged as a large group of localised cultures in the Eastern Woodlands around *c.*1000 BC, their earliest buildings appear to date from *c.*830 BC in the Scioto River Valley in Ohio (Neely 2008, 24), and they were initially a non-mound building culture. The Adena communities shared a group of common cultural traits, they were interdependent in many cases, and in certain areas appear to have co-existed with the Hopewell with whom they overlapped chronologically (*cf.* Cochran 1996). Consequently, the Adena could be considered as pre-cursors of the Hopewell or even a part of the same cultural continuum in certain areas.

The Adena inhabited an area defined by the modern states of Ohio, Indiana, West Virginia, Kentucky and parts of Pennsylvania and New York. They emerged as a cultural group during the Early Woodland Period, when pottery became more widely adopted. Earthen mounds were built towards the latter part of this period between *c.*450 BC to AD 200. However, the Adena also constructed earthwork enclosures, such as the henge-like Mount Horeb in Kentucky, located upon the summit of a hill, where a low bank encircled an inner ditch; a roughly 12m wide causeway in the west-south-west led to a circular platform which held a circular post-built enclosure some 29m in diameter (Webb 1941). Despite the construction of large communal monuments, the Adena were a people of contrasts: mobile hunter-gatherers they periodically inhabited small villages of circular houses which lay separate from the mound cemeteries; they were small-scale cultivators who used garden plots to grow marshelder, maygrass and chenopodium *etc.*, but they did not develop large fields which might have supported a more sedentary lifeway. The Adena also had extensive trade networks which presaged the "Hopewell Interaction Sphere" (see below), drawing in copper from the Great Lakes, exotic shells from the Gulf of Mexico, and mica from the Carolinas. These raw materials were crafted into various prestige goods (*e.g.* copper ornaments and mica cut-outs) many of which were finally deposited into grave assemblages.

Adena mounds ranged in diameter from 6m to 90m, and were constructed by basket-dumped earth. The time investment in such mound construction ensured that they were often re-used, and many featured sequential burials at different levels alongside the gradual enlargement of the mound. The characteristic burial rite was cremation placed within a small log-lined tomb, but rich inhumations accompanied by prestige grave goods also existed. If these burial rituals reflected the individual's status, and rich inhumations depict higher status, then it suggests that Adena society was complex and highly stratified, perhaps with wealth and status underpinned by access to, or control of, the prestige goods trade network.

However, an alternative model (*cf.* Clay 1996) suggests the Adena were an egalitarian society, and that the burial rite which emerged into the archaeological record was determined by social negotiation and was thus variable and not necessarily predicated by the social position of the deceased. Consequently, the size and complexity of the mounds are a reflection of social interaction and "less monuments to the dead"; the scale of the larger mounds is a reflection of the fact that they contained log-lined tombs. Adena mounds were "accretional" and not planned in a unified way; they began small, with a simple structure and were restricted to a few burials. Over time the mounds often acquired further burials and additional bulk to accommodate the new interments, thus their scale came to reflect the variability of local traditions. Grave accessibility was clearly an issue, and ranged from sealed internments to log-lined tombs which may have functioned as crypts. If the log-lined tombs were crypts and remained accessible until finally sealed, then they may only contain evidence of the last interments and not necessarily reflect the number of dead that may have passed through them.

Some Adena mounds were deliberately placed over circular or rectangular structures which do not contain domestic assemblages and which may have been more specialised sites. The re-use of significant cultural locations may be evidence for the continuity of special places – albeit for changing or complementary purposes (Milner 2004, 60). The presence of broken pottery sherds incorporated into the body of some Adena mounds may be evidence of further graveside ritual (Clay 1983, 113–116), or the transhipment of culturally-important earth or midden debris to create links between the settlements of the living and the mounds of the dead.

The largest Adena mound is the Grave Creek Mound in West Virginia; a late Adena Period site originally visited by Lewis and Clark, which engineers recorded in 1838 as standing 21.0m high with a diameter of 90m, and had a surrounding ditch 12m wide and 1.5m deep which was cut by a single causeway. It is estimated that the mound contains over 60,000 tons of earth, and was substantially larger than others locally. Excavations discovered the mound was built in stages between 250 BC and 150 BC, and had multiple burials at different levels within the structure (Woodward & McDonald 2002, 265–271).

The type site of Adena displayed many of the constructional and cultural traits of Adena mounds in general (*cf.* Mills 1902). This mound lay 1.5 miles (2.4km) northwest of Chilicothe in the Scioto River Valley in Ohio, and was intervisible with the later Hopewell mound group at Mound City to the north (cf. Figure 14.2), and the Chilicothe mound group to the south. At the time of excavation the mound stood 8.1m high with a circumference of 135.6m; the excavator suggested the mound had been built in two phases, although the cumulative nature of the burial record suggests a more complex and episodic construction, possibly over a number of generations. The earliest mound was constructed over a shaft-like central grave, which once sealed was surrounded by further inhumations in log-lined tombs; the twenty-one inhumations were wrapped in cloth or bark and all but one was accompanied by grave goods; all Phase 1 burials lay in the lower 1.5m of the primary mound.

The primary mound was constructed over a shallow basin, in the centre of which lay the shaft-like grave measuring 4.2m by 3.4m and 2m deep. This central grave was surrounded by displaced gravel, and lined with bark. The burial sequence appears to have been accompanied by the burning of two "great fireplaces", that on the north comprised an ash deposit 35.5cm thick which contained "a great quantity" of burnt mussel shells, calcined bones of wild turkey, trumpeter swan, Virginia deer, black bear and raccoon; a second similar fireplace was discovered on the western side of the central grave (Mills 1902, 20). Feasting or the conspicuous destruction of food resources was clearly part of the mortuary ceremonialism. The primary inhumation was an adult male who had been wrapped in three layers of bark. It would appear that the body had been de-fleshed as the leg bones had been painted with red ochre and some clothing was present. Nine Flint Ridge leaf-shaped flint knives lay at the feet, and a sharpening stone for bone tools was placed between the lower legs. Beside the right leg lay an assemblage of two further flint knives, a knife preform, several scrapers, three beaver incisors and two elk ribs – one of which had been fashioned into a comb. At the left leg lay eleven large elk bone awls and a perforated bone needle. Ranged around the head were twelve awls made from Virginia deer; on each side of the head were two perforated mountain lion canines – possibly ear ornaments. The burial was covered by many layers of bark, followed by a 7.6cm deep layer of ash which contained cremated human bones of an adult and child along with bones of deer, elk, black bear, raccoon, otter, beaver, wild turkey, trumpeter swan and great horned owl. This deposit may represent further feasting as evidenced by the adjacent hearths, with the human remains possibly representing a sacrifice (voluntary or otherwise) designed to accompany the main burial or a later death with a different burial ritual – perhaps reflecting differences in status? A layer of logs and sticks was then laid over this deposit, followed by a further unaccompanied male inhumation laid at right angles to, and above, the feet of the primary burial. The excavator found no evidence to suggest this last burial was sacrificial. This sequence was then terminated with a layer of logs.

Of the other Phase 1 burials, number 21 which lay on the north side of the mound is noteworthy for the richness of its assemblage (Mills 1902, 27–32). This inhumation lay in a log-lined tomb on a layer of bark and was adorned with some 1,500 beads forming a freshwater pearl and bone necklace and additional shell beads decorated the clothing. A shell raccoon effigy accompanied the burial, near the head lay three deer antler spear points, seven arrowheads and three knives of Flint Ridge flint; three further arrowheads lay beside the right hand. Adjacent to the left hand lay a clay effigy pipe 20cm tall, featuring a male figure with ear spool ornaments of a type common in Scioto River Valley burials. This iconic artefact has since come to typify the material manifestation of the Adena identity in many subsequent publications, and may originally have reflected the social status of the deceased.

During the excavation of the central part of the mound a "number" of hoes crafted from freshwater mussel shells were discovered (Mills 1902, 12). This assemblage may have been casual discard, although the excavator does not refer to any being found in a broken state. One interesting possibility may be evidence of a cultural taboo against removing tools used in mound construction in a similar way to that imposed upon removing tools from certain extraction sites (*cf.* Flood 1995).

The second construction phase was built over the Phase 1 mound, but eccentrically depositing more earth on the north side. The burials in this phase were scattered throughout the body of the mound, they were not entombed and only one of the twelve inhumations had evidence of a cloth wrapping or clothing; grave goods were fewer than in Phase 1, and "quite a number … had no implements or ornaments of any kind" (Mills 1902, 8), perhaps suggesting either a change in mortuary ceremonialism, or that the secondary burials reflected a change in status or social grouping amongst the deceased.

The bulk of the secondary mound must have risen around the original like a ruff collar, periodically halting to allow the staged placement of the dead, suggesting that this phase was not necessarily a single event but the result of an episodic series of communal interments which eventually led to the complete mantling of the Phase 1 mound by the secondary mound. The final formal inhumations near the summit of the secondary mound comprised an adult with four copper bracelets, to the east of whom lay an adolescent with two copper bracelets, a mica headdress, an earthen jar and a large sandstone block with "cup-shaped depressions" (Mills 1902, 11).

The mound was finally capped by earth which had a high concentration of charcoal, suggesting several episodes of conflagration (Mills 1902, 8–9); whether this represented ceremonial bonfires to dedicate the sealing of the mound, or off-site deposits designed to sediment culturally-significant places within the matrix of the mound is unclear. Near the centre of the mound a second "large pitted sandstone" was discovered, and at the summit lay a deposit of charcoal, ashes, human bones and the bones of deer and wild turkey. This deposit may represent both sacrifice and feasting at the closing of the mound. That sacrifice could form an integral part of the burial rite is graphically illustrated at the later Mississippian Mound 72 at Cahokia, where numerous individuals accompanied the primary inhumation (see below).

Adena mortuary ceremonialism included various ritualised elements. Skeletons or bodies were occasionally coated in red or yellow ochre. The construction of certain mounds involved the use of differently-coloured soils, zoned into different structural areas; certain colours were used for the mound whereas different colours were used for any surrounding earthworks. The use of coloured soils may be recording the presence of a colour-coded iconography which signposted differing levels of sacred space designed to trigger ceremonial behaviour. It is interesting to note that coloured soils were also carefully used in both Hopewell mounds and enclosures (*cf.* Lynott 2007), suggesting a longevity to this tradition and a perpetuation of the concept of embedding culturally-important deposits into important communal monuments.

HOPEWELL MOUNDS (MIDDLE WOODLAND) *c.*50 BC–AD 400

By the Middle Woodland period, mound building became common throughout the Midwest and Southeast, ranging from circular mounds no more than a few metres high to large, elongated mounds juxtaposed with geometric earthworks as can be found in Ohio. The Hopewell mounds in the Illinois and Mississippi River Valley are often located upon prominent, steep spurs overlooking the valley, although some also occupy the floodplain. The landscape setting of these mounds was clearly variable, and may have been driven as much by magico-religious beliefs as a territorial imperative designed to signpost cultural areas, although the richness of some burials makes it difficult to ignore "the powerful Hopewell ideology of individual power and prestige" (Fagan 2000, 139). The evidence for such individuality among the Hopewell is reflected not only in the burial record, but also the material culture and exchange networks, the often complex earthwork enclosures, and may have arisen from both exclusionary and corporate forms of political economies which may have existed separately, simultaneously, or as a matrix of both forms (Coon 2009). Such potentially polarised socio-economic systems would create the conditions to stimulate competition and wealth-display between inter-related but directly competing communities, which could explain the relatively discrete distributions of different enclosure forms – hilltop enclosures dominate southwestern Ohio, compared to compound geometric enclosures in south-central Ohio (*cf.* Coon 2009, 51, fig 1). Such differences may have been used to define and maintain separate cultural identities, even if the differences in material culture and burial practice were subtle.

The creation and maintenance of separate, regionalised community identities existing within the greater Hopewell cultural milieu faced certain difficulties. For example, the construction of the Hopewell enclosures – and indeed any form of communal earthwork including mounds – had to overcome the problem of a dispersed population which would have been difficult to marshal into effective "autonomous labor pools" for each construction project. However, it is likely that individuals may have been involved in the construction of several earthworks during their lifetime, and they will have provided labour to these projects "depending on the rewards offered, the varying prestige of earthwork sponsors, or the stage of a multi-earthwork ritual cycle" (W. Bernardini, lecture; SAA Annual Meeting, 25 March 1999). Such communal endeavours would provide a mechanism by which cultural traits could be developed, maintained and sedimented into an enclosure or burial mound to signpost cultural identities.

Certain large mounds were constructed over pre-existing structures (often interpreted as enclosures, charnel houses, or in the more elaborate cases complex buildings, especially at the Edwin Harness Mound (*cf.* Greber 1979, 30–31)) which contained skeletal material and grave assemblages, frequent fires in "crematory basins", both disarticulated and articulated bones, suggesting lengthy periods of use before mound construction sealed and terminated the process and monumentalised the location. The scale of interment – and thus an estimate of the uselife of these sites – can be judged by the presence of 178 individuals at the Edwin Harness mound, 132 at Seip Mound I, and 102 at Hopewell Mound 25, all in Ohio (Milner 2004, 63). Artefact assemblages are often discovered in these structures, and not always associated with burials – hoards of mica, copper gorgets and axes, or obsidian artefacts have been recovered, some wrapped in various types of fabric. As with the Adena, log-lined tombs or crypts are also found in Hopewell mounds, implying that access was required until it was decided that the sequence of mortuary ceremonialism had run its course and the mound was sealed.

At Mound City in Chilicothe, Ohio (Figure 14.1), a rectilinear, enclosed mound cemetery lies on the west bank of the Scioto River opposite the Hopeton geometric earthwork enclosures (comprising a square enclosure abutting a circular enclosure, with several smaller circular enclosures and an embanked trackway which leads from the enclosures towards the river; *cf.* Lynott 2007), suggesting the possibility of an extended ceremonial complex. Squier and Davis also recorded a further small circular enclosure 76m in diameter lying 0.4km to the northwest and adjacent to several mounds; the same distance to the southwest lay a larger sub-circular enclosure some 365m in diameter and covering an area of 11.3ha, with a central mound, six entrances, and a much smaller circle lying directly to the north. Further geometric earthwork complexes are ranged along the Scioto River, North Fork and Paint Creek, and are rarely more than 6.5km apart, creating a dense concentration of ceremonial architecture. At Mound City there is little evidence of permanent settlement in the vicinity of the cemetery, although episodic settlement is suggested, which might imply that the Hopewell mound groups and geometric enclosures were generally "vacant ceremonial centers", unused between seasonal or cultural events (Lynott & Monk 1985, 27–8). The role of such ceremonial centres must have been crucial in cementing alliances and maintaining group identity amongst what were otherwise small, dispersed communities who may only have coalesced at set times throughout the course of the year.

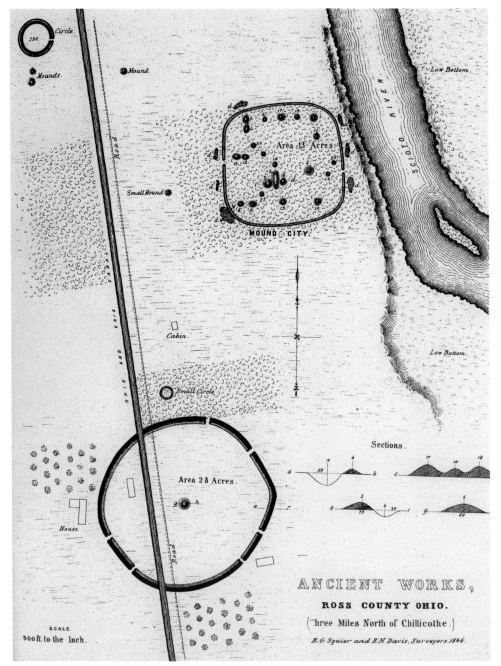

Figure 14.1: Mound City, Chilicothe, Ohio. The Squier and Davis survey of the complex Hopewell landscape surrounding Mound City enclosed cemetery as surveyed in 1846. Further complexity is added by the presence of the Hopeton earthworks located on the east bank of the Scioto River but not shown on this plan. (From Squier & Davis 1847, pl. XIX, opp. p. 54)

Figure 14.2: Mound City, Chilicothe, Ohio. Part of the enclosed mound cemetery. (Photograph: P. Topping)

Mound City derived its name from the fact that it had an unusually high concentration of mounds (Figure 14.2); Squier and Davis recorded a minimum of twenty-four mounds within a rectilinear enclosure covering some 5.3ha (Meltzer 1998, 54–55). A number of notable mound sequences were recorded at this site, some of which demonstrated the presence of pre-mound structures often interpreted as charnel houses. Mound 13 was roughly 21m in diameter, stood 0.9m high, and was discovered to have sealed a sequence of two post-built structures, the latest of which was 12.2m by 13m. The central area of the floor of this structure was littered with burnt bones, broken artefacts and mica fragments trampled into the surface. A "crematory basin" (1.8m by 1.3m) was located off-centre within the structure which had burnt and hardened the surrounding floor surface. This activity area within the final floor level was then sealed by a layer of fine sand. In the southwest corner of the structure between the wall and the crematory basin lay the primary burial deposit – the Great Mica Grave (*cf.* Brown 1979, 213–215). This grave was of the scale and shape of a crematory basin which was lined with mica sheets and had been filled with "dark earth that included many complete and broken artifacts", comprising fragments of galena, broken pipes, perforated animal teeth and beads. The observation that the dark earth contained cultural debris suggests that this deposit originated from an off-site settlement which had some social significance to the builders and created a link with the dead. Four cremations were placed in the grave with "a copper helmet headdress and a circular 'mica mirror'". A small mound 60cm high covered the grave and was mantled with sheet mica. Further cremations were placed upon mounded platforms with deliberately broken grave goods; thirteen cremations were arranged around the perimeter of the structure – only some had grave goods; at least one pit burial accompanied by

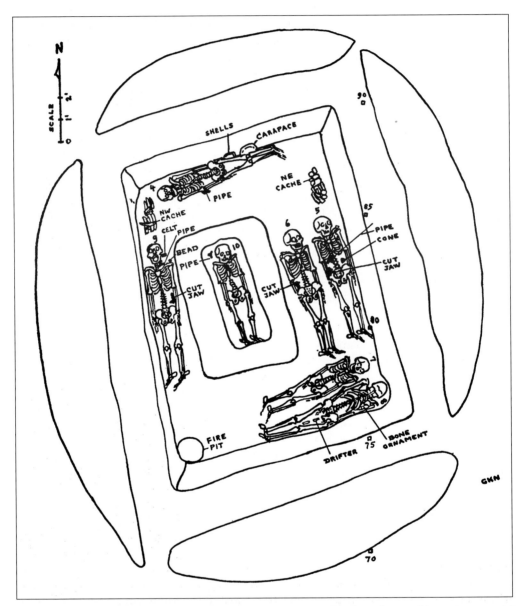

Figure 14.3: Mound Wh°6, White County, Illinois. This excavation plan shows the central log tomb surrounded by further inhumations with grave goods, caches of knapping tools and a fire pit, all within a segmented series of kidney-shaped banks. (From Neumann & Fowler 1952, pl. LXV, p. 198; Courtesy the Illinois State Museum)

grave goods was discovered; and finally the cremated remains of a child juxtaposed with broken and burnt grave goods was found in a shallow pit outside one of the corners of the structure. It has been suggested that the relative richness of these burial deposits may illustrate social stratification (Brown 1979, 115), but as proposed with the Adena burials, such graves may equally have been the result of negotiation at the time of interment and simply reflect social perceptions at that particular point in time, rather than necessarily indicate the comparative wealth of the individuals.

Not all Hopewell mounds covered structures nor contained rich burials, and a range of burial rites is evident. For example, in the Lower Wabash Valley, the Wilson Site in Emma Township comprised eleven mounds and a village site ranged along the northeast margin of the Dogtown Hills overlooking the Wabash River (*cf.* Neumann & Fowler 1952). Many of the mounds produced burials accompanied by various grave goods including pottery, copper artefacts, bone pins, mica, effigy pipes and conch shells. Mound Wh°6 was the largest of the group (Figure 14.3), some 27.5m in diameter and 4m in height, and sealed a prepared surface with a central pit 4.5m by 3.4m and 0.9m deep with its long axis aligned north-north-west to south-south-east. A smaller pit was found excavated through the floor of the first, and was some 0.9m deep, although it appears to have been empty. The displaced earth from the pits was arranged into four almost banana-shaped "ramparts" which surrounded the pit, the space between was then excavated to create a concave surface, and most of the area then covered with sheets of bark. The primary burial in the pit was a female of 65–71 years of age, in an extended position with arms at her side; a crude clay pipe lay at the right side of the head and a clam shell beside the left ankle; the burial was then covered with a layer of ash and bark. Arranged around the central pit were six extended inhumations (four adult males, two adult females), lying on the concave surface; alignments varied. A fire pit lay in the southwest corner of the concave surface, and two flint knapping kits lay in the northwest and northeast corners. A rich variety of grave goods accompanied these burials, including effigy pipes, conch shells, a turtle shell tray, a copper axe, a copper bead, shell beads, "cut bear jaws", sandstone abraders, a limestone ball and an antler handle. Log rafters sealed the tomb, which was then roofed with bark. Two secondary Hopewell burials were dug into the western side of the primary mound, and a secondary burial lay above the western "rampart" in the secondary mound (Neumann & Fowler 1952). The biography of this mound illustrates a number of interesting features. The primary burial in the pit was accompanied by relatively mundane grave goods compared to those with the burials ranged around the concave surface, which may add credence to the idea that burial deposits were socially negotiated at the time of deposition and that apparent wealth need not necessarily reflect the social position of the individual. The burials placed on the concave surface included an adult male (Wh°6–5) with a disarticulated skull which had a number of pebbles in the brain case, which might record some disturbance to this burial if the tomb had remained open for intermittent deposition. Burials Wh°6–5 and Wh°6–9 lay beside the two flint working kits which may suggest that these individuals were craft specialists; the fact that they were also accompanied by some of the most valuable grave goods (copper axe, *etc.*) could illustrate a valued position in the community. The presence of secondary interments implies that the mound retained a cultural value over successive generations, and drew further interments as a means of social renewal.

Figure 14.4: Temple Mound (A), Kolomoki, Georgia. The mound is part of a complex built by Woodland Indians of the Swift Creek and Weeden Island Cultures between c.AD250–950. The temple mound stands 17m high and covers an area of 99m north to south by 61m transversely; it towers over the plaza around which are ranged a series of six further – but smaller – mounds, some of which contained complex burials (i.e. Mound D). (Photograph: P. Topping)

Another variant of the Hopewell mortuary ritual can be seen at Trempealeau, Wisconsin, where another embankment surrounded a rectilinear pit, leaving a shelf between. The pit contained a jumble of disarticulated human bones, mostly long bones and skulls with some clustering of the latter. In contrast the shelf held discrete groupings of disarticulated bones comprising a skull and a number of long bones, each grouping regularly spaced around the south and west sides (*cf.* Milner 2004, 69, fig 47). Such deposition suggests that the central pit may have functioned as a charnel house where bodies were de-fleshed before careful arrangement into the groups on the shelf. Grave goods, including some of copper, still accompanied the deceased at Trempealeau.

At the Tremper Mound in Ohio, a sub-circular enclosure some 146m by 122m enclosed a low, amorphous mound up to 2.5m high which covered a burned, oval wooden structure defined by post-holes of a multi-chambered building roughly 61m long and 30m wide and interpreted as a great house. Unusually four communal graves were also discovered which held 375 cremations with a large number of tobacco pipes, both complete and ritually broken (both platform and effigy types). This example suggests the deliberate abandonment of a great house which was clearly also a culturally-significant location, but which maintained the importance of the location through the re-use of the site for multiple burials in the communal graves. Despite the communal nature of the burial deposits, social stratification or status was still signified by the presence of rich grave goods and elaborate ritual evidenced by the broken pipes. Hopewell mortuary ceremonialism was nothing if not varied.

During the Middle Woodland period, ceremonial platform mounds were also constructed (Figure 14.4). At Crystal River on the Gulf Coast of Florida, the local Deptford Culture developed strong contacts with the Eastern Woodlands cultures to the north and appeared to share many traits such as mortuary customs. Crystal River appears to have been a peripheral element of the Hopewell Interaction Sphere which supplied conch shells to the north, and in return received new types of pottery which was only found in mortuary contexts on site (Weisman 1995, 68), copper artefacts, steatite for bowls, quartzite for points and greenstone for axes. As such the site developed a local importance which led to a growing complexity and growth in comparison to adjacent sites which generally remained at the level of small shell middens with limited assemblages and few burials. Consequently, Crystal River clearly developed a regional importance (perhaps alongside another complex a mile downstream), it became pivotal to the shell midden sites, but may have only been used at certain times – the site thus becoming "a vacant ceremonial center for much of the year" (Weisman 1995, 83) – which might explain the lack of evidence for continuous settlement at Crystal River.

Crystal River lies on the north bank of the eponymous river and comprises two ramped "temple mounds" (A & H), a centrally-placed complex burial mound located in the plaza (C, D, E & F), a second burial mound lying to the west (G), a number of sub-circular shell middens (J & K), an irregular linear shell midden (B), and two "stelae". The layout of the complex focuses upon the plaza: the ramps of the two temple mounds lead from the plaza and are loosely aligned upon the central burial mound complex (C–F) in the centre of the plaza; overall these three mounds are roughly aligned north-north-east to south-south-west. Apart from the presence of one of the stelae, the eastern approach to the site is relatively open compared to the western where temple mound A and several others cluster together, which might suggest that the approach upstream from the coast was the most important aspect to the complex.

Mound A, the southernmost temple mound, now lies adjacent to the river bank and was originally 8.7m high with a summit platform 32.6m by 15.2m; a graduated ramp 24.3m long and 4.2m to 6.4m wide lay on the northeast side leading to/from the plaza. This mound appears to have been constructed from midden material comprising pottery, "other cultural debris", oyster shells and general food refuse; it is unclear whether this material was accumulated on site from a domestic source, or was re-deposited from an adjacent location such as the linear midden Mound B. As yet no temple structure has been found associated with this mound.

The linear midden, Mound B, was approximately 335m long and 30m wide, and meandered eastwards from Mound A. The midden has been sampled and produced an assemblage ranging from various forms of pottery, shell tools, lithics, mica, bone tools, and a faunal assemblage comprising turtle, fish, deer, bird, shark teeth and dog. Some of this assemblage was deposited during the Hopewell phase (Santa Rosa-Swift Creek Period), others afterwards, demonstrating a sequence of successive cultures at the Crystal River site. At present it is uncertain whether craft specialisation took place at the midden, and what role feasting may have played in the ceremonial life of the site – although periodic feasting would help to explain the presence of so much food debris in the absence of permanent settlement.

The main burial complex (C–F) was a multi-phase construction which consisted of a circular embankment (C) 23m in diameter and 1.8m high defining a concentric space which enclosed an irregular low mound built of sand (E) which surrounds a conical mound (F). Excavations suggest that this mound complex was initially constructed during the Hopewell period and associated with the local Santa Rosa – Swift Creek and Deptford – Swift Creek cultures, but was added to or modified during the later Weeden Island period.

Various excavations in the central mound complex (E & F) have revealed the presence of multiple burials, some 400 plus, interred during the two cultural periods. The primary burials in Mound F consisted of Hopewell-inspired grave assemblages comprising shell gorgets and cups, rock and quartz crystal pendants, soapstone pipes, painted pottery, copper ornaments, animal jaw ornaments, mica sheets and meteoric iron. "Mortuary pottery was found not as individual grave offerings but distributed throughout the associated strata" (Weisman 1995, 53), which suggests that certain elements of Hopewellian mortuary ceremonialism in the southeast did not focus upon the individual and that the role of pottery was a generic symbol that defined the general mortuary deposit and recorded its cultural affiliations and ritual or mythological aspirations. The fact that many of these mortuary artefacts were crafted from supra-regional raw materials demonstrates the wide-ranging power and influence of Hopewell culture traits emanating from the Eastern Woodlands down as far as the Southeast. Whether the mechanism for this was through contiguous community contact or simply the result of long-distance exchange networks is difficult to establish. In addition, the nature of Hopewellian influence in Florida is problematic – did it demonstrate political drivers such as alliance building or kinship networks, or was it simply a cultural aspiration of affiliation which emerged at the periphery of an extensive trade network?

Excavations in 1960 (Weisman 1995, 55) discovered that the mortuary rite in Mound F changed over time. The earliest Hopewell-influenced burials comprised extended inhumations lying upon a layer of charcoal impregnated sand, and this mortuary deposit was then sealed by a thin layer of oyster shells. The subsequent Weeden Island burials were radically different, consisting of "concentrated flexed burials sloping downwards towards the outside edge of the mound".

The later irregular Mound E produced 186 burials; most discovered lying beneath deposits of oyster shells with numerous grave goods – although these were of inferior quality to those in Mound F. This burial rite was not practiced in the earlier Hopewell-inspired graves in Mound F.

The encircling ring mound C produced burial assemblages which appeared to have cultural affiliations with the Hopewell burials in Mound F, thus creating further parallels with the widespread Hopewell tradition throughout the Eastern Woodlands.

Mound H, lying to the north, was constructed of shells and has a rectilinear plan with a ramp leading to/from the plaza. Excavations recovered pottery, bone tools, an utilised chert chip and a shell gouge but no evidence of a structure on the summit of the mound. The remaining mounds at Crystal River appear to be middens.

Roughly 1 mile downstream from Crystal River lies a second mound complex comprising large shell-built mounds, a shell ridge, and a platform/temple mound. No burials have been recorded, but the assemblages suggest that chronologically this mound group is "overlapping with Crystal River" (Weisman 1995, 83). The presence of two major mound complexes situated on the same river and in close proximity, suggests that this part of the Gulf Coast was a culturally-significant location, and clearly was a draw for exotic trade items from regional or distant communities.

EFFIGY MOUNDS (LATE WOODLAND/TRANSITION TO MISSISSIPPIAN) *c.*AD 600–AD 1200 (OR AD 700–AD 1030; *cf.* STOLTMAN & CHRISTIANSEN 2000, 507)

During the Late Woodland period the cultural phenomenon of effigy mound building became common, although conical mounds continued to be constructed (Colour Plate 12). The effigy mound builders appear to have been mobile hunter-gatherers who inhabited seasonal settlements, but did grow small amounts of cultivated plants such as maize; sunflower; squash; and sumpweed (*cf.* Stoltman & Christiansen 2000, 512–513). Effigy mounds had a tightly defined distribution westwards from Lake Michigan, including northern Illinois, southern Wisconsin, eastern Iowa and southeastern Minnesota. Occasional outliers occur in Ohio. In Wisconsin alone, it has been estimated that some 900 effigy mound centres were constructed, possibly comprising 15,000 individual mounds of which 2–3,000 were identifiable effigies – the remainder consisted of low conical, linear or oval forms often

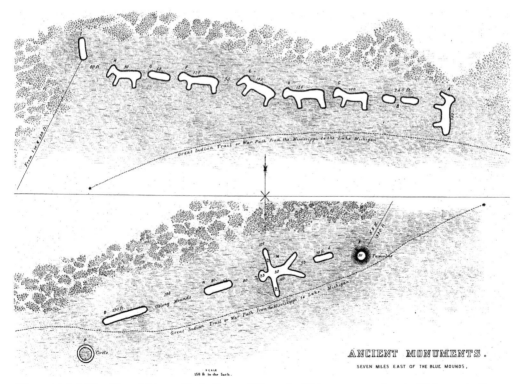

Figure 14.5: Effigy Mound Group, Dade County, Wisconsin. This group comprises six (?) bears, six linears, a conical mound, a human figure and a small circle, and it is ranged along a ridge separating the river valleys of the Rock and Wisconsin. (From Squier & Davis 1847, pl. XL, opp. p. 126)

interspersed with distinctive effigies which may have been considered more abstract motifs by their builders (Figure 14.5). The average effigy mound group contains some 20–30 mounds, but the extreme was recorded at the Harper's Ferry Great Mound Group which comprised 895. Although effigy mounds are generally less than 30m long and rarely exceed 1.5m in height, others achieve truly monumental scale: the largest surviving bird effigy lies in the grounds of Mendota State Hospital and has a wingspan of 190m, but an even larger cropmark site has been recorded in Eagle Township; a human effigy with a horn headdress in Man Mound County Park was originally 66m in length; and linear mounds juxtaposed with effigies near Lake Monona were 213m long (Birmingham & Eisenberg 2000, 109–110).

Effigy mounds are often located on high ground overlooking waterways, wetlands and lakes – all areas of rich, seasonally available resources. As such they may have been deliberately located to signpost seasonal gathering points, and/or to function as a form of monumental increase totemism. The fact that many effigy mound groups are also located near springs or other significant topographic features suggests spiritual connotations were embedded into these loci (Birmingham & Eisenberg 2000, 112). There appears to be between eight to thirteen types of effigy mound, ranging from birds, bears, deer, buffalo to panthers/water spirits to relatively abstract chain or compound mounds (*cf.* Stoltman & Christiansen 2000, 501; Birmingham & Eisenberg 2000, 113). Early commentators divided the effigy mounds into three groups correlating with the three basic elements of air, earth and water, and their role was to underpin social reproduction and world renewal. This model has been further refined into "upperworld" and "lowerworld" divisions which closely parallel the cosmology of many Midwestern Native Americans (*cf.* Hall 1993). This hypothesis places the various bird effigies symbolically inhabiting the "upperworld", contrasting with the animal and water spirit effigies in the "lowerworld", creating a sky – earth/water dichotomy. A recent survey has also concluded that most mound groups depict a pre-eminent "world" which generally includes a minority of effigies from the opposing "world", adding further weight to the suggestion that these mound groups have an integral harmony, deliberately creating a balance as part of a social process of world renewal (quoted in Birmingham & Eisenberg 2000, 11). The distribution of effigy mound groups in Wisconsin appears to show a preponderance of "lowerworld" water spirit effigies in the eastern part of the state, whereas "upperworld" groups dominated by birds are found in the west. Between these two distributions lie groups comprising both lower and "upperworld" forms. The composition of these mound groups appears to parallel ethnographic records which suggest that they also contain totemic elements representing the clan structure still evident in some Midwestern Native American communities, adding a further level of symbolic referencing (*cf.* Hall 1993).

Effigy mounds were often constructed by firstly excavating a shallow "intaglio" or footprint in the shape of the mound, thus creating an inverse representation of the effigy. The majority of intaglios were buried beneath a mound, but Antiquarian records demonstrate that eleven such sites survived in the nineteenth century in south central and eastern Wisconsin. The recorded intaglios were all lowerworld forms (Birmingham & Eisenberg 2000, 125–127); the single surviving example on the Rock River in Fort Atkinson was a "panther" or water spirit some 38m in length from head to tip of tail, and described by the Ho-Chunk (Winnebago) "as an animal that lives in the water, and crawls out at night along the bank" (Wheaton & Brown 1920, 204). This intaglio had originally been associated with seventeen burial mounds (Wheaton & Brown 1920, 207). The survival of only lowerworld intaglios may be significant. An interesting perspective on the possible social and spiritual nuances of lowerworld intaglios was provided at the dedication ceremony at Fort Atkinson in 1920 when a Ho-Chunk speaker delivered the following as part of his oration:

"Long and faithfully did they labor to carve out from the soil, this silent figure of the Wichawa, the panther, most powerful and guardian spirit of our Winnebago village.

Once in the long, long ago, a good Winnebago stood on the bank of the river, offering his devotions to the Wakanda, and fasting 20 days. Then he saw an animal rise to the surface of the water, it was a Wakanda, a water spirit. It had heard the Indian's story of his troubles and told him that it would help him and that his life thereafter would be long and happy. Then many other Indians saw the animal. As our ancestors desired its future protection and guidance, they constructed near this village, and among those of other wakandas, its likeness.

Here it is, apparently in perfect condition. O my people! and my white brothers and sisters, this is hallowed ground. Here my ancestors worshipped the spirit of the panther and believed in its protection and guidance. It is a symbol of the sacred past, of the community life of my people. Here our ancestors made their home and here we made our home; we were members of the Panther Clan; we had the panther spirit in us and were all kindred." (Wheaton & Brown 1920, 207–208).

Clearly clan symbolism played a part in the construction of these effigies, but it has also been suggested that effigy mounds showed a strong correlation between mound form and resource availability. It has been observed that turtle effigies are often discovered adjacent to rivers, lakes and wetlands, whereas bird effigies are concentrated along the Mississippi migration route (Goldstein 1995). However, this suggestion is clouded by both the quotation above, and Hall's convincing argument that the "turtle" effigies are in fact water spirits as depicted in Late Woodland material culture and Midwestern Native American beliefs. In addition, and considering the composition and distribution of the effigy mound groups, Hall suggests that they would appear to depict the "monumental constructions of the cosmology of their builders and represented the division of the world into earth/water and sky divisions" (Hall 1993, 51). A complex matrix of symbolism may thus have lain behind the choices of animal or abstract shapes, and the combinations they were used in, to create a monumentalised message which could be used to define ancestral presence, clan affiliation, resource availability, increase totemism and create zoning in the landscape.

Following the creation of the intaglio, if a mound was to be constructed, then the interment was the next stage of the process. The most numerous form of burial in effigy mounds was the secondary bundle burials (64%), followed by far fewer primary flexed inhumations (21%), a number of indeterminate remains (15%), with some evidence for cremation. These statistics might imply that the after-life of the mounds was equally important to succeeding generations. The burials, generally few in number per mound, could be placed within "accretional mounds", on the floor of the "intaglio", or within pits beneath the floor of the mound. Burials were often positioned in the head and heart areas of animal-shaped effigies and were rarely accompanied by grave goods. Hearths or "fireplace altars" and cists were common, and the burial ritual appears to have been accompanied by fires, sometimes large, which contained burned animal bone as part of the construction process of the mound. These episodic fires were placed over the head, flanks or heart of the creature depicted, and eventually became sedimented into the body of the mound. The effigy mounds were built of layered strata comprising vari-coloured soils ranging from forest brownearths to clays from riverbanks, often interspersed with the burnt material (*cf.* Stoltman & Christiansen 2000, 503–4). This construction technique ensured that culturally significant deposits of earth derived from important places such as settlements, resource locations or sites with cultural associations, could all be embedded into the body of the effigy to create an enhanced aura to the mound. The resulting mound, its group and location would then – as a matrix of cultural information – be able to transmit social narratives to the community. Some of these narratives would clearly be underpinned by oral history, so that the significance of the site was understood and passed down through the generations. Together, such encoded earthwork symbolism clearly sedimented information concerning totemism, mythologies and resource information into the cultural landscape through the medium of figurative mound building.

Different traditions of effigy mound building occurred in Ohio, which was more focussed on individual, large monuments than groups of small mounds. Arguably the most iconic example of the mound builders art is the Serpent Mound constructed in Adams County, Ohio, creating the largest recorded serpent effigy in the United States (Figure 14.6). The sinuous effigy is aligned along a narrow promontory which overlooks the Ohio Brush Creek, and is located upon an unusual geological disturbance known as a cryptoexplosion structure some 4.5 miles in diameter, which is characterised by a massive dislocation of strata intermixed with numerous faults, anticlines and synclines, together creating the impression of a "sunken mountain" (Glotzhober & Lepper 1994, 16). The unusual geomorphology of this area was obviously an attraction to local communities, which is demonstrated by the presence of two adjacent mounds attributed to the Adena, thus potentially pre-dating the serpent mound by many centuries. A third mound of elliptical form is considered contemporary with the serpent, and Squier and Davis recorded a series of "Indian Graves" lying across a ravine and opposite the head of the serpent (Meltzer 1998, fig. XXXV opp. 96). Clearly this location held a deep cultural resonance where spiritual matters and the construction of monuments to the dead coalesced. A cliff below the head of the serpent has a reptilian, lizard-like appearance which may have inspired the builders of the mound and influenced the choice of location (Glotzhober & Lepper 1994, 4). Excavations have shown that the serpent mound was constructed by Fort Ancient communities around AD 1030, and a contemporary settlement has been discovered to the south of the mound (Woodward & McDonald 2002, 121).

The body of the serpent mound measures some 410m in length. When originally surveyed by Squier and Davis in 1846, they recorded that the body was 9.1m wide and stood up to 1.5m high (Meltzer 1998, 97); since Putnam's restoration in 1887–1890, it is 6m wide and stands between 0.6m to 1.8m high (Glotzhober & Lepper 1994, 3). Excavations have discovered that the body of the mound is composed of what may be a spine of stones sealed within yellow clay, which was then capped by dark earth to create a skeuomorph of the skeleton and tissue of a snake. The design of the effigy has been variously interpreted as a serpent swallowing an egg to a mythological horned serpent swallowing a solar eclipse. The oval "egg/sun" component may be a burial mound, which when recorded by Squier

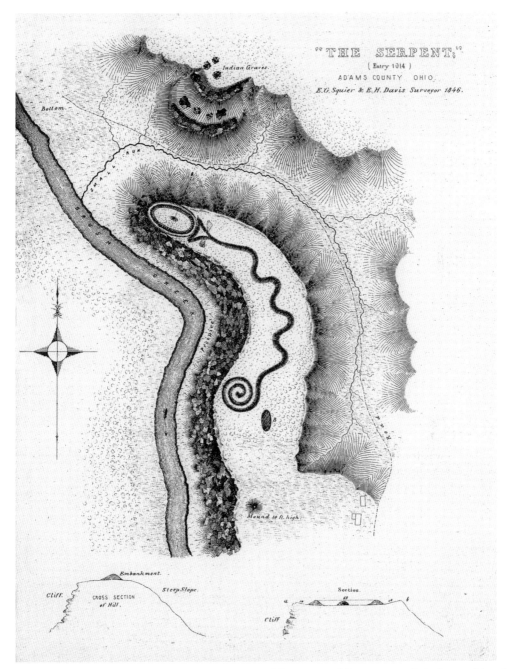

Figure 14.6: The Serpent Mound, Adams County, Ohio. The Squier and Davis survey of the Serpent Mound undertaken in 1846, and pre-dating the Putnam restoration. Note the added detail at the head and the egg/ sun earthwork with its central cairn which are now obscured. The presence of "Indian Graves" in the vicinity emphasises the special nature of this location. (From Squier & Davis 1847, pl. XXXV, opp. p. 96)

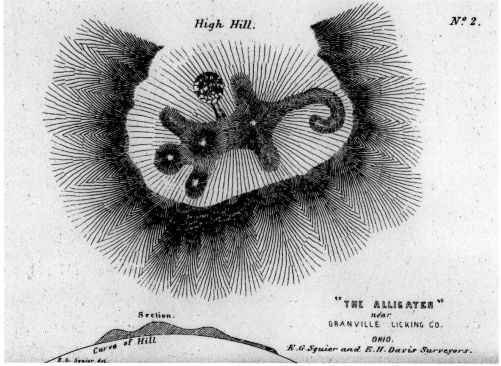

Figure 14.7: The Alligator Mound, Licking County, Ohio. This effigy mound is now considered to represent the mythical "Underwater Panther" – the most powerful underwater/underworld deity – rather than an alligator or lizard. It appears to have been constructed by Fort Ancient communities. (From Squier & Davis 1847, pl. XXXVI, opp. p. 98)

and Davis was found to contain a central cairn of "large stones much burned" which had been recently disturbed by treasure hunters (Meltzer 1998, 97).

A number of possible astronomical alignments have been claimed for the serpent mound (data from Glotzhober & Lepper 1994, 10–11), which include a sightline from roughly the centre of the serpent's head through the oval egg/sun where the lost cairn once stood creating an alignment on sunset at summer solstice. An alignment drawn from the centre of the curled tail to the centre of the serpent's head is aligned on Polaris and true north. The alignment of each of the three coils of the snake is focused upon summer solstice sunrise, equinox sunrise and winter solstice sunrise. Clearly, if these alignments are genuine, then not only might the serpent mound have had a cultural significance in terms of being a monumentalised symbolic message, juxtaposed with ancestral remains in an unusual geological setting, but the astronomical alignments would enhance it's value further by being a seasonal predictor for the local agriculturalists.

Fort Ancient farmers also appear to have constructed a second large effigy mound at Granville in Ohio, where the mound was constructed on a spur overlooking the Raccoon Creek (Figure 14.7). The clay, silt and stone mound has been described as an alligator, reptile or salamander, but recent research suggests it may have been the representation of an "underwater panther" (Woodward & McDonald 2001, 173), a spirit form familiar from the smaller effigy mounds of Wisconsin (see above). When Squier and Davis recorded this work they noted that it was 76m from nose to tail, the body was 12m wide, each limb was 11m long, and the effigy stood between 1.2m and 1.8m high. On the north side of the effigy "is an elevated circular space, covered with stones which have been much burned. This has been denominated an altar. Leading from it to the top of the effigy is a graded way, ten feet broad (3m)" (Meltzer 1998, 99). Clearly this second Fort Ancient effigy mound also had a vibrant spiritual use-life suggested by the "altar", creating a stage for ceremonial interaction with the earthen representation, the landscape and the sky world.

MISSISSIPPIAN MOUNDS (LATE WOODLAND) *c.*AD 900–AD 1600

During the earliest part of the Late Woodland, Mississippian mounds often record multiple episodes of construction in an incremental fashion, but by the later period construction had focussed upon adding to, or modifying, existing mounds as the burial rituals changed to an emphasis on the sky and sky deities (Kelly 1996; J. E. Kelly, lecture 24 March 1999). Late Woodland conical mounds are the most ubiquitous mound type and are generally found in groups located in prominent positions upon high ground overlooking rivers. Burial ceremonialism varied, but the grave assemblages are similar. The conical mounds may have been fixed aggregation points in the cultural landscape (L. Goldstein & J. Sansone, lecture 24 March 1999).

Mississippian towns and settlements were scattered throughout the Midwest, with arguably the most significant site located upon the broad floodplain of the Mississippi, or the American Bottom of Illinois, at Cahokia. Although Cahokia is a major centre and built on a grand scale, it is now generally considered to have been organised as a "very large … paramount chiefdom that in many respects resembled other known Mississippian polities" (Neusis & Gross 2007, 537); however, unlike many contemporary polities Cahokia was primarily a ritual arena (Kelly 1996, 97) which may have been organised as a "theatre state" where power was articulated through ceremonialism rather than strength of arms (Holt 2009). This chiefdom then presided over a number of smaller political centres which in turn ruled over rural homesteads. Cahokia was at the height of its power between AD 1050 and AD 1250, but during the thirteenth century the chiefdom disintegrated, probably the result of both political and economic pressures generated by the extended population buffering against adjacent cultural groups.

The Cahokia complex is spread over an area of some 10 square kilometres, comprising platform mounds, conical and ridgetop burial mounds, plazas, a palisaded enclosure or stockade, all surrounded by a number of dispersed satellite mound centres such as the Powell and Bishop Groups in the hinterland. Central Cahokia consists of 104 recorded mounds, most of which lie within 1km of Monks Mound positioned near the centre (Fowler 1989, 201). However, if one considers Cahokia and it's hinterland of East St. Louis and St. Louis, then the total number of mounds distributed over this area may be closer to 200. Considering the scale and complexity of Cahokia, the evidence for a hierarchy and elites, it is surprising to note that these developments were underpinned by an economic base of small-scale agriculturalists.

Monks Mound is the largest mound in North America and was constructed between roughly AD 900 and AD 1200 (Figure 14.8). It has four terraces; the uppermost was the

Figure 14.8: Monks Mound and Mound 51 (to right), Cahokia, Illinois. The view of Monks Mound from the southeast showing the terraces facing on to the plaza. (Photograph: P. Topping)

site of a major building 32m long by 14.6m wide and estimated to have stood some 15m high; it is assumed to have been the residence of one of the elite or a significant priest. A ramp leads from the south side of Monks Mound to the central plaza. Monks Mound covers an area of 305m north-south by 236m transversely (or 7.2ha) and stands to a height of 30.5m, creating a bulk of 624,000 cubic metres (Fowler 1989, 7). As a yardstick, this compares to Silbury Hill which has a basal diameter ranging from 135–145m, a summit diameter of 32–4m, a height of 31m and a volume of 239,133 cubic metres. Consequently, although Monks Mound is 0.5m shorter than Silbury Hill, the bulk of Monks Mound is roughly three times larger than Silbury Hill.

Monks Mound was surrounded by four plazas aligned upon the cardinal directions creating a cruciform ground plan which was further extended by alignments of mounds leading away from Monks Mound – the cross is a recurrent theme in Native American ritual and cosmology (Kelly 1996, 101). The overarching structure of Cahokia embedded traditional cosmological beliefs into a symbolic four-fold division of the world, creating northern, southern, eastern and western elements set within the vertical divisions of a lower world, the present world and an upper world (Hall 1997). The construction of the larger mounds such as Monks Mound and the Powell Mound, which both stood prominently above the surrounding prairie, may have been a deliberate attempt to bridge the void between the present world and the upper world of the sky and its deities (*cf.* Kelly 1996).

Ritual was further sedimented into the layout of Cahokia by the construction of a series of "Woodhenges" or timber circles which were clearly multi-functional. These circles often had a central post for use in calendrical and astronomical observations. One "Woodhenge" lay at the western arm of the Cahokian cruciform layout near Mound 44 and comprised a sequence of five circles; a second lay at the southern arm at Mound 72 and appears to have been the focus of rich, elite burials within the circle which were gradually monumentalised by a mound as the circle eventually became abandoned (see below); a third is postulated at the eastern arm of Cahokia adjacent to Mound 27 (*cf.* Wittry 1996; Fowler 1996). No "Woodhenge" has yet been discovered at the northern arm of the Cahokia complex.

The western "Woodhenge" created an astronomical sightline to midsummer sunrise which marked the sun's apparent emergence from the centre of Monks Mound between the first and uppermost terrace. It is possible that this observed phenomenon was purposefully chosen to create a link between the sun and the person who lived on the summit of the mound, part of embedding sky belief systems into the body of the largest mound in North America. The importance of this alignment was further enhanced by the site of a large fire adjacent to Woodhenges III and IV which had been used to seal Pit 309. This pit contained decorated fragments of a beaker which featured an elaborate cross within a circle motif – a world symbol – with a band in the southeast which may represent sunlight streaming towards the earth during a solstice at both sunrise and sunset (Wittry 1996, 29–31). This form of design appears to be a variant of the Plains Indian quartered circle device symbolising the earth, the camp circle and the sacred hearth (Hall 1985, 183–184). Sky watching and astronomical observation was clearly an important factor which underpinned not only elements of ritual, but also the foundations of the Cahokian hierarchy. However, the fact that the Woodhenges comprised complete circuits of posts when only a few would be needed for astronomical observations, suggests that these timber circles – which have some similarities to sun dance lodges – also had ceremonial functions and may have "served as symbolic world centers" (Hall 1996, 124).

The wealth and social control of the Cahokian elite is epitomised by Mound 72, lying near the southern extremity of the north-south alignment, and to date one of the richest burial sequences at this site (*cf.* Fowler *et al.* 1999). This mound began with the construction of a timber circle, Woodhenge 72, which included an original marker post (Post Pit 1) aligned on the summer solstice sunrise, which was built sometime before AD 1000. A midden developed near Post Pit 2 with other "offertory features", and a "wall trench structure" which was devoid of cultural debris and may have been a charnel house. By Phase 2 (*c.*AD 1000) significant changes occurred, including the dismantling of the putative charnel house and the superimposition of a burial group of ten to nineteen individuals with ages ranging from 15–35 plus years and accompanied by some grave goods. Post Pit 2 had its post removed and a burial pit excavated over its site which contained twenty-two extended burials oriented east-west with heads to the west; all appeared to be female interments aged 20–30 years – allowing for the limited gender and age range this burial deposit suggests a sacrificial event. A further burial pit contemporary with those above was oriented north-north-east to south southwest and contained nineteen individuals with their heads aligned to the north-north-east; twelve were female and the remainder unknown with an age range of 5–25 years; again, the factor of a mass burial, limited age range and potentially gender suggests another sacrifice. These features were then sealed beneath a rectilinear mound [72SUB2] which was modified subsequently by the construction of a terrace followed by the addition of a ramp, thus creating a miniature representation of Monks Mound – deliberately or otherwise. This mound was subsumed in the northwest part of the final mound.

Phase 3 (*c*.AD 1000) was broadly contemporary with Phase 2, but was located in the southeast area covered by the final mound. This phase saw the re-use of Post Pit 1 as a marker for the primary mound complex. The most important context during this phase was the presence of the Beaded Burial Group (BBG), a rich elite interment which was surrounded by a series of three "sacrificial" burial groups and various exotic assemblages. The BBG began with a male interment which was then masked by a shell bead cape or platform comprising at least 20,000 beads which took the shape of a bird with a down-curved beak – probably a raptor. A second male was laid on top of the shells with his head aligned to the southeast, and four adult burials were arranged around the BBG consisting of three extended and one bundle burial. The use of such raptor iconography is a relatively common Mississippian theme and can be seen in the Birdman motifs such as the Rogan copper *repoussé* plates discovered at Etowah in Georgia (*cf.* King 2004) and elsewhere, the avian and Birdman images incorporated into rock art, particularly in Missouri (Diaz-Granados 2004, 142–4), and the portable art such as engraved shell gorgets with Birdman carrying severed heads from Craighead County, Arkansas (Reilly 2004, 127). A Mississippian earthlodge at Ocmulgee in Georgia featured a clay-platform in the shape of a large raptor-like bird opposite the entrance. Such wide ranging use of this iconography had a widespread distribution and may have been founded upon earlier art circulated by the Hopewell Interaction Sphere, but this later artistic package was distributed via an elite exchange mechanism (Reilly 2004, 126).

Roughly 4m to the southwest of the BBG lay a burial deposit of seven adults accompanied by "exotic trade goods" comprising a copper staff, shell beads, chunkey stones, projectile points and a pile of uncut mica. Two of these burials were picked out for special treatment: Burial 8 had fifteen chunkey stones arranged beneath the pelvis, and 332 projectile points were "scattered around the legs of Burial 10" – almost all aligned east to southeast. A few metres to the north of the BBG lay a further extended adult burial and an empty pit lay on the south side of the mound. These various burials and deposits were then sealed beneath a second primary mound (72SUB1) which was subsequently the site of a cache pit excavated into this mound which contained 36,177 beads of various types, marine shells, copper beads and copper sheet, eight chert points, several bone harpoons and points, three chert flakes and a cache of 451 projectile points with no uniform alignment. This deposit was clearly dedicatory in nature and presumably undertaken within living memory of the interment of the elite primary burial (BBG) beneath the mound.

During Phase 4 (AD 1000+) the southeast primary mound was disturbed and a small post-pit dug into it on the west side. However, of more significance was the excavation of a large burial pit aligned northwest to southeast under a southeastern extension of the northwest primary mound which contained twenty-four interments arranged in two layers with heads to the northeast and arms at their sides. Of these burials, nine were female, eight had female indicators and seven were indeterminate. Age ranges were 10–25, and considering the restricted gender and age suggest a further sacrificial event.

The central area between the two primary mounds became the focus of Phase 5 (AD 1050+). Here a large burial pit was excavated on a northeast to southwest axis and a mass grave of fifty-three individuals with heads largely aligned to the northwest were placed in it. The age demographic was 15–30 years, and although the gender was difficult to ascertain for all interments it appeared to be predominantly female. The recurrence of age/gender restrictions again suggests sacrificial burial. Roughly 2m to the northwest a further small burial deposit of four males was encountered, but all were missing heads and hands – but with their arms interlocking, suggesting another form of sacrifice and ritualised mutilation. These two burial deposits were then sealed beneath a linear mound aligned northwest to southeast, which overlay the northwest mound and abutted the southeast mound.

Roughly a generation later, Phase 6 (*c*.AD 1100) saw three extended inhumations inserted into the southeast primary mound, all young adult/adult, and one possible female. A burial pit containing eight individuals was dug on the south side of the mound, with a demographic of one female, one possible female and six unknown gender; the age range included one child (10–15yrs), two adolescents (15–20yrs) and five uncertain; four of these burials appeared to have been bound; they were aligned northeast to southwest with heads to the northeast. An extended ?female burial was interred partly overlying the burial pit and parallel with the mound with her head to the southeast. Middens and shell heaps developed between the two primary mounds demonstrating that the generation of domestic debris or evidence of feasting formed part of the process of successive interments. A further burial pit was discovered on the southern edge of the linear mound and during the construction of the final mound. This pit contained two distinct layers of burials: the lower comprised the haphazard interment of thirty-nine individuals, but unlike the other burial pits this time the demographic was not primarily female but possibly 50–50 male to female, and with a range of ages represented. Three individuals had been decapitated, another incompletely decapitated, two projectile points were recovered and other signs of violence suggested that if these dead represented sacrifices, then the selection criteria may have changed in comparison to the other sacrificial pits. Alternatively this deposit could comprise war dead. At least two layers of organic material was deposited over these bodies before a second layer of interments was placed in this pit. The upper layer of burials consisted of ten individuals, evenly spaced but with differing alignments, six of whom had been laid in the pit on litters (the others may also have had litters which did not survive), they appeared to have been bound before interment, and represented adolescents/adults and two children of both genders.

As the final mound continued to envelope the three preceding mounds, further burials were deposited including two separate bundle burials and a small burial pit. This pit contained six disarticulated individuals with skulls arranged along the north wall and the long bones laid perpendicular to the skulls; one adult (25–30yrs) and one juvenile (15–20yrs) were identified, and the presence of teeth from a child and an infant suggest that the mixed assemblage may have originated from a charnel house.

During Phase 7 (AD 1000+), a series of burial deposits accumulated in the final mound, including nineteen burials interred over four events, an extended adult with skull aligned to the southeast, and a burial pit with two extended females, skulls aligned to the northeast and possibly holding hands. Finally, Phase 8 (AD 1000+) was also characterised by a sequence of small scale burial deposits: an extended burial with skull aligned to the northwest; a possible male bundle burial of 20–25 years with skull to the southeast; an extended male burial of 35–45 years with skull to southeast; and a pit with two individuals, a possible female of 20–25 years and an adolescent of 15–20 years. These two final phases demonstrate the continued use of the final mound as a focus for more mundane burials, which clearly signal the termination of elite deposition and sacrifice in Mound 72.

Mound 72 appears to have evolved over the course of a century or more, developing from contiguous primary mounds to increasingly larger single entities until a final ridge-top mound was created. The presence of one of the richest Mississippian burial assemblages during Phase 3, the Beaded Burial Group, and the burial pits containing apparently sacrificial victims, demonstrates the presence and power of the Cahokia elite in a monumental form. The association of this elite burial mound with the Mound 72 "Woodhenge" timber circle whose original marker post was aligned on the summer solstice sunrise and was juxtaposed with the Beaded Burial Group laid out on its falcon-like platform, created a culturally-charged location which embedded the ancestral elite in the sky-watching present.

The demographic of the interments included fifty-two extended burials, forty-one bundle burials, seven partly articulated bundle burials, four incomplete interments and a staggering 161 sacrificed individuals, bringing the total number of bodies buried in the mound to 265. Considering the high percentage of sacrifices, it is clear that the institutionalised use of lethal force played a major part in the maintenance of the Cahokia elites.

During the Mississippian Period, mound building became a focus for the maintenance and renewal of social control, facilitated through human sacrifice as part of the mortuary ceremonialism at elite burials such as Mound 72. The success of such political manipulation is evidenced by the construction of major public works ranging from the scale and complexity of the Cahokia mounds, palisaded enclosures, public spaces (plazas), "Woodhenges" to the episodic enlargement of Monks Mound (*cf*. Hall 2004, 97).

DISCUSSION

Mound building and formalised cemeteries emerged around the transition of the Middle to Late Archaic at a time of social change demonstrated in the archaeological record. The first burial mounds were constructed in river valleys where plentiful resources were available, signalling a significant shift in Archaic lifeways. Mound building became a means by which a community could legitimise kinship or clan-based claims to resources by placing built markers in the cultural landscape. By imposing the dead in prominent, formalised burials in significant locations a process began of overtly creating proto-territories, particularly in important areas such as the Illinois and Mississippi valleys which are major avian migration routes. By the Late Archaic more sedentary lifeways had developed at locations such as Poverty Point where both burial mounds and formal earthworks created a complex which provided a sedentary social context for a widely based exchange network underpinned by limited cultivation and the exploitation of wild resources. However, at Poverty Point it is unclear whether the complex was constructed by its inhabitants only, or whether it was a communal project undertaken by the population of its hinterland.

The Adena-Hopewell-Mississippian Woodland traditions emerged from long-term adaptations and cultural trends which often placed the emphasis on the individual in mortuary ceremonialism. The cultural context of these trends included an intensification of wild resource exploitation, relatively sedentary settlement patterns, extensive exchange networks and the appearance of complex social structures. Alongside this was the widespread adoption of pottery manufacture, cultivation and a deliberate move to embed social mores in burial deposits.

During the Adena Period mound building evolved into a major cultural expression, to the extent that most surviving Adena sites are mounds. Excavations have discovered that the burial rite evolved over time, beginning with relatively simple individual interments often followed by secondary burials in the same mound during the Early to Middle Adena Period. Burials at this time were often sprinkled with variously coloured ochres, graphite or manganese dioxide, accompanied by everyday tools, adorned with copper or shell beads and slate or copper gorgets, and tubular pipes. However, by the Late Adena, interments were accompanied by a richer variety of grave goods and mortuary ceremonialism was more elaborate. This elaboration took the form of large burial chambers or enclosures with one or more primary interments. The mortuary structures were often dug through, or sealed by circular buildings which were burnt down as a preliminary to mound building and which may have functioned as charnel houses as a distinct stage during the process of mourning and body preparation. The bodies or de-fleshed bones were still painted with brightly-coloured pigments but the accompanying grave goods were much richer than in the earlier period, offerings of food were placed in the grave, and certain individuals had "trophy skulls" placed on their laps. But as with the earlier period, the mound could still be the host to secondary interments suggesting continuing associations through clan or kinship affiliation. Such linkages may have been sedimented by the occasional presence of adjacent circular earthwork enclosures which appear to be formalising meeting places for affiliates, or creating pre-cursors to the "world centre shrines" such as the "Woodhenges" at Cahokia.

Hopewell mound building is one of their most conspicuous cultural trends demonstrating a high investment in the dead, often with multi-phase mound building, elaborate graves, the procurement of exotic grave goods and complex burial practices. These mounds could often be grouped to form cemeteries as at Mound City, Chilicothe, Ohio, which forms a component part of the extended cultural landscape featuring geometric enclosures and embanked trackways in the Scioto Valley (Figure 14.1). This cultural expression occurred despite limited agricultural resources derived from garden plots, and may have been stimulated by "exclusionary political strategies" in certain parts of the Hopewellian diaspora such as Hopewell and Seip; the former monopolised and depended upon the prestige goods networks to maintain leadership and demonstrate extra-community interaction and the latter developed an intensification of artefact production (Coon 2009).

Mound building and the veneration of the dead helped the Hopewell communities define their cultural identity and maintain social cohesion – "The elaboration of the mortuary complex may have been some part of an organisational solution to problems of life in a society based upon a mixture of hunting, fishing, gathering wild plant foods, and limited gardening" (Hall 1997, 156–157). Hopewell mortuary ceremonialism would have been underpinned by myth-based traditions as part of the overarching ideology, and ethnography has demonstrated that these rituals are rarely without their origin myths, which are often re-told or re-enacted during ceremonies (Hall 1997, 161). Such activities created the links between the dead, their surviving relations and the spirit world, and would have created the legitimisation to underpin kinship and clan-based networks.

By the Mississippian Period mound complexes comprised platform mounds arranged around a plaza, with a larger mound forming the residence of the paramount chief. The ancillary mounds held temples and charnel houses (Colour Plate 13). Ethnography has suggested that the layout of some complexes such as Moundville in Alabama may symbolise the clan system, and on another level also reflect political and religious organisation through the encapsulation of concepts relating to the Upper and Lower Worlds. A dichotomy developed, whereby the mound centres came to symbolise the Upper World through the presence of the upwardly thrusting mounds, whereas the structure of the rural hinterland embodied references to the Lower World and the Cahokia Fertility Cult (Kelly 1996, 97).

The general layout of Cahokia would appear to have been preordained and physically established at an early stage with a heavy emphasis upon the cardinal directions with Monks Mound lying at its centre and four plazas arranged around it to the north, east, south and west. This deliberate cruciform plan reflected a symbolically-charged motif in Native American cosmology – the cross. Interestingly, the mounds nearest Monks Mound appear to have been deliberately kept smaller in scale so as not to visibly compete with the extraordinarily prominent central mound. The general layout and planning of Cahokia parallels that of the late Emergent Mississippian village at the Range site some 20km to the south (Kelly 1996, 105–106). Both feature dualism with two distinctive halves to their layout, but this is then further complicated and enhanced by a focus upon centrality, *e.g.* the pivotal placement of Monks Mound, and the quadripartite division of the two sites by their plazas. In addition, the juxtaposition of large structures such as platform mounds, plazas and pit groups represents and contrasts symbolic representations of the Upper World and Lower World dimensions of Native American cosmology, worldviews and the conceptualisation of the universe (Hall 1996, 124). Such concepts embedded in town and village plans may parallel Osage and Ho-Chunk (Winnebago) ethnography which suggests a celestial inspiration for this duality based upon the division of patrilineal clans between the moieties of the "sky" and "earth" (Hall 1985; 1993; 1996; 2004; Kelly 1996).

The Upper World/Lower World dichotomy is expressed at Cahokia by the verticality of the mounds. The centrality of Monks Mound and the scale of its construction has created a dramatic Upper World metaphor, achieved without any apparent coercion, and possibly at the direction of an Upper World elite directing a construction crew drawn from members of the Lower World clans through the use of social position and power, thus creating a ritualised, cooperative process through the enactment of reciprocal obligations (Kelly 1996, 109). The directional arms of the Cahokia plan are emphasised by the placement of the plazas radiating from Monks Mound juxtaposed with platform mounds to establish a compartmentalisation of space into a quadripartite cross – the four cardinal directions are thus embedded into the layout of central Cahokia.

An additional symbolic element in the plan of Cahokia was the placing of the "Woodhenges" which probably functioned as symbolic world centre shrines and were not simply solar observatories (Hall 1996, 124). Such world centre shrines were a portal between the living and the spirit world at a location "which had the character of a world center" (Hall 1985, 190–191). The timber circles may also have functioned as places for the display of war trophies, particularly body parts, as depicted in mid-sixteenth century engravings (*cf.* Wittry 1996, 32, fig 3.3).

Much debate has focussed around whether Cahokia was a state formation or a complex chiefdom. Concepts such as the "Ramey State" reference the distribution of Ramey Incised Pottery (the archetypal ceremonial ware of Cahokia), believed to have been controlled by the elite at Cahokia and distributed throughout the American Bottom and adjacent uplands as far north as Wisconsin and Minnesota, and as far south as southern Illinois and southern Indiana – thus potentially demonstrating the area of political influence exerted by Cahokia. The complexity of the Cahokian social setting is evidenced by the presence of craft specialisation in the form of a potters quarter, shell bead manufacturing, *etc.*, the presence of hierarchical settlement patterns, and a rural population which provided support to the centre demonstrating that political/economic classes existed. On a socio-political level, hierarchies are recorded by the elite burials, the articulation of communal construction projects such as mound building and other public structures as part of a planned design – all underpinned by the threat of force as recorded in the episodes of mass sacrifice. The importation of exotic trade goods such as shark teeth, copper and marine shells, occurred alongside more mundane raw materials such as the local Mill Creek chert and salt. The bastions built into the line of the palisades may have been used for the secure storage of prestige goods or raw materials. The trade in non-local materials became increasingly important to the extent that fortified "frontier towns" were established at strategic points to protect the trade routes, such as Aztalan which channelled the copper, fish, fur and timber products from the north, or Dickson Mounds designed to protect the flow of animal products such as meat and buffalo hides. The Mississippian frontier towns contrasted markedly from their neighbours by following the Mississippian tradition of constructing a temple mound. The circulation of prestige goods by Mississippian communities may have been used to develop and maintain social relations, kinship links and alliances, and attract people to Cahokia.

It has been suggested that early Cahokian ideology was dominated by fertility rather than war symbolism. At Mound 72, episodes of the sacrifice of up to fifty-three individuals at a single event, the presence of the four headless and handless men, and other examples from Dickson Mounds, may be evidence of the Green Corn ceremony which is associated with fertility and world renewal (Hall 1997, 138). However, after *c.*AD 1200, warfare may have increased and become ritualised as elites competed for prestige. Such competitiveness between elites may also be demonstrated in the scale of mound building, although conversely those mounds nearest to Monks Mound were small so as not to compete with the most important mound in the complex. Nevertheless, mounds in the American Bottom "were large by Mississippian standards but only a fraction of the size of Monks Mound" (Holt 2009, 236–237).

The Cahokia Mississippians primarily exploited large alluvial river valleys such as the Mississippi and Illinois, but this became eclipsed by the beginning of the fourteenth century with the introduction of more robust varieties of maize which could be grown in a wider range of habitats. In addition, the gradual eastwards migration of the buffalo herds towards the Mississippi offered an alternative subsistence strategy which may have been more appealing than maize agriculture (Hall 1997, 152–153). By *c.*AD 1350, environmental issues, some of which were anthropogenic in origin, added to the pressures on those living in the American Bottom catchment (Holt 2009, 247), and in combination these may have led to the de-centralisation and fragmentation of the Cahokia socio-political structure and the erosion of Mississippian identity at broadly the same time as similar events were unfolding in the American Southwest amongst the ancestral Puebloans.

The abandonment of mound burial during the Late Woodland Period may have been instigated by the gradual restriction of such rites to the elites which emerged during the rise of stratified societies in the Mississippian Period. Changes in mortuary ceremonialism may have led to the uncoupling of mound construction from world renewal rites which then led to their replacement by cemetery burial for the general population (Hall 1997, 167).

CONCLUSION

At its most egocentric, mound building is a form of "signing" the land, a means of establishing a presence and physically sedimenting cultural information into the landscape. This cultural information can then signpost and legitimise claims to land or resources through embedding the dead of the community at significant locations and demonstrating the longevity of the claim – in effect "writing" the story of the land and its people with earthworks.

One recurrent trend amongst the mound builders is that of referencing earlier sites and monuments and developing sacred geographies through the creation of a structured landscape as can be seen in the Scioto Valley, Ohio or Cahokia, Illinois. Such a strategy is epitomised by the secondary burials inserted into pre-existing mounds, re-creating the ancestral past through sedimenting experience, tradition and history upon existing, culturally-charged loci. The concept of an ancestral presence embedded in a mound, or community, clan or kinship-based information presented through the juxtaposition of various forms of earthworks, helped to define "place" for the living, until they themselves died and joined the dead, entombed, completing the circle and becoming part of the past in the present. Mound building thus became an important element of the living cultural landscape, part of developing a sense of place and identity.

ACKNOWLEDGEMENTS

The editor's invitation to write this paper was too tempting to resist, although they may now regret its length – like Topsy it simply grew and grew, but still has barely scratched the surface of this massive subject. The author would like to especially thank Dr Mark Lynott of the Midwest Archeological Center for his help with this paper and providing the aerial photograph of the effigy mounds, and the two Daves – Field and McOmish – for many discussions of Native American archaeology over the years. Any errors of omission or commission are mine alone.

BIBLIOGRAPHY

Birmingham, R. A. and Eisenberg L. E. (2000) *Indian Mounds of Wisconsin*. Madison, University of Wisconsin Press.

Brown, J. A. (1979) Charnel Houses and Mortuary Crypts: Disposal of the Dead in the Middle Woodland Period. In D. S. Brose and N. Greber (eds.) *Hopewell Archaeology: The Chillicothe Conference*, 211–219. Kent, Kent State University Press.

Cochran, D. R. (1996) The Adena / Hopewell convergence in east central Indiana. In P. J. Pacheco (ed.) *A view from the core: a synthesis of Ohio Hopewell archaeology* 36–52. Columbus, Ohio Archaeological Council.

Clay, R. B. (1983) Pottery and graveside ritual in Kentucky Adena. *Midcontinental Journal of Archaeology* 8, 109–26.

Clay, R. B. (1996) Available at: http://www.gbl.indiana.edu/abstracts/adena/mounds.html (Accessed: 24 December 2008).

Coon, M. S. (2009) Variation in Ohio Hopewell political economies. *American Antiquity* 74(1), 49–76.

Diaz-Granados, C. (2004) Marking stone, land, body, and spirit: rock art and Mississippian iconography. In R. F. Townsend & R. V. Sharp (eds.) *Hero, hawk, and open hand* 139–49. New Haven, Yale University Press.

Fagan, B. M. (2000) *Ancient North America: the archaeology of a continent* (Third edition). New York, Thames & Hudson.

Flood, J. (1995) *Archaeology of the Dreamtime (Revised edition)*. London, Harper Collins.

Fowler, M. (1989) *The Cahokia atlas: a historical atlas of Cahokia archaeology*. Springfield, Illinois, Illinois Historic Preservation Agency.

Fowler, M. (1996) The Mound 72 and Woodhenge 72 area of Cahokia. *The Wisconsin Archeologist* 77(3/4), 36–59.

Fowler, M. L., Rose, J., Vander Leest, B. and Ahler, S. R. (1999) *The Mound 72 area: dedicated and sacred space in early Cahokia*. Springfield, Illinois, Illinois State Museum (Reports of Investigations 54).

Goldstein, L. (1995) Landscapes and Mortuary Practices: A Case for Regional Perspectives. In L. A. Beck (ed.) *Regional Approaches to Mortuary Analysis*, 101-120. New York, Plenum.

Glotzhober, R. C. and Lepper, B. T. (1994) *Serpent Mound: Ohio's enigmatic effigy mound*. Ohio, Columbus, Ohio Historical Society.

Greber, N. (1979) A comparative study of site morphology and burial patterns at Edwin Harness Mound and Seip Mounds 1 and 2. In D. S. Brose and N. Greber (eds.) *Hopewell archaeology: the Chillicothe Conference* 27-38. Ohio, Kent: Kent State University Press.

Hall, R. L. (1985) Medicine wheels, sun circles, and the magic of world center shrines. *Plains Anthropologist* 30(109), 181–193.

Hall, R. L. (1993) Red Banks, Oneota, and the Winnebago: views from a distant rock. *The Wisconsin Archeologist* 74, 10–79.

Hall, R. L. (1996) American Indian worlds, world quarters, world centers, and their shrines. *The Wisconsin Archeologist* 77(3/4), 120–7.

Hall, R. L. (1997) *An Archaeology of the Soul: North American Indian Belief and Ritual*. Chicago, University of Illinois Press.

Hall, R. L. (2004) The Cahokia site and its people. In R. F. Townsend and R. V. Sharp (eds.) *Hero, hawk, and open hand,* 93–103. New Haven: Yale University Press.

Holt, J. Z. (2009) Rethinking the Ramey State: was Cahokia the center of a theater state? *American Antiquity* 74(2), 231–54.

Kelly, J. E. (1996) Redefining Cahokia: principles and elements of community organisation. *The Wisconsin Archeologist* 77(3/4), 97–119.

King, A. (2004) Power and the Sacred: Mound C and the Etowah Chiefdom. In R. F. Townsend and R. V. Sharp (eds.) *Hero, hawk, and open hand* 151–165. New Haven: Yale University Press.

Lynott, M. J. and Monk, S. M. (1985) *Mound City, Ohio, archeological investigations*. Lincoln, Nebraska, Midwest Archeological Center (Occasional Studies in Anthropology 12).

Lynott, M. (2007) The Hopeton Earthworks Project: using new technologies to answer old questions. In S. W. Neusius and G. T. Gross (eds.), *Seeking our past: an introduction to North American archaeology,* 550–59. New York, Oxford University Press.

Meltzer, D. J. (ed.) (1998) *Ephraim G. Squier and Edwin H Davis: Ancient Monuments of the Mississippi Valley*. Washington, Smithsonian Institution Press.

Mills, W. C. (1902) Excavations of the Adena Mound. *Ohio Archaeological and Historical Quarterly* 10(4), 2–32.

Milner, G. R. (2004) *The Moundbuilders: ancient peoples of eastern North America*. London, Thames & Hudson.

Neely, P. (2008) Redefining the Adena. *American Archaeology* 12(2), 20–6.

Neumann, G. K. and Fowler, M. L. (1952) Hopewellian sites in the Lower Wabash Valley. In T. Deuel (ed.) *Hopewellian communities in Illinois,* 177–248. Springfield, Illinois: Illinois State Museum (Scientific Papers 5).

Neusius, S. W. and Gross, G. T. (2007) *Seeking our past: an introduction to North American archaeology*. New York, Oxford University Press.

Randall, A. R. (2008) Archaic shell mounds of the St. Johns River, Florida. *The SAA Archaeological Record* 8(5), 13–17.

Reilly III, F. K. (2004) People of Earth, People of Sky: visualizing the sacred in Native American art of the Mississippian Period. In R. F. Townsend and R. V. Sharp (eds.) *Hero, hawk, and open hand*, 125–37. New Haven: Yale University Press.

Robinson, B. S. (2008) "Archaic Period" traditions of New England and the Northeast. *The SAA Archaeological Record* 8(5), 23–46.

Russo, M. (2008) Late Archaic shell rings and society in the Southeast U.S.. *The SAA Archaeological Record* 8(5), 18–22.

Sassaman, K. E., Blessing, M. E. and Randall, A. R. (2006) Stallings Island Revisited: new evidence for occupational history, community pattern, and subsistence technology. *American Antiquity* 71(3), 539–65.

Saunders, J. W. (1997) A mound complex in Louisiana at 5400-5000 years before the present. *Science* 277, 1796–99.

Squier, A. M. and Davis, E. H. (1847) *Ancient Monuments of the Mississippi Valley: Comprising the results of extensive original surveys and explorations*. Washington, Smithsonian Contributions to Knowledge, Volume 1.

Stoltman, J. B. and Christiansen, G. W. (2000) The Late Woodland Stage in the Driftless area of the Upper Mississippi Valley. In T. E. Emerson, D. L. McElrath and A. C. Fortier (eds.) *Late Woodland societies: tradition and transformation across the midcontinent*, 497-524. Lincoln, University of Nebraska Press.

Webb, W. S. (1941) *Mt. Horeb earthworks and the Drake Mound*. Lexington, University of Kentucky, Department of Anthropology (Reports in Anthropology 5(2)).

Weisman, B. R. (1995) Crystal River: a ceremonial mound center on the Florida Gulf coast. *Florida Archaeology* 8.

Wheaton, H. and Brown, C. E. (1920) The dedication of the Fort Atkinson intaglio. *The Wisconsin Archeologist* 19(4), 197–208.

Wittry, W. L. (1996) Discovering and interpreting the Cahokia Woodhenges. *The Wisconsin Archeologist* 77(3/4), 26–35.

Woodward, S. L. and McDonald (2002). *Indian mounds of the Middle Ohio Valley*. Virginia, Blacksburg, The McDonald & Woodward Publishing Company.

Chapter 15

The Round Mound is Not a Monument

Tim Ingold

INTRODUCTION

Is a round mound an ancient monument? The answer depends, of course, on what we take to be a monument and on what we mean by antiquity. Purely for the sake of argument, I define a monument here as a structurally coherent edifice, built to the specifications of an original design, and intended by its designers and builders to last in perpetuity as a memorial to their endeavour. Having been built at a particular historical moment, the monument has a certain age. In principle, then, we can tell how old it is. In principle, too, it is set up in a landscape, and marks a site within it.

I believe that these are the characteristics that most people in contemporary western societies attribute to monuments. I have no evidence to support this claim, however, nor do I wish to become mired in definitional arguments about what the essential features of monuments might be – if indeed any such features can be identified. My purpose is rather to use this characterisation of the monument as a foil against which to mount an argument to the effect that the mound is everything that the monument is not. In brief, the argument is that the mound is not an edifice but a growth, that this growth is not obedient to the dictates of any prior design, and that its form – at least until artificially stabilised by heritage-led efforts at conservation – is not constant but ever evolving thanks to processes of deposition and erosion that are continually going on. For the same reason, the mound is not like a time capsule, in which a record of past people and events is locked for the benefit of posterity, but a place where the work of memory is forever carried on in the activities that surround it. Because of this, we cannot assign to it any determinate date of origin, or tell for sure how old it is. Nor is the mound exactly situated in a landscape. It rather constitutes a node or confluence within what I shall call an earth-sky world.

THE MOUND IS NOT AN EDIFICE

If you heap stuff up over a period of time, always adding to the top of the pile and allowing it to settle of its own accord, it will generally form a mound, roughly circular in plan and bell-shaped in elevation. On a miniature scale, we can observe this process of mound formation in the sand of an hour-glass. On a gigantic scale, it can be witnessed in the formation of volcanic cones. From mole-hills to ants' nests (Figure 15.1c), mounds are among the commonest forms in nature. They often result from human activities too

– think of shell middens, stone cairns, compost heaps, and sandcastles. In every case, the roundness of the form emerges spontaneously, due to the way in which the pressure of material added from above displaces material already deposited, equally in all directions. One could say that the mound builds up precisely because the material of which it is made is continually falling down. Each and every particle, as it falls, eventually finds its own more or less enduring place of rest.

In this respect the mound is the very opposite of the edifice (Figure 15.1b). In the construction of an edifice each successive piece is carefully laid to rest upon the last in such a way that a static equilibrium is maintained. The permanence and integrity of the structure depend on the way in which additional material is locked into position through its abutment to what has already been laid. In building a tower of stone blocks, for example, every layer of blocks has to be added so that it bears down precisely on the preceding layer, which bears in turn upon the layer before that, and so on right down to the foundations. Without fixed and solid foundations, the entire building process could not even begin. Ultimately, therefore, every edifice must rest upon foundations set in the earth. If the foundations give way, as in an earthquake, the entire structure can come crashing down. If and when it does, the result will be a mound of stones!

It would in fact be quite difficult to build an edifice in such a way as to imitate the form of a mound. One would first have to lay out the foundations by drawing a circle in the earth. The easiest way to lay out foundation lines – and by all accounts, the way most commonly employed by early architects and builders – is to stretch a string between pegs driven into the ground, much as methodical gardeners still do today. But this method yields a straight line, and not a circle. Thus the foundations of our mound-edifice could only take the form of a regular, straight-sided polygon, approximating more closely to the circle the more sides it has. To build up from these foundations one could proceed as if building a pyramid, or alternatively attempt the more complex architectural form of the dome. Either way, there is a definite point at which the structure is complete, where the final piece has been added.

But the mound is never complete. One can always carry on adding new material. As the mound consequently rises in height, it also expands at the base. Unlike the edifice, it is not tied to fixed foundations. Indeed properly speaking, it has no foundations at all. Although

Figure 15.1: Mountains, monuments and mounds. A) The Pike of Stickle, Cumbria (Photograph: D. Field); B) Pyramid of the Sun, Teotihuacán, Mexico (Photograph: F. Worley); and C) an anthill with a visitor (Photograph: D. Field). (Figure compiled by Chris Evans)

every particle of the mound comes to rest on other particles, the mound as a whole does not rest upon the earth. For it is as much of the earth as on it. Like the compost heap or the ants' nest, the mound is *becoming earth*. Indeed the mound forces us to recognise that the earth itself is not the solid and pre-existing material substrate that the edifice builder takes it to be. It is rather the source of all life and growth, "the serving bearer", as Martin Heidegger called it, "rising up into plant and animal" (Heidegger 1971, 149). Plants grow in the earth, not on it, and from these, animals – including human beings – draw their subsistence. Metabolised and decomposed by the processes of life, materials drawn from the earth are eventually returned to it, fuelling further growth. In this sense, the earth is perpetually growing over, which is why archaeologists have to dig to discover evidence of past lives (Ingold 2008, 31). Formed in the process of life becoming earth, the mound could be regarded as a growth or swelling, manifested as a bump in the ground surface. But it is not an edifice erected on it.

THE MOUND HAS NO DESIGN

Modern thinkers find it very difficult to understand how there can be form without design. To the modern mind, as David Turnbull has observed, it seems self-evident that wherever we encounter built form of even the simplest kind, it must first have been designed by an intellect (Turnbull 1993, 319, and for an example see Harvey 1972, 101). Indeed it is precisely in the extent to which a building's form is taken to be the manifestation of a prior design that it is judged to be an instance of architecture. It has, of course, long been the conceit of the architectural profession that all the creative work that goes into the fashioning of a building is concentrated in the process of design, and that the subsequent phase of construction adds up to little more than its realisation in the proverbial "bricks and mortar" of the built environment. The architect would like to think that the complete building stands as the crystallisation of an original design concept, with all its components finally fixed in their proper places.

This architectural conceit, though given a new lease of life in the European Renaissance, goes back to classical Antiquity, and was originally formulated by Aristotle in the doctrine of hylomorphism. According to Aristotle, in fashioning a monument such as a marble statue, the sculptor starts with a shapeless block of raw material (*hyle*) and an idea in mind of how the finished form (*morphe*) should look. In the course of his work, material and form are brought together: matter is formed and form rendered material. To this day, archaeological interpretation has continued to be influenced by hylomorphism to an extent that its practitioners are rarely willing to acknowledge (although see Leary, this volume Chapter 8). It is this doctrine that predisposes them to think of the mound as a sculptured earthwork. It is as though the mound-builders, as they piled up earth and stones, had an idea of how the work would finally look, and kept on piling until the height, diameter and contours of the accumulated material matched their expectations.

As a thought experiment, imagine that we are equipped with a time-machine that enables us to revisit the folk who, in the distant past, were living in and around those places where now there are round mounds. Let us ask them what they are doing. They may perhaps answer that they are burying their dead. Or perhaps that they are meeting to resolve their affairs. They might say that they are conducting ceremonies to restore the fertility of the land. They might even claim to be depositing their rubbish, or simply building and rebuilding on the same spot. The one answer, however, that they would be most unlikely to give would be "building a mound". Rather, the mound that confronts us today is the cumulative by-product of all kinds of activities, carried on over long periods of time. Nor are the activities that contributed to shaping it confined to human beings. Burrowing animals, from worms to rabbits, have continued to play their part in the evolution of the mound (Figure 15.1c). The roots of trees, bushes and grasses, threading through its volume, have helped to fix it. Last but not least the weather, and above all the rain, has shaped it internally and externally, in the creation of patterns of drainage and run-off.

Crucially, these organic and hydrological processes continue in the present as they have always done in the past. To observe the mound today is to witness their going on. The mound, we could say, presents itself in its *mounding*. This is to think of it not as a finished object, standing on foundations and set over and against its surroundings, but as a locus of growth and regeneration where materials welling up from the earth mix and mingle with the fluxes of the weather in the ongoing production of life. The mound has not turned its back on us, as we might suppose, hiding secrets within its dark, enclosed interior that we can discover only by tunnelling in. On the contrary, it is open to the world. I shall return to this point below. For the moment, suffice it to say that this argument entails a radical rejection of the hylomorphic model, and with it, the notion that the round mound is an outcome of the planned imposition of preconceived form on inert matter. It is rather the ever-emergent outcome of the interplay of cosmic forces and vital materials. The mound, as we have already observed, is not built. It grows.

THE MOUND IS NOT A MEMORIAL

History is littered with the products of monumental attempts to put an end to it. The paradox of monuments is that they can serve as memorials only because they have failed in the objective set for them by the powers that originally intended their construction. Had they succeeded – if, that is, their architects had managed to bring history to a close and thereby to secure their own immortality – then there would be no future generations to look back on them and marvel at how they had come to be built. Impressive in their permanence and solidity, monumental structures intended by their makers to confer everlasting life provide irrefutable evidence, to those who subsequently come across them, that the past is dead, over and done with. Like beached whales, they seem to have been left stranded on the shores of history, while time moves on. As it does so, the gap between a lost past and the vivid present grows ever wider.

For while the monument speaks *for* itself, calling out the names or preserving the likenesses of those whom it commemorates, it also speaks *to* itself in the idiom and language of its time. To visit a memorial is to eavesdrop on past conversations that we can no longer fully understand. They were then, we are now. This is not to deny that the memorial holds memories for us. Perhaps it stands in a place we have often visited, and that generations of our families have visited previously. We might have old photographs to prove it, and looking longingly at the figures in the photos, we exclaim that "they are us!" This kind of memory-work allows us to tell stories that flow as seamlessly from past to present as our own lives. Throughout, the monument stands as a focus. Yet what it records, if anything, or whether this record is comprehensible to anyone but the specialist antiquarian, is incidental to the stories we tell. We remember that we visited, as did others before us. It is the latter, and not the persons explicitly commemorated in the monument, that we draw into our conversations.

It is essential, therefore, to draw an analytic distinction between *places of memory* and *sites of commemoration*. The monument commemorates a remarkable event or notable personage, or perhaps many such. But it can only be a place of memory if it is frequented. Conversely, many places of memory are not – and never have been – sites of commemoration. A place may be marked by the comings and goings of previous generations, as for example the rocky outcrop at a local beauty spot on which visitors have carved their own and their sweethearts' names. Adding our own mark, we join the conversation. Perhaps, far off in the future, antiquarians will struggle to decipher these inscriptions as the commemorative insignia of a lost civilisation. Only then, however, will the rock have become a monument. And from then on, the original conversation will no longer be open to newcomers. To add marks to a monument is not to contribute to the growth of a place, but to commit an act of despoliation.

Now round mounds are clearly places of memory. The remembering goes on in the very activities that we – like our predecessors – carry on around them, in walking, cultivating, excavating and so on. All of these activities, as we have already seen, contribute to the mounds' ongoing formation. Of course as time passes, interests and priorities change, as does the character of the environment. But there is little or no evidence to suggest that at any point in their history, mounds were anything *other* than places of memory. Convinced however that they must be monuments, and thus sites of commemoration, archaeologists have long been driven by a relentless search for some commemorative secret – a kernel of meaning that the original mound-builders left inside as a record of their lives and deeds. If only something spectacular could be found at the heart of the mound, we would at last know who built them and why! More often than not, however, excavation has been unrewarded by discovery. Though mounds might draw attention to themselves as places to dig, they often turn up no more than would be uncovered by digging anywhere else. For the archaeologists of today it is precisely in the finding, and not in what (if anything) is found, that the work of memory lies. This must have been equally true for people in the past. Perhaps it was in the very process of trying to find things, or alternatively of trying to get rid of them, that – over the millennia – mounds were formed.

THE MOUND IS NOT ANCIENT

How old is a monument? How old is a mountain? The first question, at least at first glance, is simple to answer. Surely the monument dates from that defining moment when a form, which until then had been present only as an idea, was unified with hitherto formless raw material, so as to create a finished work of architecture. It might require some archaeological detective work to discover when this moment was, but we do not doubt that it existed. In the case of the mountain, however, it is quite otherwise. For the mountain was neither made nor built. Rather, it took shape, gradually and – to ordinary mortals – imperceptibly, over great aeons of geological time, through processes of deposition, compression, uplift and erosion that are still going on now much as they have always done. At no singular point in time did these processes begin, nor have they come to an end. The mountain is not, and never will be, completed. Thus, no amount of detective work on the part of the geologist will suffice to determine its age or antiquity. It is a question that cannot even be sensibly asked of the mountain, let alone answered. Monuments can be ancient, but mountains cannot (Figure 15.1, compare a and b).

What, then, of the mound? Can we say how old it is? Apparently more artificial than a mountain, but more natural than a monument, the mound seems to lie halfway between the two. Yet this very distinction between the natural and the artificial, and with it the question of antiquity, rests on the assumptions of the hylomorphic model of making. According to this model, it is the imposition of pure form that raises naturally given raw material to an artificial state. As I have already shown, however, the phenomenon of the mound obliges us to reject these assumptions. The mound differs from the mountain in that it is of a more human scale, and its formation undoubtedly owes more to the labour of human beings and other living creatures. Yet like the mountain, its form is ever-emergent through the play of forces and materials.

Moreover, once we turn this argument back on the monument, the question of its antiquity, which had initially seemed so simple, begins to look a good deal more complex. Why should we date a monument from the moment it was built? Is this not just one, relatively arbitrary point in the life of a thing, and of its constituent materials? The teams of masons employed in cutting stone to shape and assembling the pieces did not work precisely to the dictates of any architectural design. Rather, they improvised as they went along, working *with* the forms and properties of the stones available to them. Each piece was cut, shaped and – if necessary – reshaped so as to fit the space prepared for it by previous ones, and in turn preparing the spaces for those to follow. And even when the masons' work was done, the structure has ever since remained subject to the ravages of the weather, the forces of erosion and the wear and tear of use. Maintenance calls for frequent, restorative intervention. In principle, we could date the monument to any intervention, making it as old or new as we please.

Why, in the face of these observations, does archaeology remain so committed to the unequivocal determination of the antiquity of things? The answer, I think, lies in its concern to treat these things as comprising a *record* of times long past. For a structure of any kind to become part of the archaeological record, it must hold fast to a point of origin, receding ever further from the horizon of the present as the rest of the world moves on. Conversely, things that carry on, that undergo continuous generation or, in a word, that *grow* cannot be part of the record. Are they, then, of no further archaeological interest? Of course not. They are of principal interest, however, to an archaeology that is concerned with the persistence of things rather than their antiquity. Persistent things have no point of origin, no date, but seem instead to be originating all the time. Acknowledging the mound to be a thing of this kind, the antiquarian digs down in the hope of finding objects hidden *inside* the mound. But from the perspective of the archaeology of persistence such objects, even if perfectly preserved, are but ephemera, the cast-offs of time and history. What lasts is the mound itself. For unlike the long forgotten objects possibly deposited inside it, the mound is still mounding.

THE MOUND IS NOT SET IN A LANDSCAPE

Because of the kinds of houses they live in, people in modern western societies are used to looking out of windows mounted in vertical walls. If these windows afford an expansive view, then what inhabitants see is often called a landscape. Perhaps the view includes a monument seen in elevation, standing upright, pictured against the horizon. There is indeed an intrinsic connection between the idea of landscape and that of the monument: the one is supposed to provide the scenic background against which the other is displayed or "set off" to best advantage. Together, the monument and its landscape are considered to comprise a totality that is complete and fully formed. Could the same be said of the mound in relation to its surroundings?

I have already shown that the mound is not an edifice. It does not stand up on solid foundations. On the contrary, it lies down. Like a collapsed, dormant figure, it is both *on* and *of* the earth. Let us follow suit and lie down with the mound. How would we apprehend the world, as it were, from the mound's point of view? Certainly not as a landscape, in any conventional sense. Typically, the landscape includes a terrestrial vista extending to the line of the horizon, above and beyond which lies the sky. But when we lie down, the horizon disappears beyond the periphery of our visual awareness, which becomes one with the variable luminosity of sky, while at the same time we feel the embracing dampness of the earth beneath our body. Thus earth and sky, far from being divided along the line of the distant horizon, are unified at the very centre of our emplaced being. The mound's-eye view, in short, opens up not to a landscape but to an *earth-sky world*.

The psychologist James Gibson, introducing his ecological approach to visual perception, was among the first to challenge the once dominant view that people see the world in pictures, projected on the back of the retina. Gibson placed perceivers at the centre of a world that is *all around* them rather than passing by in front of their eyes. He imagined this world as comprising two hemispheres, of the sky above and the earth below. At the interface between the upper and lower hemispheres, and stretching out to the great circle of the horizon, lies the ground on which perceivers stand. Their environment, in his words, consists of "the earth and the sky with objects *on* the earth and *in* the sky, of mountains and clouds, fires and sunsets, pebbles and stars" (Gibson 1979, 66). In this evocative passage, and despite his appeal to the all-around, Gibson presents us with an environment in which everything is locked solid, whether placed on the ground or hung in the sky. This is a strange world indeed, more like a full-scale model or simulacrum than the real thing (Ingold 2008, 26).

Were we to think of the mound in Gibson's terms, it could only be as an object that had been placed fully formed upon the ground. Yet in reality, as we have seen, not only does the mound undergo continual formation, but this formative process is also one of becoming earth. Thus Gibson's static understanding of the earth-sky world needs to be replaced by a dynamic one. In this, the ground is no mere platform on which things sit or lie but a permeable zone of formative and transformative processes: a textural composite of diverse materials that are grown, deposited and woven together through the earth's exposure to light, moisture and currents of air – to sunshine, rain and wind – or in short, to the weather.

The world of earth and sky, I suggest, is a weather-world, a world of flux in which materials flow and the task of inhabitants is actively to follow them. In place of Gibson's understanding of the environment as earth and sky with objects on the earth and in the sky, I propose the notion of an *environment without objects* (EWO). In the EWO there are no objects as such, but rather gatherings, confluences, swellings and growths. The round mound may be all of these. Lying with the mound, we do not perceive it but perceive *from* it, and what it yields are not objects of sense but experiences of light, sound and feeling. The mound is present in its mounding, to borrow an expression from Heidegger, "from out of the worlding world" (Heidegger 1971, 181). As the mound mounds, the sun shines, the rain falls, the wind blows and earth rises up into plant and animal.

BIBLIOGRAPHY

Gibson, J. J. (1979) *The ecological approach to visual perception*. Boston, Houghton Mifflin.
Harvey, J. (1972) *The mediaeval architect*. London, Wayland.
Heidegger, M. (trans. A. Hofstadter) (1971) *Poetry, Language, Thought*. New York, Harper and Row.
Ingold, T. (2008) Earth, sky, wind and weather. In E. Hsu and C. Low (eds.) *Wind, life and health*, 17–35. Oxford, Blackwell.
Turnbull, D. (1993) The ad hoc collective work of building Gothic cathedrals with templates, string, and geometry. *Science, Technology and Human Values* 18(3), 315–40.

Colour Plate 1. A photograph from the main tunnel in Silbury Hill showing the northern tip of the gravel mound sitting on the old ground surface. The Lower Organic Mound material can be seen overlying the gravel mound. (Photograph: D. Stirk) © English Heritage.

Colour Plate 2. Photograph from the west lateral tunnel in Silbury Hill showing one of the pits cut into the Lower Organic Mound (it was itself cut on the eastern side by the 1849 tunnel). (Photograph: D. Fellows) © English Heritage.

Colour Plate 3 (left). Photograph of the end of the Silbury Hill tunnel showing a section through the Upper Organic Mound. (Photograph: D. Stirk) © English Heritage.

Colour Plate 4 (below). A reconstruction drawing of the Silbury enclosure. (Drawing by Judith Dobie) © English Heritage.

Colour Plate 5(above). Photograph of one of the chalk walls on the summit of Silbury Hill. A cluster of sarsen stones can be seen on the right hand side of the wall. (Photograph: J. Leary) © English Heritage.

Colour Plate 6 (right): Close-up photograph of the sarsen stones in the chalk wall and associated antler fragments. (Photograph: D. Stirk) © English Heritage.

Colour Plate 7: Photograph of Silbury Hill and its water-filled ditch at night. (Photograph: James O'Davies)
© English Heritage.

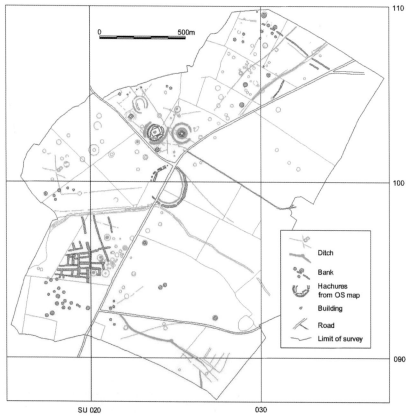

Colour Plate 8: A map compiled from the aerial photographic evidence around Knowlton shows that the henges and the Great Barrow are elements within a series of overlapping landscapes spanning the Neolithic to medieval periods. © English Heritage. NMR.

Colour Plate 9: The tree-covered mound of the Great Barrow (right) and the earthworks of the Church Circle henge (centre) are all that survives above the ground of the Neolithic and Bronze Age monument complex at Knowlton. (Photographer: Roger Featherstone. RCHME Photograph: NMR 15326/06 13 July 1995 © Crown Copyright. NMR).

Colour Plate 10: Mount Pleasant in 2004. Conquer Barrow is completely obscured by trees in the top left of the photograph. However, this photograph does emphasise the fact that parts of the henge bank have been heightened at some point in the enclosure's history – the higher parts, with clear terminals, are visible. (Photographer: Damian Grady. English Heritage Photograph: NMR 23601/32 1st September 2004 © English Heritage. NMR).

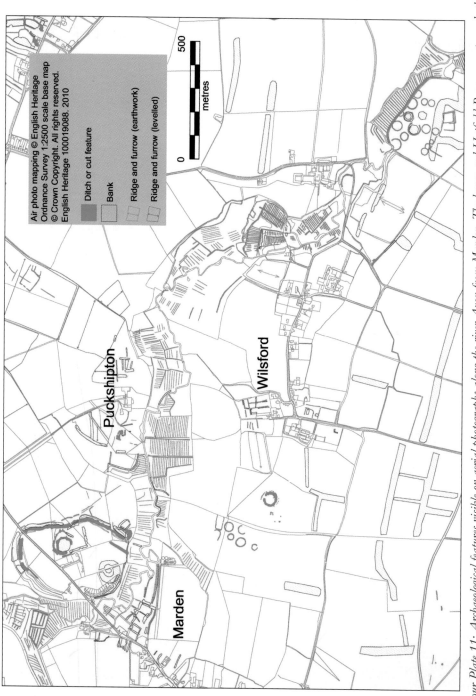

Colour Plate 11: Archaeological features visible on aerial photographs along the river Avon from Marden. The henge and Hatfield Barrow are towards the top left of the illustration. A barrow cemetery sits on a slight rise to the south of Marden. Post Medieval water meadows extend along the flood plain of the river. To the bottom right of the illustration there is a large barrow cemetery situated in the flood plain. Topographical detail based on Ordnance Survey 1:2500 scale mapping. (© Crown Copyright and database right 2009. All rights reserved. Ordnance Survey Licence number 100019088).

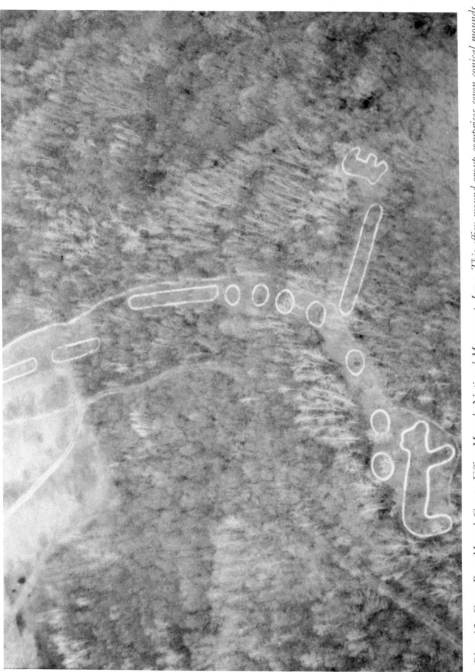

Colour Plate 12: Great Bear Mound Group, Effigy Mounds National Monument, Iowa. This effigy mound group comprises seven conical mounds, four linear mounds and two bear effigies. The larger of the two, the Great Bear is 42m long. (Photograph courtesy of the Midwest Archeological Center, National Park Service).

Plate 13: Mound C, Etowah, Georgia. A reconstruction of the burial of two figurines in a pit in
~~~~nd C following the destruction of a temple on the summit during the Late Wilibanks Phase
~~~~) of the Mississippian Climax. (Photograph: P. Topping; Etowah Indian Mounds State